Native Americans

# Cahuilla

**Barbara A. Gray-Kanatiiosh**

ABDO Publishing Company

# visit us at
# www.abdopublishing.com

Published by ABDO Publishing Company, 4940 Viking Drive, Edina, Minnesota 55435. Copyright © 2007 by Abdo Consulting Group, Inc. International copyrights reserved in all countries. No part of this book may be reproduced in any form without written permission from the publisher. The Checkerboard Library™ is a trademark and logo of ABDO Publishing Company.

Printed in the United States.

Cover Photo: ©Bowers Museum of Cultural Art/Corbis
Interior Photos: Agua Caliente Cultural Museum p. 29; AP/Wide World p. 30; Corbis pp. 4, 30
Illustrations: David Kanietakeron Fadden pp. 7, 9, 11, 13, 15, 17, 19, 21, 23, 25, 27
Editors: Rochelle Baltzer, Heidi M. Dahmes
Art Direction & Maps: Neil Klinepier
Special thanks to the Agua Caliente Cultural Museum.

**Library of Congress Cataloging-in-Publication Data**

Gray-Kanatiiosh, Barbara A., 1963-
  Cahuilla / Barbara A. Gray-Kanatiiosh.
    p. cm. -- (Native Americans)
  Includes index.
  ISBN-10 1-59197-651-0
  ISBN-13 978-1-59197-651-6
  1. Cahuilla Indians--History--Juvenile literature. 2. Cahuilla Indians--Social life and customs--Juvenile literature.
  I. Title. II. Series: Native Americans (Edina, Minn.)

E99.C155G73 2006
979.4004'9745--dc22

2005018462

## About the Author: Barbara A. Gray-Kanatiiosh, JD

Barbara Gray-Kanatiiosh, JD, Ph.D. ABD, is an Akwesasne Mohawk. She resides at the Mohawk Nation and is of the Wolf Clan. She has a Juris Doctorate from Arizona State University, where she was one of the first recipients of ASU's special certificate in Indian Law. Barbara's Ph.D. is in Justice Studies at ASU. She is currently working on her dissertation, which concerns the impacts of environmental injustice on indigenous culture. Barbara works hard to educate children about Native Americans through her writing and Web site, where children may ask questions and receive a written response about the Haudenosaunee culture. The Web site is: www.peace4turtleisland.org

## About the Illustrator: David Kanietakeron Fadden

David Kanietakeron Fadden is a member of the Akwesasne Mohawk Wolf Clan. His work has appeared in publications such as *Akwesasne Notes*, *Indian Time*, and the *Northeast Indian Quarterly*. Examples of his work have also appeared in various publications of the Six Nations Indian Museum in Onchiota, NY. His work has also appeared in "How the West Was Lost: Always the Enemy," produced by Gannett Production, which appeared on the Discovery Channel. David's work has been exhibited in Albany, NY; the Lake Placid Center for the Arts; Centre Strathearn in Montreal, Quebec; North Country Community College in Saranac Lake, NY; Paul Smith's College in Paul Smiths, NY; and at the Unison Arts & Learning Center in New Paltz, NY.

# Contents

# Where They Lived

The Cahuilla (kuh-WEE-uh) lived in southern California. Their homelands were located in present-day Riverside and San Diego **counties**. The Cahuilla's neighbors included the Gabrielino, Kumeyaay, and Tipai tribes. The Cahuilla spoke a **dialect** of the Uto-Aztecan language family.

There were many different landforms in Cahuilla territory. They included steep mountains and deep canyons. The San Bernardino Mountains reach nearly 11,500 feet (3,500 m) above sea level. And, the Salton Sink was once about 280 feet (85 m) below sea level. Deserts and forests were also found throughout the area.

Many types of trees, shrubs, berries, and wildflowers grew on Cahuilla land. Mesquite trees and oak trees were commonly

**Today, desert palm trees grow on the Agua Caliente Reservation in Palm Springs, California.**

found there. These trees provided important food sources for the tribe.

Weather conditions on Cahuilla territory changed often. Sometimes, rain flooded the area. Other times, the land experienced extreme dryness. And, high winds sometimes led to damaging sandstorms.

## Cahuilla Homelands

5

# Society

The Cahuilla lived in villages. When searching for a place to settle, they looked for areas that had access to food and water. Sometimes, they built a village in a canyon for protection from strong winds. Other times, they built a village at the base of a mountain.

Each village had a leader called a *net*. This title belonged to a family and was usually passed from father to son. The net acted as the ceremonial leader, the **economic** ruler, and the problem solver for the village. He also arranged hunting and trading trips.

The net had a helper called a *paxaa*. The paxaa assisted the net during ceremonies and **rituals**. He made sure that people followed ceremonial rules, and he punished those who did not. He helped the net organize meetings and trips, too.

Cahuilla society also had special speakers and singers. They performed ceremonial speeches and long, difficult songs. And, they passed on their knowledge to new speakers and singers. This ensured that these traditions would continue.

Healers were other important people in Cahuilla society. Doctors were usually older women. They cured the sick people.

Shamans, or medicine people, were typically men. They were believed to have supernatural powers. Shamans could cause rain, cure people, and keep away bad spirits.

**Many Cahuilla considered shamans the most respected people in their society.**

# Food

The Cahuilla ate plants and animals found in their environment. To obtain these foods, they hunted and gathered. They also planted foods such as corn, beans, squashes, and melons.

Smaller animals were abundant on Cahuilla territory. Men hunted squirrels, rabbits, mice, rats, ducks, and quail. They used traps, snares, and nets to catch most of these animals. To hunt rabbits, they often used throwing sticks. With this tool, a skilled hunter could hit a rabbit from 150 feet (46 m) away! Men used bows and arrows to hunt deer, antelope, and mountain sheep.

The Cahuilla gathered wild plants, fruits, beans, nuts, berries, and seed. Acorns were a seasonal food that they collected from oak trees. To prepare acorns for eating, women first ground them using a **pestle** and **mortar**. Then, they leached them to remove poisonous tannic acid. To do this, they placed the ground acorns in a hopper basket and poured boiling water over them.

Cahuilla women used flat stones, baskets, and pots to cook food. They roasted ground seed or made it into flour or bread. To make soup and mush, they put flour and water in a basket with hot rocks. They also dried some foods in the sun.

The Cahuilla preserved excess food in baskets or pots. They stored acorns and beans in large baskets called granaries. Granaries protected food from being eaten by insects and animals. Other foods were stored in large, round pots.

**Cahuilla women leached ground acorns to remove poisonous tannic acid. This acid is a form of tannin, which is a bitter-tasting mix of chemicals.**

9

# Homes

The Cahuilla lived in homes called *kishes*. Most *kishes* were circular with domed roofs, but a few were rectangular. Sometimes, the Cahuilla left their villages to go on gathering trips. During these times, they lived in temporary brush shelters.

Men were in charge of constructing the *kishes*. First, they dug out an area for the floor. Then, they lined the inside walls of the dug-out area with boulders. To build a frame, they placed long poles upright in the ground. The frame was about 15 to 20 feet (5 to 6 m) long. Then, the men bent the poles and tied them together at the top. This created a domed roof.

Finally, the men covered the frame with mats woven from reeds and leaves. They used willow strips or rope made from plant fibers to tie the covering to the frame.

In every Cahuilla village, there was a ceremonial house. This house was both a social and spiritual place where healings sometimes took place. The net usually lived in or near this building.  Normally, ceremonial houses were dome shaped. They were often as large as 50 feet (15 m) across the middle.

Near the ceremonial houses were sweat houses. The Cahuilla believed that **ritual** sweating helped to keep the mind and body healthy.  Sweat houses were also important meeting places for Cahuilla men. There, the men made political decisions and scheduled food-gathering trips.

Cahuilla villages consisted of family homes, ceremonial houses, and sweat houses.

# Clothing

    The Cahuilla used natural materials, such as grass, feathers, furs, and animal skins, to make their clothing. During the warmer months, the Cahuilla did not wear much clothing. Women wore skirts made from woven mesquite bark. Men wore **breechcloths** made from woven plant fibers or deerskins.

    During ceremonies, the Cahuilla wore capes, skirts, and elaborate head coverings. These pieces were usually woven from feathers. Men's ceremonial skirts were woven from both plant fibers and feathers.

    Both men and women wore two types of sandals. One type of sandal was made from animal skins. The other type was made from woven plant fibers. These plant fibers wrapped around the toe and the heel. This held the sandal in place.

    When a Cahuilla girl was about 11 years old, she received a chin **tattoo**. An aunt or a female friend gave the tattoo. She used a cactus thorn to prick holes in the chin. Then, she rubbed charcoal over the holes for coloring.

The Cahuilla wore rabbit-skin robes during cool weather.

13

# Crafts

The Cahuilla made beautiful pottery and baskets. They used pots for cooking and storing food, as well as holding water. Baskets were used for gathering, cooking, serving, and storing food. The Cahuilla also used baskets as baby cradles and hats. And sometimes, they gave baskets as gifts.

Typically, women made baskets. To weave the baskets, the women used plants such as yucca, agave, sumac, juncus, and deer grass. Sometimes they wove symbols into the baskets. These symbols included eagles, stars, and lightning bolts.

Cahuilla women made a special kind of basket for grinding foods. This hopper basket had tall sides and no bottom. The women used asphaltum to attach it to a stone **mortar**. The hopper basket's tall sides kept seed and nuts from falling out as they were ground.

Older women usually made pottery. They used clay to sculpt the pots. Sometimes, they scratched designs on them. To harden the clay, the women fired the pots in a pit. After the pots were fired, they sparkled because of the minerals in the clay. Cahuilla pots were sometimes called "red ware" because of the clay's rosy red color.

Cahuilla women showed off their creative skills by making baskets. A woman earned honors for her abilities.

# Family

Cahuilla society was divided into two groups called the Wildcats and the Coyotes. Children were the same division as their father. The Cahuilla married people of the opposite group. Both divisions were further split into **clans**. And within the clans, there were even smaller family groups.

Throughout the year, Cahuilla families traveled to hunt and gather foods. Families owned certain parts of land for these purposes. Each family cared for and protected this land.

To keep Cahuilla society successful and strong, both women and men were responsible for certain tasks. Besides cooking food and making crafts, the women gathered foods, cared for children, and made clothing.

The men hunted and made tools. They made cooking tools such as stone **mortars**, **pestles**, and bowls. And, they built traps, nets, throwing sticks, and bows and arrows. The men also dug wells to keep their gardens watered.

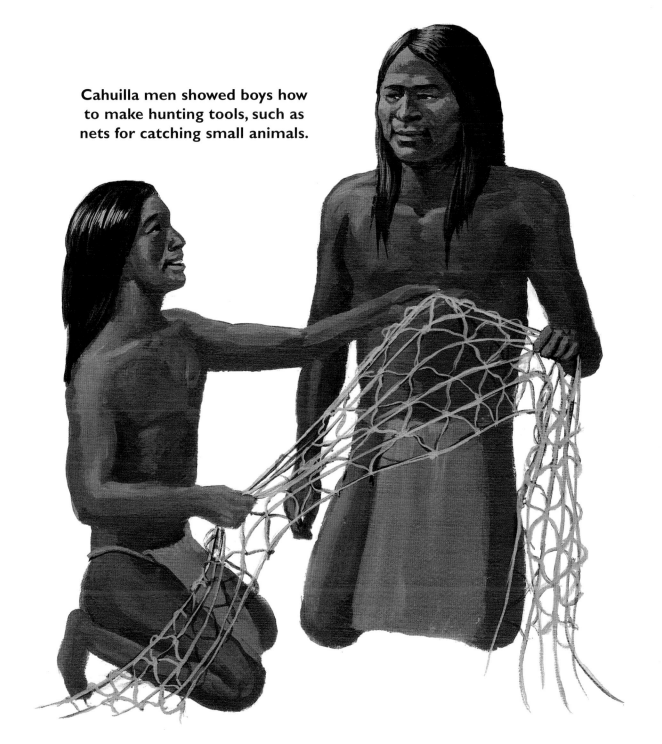

Cahuilla men showed boys how to make hunting tools, such as nets for catching small animals.

# Children

At a young age, Cahuilla children learned how to do important tasks. But, they also had plenty of time to play games. Boys wrestled and played tug-of-war. Girls spun tops, juggled, and made string figures. These games helped them gain necessary skills for their future responsibilities.

Cahuilla women taught girls how to weave baskets and make pottery. The girls learned to find clay deposits in the mountains. Then, the women showed them how to use **mortars** to grind the clay into a fine powder. The girls also learned how to cook food and care for younger children.

Men taught boys how to make hunting tools, such as rabbit sticks and bows and arrows. Bows were made from willow or mesquite wood. The string was made from **sinew** or plant fibers. The boys used a notched stone to help them make straight arrows. Then, boys learned how to use these tools to hunt for small animals.

Cahuilla elders were important keepers of knowledge, and they were highly respected. Elders taught children ceremonial songs and dances. They also showed them how to make rattles and whistles. These instruments were used during ceremonies.

**Elders often told stories to children about Cahuilla culture and history.**

19

# Myths

    The Cahuilla did not use a writing system, so they learned history through storytelling. The tribe continues to pass on myths from generation to generation. The following is a Cahuilla creation myth.

    Many years before there was life on Earth, there was nothing but light. The light was made of energy forces that raced through the sky. These forces were red, blue, white, and brown.

    One day, the lights met in the sky. They united and formed two embryos. The two embryos used their minds to communicate with each other. Eventually, they grew into powerful spiritual beings named Temayawut and Mukat. They both had the ability to create life.

    Temayawut was always in a hurry. In an attempt to make hands and feet, he made paws and webbed fingers. His creations had many legs and eyes. And, he made things with horns, thorns, bumps, and fur.

However, Mukat always took his time. He created human beings in many different sizes, shapes, and colors. Soon, the humans began to fight over where to live. Mukat called the most reasoned and strongest-voiced people *Cahuilla*. He gave them a good place to live and told them how to survive.

Energy forces in the sky produced Mukat and Temayawut. As embryos, they were in the early stages of development. Eventually, they grew to become powerful beings.

21

# War

The Cahuilla aimed to keep peaceful relations with their neighbors. Their **economy** depended on trading with bordering tribes. The Cahuilla provided furs, hides, **obsidian**, and salt for the Gabrielino. In exchange, the Gabrielino gave the Cahuilla shell beads and asphaltum.

However, the Cahuilla were prepared for battle in certain events. For example, they went to war if other tribes invaded their territory or captured their women or children. Often, the tribe attempted peaceful agreements. But when such efforts failed, war became the necessary alternative.

Prior to battle, the Cahuilla performed **rituals** to gain supernatural support. The tribe also formed a temporary war party. The leader of this group was either a net or a skilled warrior.

During battle, the Cahuilla often **ambushed** their enemies. Warriors used clubs and bows and arrows. They also used obsidian arrowheads that were dipped in poison. A poisoned arrow helped to kill the enemy.

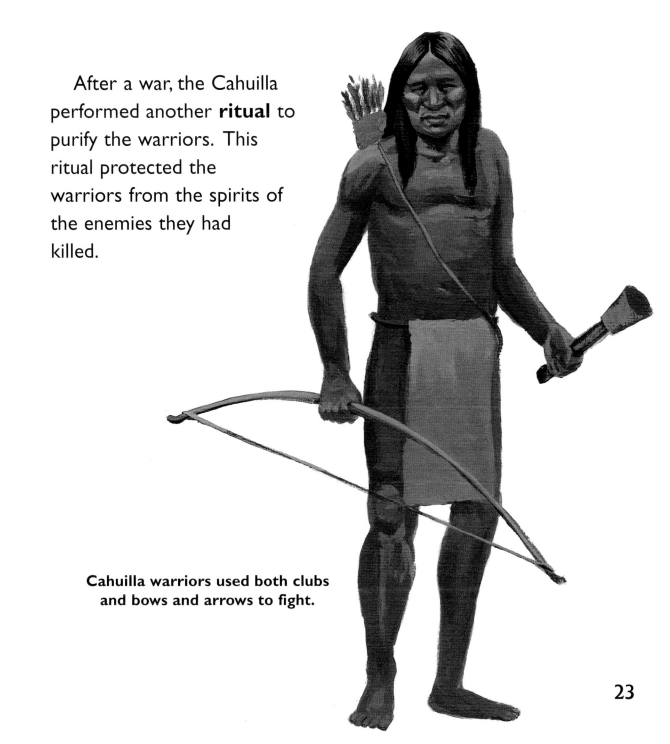

After a war, the Cahuilla performed another **ritual** to purify the warriors. This ritual protected the warriors from the spirits of the enemies they had killed.

Cahuilla warriors used both clubs and bows and arrows to fight.

23

# Contact with Europeans

The Cahuilla had their first European encounter in 1774. They met a group of Spaniards under the command of Juan Bautista de Anza. The Cahuilla had heard terrifying stories of what had happened to other tribes who had welcomed Europeans. So, they were not friendly to Anza's group.

After hostile encounters with California tribes, Europeans used Pacific Ocean routes to reach their desired lands. Cahuilla villages were far inland. So, the tribe did not experience more European contact for several years.

By the early 1800s, many Spanish **missions** had been established along the California coast. The Cahuilla had visited these missions, and some of them had even been **baptized**.

Also around this time, the Cahuilla began adopting Spanish ways of life. They started raising cattle and wearing European-style clothing. And, the men began working outside their villages for the Spanish. Despite these changes, the Cahuilla remained **economically** and politically independent.

The most damaging effect of European contact was the spread of illnesses. Europeans brought diseases that the Cahuilla had no defenses against. In 1863, a smallpox outbreak took the lives of many Cahuilla.

The first Europeans that the Cahuilla met were Spaniards with Juan Bautista de Anza's expedition.

# Famous Leaders

There have been many great Cahuilla leaders throughout the years. Chief Cabezon and **clan** leader Juan Antonio worked for peace between the Cahuilla, the Mexicans, the Spaniards, and the Americans. In 1855, Antonio was named captain general. He helped the Cahuilla develop treaties with the U.S. government.

Helen Hunt Jackson was an American poet and novelist. She was also a Native American activist. In 1881, she wrote a book titled *A Century of Dishonor*. She hoped the book would expose the unjust treatment of Native Americans.

Later, Jackson heard the story of Ramona Lubo. Lubo was a Cahuilla basket maker. In 1883 her husband, Juan Diego, rode a horse without permission. The horse belonged to a white man named Sam Temple. Temple became very angry and fatally shot Diego.

Lubo saw what had happened. But, she was not allowed to speak in court because she was Native American. Temple said he killed Diego out of self-defense, and he went free.

When Jackson heard of this, she visited Lubo. Lubo became the inspiration for her 1884 novel, *Ramona*. Jackson's books caught the attention of the public. And, her powerful words educated people about the harsh realities that Native Americans faced.

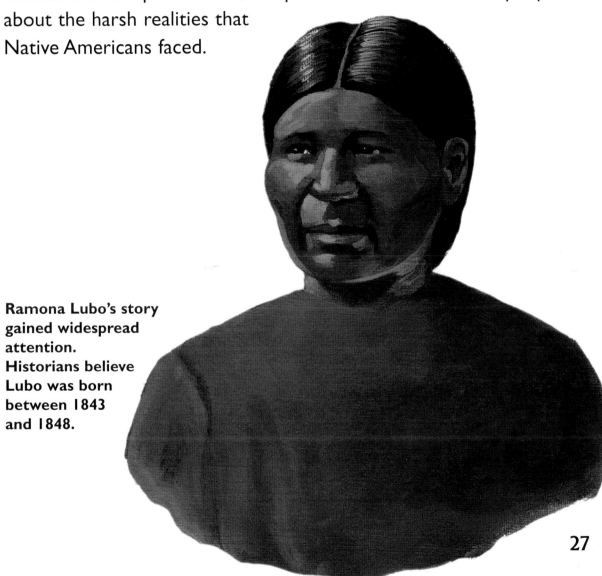

**Ramona Lubo's story gained widespread attention. Historians believe Lubo was born between 1843 and 1848.**

 # The Cahuilla Today

From 1875 to 1877, the U.S. government established **reservations** for the Cahuilla. And in 1891, it began efforts to **assimilate** Native Americans. Native Americans were educated in European ways. And, **missionaries** introduced foreign religions in an attempt to end tribal spiritual beliefs.

Today, the Cahuilla live on **federally recognized** reservations. These include Agua Caliente, Augustine, Cabazon, Cahuilla, Los Coyotes, Morongo, Ramona, Santa Rosa, and Torres-Martinez reservations. The Cahuilla share some of these reservations with other tribes. In 2000, there were 3,188 Cahuilla.

The Cahuilla work hard to preserve their traditions and protect the environment. They have opened museums to the public. The Malki Museum, the Cabazon **Cultural** Museum, and the Agua Caliente Cultural Museum offer educational programs, exhibitions, and collections.

The Cahuilla have not performed **rituals** or had a ceremonial house for many years. However, they still perform social songs and dances at celebrations. Keeping these traditions alive is important to the Cahuilla. Fiestas are still celebrated among the Cahuilla. During fiestas craftspeople show their work, and elders speak the Cahuilla language and sing traditional songs.

Every Memorial Day, the Malki Museum holds a fiesta to honor the Cahuilla men who died in service during World War II. This event is open to both Cahuilla and non-Cahuilla. Visitors can taste traditional foods, see craft samples, and observe dances.

The Agua Caliente Bird Singers performed at a festival in December 2005. Bird songs are one of the oldest Cahuilla traditions that has been passed on. The songs tell stories of history, creation, and life lessons.

This traditional Cahuilla basket was coiled. To make a coiled basket, the crafter wraps strips of materials in a bundle. The bundle circles outward in a continuous spiral.

Federal and local officials joined the Agua Caliente Cahuilla at a ceremony in December 2000. The ceremony was for the new Santa Rosa and San Jacinto Mountains National Monument in Palm Springs, California.

# Glossary

**ambush** - a surprise attack from a hidden position.

**assimilate** - to become a comfortable part of a new culture or society.

**baptize** - to be admitted into the Christian community during a ceremony involving the ritual use of water.

**breechcloth** - a piece of hide or cloth, usually worn by men, that wraps between the legs and ties with a belt around the waist.

**clan** - an extended family related by a shared symbol.

**county** - the largest local government within a state of the United States.

**culture** - the customs, arts, and tools of a nation or people at a certain time.

**dialect** - a form of a language spoken in a certain area or by certain people.

**economy** - the way a nation uses its money, goods, and natural resources.

**federal recognition** - the U.S. government's recognition of a tribe as being an independent nation. The tribe is then eligible for special funding and for protection of its reservation lands.

**mission** - a center or headquarters for religious work. A missionary is a person who spreads a church's religion.

**mortar** - a strong bowl or cup in which a material is pounded.

**obsidian** - a hard, glassy rock formed when lava cools.

**pestle** - a club-shaped tool used to pound or crush a substance.

**reservation** - a piece of land set aside by the government for Native Americans to live on.

**ritual** - a form or order to a ceremony.

**sinew** - a band of tough fibers that joins a muscle to a bone.

**tattoo** - a permanent design made on the skin.

# Web Sites

To learn more about the Cahuilla, visit ABDO Publishing Company on the World Wide Web at **www.abdopublishing.com**. Web sites about the Cahuilla are featured on our Book Links page. These links are routinely monitored and updated to provide the most current information available.

# Index

*Lab Manual to Accompany*

# Health Assessment in Nursing

**FOURTH EDITION**

**JANET WEBER, RN, MSN, EdD**
Professor
Department of Nursing
Southeast Missouri State University
Cape Girardeau, Missouri

**JANE KELLEY, RN, PhD**
Adjunct Professor
University of Mississippi Medical Center
Jackson, MS
Retired from School of Nursing
American University of Beirut
Beirut, Lebanon

**ANN SPRENGEL, RN, MSN, EdD**
Professor
Department of Nursing
Southeast Missouri State University
Cape Girardeau, Missouri

 Lippincott Williams & Wilkins
a Wolters Kluwer business
Philadelphia · Baltimore · New York · London
Buenos Aires · Hong Kong · Sydney · Tokyo

*Acquisitions Editor: Elizabeth Nieginski*
*Product Manager: Katherine Burland*
*Editorial Assistant: Laura Scott*
*Design Coordinator: Joan Wendt*
*Illustration Coordinator: Brett MacNaughton*
*Manufacturing Coordinator: Karin Duffield*
*Prepress Vendor: Macmillan Publishing Solutions*

4th edition

9  8  7  6  5

ISBN: 978-0-7817-8161-9

Care has been taken to confirm the accuracy of the information presented and to describe generally accepted practices. However, the authors, editors, and publisher are not responsible for errors or omissions or for any consequences from application of the information in this book and make no warranty, expressed or implied, with respect to the currency, completeness, or accuracy of the contents of the publication. Application of this information in a particular situation remains the professional responsibility of the practitioner; the clinical treatments described and recommended may not be considered absolute and universal recommendations.

The authors, editors, and publisher have exerted every effort to ensure that drug selection and dosage set forth in this text are in accordance with the current recommendations and practice at the time of publication. However, in view of ongoing research, changes in government regulations, and the constant flow of information relating to drug therapy and drug reactions, the reader is urged to check the package insert for each drug for any change in indications and dosage and for added warnings and precautions. This is particularly important when the recommended agent is a new or infrequently employed drug.

Some drugs and medical devices presented in this publication have Food and Drug Administration (FDA) clearance for limited use in restricted research settings. It is the responsibility of the health care provider to ascertain the FDA status of each drug or device planned for use in his or her clinical practice.

LWW.com

# Contents

# Contributors

**Suha Ballout, RN, BSN**
Masters Candidate
American University of Beirut Medical Center
Beirut, Lebanon
Chapter 8, Assessing Pain: The Fifth Vital Sign

**Linda Bugle, RN, PhD**
Associate Professor
Southeast Missouri State University
Department of Nursing
Cape Girardeau, Missouri
Chapter 34, Assessing Communities

**Cathy Young, DNSc, APRN, BC**
Associate Professor
Texas Tech University Health Sciences Center
Lubbock, Texas

**Jill C. Cash, MSN, APRN, BC**
Family Nurse Practitioner
Southern Illinois OB-GYN Associates
Carbondale, Illinois
Chapter 30, Assessing Newborns and Infants
Chapter 31, Assessing Children and Adolescents

**Crystal Denise Tripp, RN, CPN**
Missouri Delta Medical Center
Sikeston, Missouri
Case Study, Chapter 31: Assessing Children and Adolescents

**Brenda Johnson, RN, PhD**
Associate Professor
Southeast Missouri State University
Department of Nursing
Cape Girardeau, Missouri
Chapter 32, Assessing Frail Elderly Clients

# Preface

The *Lab Manual to Accompany Health Assessment in Nursing*, 4th edition, can be used as a laboratory manual and study guide for the third edition of *Health Assessment in Nursing*. Each chapter corresponds to a chapter in the textbook, and contains a **chapter pretest, interactive learner activities**, a **nursing history checklist**, a **physical assessment checklist**, a **chapter posttest, critical thinking questions, case studies**, and a **self-reflection and evaluation** tool. The lab manual can assist you with comprehending theoretical content, applying this content to acquiring history and physical assessment skills, and preparing for tests.

Prior to beginning study in each textbook chapter, take the **Chapter Pretest**. This test is designed to assess the information you may already know from a prior course. It tests basic information related to the content framework or the anatomy and physiology basic to each chapter. (Answers are located in the back of the book.) If you answer most of the questions correctly, proceed to the next section. Otherwise, review the basic framework content or anatomy and physiology found at the very beginning of the appropriate chapter.

Next read the chapter and then participate in the **Learner Activities**. These activities are designed to assist you with learning the assessment skills covered in each chapter. These activities actively involve you as a learner to promote understanding and retention of chapter content.

Then you can interview your lab partner using the **Nursing History Checklist** tool provided to document findings. After practicing the physical examination on your lab partner, you can document your findings on the **Physical Assessment Checklist** tool provided. Both of these tools serve as a reminder of the steps involved in performing a thorough nursing history and physical examination. The completed checklists can also be handed in to your nursing instructor to be evaluated for accuracy and completeness of client data.

To test your comprehension of the content provided, take the **Chapter Posttest**. Again, the test answers are provided in the back of the lab manual. To test your critical thinking abilities, answer the **Critical Thinking Questions** found after the posttest. One or two case studies follow this section to test your ability to apply new knowledge in analyzing the client data you documented from a health history interview and physical examination.

Finally, use the **Self-Reflection and Evaluation** tool to identify the degree to which you have met each of the chapter **learning objectives**. This self-evaluation will help you identify those parts of the chapter you need to review to fully comprehend the knowledge needed to effectively perform a client nursing history and physical examination.

We hope and believe this lab manual will assist you to actively learn the content and skills needed to effectively perform a Client Nursing History and Physical Examination.

Best wishes and happy learning.

Janet Weber

Jane Kelley

Ann Sprengel

# UNIT 1

# Nursing Data Collection, Documentation, and Analysis

# Nurse's Role in Health Assessment: Collecting and Analyzing Data

## Chapter Overview

The activities and quizzes that follow are designed to enhance learning about the initial step of the nursing process. Assessment involves the collection of data on which to make a nursing judgment. In practice, nurses collect data continually, beginning with initial comprehensive assessments and continuing with ongoing partial assessments, focused or problem-oriented assessments, and emergency assessments.

## CHAPTER PRETEST

### Activity A MATCHING

*Match the terms in the left column with the correct descriptions in the right column.*

**Term**

1. Assessment
2. Diagnoses
3. Planning
4. Implementation
5. Evaluation
6. Nursing diagnosis
7. Subjective data
8. Objective data
9. Collaborative problem
10. Referral problem

**Description**

a. Developing a plan of nursing care and outcome criteria
b. Carrying out the plan of care
c. Sensations or symptoms that can be verified only by the client (e.g., pain)
d. Problem that requires the attention or assistance of other health care professionals
e. Assessing whether outcome criteria have been met and revising the plan of care if necessary
f. Collection of subjective and objective data
g. Clinical judgment about individual, family, or community responses to actual or potential health problems and life processes
h. Physiologic complications that nurses monitor to detect their onset or changes in status
i. Analysis of subjective and objective data to make a professional nursing judgment
j. Findings directly observed or indirectly observed through measurements (e.g., body temperature)

**Activity B** **LEARNER ACTIVITIES**

### Working with peers in the learning lab

*After reading Chapter 1 in the textbook, participate in the following activities with your lab partner as assigned.*

1. Assess your lab partner's dietary intake for yesterday and his or her satisfaction with the intake.

2. Share with your lab partner the last time you went to a physician. Describe your reason for seeing the physician. What examinations did the physician perform? What conclusions were made? Discuss how the focus of a nursing assessment would differ from the physician's assessment. Discuss how the conclusions would differ.

3. Make an observation about your lab partner. Now make a judgment based on that observation, and validate the observation with your partner. For example, "You look tired today. Do you feel tired? Describe to me your patterns of sleeping and resting."

4. Role-play how Florence Nightingale would have performed a nursing assessment in her era. Then role-play how a nurse today would approach that assessment from a different perspective (e.g., type of equipment used, type of questions asked). Next, brainstorm with your lab partner how a nursing assessment might change in the future—20 years from now.

## CHAPTER POSTTEST

**Activity C** **MULTIPLE CHOICE**

*Choose one best answer for each of the following multiple-choice questions.*

 1. A medical examination differs from a comprehensive nursing examination in that the medical examination focuses primarily on the client's
   a. physiologic status.
   b. holistic wellness status.
   c. developmental history.
   d. level of functioning.

 2. The result of a nursing assessment is the
   a. prescription of treatment.
   b. documentation of the need for a referral.
   c. client's physiologic status.
   d. formulation of nursing diagnoses.

 3. Although the assessment phase of the nursing process precedes the other phases, the assessment phase is
   a. continuous.
   b. completed on admission.
   c. linear.
   d. performed only by nurses.

 4. When a client first enters the hospital for an elective surgical procedure, the nurse should perform an assessment termed
   a. entry.
   b. exploratory.
   c. focused.
   d. comprehensive.

**5.** An ongoing or partial assessment of a client
   **a.** focuses on a specific problem of the client.
   **b.** includes a comprehensive overview of all body systems.
   **c.** is usually performed by another health care worker.
   **d.** includes a brief reassessment of the client's normal body system.

**6.** To prepare for the assessment of a client visiting a neighborhood health care clinic, the nurse should first
   **a.** discuss the client's symptoms with other team members.
   **b.** plan for potential laboratory procedures.
   **c.** review the client's health care record.
   **d.** determine potential health care resources.

**7.** The nurse is preparing to meet a client in the clinic for the first time. After reviewing the client's record, the nurse should
   **a.** analyze data that have already been collected.
   **b.** review any past collaborative problems.
   **c.** avoid premature judgments about the client.
   **d.** consult with the client's family members.

**8.** Before beginning a comprehensive health assessment of an adult client, the nurse should explain to the client that the purpose of the assessment is to
   **a.** arrive at conclusions about the client's health.
   **b.** document any physical symptoms the client may have.
   **c.** contribute to the medical diagnosis.
   **d.** validate the data collected.

**9.** To arrive at a nursing diagnosis or a collaborative problem, the nurse goes through the steps of analysis of data. After proposing possible nursing diagnoses, the nurse should next
   **a.** cluster the data collected.
   **b.** draw inferences and identify problems.
   **c.** document conclusions.
   **d.** check for the presence of defining characteristics.

**10.** The depth and scope of nursing assessment has expanded significantly over the past several decades primarily because of
   **a.** the growing elderly population with chronic illness.
   **b.** rapid advances in biomedical knowledge and technology.
   **c.** an increase in the number of baccalaureate programs in nursing.
   **d.** an increase in the number of nurse practitioners.

**Activity D** **ESSAY QUESTIONS**

**1.** Discuss ways in which expanding technology will change the future role of the nurse in health assessment.

**2.** Compare and contrast a nursing assessment with a medical assessment.

# SELF-REFLECTION AND EVALUATION OF LEARNER OBJECTIVES

After reading Chapter 1 in the text and completing the above reviews, please identify to what degree you have met each of the following chapter learning objectives. For those objectives that you have met partially or not at all, you will want to review the chapter content for that learning objective.

| Objective | Very Much | Somewhat | Not At All |
|---|---|---|---|
| 1. Explain how assessment is applicable to every situation the nurse encounters. | | | |
| 2. Differentiate between a nursing assessment and a medical assessment. | | | |
| 3. Describe how assessment fits into the total nursing process. | | | |
| 4. List and describe the steps of the nursing process: subjective data collection; objective data collection; validation of data; documentation of data. | | | |
| 5. Describe the steps of the analysis phase of the nursing process. | | | |
| 6. Explain how the nurse's role in assessment has changed over the past century. Discuss what the nurse's role might be 25 years from now. | | | |

## CHAPTER 2

# Collecting Subjective Data

## Chapter Overview

Let the pages of this chapter help you review information about the health history interview techniques related to obtaining subjective data during the nursing assessment. Subjective data may be sensed or reported by the client or significant other people, such as family or friends or health care personnel. Subjective data often are not observable or measurable.

## CHAPTER PRETEST

### Activity A  MULTIPLE CHOICE

*Choose one best answer for each of the following multiple-choice questions.*

**1.** During an interview, the nurse collects both subjective and objective data from an adult client. Subjective data would include the client's

   **a.** perception of pain.

   **b.** height.

   **c.** weight.

   **d.** temperature.

**2.** During an interview with an adult client, the nurse can keep the interview from going off course by

   **a.** using open-ended questions.

   **b.** rephrasing the client's statements.

   **c.** inferring information.

   **d.** using closed-ended questions.

**3.** The nurse has interviewed a Hispanic client with limited English skills for the first time. The nurse observes that the client is reluctant to reveal personal information and believes in a hot–cold syndrome of disease causation. The nurse should

   **a.** indicate acceptance of the client's cultural differences.

   **b.** request a family member to interpret for the client.

   **c.** use slang terms to identify certain body parts.

   **d.** remain in a standing position during the interview.

C   4. For a nurse to be therapeutic with clients when dealing with sensitive issues such as terminal illness or sexuality, the nurse should have

   a. advanced preparation in this area.

   b. experience in dealing with these types of clients.

   c. knowledge of his or her own thoughts and feelings about these issues.

   d. personal experiences with death, dying, and sexuality.

 5. The nurse is interviewing a client in the clinic for the first time. The client appears to have a very limited vocabulary. The nurse should plan to

   a. use very basic lay terminology.

   b. have a family member present during the interview.

   c. use standard medical terminology.

   d. show the client pictures of different symptoms, such as the "faces pain chart."

d   6. The nurse is interviewing a client in the clinic for the first time. When the client tells the nurse that he smokes "about two packs of cigarettes a day," the nurse should

   a. look at the client with a frown.

   b. tell the client that he is spending a lot of money foolishly.

   c. provide the client with a list of dangers associated with smoking.

   d. encourage the client to quit smoking.

 7. During a client interview, the nurse uses nonverbal expressions appropriately when the nurse

   a. avoids excessive eye contact with the client.

   b. remains expressionless throughout the interview.

   c. uses touch in a friendly manner to establish rapport.

   d. displays mental distancing during the interview.

b   8. During the interview of an adult client, the nurse should

   a. use leading questions for valid responses.

   b. provide the client with information as questions arise.

   c. read each question carefully from the history form.

   d. complete the interview as quickly as possible.

 9. While interviewing a client for the first time, the nurse is using a standardized nursing history form. The nurse should

   a. maintain eye contact while asking the questions from the form.

   b. read the questions verbatim from the form.

   c. ask the client to complete the form.

   d. ask leading questions throughout the interview.

a  10. The nurse is interviewing a 78-year-old client for the first time. The nurse should first

   a. assess the client's hearing acuity.

   b. establish rapport with the client.

   c. obtain biographic data.

   d. use medical terminology appropriately.

**Activity B** **LEARNER ACTIVITIES**

1. Obtain permission to observe client interviews in a clinic. Observe the clients' nonverbal communications. Notice the different nonverbal responses of clients. Notice differences between male and female, elderly and young, and ethnically different clients.

2. Practice using the COLDSPA mnemonic with peers or friends who are experiencing pain or other symptoms.

3. Read the section in the text on verbal communications to avoid. Give examples of each and describe how each blocks effective communication.

4. Practice with a peer or lab partner collecting information from a selected portion of the health history. First, use the structural form and questions for the section. Next, repeat data collection for the section, but this time do not use any structured questions. Use only broad open-ended questions, such as "Tell me about ..." and "Can you think of anything else?"

5. Collect a complete health history of a lab partner or peer using the health history portion of the nursing assessment tool in Chapter 28 of the textbook *Sample Adult Nursing Health History and Physical Assessment*.

**Activity C** **CASE STUDY**

*Read the following and analyze how the client's lifestyle might affect her health.*

Stacey Kline is a 29-year-old graphic artist. She is single and lives in a one-bedroom apartment in the city. She has an extensive social network in the city and goes out to clubs and bars until at least midnight about four nights a week. Her work is very fulfilling for her, and she rates her stress level as moderate. She eats two meals a day (usually out), drinks "a lot" of coffee, smokes a pack of "light" cigarettes a day, and drinks whenever she goes out with friends. Stacey does not have a serious boyfriend at present, but she is taking birth control pills "to prevent a disaster with some guy I don't care about." She has a good supportive relationship with her family, who live 15 minutes away. She visits them at least twice a week. She is a Roman Catholic and tries to go to Mass every other week. She says her faith is important to her but it does not rule her life.

# CHAPTER POSTTEST

**Activity D** **MULTIPLE CHOICE**

*Choose one best answer for each of the following multiple-choice questions.*

1. During an interview with an adult client for the first time, the nurse can clarify the client's statements by
   a. offering a "laundry list" of descriptors.
   b. rephrasing the client's statements.
   c. repeating verbatim what the client has said.
   d. inferring what the client's statements mean.

2. During an interview between a nurse and a client, the nurse and the client collaborate to identify problems and goals. This occurs during the phase of the interview termed
   a. introductory.
   b. ongoing.
   c. working.
   d. closure.

**3.** The nurse is preparing to interview an adult client for the first time. The nurse observes that the client appears very anxious. The nurse should

  **a.** allow the client time to calm down.

  **b.** avoid discussing sensitive issues.

  **c.** set time limits with the client.

  **d.** explain the role and purpose of the nurse.

**4.** The nurse is beginning a health history interview with an adult client who expresses anger at the nurse. The best approach for dealing with an angry client is for the nurse to

  **a.** allow the client to ventilate his or her feelings.

  **b.** offer reasons why the client should not feel angry.

  **c.** provide structure during the interview.

  **d.** refer the client to a different health care provider.

**5.** The nurse is planning to interview a client who is being treated for depression. When the nurse enters the examination room, the client is sitting on the table with shoulders slumped. The nurse should plan to approach this client by

  **a.** providing the client with simple explanations.

  **b.** offering to hold the client's hand.

  **c.** using a highly structured interview process.

  **d.** expressing interest in a neutral manner.

**6.** The nurse is planning to interview a client who has demonstrated manipulative behaviors during past clinic visits. During the interview process, the nurse should plan to

  **a.** give the client rules with which he must agree to comply.

  **b.** provide structure and set limits with the client.

  **c.** tell the client that the nurse is aware of his past behaviors.

  **d.** approach the client in an authoritative manner.

**7.** During a client interview, the nurse asks questions about the client's past health history. The primary purpose of asking about past health problems is to

  **a.** determine whether genetic conditions are present.

  **b.** summarize the family's health problems.

  **c.** evaluate how the client's current symptoms affect his or her lifestyle.

  **d.** identify risk factors to the client and his or her significant others.

**8.** While interviewing an adult client about her nutrition habits, the nurse should

  **a.** ask the client for a 3-day recall of food intake.

  **b.** review the food pyramid with the client.

  **c.** ask the client about limitations to activity.

  **d.** encourage the client to drink three to four glasses of water daily.

**9.** While interviewing an adult client about the client's stress levels and coping responses, an appropriate question by the nurse is

  **a.** "Do you feel stress at work?"

  **b.** "How often do you feel stressed?"

  **c.** "Is stress a problem in your life?"

  **d.** "How do you manage your stress?"

**Activity E** **MATCHING**

*Match the terms in the left column with the correct description in the right column.*

**Term**

6 **1.** Biographic data

3 **2.** Reason for seeking health care

___ **3.** History of present concern

7 **4.** Past health history

5 **5.** Family health history

___ **6.** Review of body systems for current health problem

2 **7.** Lifestyle and health practices

4 **8.** Developmental level

**Description**

a 1 • No previous problems; occasional breast soreness before menstruation

b 2 • Exercises three times a week; drinks "a lot" of caffeine to keep alert and on the go for long busy days; high stress (from work); good relationships with husband and children

c 3 • Felt lump in right breast while doing BSE

d 4 • Middlescent: generativity versus stagnation

e 5 • Great-aunt had breast cancer; sister has fibrocystic breast disease

f 6 • Female client; aged 42; married; two children

g 7 • All childhood diseases; one hospitalization to set a badly broken arm (car accident); two normal vaginal deliveries

# SELF-REFLECTION AND EVALUATION OF LEARNER OBJECTIVES

After reading Chapter 2 in the text and completing the above exercises, please identify to what degree you have met each of the following chapter learning objectives. For those objectives that you have met partially or not at all, you will want to review the chapter content.

| Objective | Very Much | Somewhat | Not At All |
|---|---|---|---|
| *Interviewing* | | | |
| 1. Describe the three phases of an interview. | | | |
| 2. Describe the use of nonverbal communication during an interview. | | | |
| 3. Describe the use of effective verbal communication during a client interview. | | | |
| 4. Describe types of verbal communication that should be avoided in client interviews. | | | |
| 5. Describe how communication should be varied to communicate with elderly clients. | | | |
| 6. Describe how ethnicity can affect communication. | | | |
| 7. Describe appropriate ways to modify communication with clients who have emotional conditions. | | | |

| Objective | Very Much | Somewhat | Not At All |
|---|---|---|---|
| *Taking the Health History* | | | |
| 8. Identify the major categories of a complete health history. | | | |
| 9. Describe key sources of biographic data. | | | |
| 10. Describe types of biographic data to be collected. | | | |
| 11. Obtain an accurate nursing history of a client, omitting (at this time) the review of body systems. | | | |
| 12. Use the COLDSPA format to collect information about a health concern. | | | |
| 13. Construct a genogram to identify patterns within family history. | | | |
| 14. Identify information to be obtained in a review of body systems. | | | |
| 15. Describe the relationship of the lifestyle and health practices profile with health status. | | | |

# Collecting Objective Data

The pages of this chapter can help you review the reasons and techniques for obtaining objective assessment data (data that are observable and/or measurable).

## CHAPTER PRETEST

**Activity A** MATCHING

*Match the terms in the left column with the correct description in the right column.*

**Term**

_b_ **1.** Sims' position

_c_ **2.** Sitting position

_d_ **3.** Supine position

_f_ **4.** Standing position

_h_ **5.** Prone position

_k_ **6.** Lithotomy position

_g_ **7.** Fingerpads

_i_ **8.** Ulnar surface or palm of hand

_a_ **9.** Dorsal surface of hand

_j_ **10.** Bell of stethoscope

_e_ **11.** Diaphragm of stethoscope

**Description**

✓ **a.** Part of examiner's hand used to feel for temperature

✓ **b.** Side-lying position used during the rectal examination

**c.** Position used during much of the physical examination including examination of the head, neck, lungs, chest, back, breast, axilla, heart, vital signs, and upper extremities

✓ **d.** Back-lying position used for examination of the abdomen (with one small pillow under the head and another under knees); this position also allows easy access for palpation of peripheral pulses

**e.** Larger end of stethoscope used to detect breath sounds, normal heart sounds, and bowel sounds

**f.** Position used to examine male genitalia and to assess gait, posture, and balance

**g.** Part of examiner's hand used to feel for fine discriminations: pulses, texture, size, consistency, shape, and crepitus

**h.** Client lies on abdomen with head turned to side; may be used to assess back and mobility of hip joint

**i.** Part of examiner's hand used to feel for vibration, thrills, or fremitus

**j.** Smaller end of stethoscope used to detect low-pitched sounds (abnormal heart sounds and bruits)

**k.** Back-lying position with hips at edge of examining table and feet supported in stirrups; used for examination of female genitalia, reproductive tract, and rectum

# LEARNER ACTIVITIES

**Activity B**  **WORKING WITH PEERS IN THE LEARNING LAB**

*After reading Chapter 3, participate in the following activities with your lab partner as assigned.*

1. Recall a time when you were about to have a physical examination. Remember the anxieties and concerns you were feeling. What were your greatest fears? Share these feelings with your lab partner.

2. Now practice verbally preparing your lab partner for a physical examination. Explain the privacy, confidentiality, time, positioning, and purpose of the examination.

3. Inspect the forearm of your lab partner. Do you have sufficient lighting? Explain. Now use Table 3-2 in the textbook to use various parts of your hand to palpate pulses, texture, shape, and temperature of the forearm.

4. Practice indirect percussion (see Fig. 3-6) on your lab partner to determine the various percussion tones listed in Table 3-3. Use studs in walls to percuss flat and dull tones. Fill a milk carton partway with water and percuss it. Now percuss an empty milk carton and notice the difference. What different types of percussion notes are you hearing?

5. Read Equipment Spotlight 3.1, "How to Use the Stethoscope." Discuss with your lab partner whether this is how you normally use a stethoscope. What did you learn?

6. Use Table 3-1, "Equipment Needed for Physical Examinations," to identify the equipment pieces needed. Find each of these pieces of equipment in your learning lab and discuss its purpose and how to use it with your lab partner.

# CHAPTER POSTTEST

**Activity C**  **MULTIPLE CHOICE**

*Choose one best answer for each of the following multiple-choice questions.*

1. Before beginning a physical assessment of a client, the nurse should first
   **a.** wash both hands with soap and water.
   **b.** determine whether the client is anxious.
   **c.** ask the client to remove all clothing.
   **d.** request a family member to be present.

2. To alleviate a client's anxiety during a comprehensive assessment, the nurse should
   **a.** begin with intrusive procedures first to get them completed quickly.
   **b.** explain each procedure being performed and the reason for the procedure.
   **c.** remain in the examination room while the client changes into a gown.
   **d.** ask the client to sign a consent for the physical examination.

3. While performing a physical examination on an older adult, the nurse should plan to
   **a.** complete the examination as quickly as possible.
   **b.** ask the client to change positions frequently.
   **c.** provide only minimal teaching related to health care.
   **d.** use minimal position changes.

4. During a comprehensive assessment, the primary technique used by the nurse throughout the examination is
   **a.** palpation.
   **b.** percussion.
   **c.** auscultation.
   **d.** inspection.

**5.** While examining a client, the nurse plans to palpate temperature of the skin by using the
   **a.** fingertips of the hand.
   **b.** ulnar surface of the hand.
   **c.** dorsal surface of the hand.
   **d.** palmar surface of the hand.

 **6.** During palpation of a client's organs, the nurse palpates the spleen by applying pressure between 2.5 and 5 cm. The nurse is performing
   **a.** light palpation.
   **b.** moderate palpation.
   **(c.)** deep palpation.
   **d.** very deep palpation.

 **7.** While performing a physical examination on an adult client, the nurse can detect the density of an underlying structure by using
   **a.** inspection.
   **b.** palpation.
   **c.** Doppler magnification.
   **d.** percussion.

**8.** When the nurse places one hand flat on the body surface and uses the fist of the other hand to strike the back of the hand flat on the body surface, the nurse is using
   **a.** firm percussion.
   **b.** direct percussion.
   **c.** indirect percussion.
   **d.** blunt percussion.

 **9.** An adult client visits a clinic and tells the nurse that she suspects she has a urinary tract infection. To detect tenderness over the client's kidneys, the nurse should instruct the client that he or she will be performing
   **a.** moderate palpation.
   **b.** deep palpation.
   **c.** indirect percussion.
   **d.** blunt percussion.

 **10.** The most commonly used method of percussion is
   **a.** direct percussion.
   **b.** mild percussion.
   **c.** indirect percussion.
   **d.** blunt percussion.

 **11.** During a comprehensive assessment of the lungs of an adult client with a diagnosis of emphysema, the nurse anticipates that during percussion the client will exhibit
   **a.** hyperresonance.
   **b.** tympany.
   **c.** dullness.
   **d.** flatness.

_b_  **12.** While percussing an adult client during a physical examination, the nurse can expect to hear flatness over the client's

    **a.** lungs.

    **b.** bone.

    **c.** liver.

    **d.** abdomen.

_b_  **13.** During a comprehensive assessment of an adult client, the nurse can best hear high-pitched sounds by using a stethoscope with a

    **a.** 1-inch bell.

    **b.** $1\frac{1}{2}$-inch diaphragm.

    **c.** 15-inch flexible tubing.

    **d.** 1-inch diaphragm.

**Activity D** **ESSAY QUESTIONS**

**1.** When might you use deep palpation during a physical examination? Bimanual palpation? Direct percussion? Indirect percussion?

**2.** Explain how the universal precautions and infection control guidelines would apply to the physical examination techniques of inspection, percussion, palpation, and auscultation.

**3.** Describe how you would prepare yourself to perform a total physical examination of a client of the opposite sex. Describe how you would prepare the client both emotionally and physically.

# SELF-REFLECTION AND EVALUATION
# OF LEARNER OBJECTIVES

After reading Chapter 3 in the text and completing the above reviews, please identify to what degree you have met each of the following chapter learning objectives. For those objectives that you have met partially or not at all, you will want to review the chapter content.

| Objective | Very Much | Somewhat | Not At All |
|---|---|---|---|
| 1. Describe ways to prepare the physical environment and make it conducive to a physical examination. | | | |
| 2. Explain ways to prepare a client for a physical examination. | | | |
| 3. Describe the various positions used to perform a physical examination. | | | |
| 4. Demonstrate the correct method used for inspection during a physical examination. | | | |
| 5. Explain the purpose and differences between light, deep, and bimanual palpation. | | | |
| 6. Demonstrate correct direct, indirect, and blunt percussion techniques used during a physical examination. | | | |
| 7. Explain the correct use of a stethoscope and the purpose of the bell and the diaphragm. | | | |
| 8. Survey the various pieces of equipment used to perform a physical examination. | | | |

# 4

# Validating and Documenting Data

## Chapter Overview

After you collect assessment data, what do you do with them? How do you know that they are reliable information? How do they become part of the client's record? Use the following activities to review and enhance the validation and documentation process.

## CHAPTER PRETEST

### Activity A  MULTIPLE CHOICE

*Choose one best answer for each of the following multiple-choice questions.*

_____ 1. If the nurse makes an error while documenting findings on a client's record, the nurse should

  a. erase the error and make the correction.

  b. obliterate the error and make the correction.

  c. draw a line through the error and have it witnessed.

  d. draw a line through the error, writing "error" and initialing.

_____ 2. The nurse is preparing to document assessment findings in a client's record. The nurse should

  a. write in complete sentences with few abbreviations.

  b. avoid slang terms or labels unless they are direct quotes.

  c. record how the data were collected.

  d. use the term normal for normal findings.

_____ 3. The nurse has assessed the breath sounds of an adult client. The best way for the nurse to document these findings on a client is to write

  a. "Bilateral lung sounds clear."

  b. "The client's lung sounds were clear on both sides."

  c. "Client's lung sounds were auscultated with stethoscope and were clear on both sides."

  d. "After listening to client's lung sounds, both lungs appeared clear."

---- **4.** An example of an objective finding in an adult client is

    **a.** a client's symptom of pain.

    **b.** family history data.

    **c.** genetic disorders.

    **d.** vital signs.

---- **5.** While recording the subjective data of an adult client who complains of pain in his lower back, the nurse should include the location of the pain and the

    **a.** cause of the pain.

    **b.** client's caregiver.

    **c.** client's occupation.

    **d.** pain relief measures.

---- **6.** One disadvantage of the open-ended assessment form is that it

    **a.** does not allow for individualization.

    **b.** asks standardized questions.

    **c.** requires a lot of time to complete.

    **d.** does not provide a total picture of the client.

---- **7.** The nurse is recording admission data for an adult client using a cued or checklist type of assessment form. This type of assessment form

    **a.** prevents missed questions during data collection.

    **b.** covers all the data that a client may provide.

    **c.** clusters the assessment data with nursing diagnoses.

    **d.** establishes comparability of data across populations.

---- **8.** One advantage for an institution to use an integrated cued/checklist type of assessment data form is that it

    **a.** allows a comprehensive and thorough picture of the client's symptoms.

    **b.** may be easily used by different levels of caregivers, which enhances communication.

    **c.** provides for easy and rapid documentation across clinical settings and populations.

    **d.** includes the 11 health care patterns in an easily readable format.

---- **9.** An assessment form commonly used in long-term care facilities is the nursing minimum data set. One primary advantage to this type of assessment form is that it

    **a.** establishes comparability of nursing data across clinical populations.

    **b.** clusters all the nursing and medical diagnoses in one place.

    **c.** allows for individualization for each client in the health care setting.

    **d.** uses a flowchart format for easy documentation of objective data.

---- **10.** In some health care settings, the institution uses an assessment form that assesses only one part of a client. These types of forms are termed

    **a.** progressive.

    **b.** specific.

    **c.** checklist.

    **d.** focused.

____ **11.** The nurse is planning to assess a newly admitted adult client. While gathering data from the client, the nurse should

    **a.** validate all data before documentation of the data.

    **b.** document the data after the entire examination process.

    **c.** record the nurse's understanding of the client's problem.

    **d.** use medical terms that are commonly used in health care settings.

**Activity B** **LEARNER ACTIVITIES**

*Working with peers in the learning lab*

*After reading Chapter 4 in the text, participate in the following activities with your lab partner as assigned.*

**1.** Select a case from the end of one of the body systems chapters in the textbook (e.g., Chapter 13 or Chapter 14) and read it. Separate the objective from the subjective data. Now determine what data need to be validated. How would you validate them?

**2.** Interview your lab partner to determine how his or her physical and mental health has been during the past month. Do this beginning with five basic questions:

    **a.** How have you felt during the past month?

    **b.** Have you had any major illnesses during this time?

    **c.** Have you had any minor illnesses during this time?

    **d.** Rate your current health on a scale of 1 to 10 (with 1 being poor and 10 being great).

    **e.** How would you like your health to improve?

# CHAPTER POSTTEST

**Activity C** **MATCHING**

*Identify the following items as either subjective (S) or objective (O) data by writing "S" or "O" on each line.*

____ **1.** Describes severe right-sided headache

____ **2.** Reddened, raised, indurated area on deltoid area of left arm

____ **3.** Cannot eat seeds or uncooked grains without abdominal discomfort

____ **4.** Passing flatus

____ **5.** Bowel sounds present in all four quadrants

____ **6.** Complains of lower back pain on movement

____ **7.** Pattern of request for pain medication every 2 hours

____ **8.** Pale, clammy, and diaphoretic

____ **9.** Feels nauseated and dizzy

____ **10.** Emesis of 200 mL light beige thin liquid

**Activity D** **ESSAY QUESTIONS**

**1.** Discuss the possible results of failing to document data. How could this affect the client? The nurse?

**2.** Discuss a variety of ways to validate client data obtained during a nursing history interview.

**3.** Document narrative progress notes using the following client information, adding hypothetical details as needed for a complete entry.

Mrs. Jones arrives in room 2344. Headache; flushed, cool skin; pale; nausea and vomiting; temperature normal; blood pressure 136/85 mm Hg; pulse rapid; respirations rapid. Requesting pain medication.

# SELF-REFLECTION AND EVALUATION OF LEARNER OBJECTIVES

After reading Chapter 4 in the text and completing the above reviews, please identify to what degree you have met each of the following chapter learning objectives. For those objectives that you have met partially or not at all, you will want to review the chapter content for that learning objective.

| Objective | Very Much | Somewhat | Not At All |
|---|---|---|---|
| 1. Define validation of data. | | | |
| 2. Describe the steps of the validation process. | | | |
| 3. Describe conditions that require data to be rechecked and validated. | | | |
| 4. Discuss several ways to validate data. | | | |
| 5. Describe the purposes of documenting assessment data. | | | |
| 6. Describe the general guidelines and rules for documenting data. | | | |
| 7. Describe the three types of standardized assessment forms for documenting data. | | | |
| 8. Document assessment findings, using a variety of assessment forms (e.g., narrative progress notes, flow sheets). | | | |
| 9. Discuss the significance of documentation as specified by your state nurse practice act and JCAHO standards. | | | |

# Analyzing Data Using Critical Thinking Skills

## Chapter Overview

Initially, sorting through nursing assessment data may seem to be an overwhelming task. Use the exercises that follow to divide the process known as diagnostic reasoning into doable components. Use the activities to review the steps of critical thinking and diagnostic reasoning, to differentiate normal findings from abnormal findings, to draw inferences, to make nursing diagnoses, and to confirm or rule out conclusions.

## CHAPTER PRETEST

### Activity A  MATCHING

*Match the terms in the left column with the correct description in the right column.*

**Term**

____ **1.** Critical thinking

____ **2.** Intuition

____ **3.** Wellness nursing diagnosis

____ **4.** Collaborative problem

____ **5.** Risk nursing diagnosis

____ **6.** Actual nursing diagnosis

____ **7.** Knowledge

____ **8.** Cognitive abilities

____ **9.** Analysis of data

**Description**

**a.** A nursing diagnosis that indicates the client has an opportunity to enhance a health status

**b.** Certain physiologic complications that nurses monitor to detect their onset or change in status

**c.** Aptitude involving the act or process of knowing, including both awareness and judgment

**d.** The fact or condition of knowing something with familiarity gained through experience or association

**e.** Quick and ready insight

**f.** The way in which one processes information using knowledge, past experience, intuition, and cognitive abilities to formulate conclusions or diagnoses

**g.** Diagnostic phase of the nursing process

**h.** A nursing diagnosis that indicates the client does not currently have a problem but is at high risk for developing it

**i.** A nursing diagnosis that indicates the client is currently experiencing the stated problem or has a dysfunctional pattern

**Activity B** **LEARNER ACTIVITIES**

### Working with peers in the learning lab

*After reading Chapter 5 in the text, participate in the following activities with your lab partner as assigned.*

1. Refer to the first page of Chapter 5 and ask yourself the 10 questions presented to determine your level of critical thinking. Discuss with your peers ways to improve your critical thinking based on these questions.

2. Interview your lab partners to assess their current level of well-being for the day. Use the seven steps for analyzing data to draw conclusions. Can you identify any nursing diagnoses or collaborative problems?

3. Review the diagnostic reasoning pitfalls in Chapter 5. Discuss with your partners which pitfalls you feel you will make most frequently. How will experience help you to avoid these pitfalls?

# CHAPTER POSTTEST

**Activity C** **MULTIPLE CHOICE**

*Choose one best answer for each of the following multiple-choice questions.*

_____ **1.** One characteristic of a nurse who is a critical thinker is the ability to
  **a.** form an opinion quickly.
  **b.** offer advice to clients.
  **c.** be right most of the time.
  **d.** validate information and judgments.

_____ **2.** Before the nurse analyzes the data collected, the nurse should
  **a.** determine collaborative problems with the health care team.
  **b.** group the data into clusters or groups of problems.
  **c.** generate possible hypotheses for the client's problems.
  **d.** perform the steps of the assessment process accurately.

_____ **3.** The nurse is caring for an adult client who tells the nurse "For weeks now, I've been so tired. I just can't get to sleep at night because of all the noise in my neighborhood." An actual nursing diagnosis for this client is
  **a.** fatigue related to excessive noise levels as manifested by client's statements of chronic fatigue.
  **b.** sleep deprivation related to noisy neighborhood and inability to sleep.
  **c.** chronic fatigue syndrome related to excessive levels of noise in neighborhood.
  **d.** readiness for enhanced sleep related to control of noise level in the home.

_____ **4.** A common error for beginning nurses who are formulating nursing diagnoses during data analysis is to
  **a.** formulate too many nursing diagnoses for the client and family.
  **b.** include too much data about the client in the history.
  **c.** obtain an insufficient number of cues and cluster patterns.
  **d.** quickly make a diagnosis without hypothesizing several diagnoses.

**Activity D** **ESSAY QUESTIONS**

1. Discuss how critical thinking is used in the assessment phase of the nursing process.

2. Describe the steps you go through to draw conclusions from gathered data.

**3.** Read the following case study. Identify a cue cluster and possible diagnostic conclusion(s) (wellness, risk, or actual nursing diagnosis). Describe your critical thinking process.

Mrs. Phillips has smoked three packs of cigarettes a day for 50 years. She complains of difficulty fixing her own meals and bathing and dressing herself because of fatigue and shortness of breath. She has a nonproductive congested-sounding cough, a respiratory rate of 26 beats/minute, a shallow breathing pattern, an oral temperature of 97.8°F, and a blood pressure of 140/92 mm Hg. Height 5 feet, 3 inches; weight 127 pounds.

# SELF-REFLECTION AND EVALUATION
# OF LEARNER OBJECTIVES

After reading Chapter 5 in the text and completing the above reviews, please identify to what degree you have met each of the following chapter learning objectives. For those objectives that you have met partially or not at all, you will want to review the chapter content for that learning objective.

| Objective | Very Much | Somewhat | Not At All |
|---|---|---|---|
| 1. Describe how critical thinking relates to diagnostic reasoning. | | | |
| 2. Determine your own ability to think critically. | | | |
| 3. Describe seven essential critical thinking characteristics. | | | |
| 4. List the six essential components of the diagnostic phase of the nursing process. | | | |
| 5. List the seven distinct steps used in this text to perform data analysis. | | | |
| 6. Describe and give examples of wellness, risk, and actual nursing diagnoses. | | | |
| 7. Give examples of collaborative problems. | | | |
| 8. Explain why experienced expert nurses have an advantage over novice nurses in making accurate diagnoses. | | | |
| 9. Describe diagnostic reasoning pitfalls. | | | |

# UNIT II

# Integrative Holistic Nursing Assessment

# Assessing Mental Status and Psychosocial Developmental Level

Your evaluation of the client's mental status and psychosocial developmental level will provide you with information regarding the client's level of cognitive functioning and emotional stability. These data will be useful to you to determine the reliability of the client's responses throughout the rest of the examination. That is why it is important to begin your examination with an assessment of the client's mental status and developmental level.

## CHAPTER PRETEST

**Activity A** MATCHING

*Match the terms in the left column with the correct description in the right column.*

**Term**

_____ **1.** Score of 28

_____ **2.** Score of 23

_____ **3.** Lethargy

_____ **4.** Obtunded

_____ **5.** Stupor

_____ **6.** Coma

_____ **7.** Adolescent

_____ **8.** Young adult

_____ **9.** Middlescent

_____ **10.** Older adult

**Description**

**a.** Slow response, opens eyes to loud voice

**b.** Awakens to painful stimuli and then goes back to sleep

**c.** Unresponsive to all stimuli

**d.** Normal SLUMS score for client with high school education

**e.** Normal SLUMS score for client with less than high school education

**f.** Opens eyes and answers questions but falls back asleep

**g.** Intimacy

**h.** Identity

**i.** Ego-integrity

**j.** Generativity

**Activity B** **LEARNER ACTIVITIES**

*After reading Chapter 6 in the text, participate in the following activities:*

**1.** Go to a community shopping mall during a busy time of the day. Sit and observe those who pass by, noting their hygiene, behaviors, facial expressions, mannerisms, and speech.

**2.** Pair up with a peer and take turns role-playing the various levels of consciousness (LOC): lethargy, obtunded, stupor, and coma. While one person portrays these various levels as the client, the other will be the nurse who will assess and record the client's LOC.

**3.** Practice assessing your own developmental level. Then assess one of your peers' developmental level. Practice recording your findings.

**Activity C** **INTERVIEWING AND RECORDING ASSESSMENT FINDINGS**

Use the following Nursing History checklist as your guide to interviewing and recording your findings in your assessment of mental status and developmental level.

### Nursing History Checklist

| Questions | Satisfactory Data | Needs Additional Data | Data Missing |
|---|---|---|---|
| *Biographic Data* | | | |
| 1. Name, address, phone numbers. | | | |
| 2. Age stated by client. | | | |
| 3. Marital status. | | | |
| 4. Place of employment. | | | |
| 5. Educational level. | | | |
| *Present History* | | | |
| 1. Most current health concern at this time. | | | |
| 2. Reason for seeking health care? | | | |
| *(Apply COLDSPA here as appropriate)* | | | |
| *Past Health History* | | | |
| 1. Head injuries, meningitis, encephalitis, stroke? Effects on health? | | | |
| 2. Past medical diagnoses, surgeries. | | | |
| 3. Past counseling services received? Results? | | | |
| 4. Headaches? Describe. | | | |
| 5. Served in active duty in armed forces? | | | |
| 6. Breathing difficulties? | | | |
| 7. Heart palpitations? | | | |
| 8. Exposure to environmental toxins? | | | |
| *Family History* | | | |
| 1. Family history of mental health problems? | | | |
| 2. Family history of psychiatric disorders, dementia, brain tumors? | | | |

| Questions | Satisfactory Data | Needs Additional Data | Data Missing |
|---|---|---|---|
| *Lifestyle and Health Practices* | | | |
| 1. Describe typical activities in a day. | | | |
| 2. Energy level with ADLs? | | | |
| 3. Typical eating habits? | | | |
| 4. Amount of alcohol consumed daily? Any use of recreational drugs (i.e., marijuana, tranquilizers, barbiturates, cocaine, methamphetamines)? | | | |
| 5. Sleep patterns. | | | |
| 6. Typical bowel elimination patterns. | | | |
| 7. Exercise patterns. | | | |
| 8. Use of prescribed or OTC drugs. | | | |
| 9. Religious practices and activities? | | | |
| 10. Role in family and community? | | | |
| 11. Relationships with others (family members, coworkers, neighbors)? | | | |
| 12. Perception of self and relationship with others? | | | |
| 13. View of one's future? Life goals? | | | |

## Activity D PERFORMING PHYSICAL ASSESSMENT

Practice recording the client's mental status and developmental level. Use the following checklist to assess a peer, friend, or family member. Column 1 may be used to guide your examination. Column 2 may be used by your instructor to provide you feedback regarding ways to enhance your skills.

### Physical Assessment Checklist

| Assessment Skill | Findings (Normal or Abnormal) and Notes | | Performance (Satisfactory, Needs Improvement, Unsatisfactory) | | |
|---|---|---|---|---|---|
| | N | A | S | N | U |
| When time is limited, use the Saint Louis University Mental Status (SLUMS) examination (Assessment Tool 6–1 in the 4th edition of *Health Assessment in Nursing*). Report Client's SLUMS score and client's level of education. Other wise, complete observations #1 to 10 below. | | | | | |
| 1. Observe level of consciousness. Ask for name, address, and phone number as appropriate. If no response: • Call name louder. • Next shake gently. • If still no response, apply painful stimulus. | ☐ | ☐ | ☐ | ☐ | ☐ |

| Assessment Skill | Findings (Normal or Abnormal) and Notes | | Performance (Satisfactory, Needs Improvement, Unsatisfactory) | | |
|---|---|---|---|---|---|
| | N | A | S | N | U |
| Use Glasgow Coma Scale (Assessment Tool 6.3 in the 4th edition of *Health Assessment in Nursing*) for high-risk clients. | | | | | |
| 2. Note posture, gait, and body movements. | ☐ | ☐ | ☐ | ☐ | ☐ |
| 3. Observe behavior and the client's affect. | ☐ | ☐ | ☐ | ☐ | ☐ |
| 4. Note dress, grooming, and hygiene. | ☐ | ☐ | ☐ | ☐ | ☐ |
| 5. Observe facial expression. | ☐ | ☐ | ☐ | ☐ | ☐ |
| 6. Observe speech. | ☐ | ☐ | ☐ | ☐ | ☐ |
| 7. Note mood, feelings, and expressions. Use Depression Questionnaire (Self-Assessment 6.1 in the 4th edition of *Health Assessment in Nursing*) if depression is suspected. Use Geriatric Depression scale (Self-Assessment 32.1 in the 4th edition of *Health Assessment in Nursing*) in older adults. | ☐ | ☐ | ☐ | ☐ | ☐ |
| 8. Note thought processes and perceptions. | ☐ | ☐ | ☐ | ☐ | ☐ |
| 9. Observe for any destructive or suicidal tendencies. | ☐ | ☐ | ☐ | ☐ | ☐ |
| 10. Observe the following cognitive abilities: <br>• Orientation to person, time, and place <br>• Concentration and attentiveness <br>• Recent memory <br>• Remote memory <br>• Memory to learn new information <br>• Abstract reasoning <br>• Judgment <br>• Visual and constructional ability | ☐ | ☐ | ☐ | ☐ | ☐ |
| *Determine the client's psychosocial developmental level* based on both the subjective and objective data you have obtained at this point. You may have to ask the client or family further questions or make additional objective observations to determine the client's stage of development. | | | | | |
| Does the Young Adult (*Intimacy versus Isolation*): <br>• Accept self? <br>• Have independence? <br>• Express love? Responsibly? <br>• Have friends and close relationships? <br>• Have a philosophy of life? <br>• Have a career or meaningful work? <br>• Independently solve typical everyday living problems? | ☐ | ☐ | ☐ | ☐ | ☐ |
| Does the Middle-Aged Adult (*Generativity versus Stagnation*): <br>• Have a healthy lifestyle? <br>• Contribute to the growth of others? <br>• Have intimate long-term relationship? <br>• Maintain stable home? <br>• Like work or career? <br>• Feel proud of family and accomplishments? <br>• Contribute to one's community? | ☐ | ☐ | ☐ | ☐ | ☐ |

| Assessment Skill | Findings (Normal or Abnormal) and Notes | | Performance (Satisfactory, Needs Improvement, Unsatisfactory) | | |
|---|---|---|---|---|---|
| | N | A | S | N | U |
| Does the Older Adult (*Integrity versus Despair*): <br> • Adjust to physical changes? <br> • Recognize aging effects on relationships and activities? <br> • Maintain relationships with family? <br> • Continue interests outside self and home? <br> • Retire and transition to new activities? <br> • Adjust to deaths of relatives and friends? <br> • Maintain optimum level of function through diet, exercise, and hygiene? <br> • Find meaning in past life and face inevitable mortality? <br> • Integrate values to understand self and be comforted? <br> • Review accomplishments and contributions to others? | ☐ | ☐ | ☐ | ☐ | ☐ |
| *Analysis of Date* | | | | | |
| 1. Formulate nursing diagnoses. | ☐ | ☐ | ☐ | ☐ | ☐ |
| 2. Formulate collaborative problems. | ☐ | ☐ | ☐ | ☐ | ☐ |
| 3. Make necessary referrals. | ☐ | ☐ | ☐ | ☐ | ☐ |

# CHAPTER POSTTEST

### Activity E MULTIPLE CHOICE

*Choose the best answer for each of the following multiple-choice questions.*

_____ **1.** The nurse assesses a client using the Glasgow Coma Scale. Which of the following indicators will be used to determine the score?

   **a.** eye opening, and appropriateness of verbal and motor responses.

   **b.** ability to recall recent and remote memories, and to use abstract reasoning.

   **c.** assessment of the 12 cranial nerves.

   **d.** naming of objects, recall of three words, and ability to redraw a design.

_____ **2.** The client's daughter asks the nurse why the nurse is asking her mother depression-related questions. The nurse explains that even though the client has symptoms of dementia, the Geriatric Depression Scale is being used because

   **a.** depression and dementia are one in the same disorder.

   **b.** finding out why she is depressed will help determine the cause of her dementia.

   **c.** depression often mimics signs and symptoms of dementia.

   **d.** it is the most accurate tool to determine the stage of dementia.

_____ **3.** The nurse documents findings from the client's Mini-Mental State Examination. The following information will be documented as a result of this test:

   **a.** mood, feelings, expressions, and perceptions.

   **b.** orientation, memory, and cognitive function.

   **c.** energy level, satisfaction, and social participation.

   **d.** appropriateness of dress, grooming, and eye contact.

___ **4.** As part of assessing the client's level of consciousness, the nurse asks questions related to person, place, and time. Which of these statements is true?

    **a.** Orientation to person is usually lost first and orientation to time is usually lost last.

    **b.** Orientation to time is usually lost first and orientation to person is usually lost last.

    **c.** Orientation to person is usually lost first and orientation to place is usually lost last.

    **d.** Orientation to time is usually lost first and orientation to place is usually lost last.

___ **5.** When the nurse asks the client to explain similarities and differences between objects, what abilities are being tested?

    **a.** judgment.

    **b.** concentration.

    **c.** memory to learn new information.

    **d.** abstract reasoning.

___ **6.** The nurse completes her interview on a 39-year-old female client who seems happily married with four healthy children who are doing very well in school and who works part time as a college professor. The nurse would be able to conclude that this client is in which of the following psychosocial developmental stages?

    **a.** intimacy.

    **b.** isolation.

    **c.** generativity.

    **d.** stagnation.

**Activity F**   **CRITICAL THINKING**

**1.** Explain some "normal variations" that may be observed in the mental status exam of different clients.

**2.** Explain some "normal" variations that may be observed in the psychosocial developmental levels of clients from different cultures.

# SELF-REFLECTION AND EVALUATION OF LEARNER OBJECTIVES

After reading Chapter 6 in the text and completing the above reviews, please identify to what degree you have met each of the following chapter learning objectives. For those objectives that you have met partially or not at all, you will want to review the chapter content for that objective.

| Objective | Very Much | Somewhat | Not At All |
|---|---|---|---|
| 1. Assess the client's mental status using the Mini-Mental State Examination Tool. | | | |
| 2. Assess the client's mental status using the in-depth step-by-step assessment. Include LOC, posture, gait, movements, dress, hygiene, facial expressions, speech, behaviors, thought patterns, mood, feelings, and eight cognitive abilities. | | | |
| 3. Identify and describe five levels of consciousness. | | | |
| 4. Explain how to use the Glascow Coma Scale with a client. | | | |

| Objective | Very Much | Somewhat | Not At All |
|---|---|---|---|
| 5. Describe eight tests to complete to determine the client's cognitive ability. | | | |
| 6. Describe Erikson's developmental tasks for the Young Adult, Middle-Aged Adult, and Older Adult. | | | |
| 7. Describe how to assess the client's psychosocial developmental level. | | | |
| 8. Describe the seven warning signs of Alzheimer's disease. | | | |
| 9. Use the Depression Questionnaire to assess for depression. | | | |
| 10. Assess for depression in elderly clients with the Geriatric Depression Scale. | | | |

# Assessing General Health Status and Vital Signs

## Chapter Overview

Your initial evaluation of the client's general health status and vital signs gives you a baseline for assessment. The following exercises and quizzes can help you review the basics.

## CHAPTER PRETEST

### Activity A  CHOICE

*Choose one best answer for each of the following multiple-choice questions.*

1. The nurse is preparing to assess an adult client in the clinic. The nurse observes that the client is wearing lightweight clothing although the temperature is below freezing outside. The nurse anticipates that the client may be

    **a.** abusing drugs.

    **b.** a victim of abuse.

    **c.** lacking adequate finances.

    **d.** anxious.

2. An elderly client is seen by the nurse in the neighborhood clinic. The nurse observes that the client is dressed in several layers of clothing, although the temperature is warm outside. The nurse suspects that the client's cold intolerance is a result of

    **a.** decreased body metabolism.

    **b.** neurologic deficits.

    **c.** recent surgery.

    **d.** pancreatic disease.

## Activity B MATCHING

*Match the terms in the left column with the correct description in the right column.*

**Term**

c **1.** 36.5°C to 37.0°C (96.0°F to 99.9°F)

f **2.** 60 to 100 beats/minute

e **3.** 12 to 20/minute

g **4.** Highest pressure exerted on artery walls

b **5.** Lowest pressure exerted on artery walls

h **6.** Difference between systolic and diastolic pressure

i **7.** Skin color, hygiene, posture, gait, physical build, and development

j **8.** Pain

d **9.** less than 120 mm Hg

a **10.** less than 80 mm Hg

**Description**

**a.** Normal diastolic blood pressure range

**b.** Diastolic blood pressure

**c.** Normal oral temperature

**d.** Normal systolic blood pressure range

**e.** Normal respiratory rate

**f.** Normal pulse

**g.** Systolic blood pressure

**h.** Pulse pressure

**i.** Overall impression

**j.** Fifth vital sign

## Activity C LEARNER ACTIVITIES

1. Go to a public place, such as a store or a shopping mall, and practice observing passersby. Look for general characteristics of physical and sexual development. Observe color, dress, hygiene, posture and gait, body build, comfort level, behavior, facial expression, and speech.

2. Practice taking vital signs and anthropometric measurements on peers, friends, and family members. Try to find a variety of people: obese, thin, elderly, young. Practice recording your findings on flowcharts.

3. Using COLDSPA, document the most severe pain you have ever experienced. Then, assess your lab partner for his or her worst experience with pain and document his or her experience using COLDSPA. (More in-depth information on pain assessment is provided in Chapter 8.)

### INTERVIEWING AND RECORDING ASSESSMENT FINDINGS

Use the following Nursing History Checklist as your guide to interviewing and recording your findings in your general survey and assessment of mental status and vital signs.

### Nursing History Checklist

| Questions | Satisfactory Data | Needs Additional Data | Data Missing |
|---|---|---|---|
| *Present History* | | | |
| 1. Height? | | | |
| 2. Weight? | | | |
| 3. Fever? | | | |
| 4. Pain? (COLDSPA) | | | |
| 5. Allergies? | | | |
| 6. Present health concerns? | | | |

| Questions | Satisfactory Data | Needs Additional Data | Data Missing |
|---|---|---|---|
| *Past History* | | | |
| 1. Weight gains or losses? | | | |
| 2. Previous high fevers, cause, and treatment? | | | |
| 3. History of abnormal pulse? | | | |
| 4. History of abnormal respiratory rate or character? | | | |
| 5. Usual blood pressure, who checked it last, and when? | | | |
| 6. History of pain and treatment? | | | |
| *Family History* | | | |
| 1. Hypertension? | | | |
| 2. Metabolic/growth problems? | | | |
| *Lifestyle and Health Practices* | | | |
| 1. Religious affiliation? | | | |

## Activity D  PERFORMING PHYSICAL ASSESSMENT

Practice recording general survey findings. Use the following Physical Assessment Checklist to assess a peer, friend, or family member. Column 1 can be used by you to guide your physical assessment. Column 2 may be used by your instructor to evaluate your skills as necessary.

### Physical Assessment Checklist

| Assessment Skill | Findings (Normal or Abnormal) and Notes | | Performance (Satisfactory, Needs Improvement, Unsatisfactory) | | |
|---|---|---|---|---|---|
| | N | A | S | N | U |
| *Overall Impression of the Client* | | | | | |
| 1. Observe physical development (appears to be chronologic age) and sexual development (appropriate for gender and age). | ☐ | ☐ | ☐ | ☐ | ☐ |
| 2. Observe skin (generalized color, color variation, and condition). | ☐ | ☐ | ☐ | ☐ | ☐ |
| 3. Observe dress (occasion and weather appropriate). | ☐ | ☐ | ☐ | ☐ | ☐ |
| 4. Observe hygiene (cleanliness, odor, grooming). | ☐ | ☐ | ☐ | ☐ | ☐ |
| 5. Observe posture (erect and comfortable) and gait (rhythmic and coordinated). | ☐ | ☐ | ☐ | ☐ | ☐ |
| 6. Observe body build (muscle mass and fat distribution). | ☐ | ☐ | ☐ | ☐ | ☐ |
| 7. Observe consciousness level (alertness, orientation, appropriateness). | ☐ | ☐ | ☐ | ☐ | ☐ |
| 8. Observe comfort level. | ☐ | ☐ | ☐ | ☐ | ☐ |
| 9. Observe behavior (body movements, affect, cooperativeness, purposefulness, and appropriateness). | ☐ | ☐ | ☐ | ☐ | ☐ |

| Assessment Skill | Findings (Normal or Abnormal) and Notes | | Performance (Satisfactory, Needs Improvement, Unsatisfactory) | | |
|---|---|---|---|---|---|
| | N | A | S | N | U |
| 10. Observe facial expression (culture-appropriate eye contact and facial expression). | ☐ | ☐ | ☐ | ☐ | ☐ |
| 11. Observe speech (pattern and style). | ☐ | ☐ | ☐ | ☐ | ☐ |
| *Vital Signs* | | | | | |
| 1. Gather equipment (thermometer, sphygmomanometer, stethoscope, and watch). | ☐ | ☐ | ☐ | ☐ | ☐ |
| 2. Measure temperature (oral, axillary, rectal, tympanic). | ☐ | ☐ | ☐ | ☐ | ☐ |
| 3. Measure radial pulse (rate, rhythm, amplitude and contour, and elasticity). | ☐ | ☐ | ☐ | ☐ | ☐ |
| 4. Monitor respirations (rate, rhythm, and depth). | ☐ | ☐ | ☐ | ☐ | ☐ |
| 5. Measure blood pressure. | ☐ | ☐ | ☐ | ☐ | ☐ |
| *Analysis of Data* | | | | | |
| 1. Formulate nursing diagnoses (wellness, risk, actual). | ☐ | ☐ | ☐ | ☐ | ☐ |
| 2. Formulate collaborative problems. | ☐ | ☐ | ☐ | ☐ | ☐ |
| 3. Make necessary referrals. | ☐ | ☐ | ☐ | ☐ | ☐ |

# CHAPTER POSTTEST

**Activity E**   MULTIPLE CHOICE

*Choose one best answer for each of the following multiple-choice questions.*

1. The nurse is assessing an elderly postsurgical client in the home. To begin the physical examination, the nurse should first assess the client's
   a. height and weight.
   b. ability to swallow.
   c. vital signs.
   d. gait.

2. While caring for an 80-year-old client in his home, the nurse determines that the client's temperature is 96.5°F. The nurse determines that the client is most likely exhibiting
   a. normal changes that occur with the aging process.
   b. hypothermia that occurs before an infectious process.
   c. a metabolic disorder resulting in circulatory changes.
   d. an immune disorder resulting in low platelet count.

3. The nurse is preparing to assess the respirations of an alert adult client. The nurse should
   a. explain to the client that he or she will be counting the client's respirations.
   b. observe for equal bilateral chest expansion of 1 to 2 inches.
   c. count for 15 seconds and multiply the number by 4 to obtain the rate.
   d. ask the client to lie in a supine position, which makes counting the respirations easier.

*A*   **4.** While assessing an older adult client's respirations, the nurse can anticipate that the respiratory pattern may exhibit a
   **a.** shorter inspiratory phase.
   **b.** longer inspiratory phase.
   **c.** shorter expiratory phase.
   **d.** longer expiratory phase.

*C*   **5.** The nurse is caring for a client who is having nothing by mouth (NPO) on the first postoperative day. The client's blood pressure was 120/80 mm Hg approximately 4 hours ago, but it is now 140/88 mm Hg. The nurse should ask the client which of the following questions?
   **a.** "Are you taking any medications for hypertension?"
   **b.** "Do you have enough blankets to stay warm?"
   **c.** "Are you having pain from your surgery?"
   **d.** "What is your typical blood pressure reading?"

*b*   **6.** A normal pulse pressure range for an adult client is typically
   **a.** 20 to 40 mm Hg.
   **b.** 30 to 50 mm Hg.
   **c.** 40 to 60 mm Hg.
   **d.** 60 to 80 mm Hg.

## Activity F   CRITICAL THINKING AND CASE STUDY

**1.** On the basis of the following case study assessment information, work through the steps of analyzing the data. Identify abnormal data and strengths in **subjective and objective findings**, assemble **cue clusters**, draw **inferences**, make possible **nursing diagnoses**, identify **defining characteristics**, **confirm or rule out** the diagnoses, and **document** your conclusions.

Use the blank diagnostic analysis charts provided at the end of this book to guide your thinking. You may want to write on the chart or use separate paper. In either case, propose nursing diagnoses that are specific to the client in the case study. Identify collaborative problems, if any, for this client. Finally, identify data, if any, that point toward a medical problem requiring a referral.

Steve Marin is a 36-year-old white man who comes to the employee health center for advice. He says he has been under a lot of stress lately. He believes he is drinking too much coffee (12 cups daily) and smoking more than usual (2 packs daily). He is neatly and appropriately dressed in a business suit. His posture is erect, and his gait is smooth. His hands are trembling. He has excess subcutaneous fat, distributed primarily around the waist. Mr. Marin appears tired, anxious, and hurried. He is cooperative, maintains good eye contact, and answers questions quickly. His speech is clear and fast paced.

### Vital Signs

Oral temperature: 98.68F

Radial pulse: 92 beats/minute, strong but irregular

Respirations: 23 breaths/minute, shallow, and somewhat labored

Blood pressure: sitting, right arm 160/110 mm Hg, left arm 162/112 mm Hg; standing, 155/100 mm Hg (standing BP taken in either arm due to similarity of sitting BPs)

No pain

Score on Saint Louis University Mental Status (SLUMS) Examination: 28

# SELF-REFLECTION AND EVALUATION
# OF LEARNER OBJECTIVES

After reading Chapter 7 in the text and completing the above reviews, please identify to what degree you have met each of the following chapter learning objectives. For those objectives that you have met partially or not at all, you will want to review the chapter content for that objective.

| Objective | Very Much | Somewhat | Not At All |
|---|---|---|---|
| 1. Explain how to prepare the client for a survey of general health status. | | | |
| 2. Assess the client's physical development and body build. | | | |
| 3. Assess the overall appearance and color of the skin; dress; and the client's hygiene, posture, and gait. | | | |
| 4. Assess apparent gender and sexual development. | | | |
| 5. Compare "reported" age to apparent age. | | | |
| 6. Obtain accurate vital signs. Assess level of consciousness, behaviors, facial expression, and speech. | | | |
| 7. Identify and explain how to use the equipment needed to obtain vital signs and temperature. | | | |
| 8. Describe temperature variations in an older adult. | | | |
| 9. Discuss how to obtain accurate measurement of the radial and apical pulses. | | | |
| 10. Obtain an accurate respiratory rate, and describe expected changes that may be apparent in the assessment of an older client's pulse, respiratory rate, and blood pressure. | | | |
| 11. Obtain an accurate measurement of blood pressure, and discuss the parameters for blood pressure (normal as well as the four stages of hypertension). | | | |
| 12. Assess for orthostatic (postural) hypotension if the client is taking antihypertensive drugs or has a history of fainting or dizziness. | | | |
| 13. Assess for the presence of pain as a "fifth vital sign." | | | |
| 14. Discuss possible nursing diagnoses and collaborative problems that may emerge after a general survey. | | | |

# Assessing Pain: The Fifth Vital Sign

## CHAPTER OVERVIEW

Pain is the fifth vital sign. It is a subjective phenomenon, and the main assessment tool is the client's reporting. The exact words used to describe the experience of pain are used to help in the diagnosis and management of the pain.

## CHAPTER PRETEST

### Activity A MULTIPLE CHOICE

*Choose one best answer for each of the following multiple-choice questions.*

_____ 1. When assessing the client for pain, the nurse should
  a. doubt the client when he or she describes the pain.
  b. assess for underlying causes of pain, then believe the client.
  c. believe the client when he or she claims to be in pain.
  d. assess for the presence of physiologic indicators (such as diaphoresis, tachycardia, etc.), then believe the client.

_____ 2. Acute pain can be differentiated from chronic pain because
  a. acute pain always scores more on the visual analog scale than chronic pain.
  b. acute pain is associated with a recent onset of illness or injury with a duration of less than 6 months, whereas chronic pain persists longer than 6 months.
  c. acute pain is not treated and left to subside on its own, whereas chronic pain is referred for treatment.
  d. acute pain occurs only in persons aged less than 45 years, whereas chronic pain occurs in persons aged 46 or above.

_____ 3. One of the body's normal physiologic responses to pain is
  a. hypotension.
  b. pulse rate below 50/minute.
  c. diaphoresis.
  d. hypoglycemia.

_____ 4. After assessing a client in pain, the nurse

    **a.** documents the exact description given by the client.

    **b.** chooses from the list of pain descriptors what best reflects the client's description.

    **c.** asks the family to describe how they view the client's pain.

    **d.** documents how he or she best sees the client's pain.

## Activity B  LEARNER ACTIVITIES

*Working with peers in learning lab*

*After reading Chapter 8, participate in the following learning activities.*

1. Clients who describe pain as their main problem are seen on an inpatient or outpatient basis. Choose a client being seen inpatient who describes pain as his or her main problem. Conduct an interview (collecting subjective and objective data) followed by a focused physical assessment. Document your findings.

2. If possible, also choose a client in an outpatient situation who is experiencing pain and who is referred to a pain clinic for pain management or follow-up. Conduct an interview (collecting subjective and objective data) and a focused physical assessment, and then record your findings. Then discuss the differences you encountered between interviewing an inpatient and an outpatient.

3. Recall a pain experience you had in the past or are currently experiencing. Have your lab partner be the nurse to assess your current or past pain. Repeat this exercise with you being the nurse and your lab partner being the client.

## Activity C  INTERVIEWING AND RECORDING ASSESSMENT FINDINGS

Use the following Nursing History Checklist as your guide to interviewing and recording your findings in a pain assessment.

### Nursing History Checklist

| Questions | Satisfactory Data | Needs Additional Data | Data Missing |
|---|---|---|---|
| *Current Symptoms* | | | |
| 1. Are you experiencing pain now or have you had pain in the past 24 hours? | | | |
| 2. Where is the pain located? | | | |
| 3. Does it radiate or spread? | | | |
| 4. Are there any other concurrent symptoms accompanying the pain? | | | |
| 5. When did the pain start? | | | |
| 6. What were you doing when the pain first started? | | | |
| 7. Is the pain continuous or intermittent? | | | |
| 8. (*Ask for intermittent pain.*) How often do the episodes occur and how long do they last? | | | |
| 9. Describe in your own words the quality of pain. | | | |
| 10. What factors relieve your pain? | | | |
| 11. What factors increase your pain? | | | |
| 12. Are you on any therapy to manage your pain? | | | |

| Questions | Satisfactory Data | Needs Additional Data | Data Missing |
|---|---|---|---|
| *Past History* | | | |
| 1. Have you had any previous experience with pain? | | | |
| *Family History* | | | |
| 1. Does anyone in your family experience pain? | | | |
| 2. How does pain affect your family? | | | |
| *Lifestyles and Health Practices* | | | |
| 1. What are your concerns about pain? | | | |
| 2. What are your concerns about the pain's effect on<br>  a. General activity<br>  b. Mood/emotions<br>  c. Concentration<br>  d. Physical ability<br>  e. Work<br>  f. Relations with other people<br>  g. Sleep<br>  h. Appetite<br>  i. Enjoyment of life | | | |

## Activity D  PERFORMING PHYSICAL ASSESSMENT

Use the following Physical Assessment Checklist as your guide to performing a pain assessment. Column 1 can be used by you to guide your physical assessment. Column 2 may be used by your instructor to evaluate your skills as necessary.

### Physical Assessment Checklist

| Assessment Skill | Findings (Normal or Abnormal) and Notes | | Performance (Satisfactory, Needs Improvement, Unsatisfactory) | | |
|---|---|---|---|---|---|
| | N | A | S | N | U |
| *General Observations* | | | | | |
| 1. Observe posture. | ☐ | ☐ | ☐ | ☐ | ☐ |
| 2. Observe facial expression. | ☐ | ☐ | ☐ | ☐ | ☐ |
| 3. Inspect joints and muscles. | ☐ | ☐ | ☐ | ☐ | ☑ |
| 4. Observe skin for scars, lesions, rashes, changes, or discoloration. | ☐ | ☐ | ☐ | ☐ | ☐ |
| *Vital Signs* | | | | | |
| 1. Measure heart rate. | ☐ | ☐ | ☐ | ☐ | ☐ |
| 2. Measure respiratory rate. | ☐ | ☐ | ☐ | ☐ | ☐ |
| 3. Measure blood pressure. | ☐ | ☐ | ☐ | ☐ | ☐ |
| *Using the client's description of pain and your findings above, continue the assessment. Refer to the physical assessment chapter appropriate for the affected body area.* | | | | | |

# CHAPTER POSTTEST

### Activity E   MATCHING

*Please match the terms on the left with the correct descriptions in the right column.*

**Term**

___ **1.** Nociceptors

___ **2.** Substance P

___ **3.** Hypothalamus and limbic system

___ **4.** Noxious stimuli

___ **5.** Frontal cortex

___ **6.** Transmission

___ **7.** A-delta and C-fibers

**Description**

**a.** Conduction of an impulse in the primary afferent neurons to the dorsal horn of the spinal cord

**b.** Initiation of a painful stimulus resulting in an inflammatory process

**c.** Primary afferent nociceptors

**d.** Responsible for the emotional aspect of the pain perception

**e.** Primary afferent nerves for receiving painful stimuli

**f.** Enhances nociception, causing vasodilatation, increased blood flow, and edema, with further release of bradykinin, serotonin from platelets, and histamine from mast cells

**g.** Responsible for rational interpretation and response to pain

### Activity F   CROSSWORD PUZZLE

*Complete the following crossword puzzle to become more familiar with the pathophysiology of pain.*

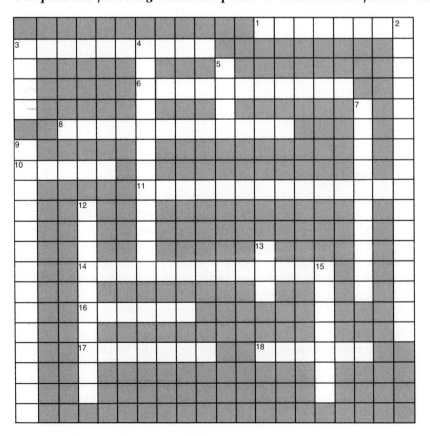

**ACROSS**

1. Stimuli transmitted by A-delta fibers are felt as _____, sharp, or electric-quality sensations and usually are caused by mechanical or thermal stimuli

3. The process of pain _____ is still poorly understood; studies have shown that it is affected by emotional status

6. Factors that increase pain

8. Process of pain that begins when a mechanical, thermal, or chemical stimulus results in tissue injury or damage stimulating the nociceptors, which are the primary afferent nerves for receiving painful stimuli

10. Category of pain that is usually associated with an injury with a recent onset and duration of less than 6 months and usually less than a month

11. Tract that ascends to the reticular formation, the pontine, medullary areas, and medial thalamic nuclei

14. Tract that ascends through the lateral edge of the medulla, lateral pons, and midbrain to the thalamus and then to the somatosensory cortex

16. Primary afferent fibers that transmit fast pain to the spinal cord within 0.1 second

17. Category of pain that is usually associated with a specific cause or injury and is described as a constant pain that persists more than 6 months

18. Psychologic response elicited by pain

**DOWN**

2. Theory that emphasizes the importance of the central nervous system mechanisms of pain, which had an influence on pain research and treatment

3. An unpleasant sensory and emotional experience that we primarily associate with tissue damage or describe in terms of such damage, or both

4. Process that results in the conduction of an impulse in the primary afferent neurons to the dorsal horn of the spinal cord

5. Histamines are released from _____ cells

7. Phenomenon that involves the body's own endogenous neurotransmitters (endorphins, enkephalins, and serotonin) in the course of processing pain stimuli

9. Substance P enhances nociception, causing _____, increased blood flow, and edema

12. Released by the nociceptors, enhancing nociception

13. Abbreviation of a pain assessment scale that rates pain on a 10-cm continuum

15. Primary afferent fibers that transmit slow pain within 1 second

**Activity G CRITICAL THINKING AND CASE STUDIES**

1. On the basis of the following case study assessment information, work through the steps of analyzing the data. Identify abnormal data and strengths in **subjective and objective findings**, assemble **cue clusters**, draw **inferences**, make possible **nursing diagnoses**, identify **defining characteristics**, **confirm or rule out** the diagnoses, and **document** your conclusions. Use the blank diagnostic analysis charts provided at the end of this book to guide your thinking. You may want to write on the chart or use separate paper. In either case, propose nursing diagnoses that are specific to the client in the case study. Identify collaborative problems, if any, for this client. Finally, identify data, if any, that point toward a medical problem requiring a referral.

Mr. F.S. is a 38-year-old architect. He is still single and is enjoying his bachelor life. He is a non-smoker but drinks alcohol—"occasionally two to three drinks." Later he says he has drunk this amount almost daily for the past 10 years. Since his appendectomy around 13 years ago, he has not had any medical examination. "The past few months have been stressful at work and my eating habits have been irregular. Sometimes I have occasional nausea and vomiting." This has advanced from being a mild epigastric upset to constant mid-epigastric pain radiating to the back.

This pain at first was relieved by pain medications, but "now it is not relieved by anything, although I realized that sitting forward helps me to relax a little bit while waiting in the doctor's clinic for my turn." The clinic desk clerk described that Mr. F.S. entered the doctor's clinic walking bent forward with his hands holding his epigastric area. During the examination, he reported severe pain (9/10) with abdominal guarding and with purplish discoloration of the periumbilical area. His respirations were shallow with a rate of 26/minute. Heart rate was 110 beats/minute with a BP = 120/80 mm Hg. (He was diagnosed with acute pancreatitis.)

# SELF-REFLECTION AND EVALUATION OF LEARNER OBJECTIVES

After you have read Chapter 8 and completed the above quizzes and activities, please identify to what extent you have met each of the following chapter learning objectives. For those you have met partially or not at all, you will want to review chapter content for that learning objective.

| Objective | Very Much | Somewhat | Not At All |
|---|---|---|---|
| 1. Identify pain as the fifth vital sign. | | | |
| 2. Explain the pathophysiology of pain. | | | |
| 3. Classify pain into acute and chronic pain. | | | |
| 4. Name the different physiologic responses to pain. | | | |
| 5. Interview a client experiencing pain, collecting subjective and objective data. | | | |
| 6. Perform a physical assessment on a client who is experiencing pain. | | | |
| 7. Analyze data collected from clients to formulate valid nursing diagnoses. | | | |

# Assessing Victims of Violence

## Chapter Overview

Use this chapter to assist you in understanding the nature of violence and how to assess victims of violence. Violence may occur across the life span and includes physical abuse, psychologic abuse, economic abuse, and/or sexual abuse.

## CHAPTER PRETEST

### Activity A TRUE/FALSE

*Circle True (T) or False (F) for each statement.*

1. T F   Family violence is limited to lower socioeconomic groups.

2. T F   Family violence refers mainly to the infliction of harm to children.

3. T F   The cause of violence in the United States is clearly understood.

4. T F   Violence has been present in the United States throughout its recorded history.

5. T F   Intimate partner violence continues to be condoned and sanctioned in many societies.

6. T F   Children raised in homes of domestic violence are more aware and, therefore, less likely to engage in it as adults.

7. T F   Theoretically, abuse often occurs in a predictable pattern or cycle.

8. T F   Nurses are more apt to report abuse in lower socioeconomic levels.

9. T F   Physical abuse may start any time during a relationship.

### Activity B LEARNER ACTIVITIES

**Working with peers in learning lab**

*After reading Chapter 9 in the textbook, participate in the following activities with your lab partner as assigned.*

1. Consider that, statistically, one out of every six persons in your classroom may be a victim of violence. This is a very sensitive topic for anyone to address. Frequently, individuals, including health care professionals, may not recognize that they are victims of abuse. Yet it is essential that

health care professionals be aware of their own past experience with violence in order to effectively assess the presence of violence in their clients. Use the screening tool provided in Assessment Tool 9.1 in your textbook to assess for the presence of violence in your own life. If you find that you are a victim of violence, you will want to share this with your nursing instructor or another health care professional.

## Activity C  INTERVIEWING AND RECORDING ASSESSMENT FINDINGS

Use the following Nursing History Checklist as your guide to interviewing and recording your findings in assessment of family violence.

### Nursing History Checklist

| Questions | Satisfactory Data | Needs Additional Data | Data Missing |
|---|---|---|---|
| *Intimate Partner Abuse Screening for Women* | | | |
| 1. Physically hurt by anyone in the past year? By whom? | | | |
| 2. Fears of others at home or elsewhere? Be sure to acknowledge abuse if present, be supportive, and help the client develop a safety plan. | | | |
| *Elder Abuse Screening for Geriatric Clients* | | | |
| 1. Activities in a typical day? | | | |
| 2. Hurt by anyone in the past? Threats by anyone in the past? | | | |
| 3. Afraid of anyone at home? | | | |
| 4. Client ever made to do anything he or she did not want to do? | | | |
| 5. Ever touched without permission? | | | |
| 6. Belongings taken without permission? | | | |
| 7. Made to sign papers without understanding them? | | | |
| 8. Often alone? | | | |
| 9. Has help ever been refused when needed? | | | |
| 10. Has anyone ever refused to give or let the client take medications as needed? | | | |
| *Child Abuse Screening for Children and Adolescents* | | | |
| Determine developmental level by asking: 1. What is your name? Please spell it. 2. When is your birthday? 3. How many eyes do you have? Using the child or adolescent's answers, formulate developmentally appropriate questions to determine if the child or adolescent was ever abused physically, emotionally, or sexually. | | | |

**Activity D** **PHYSICAL ASSESSMENT CHECKLIST**

Use the following Physical Assessment Checklist as your guide to performing an assessment for family violence.

**Physical Assessment Checklist**

| Assessment Skill | Findings (Normal or Abnormal) and Notes | | Performance (Satisfactory, Needs Improvement, Unsatisfactory) | | |
|---|---|---|---|---|---|
| | N | A | S | N | U |
| 1. General survey. | ☐ | ☐ | ☐ | ☐ | ☐ |
| 2. Assess mental status. | ☐ | ☐ | ☐ | ☐ | ☐ |
| 3. Evaluate vital signs. | ☐ | ☐ | ☐ | ☐ | ☐ |
| 4. Inspect skin. | ☐ | ☐ | ☐ | ☐ | ☐ |
| 5. Inspect head and neck. | ☐ | ☐ | ☐ | ☐ | ☐ |
| 6. Inspect eyes. | ☐ | ☐ | ☐ | ☐ | ☐ |
| 7. Assess ears. | ☐ | ☐ | ☐ | ☐ | ☐ |
| 8. Assess abdomen. | ☐ | ☐ | ☐ | ☐ | ☐ |
| 9. Assess genitalia and rectal area. | ☐ | ☐ | ☐ | ☐ | ☐ |
| 10. Assess musculoskeletal system. | ☐ | ☐ | ☐ | ☐ | ☐ |
| 11. Assess neurologic system. | ☐ | ☐ | ☐ | ☐ | ☐ |

# CHAPTER POSTTEST

**Activity E** **MULTIPLE CHOICE**

*Choose one best answer for each of the following multiple-choice questions.*

_____ 1. When interviewing a pediatric client and attempting to determine the presence of abuse, the nurse should

   a. confine the interview to yes/no questions to keep the interview simple.

   b. remain calm and accepting in response to any information the client discloses.

   c. ask leading question to convince the child to offer information.

   d. offer a reward to the child for answering difficult questions.

_____ 2. The nurse is interviewing Mr. Jenkins and, due particularly to his nervous affect and his reaction when his son is mentioned, suspects potential elder abuse. In assessing Mr. Jenkins, the nurse should

   a. focus exclusively on the physical examination, as elder abuse is primarily physical in nature.

   b. make sure that the assessment includes questions to ensure that Mr. Jenkins has access to food and needed medication.

   c. ask to speak to Mr. Jenkins' son directly, to ask him candidly about the potential abuse.

   d. keep in mind that elder abuse is usually reported, and that, for that reason, Mr. Jenkins is not likely a victim.

_____ **3.** Which of the following is a stage in Walker's Cycle of Violence?

    **a.** reporting the problem.

    **b.** hiding the abuse.

    **c.** period of reconciliation.

    **d.** ending the relationship.

## Activity F CRITICAL THINKING AND CASE STUDIES

**1.** Describe various interview techniques you might attempt to use when you highly suspect that your client is a victim of abuse but he or she is not willing to disclose this information to you.

**2.** Explain differences in screening for violence in adults, children, and the elderly.

**3.** With your lab partner, create a safety plan for the following woman and her child:

Mrs. Smith is a 33-year-old white you see in the emergency department with the presenting history of "fell on sidewalk and injured her arm." X-rays revealed a spiral fracture that was inconsistent with her history of falling. Her 10-year-old son who accompanied her has a visible rope burn on his neck, and when you question him about your observation, he states, "I hurt my neck when I was playing." When asked if she and her son are alone, she tells you that her husband is waiting in the car. When you ask Mrs. Smith for more details about how these injuries occurred, she begins to cry and says, "There is nothing I can do about this."

**4.** On the basis of the following case study assessment information, work through the steps of analyzing the data. Identify abnormal data and strengths in **subjective and objective findings**, assemble **cue clusters**, draw **inferences**, make possible **nursing diagnoses**, identify **defining characteristics**, **confirm or rule out** the diagnoses, and **document** your conclusions. Use the blank diagnostic analysis charts provided at the end of this book to guide your thinking. You may want to write on the chart or use separate paper. In either case, propose nursing diagnoses that are specific to the client in the case study. Identify collaborative problems, if any, for this client. Finally, identify data, if any, that point toward a medical problem requiring a referral.

Tommy Johnson is an 18-month boy. His mother brings him to the doctor because he is "being difficult" and refuses to be toilet trained. Mrs. Johnson states, "He is deliberately not going when I put him on the toilet and then soiling his diapers. He is doing it just to be a pest." She tells you that Tommy also refuses to eat and will not drink anything but fruit punch and lemonade from his bottle. While she is explaining this, Tommy just stares at the wall. When asked about their daily activities, she says that he wakes at about 7:00 a.m., but usually cries himself back to sleep. When she gets him out of bed, she gives him a bottle and sets him in front of the TV, while she does other things around the house. She tries to feed him lunch but he usually eats very little. The rest of the afternoon is spent napping or watching TV.

Mrs. Johnson tells you that she did not expect having a child would be this hard. Mr. Johnson no longer lives with his wife and child. He is behind in his child support payments, and Mrs. Johnson tells you that she is struggling to pay the bills.

You examine Tommy and find that he is frail and thin looking. It is chilly outside and he is wearing only a thin tee-shirt and diaper. Tommy's hair is matted and uncombed. He is in the 2nd percentile for both height and weight. He has multiple bruises on his arms, back, and legs. The bruises are in various stages of healing. Tommy is not meeting the developmental milestones for his age. He also does not interact with you at all while you are examining him.

# SELF-REFLECTION AND EVALUATION OF LEARNER OBJECTIVES

After you have read Chapter 9 and completed the above quizzes and activities, please identify to what extent you have met each of the following chapter learning objectives. For those you have met partially or not at all, you will want to review chapter content for that learning objective.

| Objective | Very Much | Somewhat | Not At All |
|---|---|---|---|
| 1. Describe how to prepare a physically and emotionally safe environment for a client who has experienced domestic violence. | | | |
| 2. Correctly use domestic violence screening tools provided in the textbook to identify victims of violence across the life span. | | | |
| 3. Describe how to teach clients at risk for violence and how to develop a safety plan. | | | |
| 4. Discuss the significance of accurate and objective documentation of physical findings in clients who have experienced abuse. | | | |
| 5. Accurately document abusive physical findings using injury maps. | | | |

# Assessing Culture

## Chapter Overview

The population of the United States has changed a great deal since World War II. The number of immigrants and the number of the countries from which they have come have increased dramatically. The predominant cultures that make up the U.S. population are whites of European descent comprising many varied cultures; African Americans; and Hispanics, from various Latin American countries. However, the Asian American population is rapidly increasing, and there is a substantial group of Native Americans of different tribal affiliations. It is not unusual for both clients and caregivers to be from different cultural groups. Because cultural beliefs and behaviors affect health and health behaviors, it is essential that nurses understand how to interact with people from many different cultures.

## CHAPTER PRETEST

### Activity A   MATCHING

*Match the terms in the left column with the correct description in the right column.*

**Term**

_____ 1. Culture

_____ 2. Ethnocentrism

_____ 3. Ethnicity

_____ 4. Race

_____ 5. Minority

**Description**

a. A socially constructed concept that has meaning for a larger group

b. A shared set of values, beliefs, and learned pattern of behavior

c. The belief that one's beliefs, values, and sanctioned behaviors are superior to others

d. A group with less power or prestige within a society

e. Exists when a socially, politically, or culturally constructed group holds a common set of characteristics not shared by others

### Activity B   LEARNER ACTIVITIES

#### Working with peers in learning lab

*After reading Chapter 10 in the textbook, participate in the following activities with your lab partner as assigned.*

1. Discuss the purpose and benefits of a cultural assessment. When would you perform the assessment? Explain.

2. Describe the elements of cultural competence. Evaluate yourself and the level of cultural competence you have now. Compare with your lab partner. Working together, make a plan to increase your cultural competence.

3. With lab partner, make a list of ways in which culture can affect health.

4. Get together with a small group of friends or lab partners to compare beliefs and behaviors related to health and illness. Make a list to see whether there is variation within the groups. Ask each group member the following:

   a. What do you do to stay healthy?

   b. What do you do to feel better when you have a cold?

   c. When do you seek help from a health care professional?

   d. What home remedies do you use? Vitamins/minerals? Herbs? Yoga? Tai chi? Special foods or diets? Alternative or complementary therapies? What home remedies do your family members use?

   e. Do you like to be left alone or have many visitors when you are ill?

   f. What do you believe causes illness?

5. Discuss how family beliefs, habits, roles, and interactions could affect your (or another family member's) health status.

6. Define "culture-bound syndromes." Which clients might experience them?

7. Discuss with lab partner the aspects of interviewing that have to be considered when assessing a client from a culture different from your own. Choose three of the ways cultural difference can affect interviews. Have each lab partner play a role as a client from a culture that affects the interview (e.g., silence) and role-play the interview. Choose different interview elements and change nurse–client roles for role-play.

8. In a clinical setting with clients from various cultures, observe a nursing assessment of a client from a culture different from your own. What variations in communication do you notice (of nurse or client)? What assessment areas would you wish to modify? Explain you answer. What areas of assessment would you like to add? Explain.

### Activity C  INTERVIEWING AND RECORDING ASSESSMENT FINDINGS

Use the following Nursing History Checklist as your guide to interviewing and recording your findings in cultural assessment. The checklist is only a beginning list of suggestions to elicit cultural behaviors and beliefs relating to health and illness. Refer to the text for the many areas of communication, biological variation, and categories of cultural variation that may be incorporated in a complete cultural assessment.

**Nursing History Checklist**

| Questions | Satisfactory Data | Needs Additional Data | Data Missing |
|---|---|---|---|
| *Current Symptoms (ask client)* | | | |
| 1. What has brought you to the clinic today? | | | |
| 2. What do you believe has caused this illness? | | | |
| 3. What have you done to treat it? Are there family remedies that you usually use for this illness? Have they worked for other family members or for you in the past? | | | |
| 4. What do you believe that health care providers can do that will help you? (*If appropriate, use COLDSPA for symptom analysis*) | | | |
| 5. Are you taking any medications? Do you have allergies or reactions to any medications or foods? | | | |

| Questions | Satisfactory Data | Needs Additional Data | Data Missing |
|---|---|---|---|
| *Affect and Behaviors (observe)* | | | |
| 1. Does affect correspond to verbal expressions? | | | |
| 2. Does pattern of eye contact correspond to the client's culture or to the majority culture? | | | |
| 3. Does the client divulge information readily or with reluctance? | | | |
| 4. Does the client seem to accept you (gender, age) as a caregiver? | | | |
| 5. Does space appear to be an issue with the client? | | | |
| 6. Are there any other communication patterns that seem to be relevant to this interview? | | | |
| *Past History (ask client)* | | | |
| 1. What has been your experience with health care professionals in the past? | | | |
| 2. Have you used community caregivers? | | | |
| 3. Have you had any illnesses like this one before? | | | |
| 4. Do you have or have you experienced any other illnesses in the past? | | | |
| 5. What types of illnesses have gotten you to go to a doctor or nurse in the past? | | | |
| *Family History* | | | |
| 1. How many family members live in the community? In the household? | | | |
| 2. Are the family members healthy? Have illnesses? Able to provide support to you? | | | |
| *Lifestyle and Health Practices* | | | |
| 1. Do you believe that exercise is important to health? How much exercise do you get each day? Week? | | | |
| 2. Do you smoke? Drink alcohol? If yes, how much or how often? | | | |
| 3. Do you participate in religious practices? Do your beliefs and practices provide strength and comfort? Are they essential to your well-being? | | | |
| 4. Do you have beliefs that would conflict with treatments or procedures? | | | |
| 5. What type of diet do you eat? Is it restricted in any way by religious or cultural beliefs? Are their foods that you believe help to make you healthy? Ill? | | | |

[Refer to the text for each physiologic system and its potential biomedical variations as you assess the physiologic systems.]

# CHAPTER POSTTEST

## Activity D  MULTIPLE CHOICE

*Choose one best answer for each of the following multiple-choice questions.*

____  1. Stereotyping is defined as

     **a.** the belief that one's cultural values are superior to all others.

     **b.** a worldview that each of us forms values and beliefs based on our own culture.

     **c.** a culture-bound syndrome found in many cultural groups.

     **d.** expecting all members of a cultural group to hold the same beliefs and behave in the same way.

____  2. Suzie is a 16-year-old daughter in the Hanes family. She is the youngest of five children. She has had a series of illnesses and does not seem to be regaining her strength. She likes school but is falling behind a bit. Her mother is very attentive to her needs but does not seem overly concerned with the continuing pattern of illness. Which of the following is most likely a Hanes family belief?

     **a.** Fathers are not involved with their children.

     **b.** Education is highly valued for sons and daughters.

     **c.** The family values taking sick roles and caregiver roles.

     **d.** Self-care is highly valued in the Hanes family.

____  3. Which of the following statements is true about biological variation.

     **a.** Both genetics and environment produce biological variation.

     **b.** Cultural practices produce biological variation.

     **c.** Race is based on physical variations.

     **d.** Drug metabolism differences are not culture based.

## Activity E  CHOOSING

*Select "Do" or "Don't" by checking the appropriate column for each behavior.*

| Do | Don't | |
|----|-------|---|
| | | a. Be aware that some nonverbal communication may be insulting to some cultural groups (e.g., direct eye contact). |
| | | b. Assume that a person who looks and behaves much as you do has no cultural differences. |
| | | c. Assume that a negative or hostile communication from a client is directed at you personally as an insult. |
| | | d. Seek feedback and constructive criticism on the transcultural interactions you have with clients. |
| | | e. Recognize and value differences. |
| | | f. Recognize there is variation within all cultural and ethnic groups, often more variation within than between groups. |
| | | g. Seek many opportunities to interact with persons of different cultures, even if it makes you uncomfortable at first. |

**Activity F** **MATCHING**

*Match the terms in the left column with the correct description in the right column.*

**Term**

____ **1.** Sickle cell disease

____ **2.** Empacho

____ **3.** Low salt sweat

____ **4.** Ethnic group

____ **5.** Culture-bound syndrome

____ **6.** Skin color

**Description**

**a.** "Blocked intestine," a culture-bound syndrome thought to result from a food lump sticking to the intestinal wall

**b.** Often found in black Africans and those whites acclimatized to the tropics

**c.** A malaria-related condition in mosquito-infected areas of the Mediterranean

**d.** A result of genetic variation across a continuum associated with distance from the equator

**e.** Concerned with learned behavior independent of genetics or nationality

**f.** Illness that is defined by a specific cultural group and may not be interpreted as an illness by other groups

# SELF-REFLECTION AND EVALUATION OF LEARNER OBJECTIVES

After reading Chapter 10 in the text and completing the above reviews, please identify to what degree you have met each of the following chapter learning objectives. For those objectives that you have met partially or not at all, you will want to review the chapter content for the learning objective.

| Objective | Very Much | Somewhat | Not At All |
|---|---|---|---|
| 1. Explain how culture, genetics, and environment interact to affect health status. | | | |
| 2. Define *culture* and describe its basic characteristics. | | | |
| 3. Discuss the role of cultural competence of the caregiver in nursing assessment. | | | |
| 4. Describe how the assessment interview needs to be modified to consider cultural variations. | | | |
| 5. Recognize culture-based syndromes and the cultural groups most likely to accept them as diseases. | | | |
| 6. Recognize your own tendency to stereotype. | | | |
| 7. Recognize your own level of ethnocentrism. | | | |
| 8. Recognize your own level of cultural competence. | | | |
| 9. Describe the parts of a cultural assessment. | | | |
| 10. Complete a cultural health assessment on a person of a different culture. | | | |

## CHAPTER 11

# Assessing Spirituality and Religious Practices

## Chapter Overview

A large number of Americans profess a belief in God, pray on a regular basis, and frequently use spiritual resources during times of high stress, but how clients use and view spirituality and religion varies immensely. It is important to consider spirituality within the context of client care, but in whatever form spirituality is incorporated into an assessment, the nurse must remain respectful and open. The following activities and questions are provided as a review and to stimulate thoughts regarding spiritual assessment of a client.

## CHAPTER PRETEST

### Activity A  MATCHING

*Match the terms in the left column with the correct description in the right column.*

**Term**

____ **1.** Spirituality

____ **2.** Religion

____ **3.** Spiritual assessment

____ **4.** Spiritual care

**Description**

**a.** Shared practices and rituals used to express one's faith

**b.** Used to determine the client's spiritual needs

**c.** Actions used to assist the client in meeting spiritual needs

**d.** One's search for life's meaning and purpose

### Activity B  LEARNER ACTIVITIES

**Working with peers in learning lab**

*After reading Chapter 11 in the textbook, participate in the following activities with your lab partner as assigned.*

**1.** Discuss the purpose and benefits of a spiritual assessment. When would you perform this assessment? Explain.

**2.** On your own, complete and score yourself on the following assessment tools found in the textbook:

　**a.** *FICA Spiritual Assessment Tool* (Assessment Tool 11.1)

　**b.** *Daily Spiritual Experiences Scale* (Assessment Tool 11.2)

　**c.** *Brief Religious Coping Questionnaire (RCOPE)* (Assessment Tool 11.3)

3. With your lab partner, discuss your findings from activity #2. Did the tools accurately reflect your beliefs? Why or why not? Which tool did you find most useful in obtaining spiritual information? Were there questions you had difficulty answering? If yes, explain. Were there questions that made you uncomfortable? If yes, explain. Explain how you could make these questions more comfortable for your client.

4. Think about interacting with clients of each of the major world religions, using information from your own experiences and from the textbook Table 11-1, "Major World Religions and Common Health Beliefs." Consider appropriate interview questions based on your knowledge of each of these faiths.

## Activity C  INTERVIEWING AND RECORDING ASSESSMENT FINDINGS

Use the following Nursing History Checklist as your guide to interviewing and recording your findings in spiritual assessment.

### Nursing History Checklist

| Questions | Satisfactory Data | Needs Additional Data | Data Missing |
|---|---|---|---|
| *Current Symptoms* | | | |
| 1. Affect corresponding to attitude? | | | |
| 2. Culturally appropriate eye contact when describing spiritual beliefs? | | | |
| 3. Sense of hope for future and comfort from beliefs? | | | |
| 4. Ease with which client divulges information? | | | |
| 5. Perceived stress level? | | | |
| 6. Presence of spiritual conflicts/struggles? | | | |
| 7. Display of religious articles? | | | |
| 8. Desire to participate in usual religious practices? | | | |
| *Past History* | | | |
| 1. Coping mechanisms? | | | |
| 2. Adherence to health promotion activities? | | | |
| *Family History* | | | |
| 1. Strength of social and spiritual support systems? | | | |
| 2. Religious ties? | | | |
| *Lifestyle and Health Practices* | | | |
| 1. Frequency attending religious service/activities? | | | |
| 2. Strength of religious group connection? | | | |
| 3. Congruency of beliefs with health care treatments? | | | |
| 4. Motivation to participate in health promotion activities? | | | |

# CHAPTER POSTTEST

## Activity D MULTIPLE CHOICE

*Choose the one best answer for each of the following multiple-choice questions.*

_____ 1. During a thorough spiritual assessment, the nurse understands that the questions asked are designed to

   **a.** encourage the client to explore other religions.

   **b.** cause the client to question long-held beliefs.

   **c.** determine if the client and nurse have similar beliefs.

   **d.** reveal beliefs that might affect client care.

_____ 2. Loss of connection with one's spiritual support most often leads to

   **a.** a new-found sense of liberation.

   **b.** spiritual distress.

   **c.** improved sense of health and well-being.

   **d.** increased adherence to religious practices.

_____ 3. Knowledge of the client's beliefs in the cause of illness can be useful to the nurse in order to

   **a.** encourage new beliefs.

   **b.** dispel religious teachings if they conflict with the nurse's belief system.

   **c.** promote harmony between health and spirituality.

   **d.** raise doubt and point out flaws in one's faith.

_____ 4. Because the nurse realizes that spirituality varies, information gained will assist the nurse in

   **a.** individualizing interventions to meet specific needs.

   **b.** diagnosing the client with spiritual distress.

   **c.** teaching strict adherence to rituals and practices to improve outcomes.

   **d.** providing an overview of widely held beliefs from the major religions.

## Activity E TRUE/FALSE

*Circle True (T) or False (F) for each statement.*

**1.** T F   For a client in spiritual distress, both the positive and negative effects of their beliefs must be considered.

**2.** T F   Depression can be the result of unmet religious group expectations.

**3.** T F   A self-evaluation of the nurse's own beliefs and biases is important in realizing the relationship between spirituality/religion and health.

**4.** T F   A client's spiritual beliefs have little influence on his or her decision-making process regarding health care.

**5.** T F   The nurse needs to be spiritual to perform a spiritual assessment.

**6.** T F   Facing chronic illness with a strong sense of religion and spirituality has been related to a greater sense of well-being.

## Activity F CRITICAL THINKING AND CASE STUDIES

**1.** Describe expected assessment findings of a client in spiritual distress.

**2.** Select a spiritual assessment tool from the text (Assessment Tools 11.1, 11.2, or 11.3) and discuss the benefits/constraints of using this tool to obtain a useful spiritual assessment. How would you use this tool to perform a spiritual assessment?

**3.** On the basis of the following case study assessment information, work through the steps of analyzing the data. Identify abnormal data and strengths in **subjective and objective findings**, assemble **cue clusters**, draw **inferences**, make possible **nursing diagnoses**, identify **defining characteristics**, **confirm or rule out** the diagnoses, and **document** your conclusions. Use the blank diagnostic analysis charts provided at the end of this book to guide your thinking. You may want to write on the chart or use separate paper. In either case, propose nursing diagnoses that are specific to the client in the case study. Identify collaborative problems, if any, for this client. Finally, identify data, if any, that point toward a medical problem requiring a referral.

Rhonda Logan is a 51-year-old divorced woman with no children. She teaches in a parochial elementary school, attends church regularly, and is the primary caregiver for an aging father in ill health. Rhonda is seeking health care related to difficulty going to sleep and staying asleep. She also reports frequent headaches, lack of appetite and motivation, and difficulty concentrating.

When interviewed, Rhonda relates that she initiated the divorce 6 months ago, ending a 25-year marriage from an alcoholic, verbally abusive husband. She states that she feels guilty over her decision to divorce because of her religious beliefs. Rhonda states she cannot understand how a loving God would have placed her in such a loveless relationship. She indicates that if she had tried harder to involve Mr. Logan in marriage counseling, perhaps things would have turned out differently. She further reflects that if she had been able to have children or had devoted less time to her father, her ex-husband would not have drunk so much.

During the interview with the nurse, Rhonda revealed that she fears that she may lose her job because of the Church's view on divorce. She states that her students are the only thing that keeps her "sane." Rhonda perceives less support from her colleagues during and after the divorce. She states that she is disappointed in their lack of Christian support during these "dark times." She states that she believes their behavior is hypocritical because she is hurting and most of the faculty is not acting in a caring way. Though she attends church regularly, she reveals that she is "going through the motions" but is feeling less and less connected to her congregation. The analogy that she shared was of an empty eggshell, void on the inside, fragile on the outside, yet looking whole and strong to onlookers. The nurse noted varied changes in her mood, vacillating among anxiety, anger, preoccupation, sadness, and crying.

# SELF-REFLECTION AND EVALUATION OF LEARNER OBJECTIVES

After you have read Chapter 11 and completed the above quizzes and activities, please identify to what extent you have met each of the following chapter learning objectives. For those you have met partially or not at all, you will want to review the chapter content for that learning objective.

| Objective | Very Much | Somewhat | Not At All |
|---|---|---|---|
| 1. Describe the difference between *spirituality* and *religion*. | | | |
| 2. Explain how understanding spirituality can assist the nurse in identifying the client's coping responses and support systems. | | | |
| 3. Explain how spiritual beliefs can influence one's decision-making relative to health care. | | | |
| 4. Discuss why it is important that nurses be aware of their own spiritual beliefs and biases as they relate to health care. | | | |

# Assessing Nutrition

## Chapter Overview

Nutritional assessment helps the nurse to identify risk factors for obesity and to promote health. The following activities and questions are provided as a review and, also, to stimulate your thoughts regarding nutritional assessment of the client.

## CHAPTER PRETEST

### Activity A  MATCHING

*Match the terms in the left column with the correct description in the right column.*

**Term**

_____ **1.** Body mass index (BMI)

_____ **2.** Visceral fat

_____ **3.** Triceps skin-fold

_____ **4.** Mid-arm circumference

**Description**

**a.** Used to evaluate subcutaneous fat stores

**b.** Used to assess skeletal muscle mass

**c.** Excess fat within the abdominal cavity

**d.** Estimate of total body fat

### Activity B  LEARNER ACTIVITIES

**Working with peers in learning lab**

*After reading Chapter 12 in the textbook, participate in the following activities with your lab partner as assigned.*

1. Using the Speedy Checklist for Nutritional Health (Assessment Tool 12.2), calculate your lab partner's as well as your own score to determine if there is a nutritional risk. Discuss your findings.

2. Practice taking anthropometric measurements on peers, friends, and family members. Try to find a variety of people: obese, thin, elderly, young. Using the tables in the textbook, locate your findings on standardized tables (below, average, or above national standards). Using the Physical Assessment Checklist in this chapter, record your anthropometric measurements.

3. Interview individuals from varying ethnic communities regarding their traditional ethnic diets. Refer to the Asian, Latin American, Mediterranean, Canadian, American, and Vegetarian food pyramids or guides to assist you in asking questions. What similarities and differences did you find?

**Activity C** INTERVIEWING AND RECORDING ASSESSMENT FINDINGS

Use the following Nursing History Checklist as your guide to interviewing and recording your findings in a nutritional assessment.

### Nursing History Checklist

| Questions | Satisfactory Data | Needs Additional Data | Data Missing |
|---|---|---|---|
| Current Symptoms | | | |
| 1. Appetite changes? | | | |
| 2. Weight changes in last 6 months? | | | |
| 3. Problems with indigestion, heartburn, bloating, gas? | | | |
| 4. Constipation or diarrhea? | | | |
| 5. Dental problems? | | | |
| Past History | | | |
| 1. Food allergies? | | | |
| 2. Conditions/diseases affecting intake or absorption? | | | |
| 3. Frequency of dieting? | | | |
| Family History | | | |
| 1. Chronic diseases? | | | |
| 2. Weight issues? | | | |
| Lifestyle and Health Practices | | | |
| 1. Average daily food and beverage intake? | | | |
| 2. Type of beverages consumed? | | | |
| 3. Dine alone or with others? | | | |
| 4. Number of meals and snacks per day? | | | |
| 5. Food preferences? | | | |
| 6. Frequency of eating out? | | | |
| 7. Long work hours? | | | |
| 8. Sufficient income for food? | | | |

**Activity D** PERFORMING PHYSICAL ASSESSMENT

Use the following Physical Assessment Checklist as your guide to performing a nutritional assessment. Column 1 can be used by you to guide your physical assessment. Column 2 may be used by your instructor to evaluate your skills as necessary.

**Physical Assessment Checklist**

| Assessment Skill | Findings (Normal or Abnormal) and Notes | | Performance (Satisfactory, Needs Improvement, Unsatisfactory) | | |
|---|---|---|---|---|---|
| | N | A | S | N | U |
| 1. Gather equipment (balance beam scale with height attachment, metric measuring tape, marking pencil, and skin-fold calipers). | ☐ | ☐ | ☐ | ☐ | ☐ |
| 2. Measure height. | ☐ | ☐ | ☐ | ☐ | ☐ |
| 3. Measure weight (1 kg = 2.205 lb). | | | | | |
| 4. Determine body mass index (BMI = weight in kilograms/ height in meters squared or use the NIH website: http//nhlbisupport.com/bmi/bmicalc.htm). Compare results to BMI in Table 12-1. | ☐ | ☐ | ☐ | ☐ | ☐ |
| 5. Measure waist circumference and compare findings to Table 12-4. | ☐ | ☐ | ☐ | ☐ | ☐ |
| 6. Measure mid-arm circumference (MAC) and compare findings to Table 12-5. | ☐ | ☐ | ☐ | ☐ | ☐ |
| 7. Measure triceps skin-fold thickness (TSF) and compare to Table 12-6. | ☐ | ☐ | ☐ | ☐ | ☐ |
| 8. Calculate mid-arm muscle circumference (MAMC), MAMC (cm) = MAC (cm) – (0.314 × TSF). Refer to Table 12-7 for interpretation. | ☐ | ☐ | ☐ | ☐ | ☐ |
| *Analysis of Data* | | | | | |
| 1. Formulate nursing diagnoses (wellness, risk, actual). | ☐ | ☐ | ☐ | ☐ | ☐ |
| 2. Formulate collaborative problems. | ☐ | ☐ | ☐ | ☐ | ☐ |
| 3. Make necessary referrals. | ☐ | ☐ | ☐ | ☐ | ☐ |

# CHAPTER POSTTEST

**Activity E**  **MULTIPLE CHOICE**

*Choose the one best answer for each of the following multiple-choice questions.*

_____ **1.** The nurse is caring for an adult female client whose BMI is 38.7. The nurse should instruct the client that she is at greater risk for

    **a.** heart attack.

    **b.** osteoporosis.

    **c.** rheumatoid arthritis.

    **d.** stomach cancer.

_____ **2.** Waist circumference guidelines may not be accurate for adult clients who are shorter than 5 feet in height. This restriction is also a concern for which other anthropometric measurement?

    **a.** ideal weight.

    **b.** mid-arm circumference.

    **c.** body mass index (BMI).

    **d.** triceps skin-fold measurements.

_____ **3.** Based only on anthropometric measurements, which set of clients listed below are at the greatest risk for diabetes and cardiovascular disease?

   **a.** clients with a BMI of 23.

   **b.** females with 35 inches or greater waist circumference.

   **c.** males with 35 inches or greater waist circumference.

   **d.** clients with a BMI of 20.

_____ **4.** What is the most common measurement used to determine abdominal visceral fat?

   **a.** waist circumference.

   **b.** body mass index (BMI).

   **c.** subcutaneous fat determination.

   **d.** triceps skin-fold thickness.

_____ **5.** Because BMI is calculated using only height and weight, the nurse knows that inaccurate findings would most likely occur in a client

   **a.** with diabetes.

   **b.** who is 6 feet tall.

   **c.** with osteoarthritis.

   **d.** who is a bodybuilder.

_____ **6.** The nurse documents that a 45-year-old male is 5 feet 10 inches tall and weighs 215 pounds. He tells the nurse that he "has a good appetite, but doesn't get much exercise because of his busy work schedule." An appropriate NANDA nursing diagnosis for this client is

   **a.** normal body nutrition related to healthy eating patterns and good appetite.

   **b.** altered nutrition, more than body requirements related to intake greater than calories expended.

   **c.** risk for altered nutrition, more than body requirements related to lack of routine exercise.

   **d.** obesity related to lack of exercise.

_____ **7.** The nurse is preparing to measure the triceps skin-fold of an adult client. The nurse should

   **a.** ask the client to assume a sitting position.

   **b.** measure the triceps skin-fold in the dominant arm.

   **c.** repeat the procedure three times and average the measurements.

   **d.** pull the skin toward the muscle mass of the arm.

### Activity F  CRITICAL THINKING AND CASE STUDIES

**1.** Discuss why determining the presence and extent of abdominal visceral fat is significant during an assessment? Explain.

**2.** Describe the procedures that you would use to determine the client's body composition.

**3.** Discuss expected changes in height and weight associated with the aging process. How does this affect the BMI accuracy? Why?

**4.** Explain how an obese client may be undernourished in spite of ample weight and intake. What nursing diagnosis might you make?

**5.** On the basis of the following case study assessment information, work through the steps of analyzing the data. Identify abnormal data and strengths in **subjective and objective findings**, assemble **cue clusters**, draw **inferences**, make possible **nursing diagnoses**, identify **defining characteristics**, **confirm or rule out** the diagnoses, and **document** your conclusions. Use the blank diagnostic analysis charts provided at the end of this book to guide your thinking. You may want to write on the chart or use separate paper. In either case, propose nursing diagnoses that are specific to the client in the case study. Identify collaborative problems, if any, for this client. Finally, identify data, if any, that point toward a medical problem requiring a referral.

Gina Riley is a 43-year-old married woman who has been newly diagnosed with diabetes mellitus. She is 5 feet 2 inches tall, weighs 236 pounds, and has elevated blood glucose levels, cholesterol, and triglyceride levels. Gina has a college education and two teenage children, one of whom is away at college. Her husband is on permanent disability resulting from alcohol-induced cirrhosis. Gina works with an enrichment program for parents of preschoolers. Because she works in a rural area, she spends a large amount of time driving between client home visits.

When interviewed, Gina states that 3 years ago she was diagnosed with a brain tumor but was successfully treated with surgery, radiation, and chemotherapy. She remains on a maintenance dose of prednisone, which she reports stimulates her appetite and has caused her to develop diabetes. Gina takes metformin (Glucophage) to reduce her blood sugar. She correctly states that this medication can also suppress appetite and promote weight loss. When questioned about snacks, she reports that she ate half a box of cookies last evening, but clarified this by stating that they were low-fat cookies.

Further interviewing revealed that Gina knows she must lose weight but states it is difficult because she spends much of her day traveling, has little, if any, time to exercise, and works long hours, so she and her husband eat out frequently. She denies smoking or drinking. Gina reports few social contacts due to her husband's illness. She appears very devoted to her children and her client families that she serves. During the interview, she further states that food was her only pleasure and now that too has been taken away due to dietary restrictions. Though often smiling during the interview, Gina shares that life would have been simpler if her husband had died last summer when he was so critically ill.

# SELF-REFLECTION AND EVALUATION
# OF LEARNER OBJECTIVES

After you have read Chapter 12 and completed the above quizzes and activities, please identify to what extent you have met each of the following chapter learning objectives. For those you have met partially or not at all, you will want to review the chapter content for that learning objective.

| Objective | Very Much | Somewhat | Not At All |
|---|---|---|---|
| 1. Assess the overall appearance as well as the client's body build, muscle mass, and fat distribution. | | | |
| 2. Describe the equipment needed to perform anthropometric measurement, and obtain accurate measurements (height, weight, BMI, waist circumference, mid-arm circumference, triceps skin-fold thickness, and mid-arm muscle circumference). | | | |
| 3. Calculate a client's BMI. | | | |
| 4. Describe expected changes with height and weight associated with the aging process. | | | |
| 5. Explain the importance of BMI, waist circumference, mid-arm circumference, triceps skin-fold thickness, and mid-arm muscle circumference in a health assessment. | | | |
| 6. Discuss clusters of signs and symptoms that may indicate changes in hydration status. | | | |
| 7. Discuss possible nursing diagnoses and collaborative problems that may emerge after a nutritional assessment. | | | |

# UNIT III

# Nursing Assessment of Physical Systems

# Skin, Hair, and Nails

## Chapter Overview

In any kind of nursing assessment, the client's skin, hair, and nails are among the most easily observed characteristics. They also provide clues to the client's general health condition. The following questions and exercises are presented to help you review your observation and other assessment skills. You will also be helped, both in your studies and in your practice, by the directions for performing a skin self-assessment, which may be found at the end of this chapter.

## CHAPTER PRETEST

### Activity A MULTIPLE CHOICE

*Choose the one best answer for each of the following multiple-choice questions.*

____ **1.** Connecting the skin to underlying structures is/are the

   **a.** papillae.

   **b.** sebaceous glands.

   **c.** dermis layer.

   **d.** subcutaneous tissue.

____ **2.** The skin plays a vital role in temperature maintenance, fluid and electrolyte balance, and synthesis of vitamin

   **a.** A.

   **b.** $B_{12}$.

   **c.** C.

   **d.** D.

____ **3.** The only layer of the skin that undergoes cell division is the

   **a.** innermost layer of the epidermis.

   **b.** outermost layer of the epidermis.

   **c.** innermost layer of the dermis.

   **d.** outermost layer of the dermis.

___ **4.** A client's skin color depends on melanin and carotene contained in the skin, and the
  **a.** client's genetic background.
  **b.** volume of blood circulating in the dermis.
  **c.** number of lymph vessels near the dermis.
  **d.** vascularity of the apocrine glands.

___ **5.** Hair follicles, sebaceous glands, and sweat glands originate from the
  **a.** epidermis.
  **b.** eccrine glands.
  **c.** keratinized tissue.
  **d.** dermis.

___ **6.** The apocrine glands are dormant until puberty and are concentrated in the axillae, the perineum, and the
  **a.** areola of the breast.
  **b.** entire skin surface.
  **c.** soles of the feet.
  **d.** adipose tissue.

___ **7.** Short, pale, and fine hair that is present over much of the body is termed
  **a.** vellus.
  **b.** dermal.
  **c.** lanugo.
  **d.** terminal.

___ **8.** A primary function of hair in the nose and eyelashes is to serve as a
  **a.** response to cold.
  **b.** filter for dust.
  **c.** pigment producer.
  **d.** response to fright.

___ **9.** The nails, located on the distal phalanges of the fingers and toes, are composed of
  **a.** ectodermal cells.
  **b.** endodermal cells.
  **c.** keratinized epidermal cells.
  **d.** stratum cells.

## Activity B LABELING ACTIVITIES

*Label the following skin structures.*

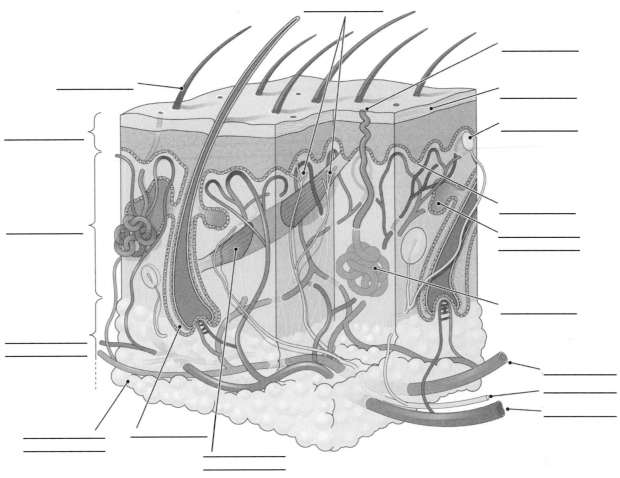

Skin and hair follicles and related structures.

*Label the structure indicated by the line; then match your answer with the label on the matching figure in Chapter 13 of your textbook.*

*Label the following nail structures.*

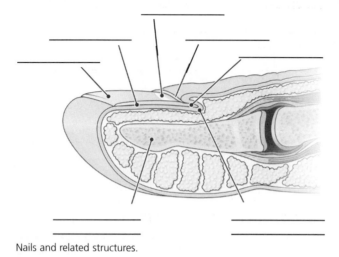

Nails and related structures.

*Label the structure indicated by the line; then match your answer with the label on the matching figure in Chapter 13 of your textbook.*

**Activity C** LEARNER ACTIVITIES

### Working with peers in learning lab

1. Review the information in "Promote Health: Skin Cancer." Then, determine your own risk for skin cancer. Next, identify and discuss ethnic groups that are at highest risk for skin cancer.

2. Practice recording the descriptions of various common skin lesions on your own arms and legs (freckles, warts, moles, and sores) by examining the color, size, configuration, and shape of any lesion you find.

3. Find an elderly client or friend or relative who will let you examine his or her skin, hair, and nails. Report your findings as they compare with those of a younger person's skin, hair, and nails.

**Activity D** INTERVIEWING AND RECORDING ASSESSMENT FINDINGS

Use the following Nursing History Checklist as your guide to interviewing and recording your findings in skin, hair, and nail assessment.

### Nursing History Checklist

| Questions | Satisfactory Data | Needs Additional Data | Data Missing |
|---|---|---|---|
| *Current Symptoms* | | | |
| 1. Skin problems (rashes, lesions, dryness, oiliness, drainage, bruising, swelling, pigmentation) | | | |
| 2. Changes in lesion appearance | | | |
| 3. Feeling changes (pain, pressure, itch, tingling) | | | |
| 4. Hair loss or changes | | | |
| 5. Nail changes | | | |
| 6. Body odor problems | | | |

| Questions | Satisfactory Data | Needs Additional Data | Data Missing |
|---|---|---|---|
| *Past History* | | | |
| 1. Previous problems with skin, hair, or nails (treatment and surgery) | | | |
| 2. Allergic reactions | | | |
| *Family History* | | | |
| 1. Family history of skin problems or skin cancer | | | |
| *Lifestyle and Health Practices* | | | |
| 1. Exposure to sun or chemicals | | | |
| 2. Daily care of skin, hair, and nails | | | |
| 3. Usual diet and exercise patterns | | | |

### Activity E PERFORMING PHYSICAL ASSESSMENT

Use the following Physical Assessment Checklist as your guide to performing skin, hair, and nail assessment. Column 1 can be used by you to guide your physical assessment. Column 2 may be used by your instructor to evaluate your skills as necessary.

### Physical Assessment Checklist

| Assessment Skill | Findings (Normal or Abnormal) and Notes | | Performance (Satisfactory, Needs Improvement, Unsatisfactory) | | |
|---|---|---|---|---|---|
| | N | A | S | N | U |
| 1. Gather equipment (gloves, exam light, penlight, magnifying glass, centimeter ruler, Wood's lamp if available). | ☐ | ☐ | ☐ | ☐ | ☐ |
| 2. Explain procedure to client. | ☐ | ☐ | ☐ | ☐ | ☐ |
| 3. Ask client to gown. | ☐ | ☐ | ☐ | ☐ | ☐ |
| *Skin* | | | | | |
| 1. Note any distinctive odor. | ☐ | ☐ | ☐ | ☐ | ☐ |
| 2. Inspect for generalized color variations (brownness, yellow, redness, pallor, cyanosis, jaundice, erythema, vitiligo). | ☐ | ☐ | ☐ | ☐ | ☐ |
| 3. Inspect for skin breakdown (use staging criteria given in Chapter 13). | ☐ | ☐ | ☐ | ☐ | ☐ |
| 4. Inspect for primary, secondary, or vascular lesions. (Note size, shape, location, distribution, and configuration.) Use Wood's lamp if fungus is suspected. | ☐ | ☐ | ☐ | ☐ | ☐ |
| 5. Palpate lesions. | ☐ | ☐ | ☐ | ☐ | ☐ |
| 6. Palpate texture (rough, smooth) of skin, using palmar surface of three middle fingers. | ☐ | ☐ | ☐ | ☐ | ☐ |
| 7. Palpate temperature (cool, warm, hot) and moisture (dry, sweaty, oily) of skin, using dorsal side of hand. | ☐ | ☐ | ☐ | ☐ | ☐ |

| Assessment Skill | Performance (Normal or Abnormal) and Notes | | (Satisfactory, Needs Improvement, Unsatisfactory) | | |
|---|---|---|---|---|---|
| | N | A | S | N | U |
| 8. Palpate thickness of skin with fingerpads. | ☐ | ☐ | ☐ | ☐ | ☐ |
| 9. Palpate mobility and turgor by pinching up skin over sternum. | ☐ | ☐ | ☐ | ☐ | ☐ |
| 10. Palpate for edema, pressing thumbs over feet or ankles. | ☐ | ☐ | ☐ | ☐ | ☐ |
| *Scalp and Hair* | | | | | |
| 1. Inspect color. | ☐ | ☐ | ☐ | ☐ | ☐ |
| 2. Inspect amount and distribution. | ☐ | ☐ | ☐ | ☐ | ☐ |
| 3. Inspect and palpate for thickness, texture, oiliness, lesions, and parasites. | ☐ | ☐ | ☐ | ☐ | ☐ |
| *Nails* | | | | | |
| 1. Inspect for grooming and cleanliness. | ☐ | ☐ | ☐ | ☐ | ☐ |
| 2. Inspect for color and markings. | ☐ | ☐ | ☐ | ☐ | ☐ |
| 3. Inspect shape. | ☐ | ☐ | ☐ | ☐ | ☐ |
| 4. Palpate texture and consistency. | ☐ | ☐ | ☐ | ☐ | ☐ |
| 5. Test for capillary refill. | ☐ | ☐ | ☐ | ☐ | ☐ |
| *Analysis of Data* | | | | | |
| 1. Formulate nursing diagnoses (wellness, risk, actual). | ☐ | ☐ | ☐ | ☐ | ☐ |
| 2. Formulate collaborative problems. | ☐ | ☐ | ☐ | ☐ | ☐ |
| 3. Make necessary referrals. | ☐ | ☐ | ☐ | ☐ | ☐ |

# CHAPTER POSTTEST

### Activity F MULTIPLE CHOICE

*Choose the one best answer for each of the following multiple-choice questions.*

_____ 1. An adult female client visits the clinic for the first time. The client has many bruises around her neck and face, and she tells the nurse that the bruises are the "result of an accident." The nurse suspects that the client may be experiencing

  **a.** leukemia.

  **b.** diabetes mellitus.

  **c.** melanoma.

  **d.** domestic abuse.

_____ 2. An adult male client visits the outpatient center and tells the nurse that he has been experiencing patchy hair loss. The nurse should further assess the client for

  **a.** symptoms of stress.

  **b.** recent radiation therapy.

  **c.** pigmentation irregularities.

  **d.** allergies to certain foods.

____ **3.** The nurse is instructing a group of high school students about risk factors associated with various skin cancers. The nurse should instruct the group that

    **a.** melanoma skin cancers are the most common type of cancers.

    **b.** African-Americans are the least susceptible to skin cancers.

    **c.** usually there are precursor lesions for basal cell carcinomas.

    **d.** squamous cell carcinomas are most common on body sites with heavy sun exposure.

____ **4.** Squamous cell carcinoma is associated with

    **a.** overall amount of sun exposure.

    **b.** intermittent exposure to ultraviolet rays.

    **c.** precursor lesions.

    **d.** an increase in the rates of melanoma.

____ **5.** The nurse is assessing an African-American client's skin. After the assessment, the nurse should instruct the client that African-American persons are more susceptible to

    **a.** skin cancers than persons of European origin.

    **b.** melanomas if they reside in areas without ozone depletion.

    **c.** chronic discoid lupus erythematosus.

    **d.** genetic predisposition to melanomas.

____ **6.** A 20-year-old client visits the outpatient center and tells the nurse that he has been experiencing sudden generalized hair loss. After determining that the client has not received radiation or chemotherapy, the nurse should further assess the client for signs and symptoms of

    **a.** hypothyroidism.

    **b.** hyperthyroidism.

    **c.** infectious conditions.

    **d.** hypoparathyroidism.

____ **7.** A client visits the clinic for a routine physical examination. The nurse prepares to assess the client's skin. The nurse asks the client if there is a family history of skin cancer and should explain to the client that there is a genetic component with skin cancer, especially

    **a.** basal cell carcinoma.

    **b.** actinic keratoses.

    **c.** squamous cell carcinoma.

    **d.** malignant melanoma.

____ **8.** A female client visits the clinic and complains to the nurse that her skin feels "dry." The nurse should instruct the client that skin elasticity is related to adequate

    **a.** calcium.

    **b.** vitamin D.

    **c.** carbohydrates.

    **d.** fluid intake.

____ **9.** An adult white client visits the clinic for the first time. During assessment of the client's skin, the nurse should assess for central cyanosis by observing the client's

    **a.** nailbeds.

    **b.** oral mucosa.

    **c.** sclera.

    **d.** palms.

____ **10.** To assess for anemia in a dark-skinned client, the nurse should observe the client's skin for a color that appears

    **a.** greenish.

    **b.** ashen.

    **c.** bluish.

    **d.** olive.

____ **11.** The nurse is assessing a dark-skinned client who has been transported to the emergency room by ambulance. When the nurse observes that the client's skin appears pale, with blue-tinged lips and oral mucosa, the nurse should document the presence of

    **a.** a great degree of cyanosis.

    **b.** a mild degree of cyanosis.

    **c.** lupus erythematosus.

    **d.** hyperthyroidism.

____ **12.** A dark-skinned client visits the clinic because he "hasn't been feeling well." To assess the client's skin for jaundice, the nurse should inspect the client's

    **a.** abdomen.

    **b.** arms.

    **c.** legs.

    **d.** sclera.

____ **13.** While assessing the skin of an older adult client, the nurse observes that the client has small yellowish brown patches on her hands. The nurse should instruct the client that these spots are

    **a.** signs of an infectious process.

    **b.** caused by aging of the skin in older adults.

    **c.** precancerous lesions.

    **d.** signs of dermatitis.

____ **14.** While assessing an adult client's feet for fungal disease using a Wood's light, the nurse documents the presence of a fungus when the fluorescence is

    **a.** blue.

    **b.** red.

    **c.** yellow.

    **d.** purple.

____ **15.** The nurse assesses an older adult bedridden client in her home. While assessing the client's buttocks, the nurse observes that a small area of the skin is broken and resembles an erosion. The nurse should document the client's pressure ulcer as

    **a.** stage I.

    **b.** stage II.

    **c.** stage III.

    **d.** stage IV.

____ **16.** To assess an adult client's skin turgor, the nurse should

    **a.** press down on the skin of the feet.

    **b.** use the dorsal surfaces of the hands on the client's arms.

    **c.** use the fingerpads to palpate the skin at the sternum.

    **d.** use two fingers to pinch the skin under the clavicle.

____ **17.** While assessing the nails of an adult client, the nurse observes Beau's lines. The nurse should ask the client if he has had

    **a.** chemotherapy.

    **b.** radiation.

    **c.** a recent illness.

    **d.** steroid therapy.

____ **18.** While assessing the nails of an older adult, the nurse observes early clubbing. The nurse should further evaluate the client for signs and symptoms of

    **a.** hypoxia.

    **b.** trauma.

    **c.** anemia.

    **d.** infection.

____ **19.** While assessing an adult client, the nurse observes freckles on the client's face. The nurse should document the presence of

    **a.** macules.

    **b.** papules.

    **c.** plaques.

    **d.** bulla.

____ **20.** While assessing an adult client, the nurse observes an elevated, palpable, solid mass with a circumscribed border that measures 1 cm. The nurse documents this as a

    **a.** plaque.

    **b.** macule.

    **c.** papule.

    **d.** patch.

____ **21.** The nurse is preparing to examine the skin of an adult client with a diagnosis of herpes simplex. The nurse plans to measure the client's symptomatic lesions and measure the size of the client's

    **a.** nodules.

    **b.** bullae.

    **c.** vesicles.

    **d.** wheals.

____ **22.** An adult male client visits the clinic and tells the nurse that he believes he has athlete's foot. The nurse observes that the client has linear cracks in the skin on both feet. The nurse should document the presence of

    **a.** ulcers.

    **b.** erosion.

    **c.** scales.

    **d.** fissures.

____ **23.** An African-American female client visits the clinic. She tells the nurse that she had her ears pierced several weeks ago, and an elevated, irregular, reddened mass has now developed at the earlobe. The nurse should document a

    **a.** cyst.

    **b.** lichenification.

    **c.** bulla.

    **d.** keloid.

_____ **24.** A client who is an active outdoor swimmer recently received a diagnosis of discoid systemic lupus erythematosus. The client visits the clinic for a routine examination and tells the nurse that she continues to swim in the sunlight three times per week. She has accepted her patchy hair loss and wears a wig on occasion. A priority nursing diagnosis for the client is

   **a.** ineffective individual coping related to changes in appearance.

   **b.** anxiety related to loss of outdoor activities and altered skin appearance.

   **c.** dry flaking skin and dull dry hair as a result of disease.

   **d.** risk for ineffective health maintenance related to deficient knowledge of effects of sunlight on skin lesions.

## Activity G  CROSSWORD PUZZLE

*Complete the following crossword puzzle to become more familiar with the terminology used with assessment of the skin, hair, and nails.*

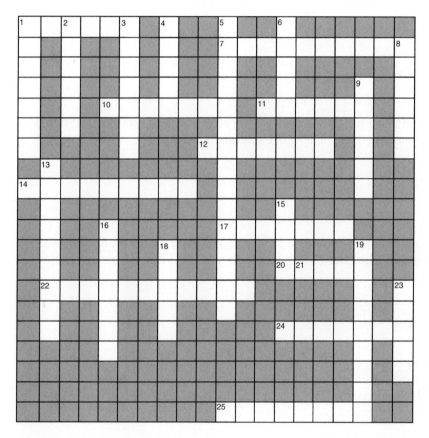

**Across**

   **1.** Solid, elevated, circumscribed, superficial lesion; 1 cm or less in diameter

   **7.** Hardening of the skin, usually caused by edema

   **10.** Linear crack in the skin

   **11.** Flat circumscribed lesion of the skin or mucous membrane; 1 cm or less in diameter

   **12.** Spread out, widely dispersed

**Down**

   **1.** Vesicle or bulla that contains pus

   **2.** Solid, elevated, circumscribed superficial lesion; more than 1 cm in diameter

   **3.** Wearing away or destruction of the mucosal or epidermal surface, often develops into an ulcer

   **4.** Congenital pigmented area on the skin, for example, mole, birthmark

**Across**

**14.** Swelling, discoloration, and pain without a break in the skin; a bruise

**17.** Describes a lesion that forms a ring around a clear center of normal skin

**20.** Solid skin elevation extending into the dermal layer; more than 1 cm in diameter

**22.** Scratch or abrasion on the skin surface

**24.** Fluid-filled, elevated, superficial lesion; 1 cm or less in diameter

**25.** Tiny, flat, purple, or red spots on the surface of the skin resulting from minute hemorrhage

**Down**

**5.** Thickening of the skin characterized by accentuated skin markings

**6.** An elevated, circumscribed, fluid-filled lesion; greater than 1 cm in diameter

**8.** Solid skin elevation that extends into the dermal layer; 1 cm or less in diameter

**9.** Hypertrophic scar tissue; prevalent in non-white races

**13.** Describes lesions that run together

**15.** Dried serum, blood, or purulent exudate on the skin

**16.** Decrease in size, or wasting

**18.** Small thin flakes of epithelial cells

**19.** Hives; pruritic wheals, often transient and allergic in origin

**21.** Circumscribed crater on the surface of the skin or mucous membrane that leaves a wound

**23.** Elevated, solid, transient lesion; often irregularly shaped; an edematous response

## Activity H  CRITICAL THINKING AND CASE STUDIES

**1.** Discuss how you would assess for pallor, cyanosis, jaundice, and erythema in a dark-skinned client.

**2.** Read the following case study. Then analyze the client's risk for skin cancer.

Mike McDaniel is a 47-year-old construction worker who has lived for 20 years in southern Florida. He has blond hair and tanned, leathery, freckled skin. He is 5 feet 10 inches tall and weighs 200 pounds. He smokes two packs of cigarettes and drinks a six-pack of beer per day. He describes himself as a "meat and potatoes man." He has a history of mild hypertension, and several members of his family have heart disease.

**3.** On the basis of the following case study assessment information, work through the steps of analyzing the data. Identify abnormal data and strengths in **subjective and objective findings**, assemble **cue clusters**, draw **inferences**, make possible **nursing diagnoses**, identify **defining characteristics**, **confirm or rule out** the diagnoses, and **document** your conclusions. Use the blank diagnostic analysis charts provided at the end of this book to guide your thinking. You may want to write on the chart or use separate paper. In either case, propose nursing diagnoses that are specific to the client in the case study. Identify collaborative problems, if any, for this client. Finally, identify data, if any, that point toward a medical problem requiring a referral.

Evelyn Vaughn is a 47-year-old white woman who comes to the clinic for evaluation. She is a single mother and sells cosmetics in her home. She is lethargic and walks slowly into the room. She asks if she can have some "special lotion" for her dry skin.

When interviewed, Evelyn states that her skin has been dry and scaly for the past several months, unrelieved by numerous moisturizers. She expresses concern about "fly-away hair that I can't do anything with" and about brittle, easily broken fingernails. When asked about medications, she explains that she is supposed to take Synthroid daily for "my low thyroid" but cannot afford to get the prescription filled. She has a poor appetite, and with "not enough money to go around," she has been nibbling on crackers, lunch meat, and sodas daily. Exercise is out of the question because she lacks energy, and she is rarely able to get through a day without one or two 30-minute naps. Evelyn takes a shower and washes her hair using Ivory soap and baby shampoo. She applies moisturizer to her skin and conditioner to her hair but states that neither helps for any length of time. She keeps her nails cut short because they break so easily. She states that she has cut down on her cosmetic sales appointments because "I look like I never use my own products."

Your physical assessment reveals dry flaking skin that is cool to the touch and yellow tinged. Facial and periorbital edema are present. The client's facial expression is blank. She has multiple bruises on both forearms and anterior lower legs, which are in various stages of healing and tender when touched. Her scalp hair is dry and dull and breaks easily. Her scalp is scaling. Sparse hair is noted in the axillae and the pubic area. Her fingernails are short and dry; her cuticles are dry and torn. Her toenails are thick and yellow.

# SELF-REFLECTION AND EVALUATION OF LEARNER OBJECTIVES

After you have read Chapter 13 and completed the above quizzes and activities, please identify to what degree you have met each of the following chapter learning objectives. For those objectives that you have met partially or not at all, you will want to review the chapter content for that learning objective.

| Objective | Very Much | Somewhat | Not At All |
|---|---|---|---|
| 1. Describe the structures and functions of the skin. | | | |
| 2. Discuss risk factors for skin cancer and ways to reduce these risk factors. | | | |
| 3. Discuss the incidence of skin cancer across cultures. | | | |
| 4. Obtain an accurate nursing history of the client's skin, hair, and nails. | | | |
| 5. Explain how to prepare the client and the equipment necessary to perform a skin, hair, and nail assessment. | | | |
| 6. Describe the two physical examination techniques used to assess the skin. | | | |
| 7. Assess the skin for color, breakdown, lesions, moisture, turgor, and edema. | | | |
| 8. Describe the two physical examination techniques used to assess the hair and nails. | | | |
| 9. Assess the scalp and hair for color, amount, distribution, condition, and texture. | | | |
| 10. Assess the nails for grooming, color, markings, shape, texture, consistency, and capillary refill. | | | |
| 11. Describe differences in hair color and texture that may be seen in ethnic groups. | | | |
| 12. Describe changes that are common with aging of the skin, hair, and nails. | | | |

***Label the structure indicated by the line; then match your answer with the label on the matching figure in Chapter 14 of your textbook.***

***Label the lymph nodes in the neck in the following figure.***

Lymph nodes in the neck.

***Label the structure indicated by the line; then match your answer with the label on the matching figure in Chapter 14 of your textbook.***

### Activity C LEARNER ACTIVITIES

#### Working with peers in learning lab

1. Refer to Table 14-1 in the textbook, "Kinds and Characteristics of Headaches." Interview your lab partner to determine whether he or she has ever had a headache. Determine the type it might have been, based on the information in Table 14-1.

2. Practice the correct method for palpating the thyroid gland on your lab partner. Discuss your findings: size, texture, smoothness, presence of nodules or masses.

3. Auscultate your lab partner's thyroid gland and carotid arteries. Discuss the significance of this exam and what would indicate an abnormality.

4. Demonstrate on your lab partner how to inspect and palpate the C7 vertebra. Discuss the changes that may occur with aging, such as kyphosis of the spine or dowager's hump.

5. Assess the lymph nodes of your lab partner. Discuss the normal and abnormal characteristics of the lymph nodes.

**Activity D** INTERVIEWING AND RECORDING ASSESSMENT FINDINGS

Use the following Nursing History Checklist as your guide to interviewing and recording your findings in a head and neck assessment.

### Nursing History Checklist

| Questions | Satisfactory Data | Needs Additional Data | Data Missing |
|---|---|---|---|
| *Current Symptoms* | | | |
| 1. Lumps or lesions on head or neck that do not heal or disappear. | | | |
| 2. Difficulty moving head or neck. | | | |
| 3. Facial or neck pain or frequent headaches. | | | |
| 4. Dizziness, lightheadedness, spinning sensation, or loss of consciousness. | | | |
| *Past History* | | | |
| 1. Previous head or neck problems/trauma/injury (surgery, medication, physical or radiation therapy); results. | | | |
| *Family History* | | | |
| 1. Family history of head and/or neck cancer. | | | |
| 2. Family history of migraine headaches. | | | |
| *Lifestyle and Health Practices* | | | |
| 1. Do you smoke or chew tobacco? Amount? Secondhand smoke? | | | |
| 2. Do you wear a helmet or hard hat? | | | |
| 3. Typical posture when relaxing, during sleep, and when working. | | | |
| 4. Type of recreational activities. | | | |
| 5. Satisfaction with appearance. | | | |

**Activity E** PERFORMING PHYSICAL ASSESSMENT

Use the following Physical Assessment Checklist as your guide to performing a head and neck physical assessment. Column 1 can be used by you to guide your physical assessment. Column 2 may be used by your instructor to evaluate your skills as necessary.

### Physical Assessment Checklist

| Assessment Skill | Findings (Normal or Abnormal) and Notes | | Performance (Satisfactory, Needs Improvement, Unsatisfactory) | | |
|---|---|---|---|---|---|
| | N | A | S | N | U |
| 1. Gather equipment (gloves, penlight or flashlight, small glass of water, stethoscope). | ☐ | ☐ | ☐ | ☐ | ☐ |
| 2. Explain procedure to client. | ☐ | ☐ | ☐ | ☐ | ☐ |

| Assessment Skill | Findings (Normal or Abnormal) and Notes | | Performance (Satisfactory, Needs Improvement, Unsatisfactory) | | |
|---|---|---|---|---|---|
| | N | A | S | N | U |
| *Head and Face* | | | | | |
| 1. Inspect head for size, shape, and configuration. | ☐ | ☐ | ☐ | ☐ | ☐ |
| 2. Palpate head for consistency while wearing gloves. | ☐ | ☐ | ☐ | ☐ | ☐ |
| 3. Inspect face for symmetry, features, movement, expression, and skin condition. | ☐ | ☐ | ☐ | ☐ | ☐ |
| 4. Palpate temporal artery for tenderness and elasticity. | ☐ | ☐ | ☐ | ☐ | ☐ |
| 5. Palpate temporomandibular joint for range of motion, swelling, tenderness, or crepitation by placing index finger over the front of each and asking client to open mouth. Ask if client has history of frequent headaches. | ☐ | ☐ | ☐ | ☐ | ☐ |
| *Neck* | | | | | |
| 1. Inspect neck while it is in a slightly extended position (and using a light) for position, symmetry, and presence of lumps and masses. | ☐ | ☐ | ☐ | ☐ | ☐ |
| 2. Inspect movement of thyroid and cricoid cartilage and thyroid gland by having client swallow a small sip of water. | ☐ | ☐ | ☐ | ☐ | ☐ |
| 3. Inspect cervical vertebrae by having client flex neck. | ☐ | ☐ | ☐ | ☐ | ☐ |
| 4. Inspect neck range of motion by having client turn chin to right and left shoulder, touch each ear to the shoulder, touch chin to chest, and lift chin to ceiling. | ☐ | ☐ | ☐ | ☐ | ☐ |
| 5. Palpate trachea by placing your finger in the sternal notch, feeling to each side, and palpating the tracheal rings. | ☐ | ☐ | ☐ | ☐ | ☐ |
| 6. Palpate the thyroid gland. | ☐ | ☐ | ☐ | ☐ | ☐ |
| 7. Auscultate thyroid gland for bruits if the gland is enlarged (use bell of stethoscope). | ☐ | ☐ | ☐ | ☐ | ☐ |
| 8. Palpate lymph nodes for size/shape, delimination, mobility, consistency, and tenderness (refer to display on characteristics of lymph nodes). | ☐ | ☐ | ☐ | ☐ | ☐ |
|    a. Preauricular nodes (front of ears) | ☐ | ☐ | ☐ | ☐ | ☐ |
|    b. Postauricular nodes (behind the ears) | ☐ | ☐ | ☐ | ☐ | ☐ |
|    c. Occipital nodes (posterior base of skull) | ☐ | ☐ | ☐ | ☐ | ☐ |
|    d. Tonsillar nodes (angle of the mandible, on the anterior edge of the sternocleidomastoid muscle) | ☐ | ☐ | ☐ | ☐ | ☐ |
|    e. Submandibular nodes (medial border of the mandible); do not confuse with the lobulated submandibular gland | ☐ | ☐ | ☐ | ☐ | ☐ |
|    f. Submental nodes (a few centimeters behind the tip of the mandible); use one hand | ☐ | ☐ | ☐ | ☐ | ☐ |
|    g. Superficial cervical nodes (superficial to the sternomastoid muscle) | ☐ | ☐ | ☐ | ☐ | ☐ |
|    h. Posterior cervical nodes (posterior to the sternocleidomastoid and anterior to the trapezius in the posterior triangle) | ☐ | ☐ | ☐ | ☐ | ☐ |
|    i. Deep cervical chain nodes (deep within and around the sternomastoid muscle) | ☐ | ☐ | ☐ | ☐ | ☐ |
|    j. Supraclavicular nodes (hook fingers over clavicles and feel deeply between the clavicles and the sternomastoid muscles) | ☐ | ☐ | ☐ | ☐ | ☐ |

| Assessment Skill | Findings (Normal or Abnormal) and Notes | | Performance (Satisfactory, Needs Improvement, Unsatisfactory) | | |
|---|---|---|---|---|---|
| | N | A | S | N | U |
| *Analysis of Data* | | | | | |
| 1. Formulate nursing diagnoses (wellness, risk, actual). | ☐ | ☐ | ☐ | ☐ | ☐ |
| 2. Formulate collaborative problems. | ☐ | ☐ | ☐ | ☐ | ☐ |
| 3. Make necessary referrals. | ☐ | ☐ | ☐ | ☐ | ☐ |

# CHAPTER POSTTEST

**Activity F** **MULTIPLE CHOICE**

*Choose the one best answer for each of the following multiple-choice questions.*

_a_ 1. The nurse assesses an adult client's head and neck. While examining the carotid arteries, the nurse assesses each artery individually to prevent a

    **a.** reduction of the blood supply to the brain.

    **b.** rapid rise in the client's pulse rate.

    **c.** premature ventricular heart sound.

    **d.** decreased pulse pressure.

_b_ 2. A client visits the outpatient center with a complaint of sudden head and neck pain and stiffness. The client's oral temperature is 100°F. The nurse suspects the client is experiencing symptoms of

    **a.** migraine headache.

    **b.** meningeal irritation.

    **c.** trigeminal neuralgia.

    **d.** otitis media.

_d_ 3. While assessing the head and neck of an adult client, the client tells the nurse that she has been experiencing sharp shooting facial pains that last from 10 to 20 seconds but are occurring more frequently. The nurse should refer the client for possible

    **a.** cancerous lesions.

    **b.** arterial occlusion.

    **c.** inner ear disease.

    **d.** trigeminal neuralgia.

_a_ 4. A female client visits the clinic and tells the nurse that she frequently experiences severe recurring headaches that sometimes last for several days and are accompanied by nausea and vomiting. The nurse determines that the type of headache the client is describing is a

    **a.** migraine headache.

    **b.** cluster headache.

    **c.** tension headache.

    **d.** tumor-related headache.

5. An adult client visits the clinic and tells the nurse that she has had headaches recently that are intense and stabbing and often occur in the late evening. The nurse should document the presence of

    **a.** cluster headaches.

    **b.** migraine headaches.

    **c.** tension headaches.

    **d.** tumor-related headaches.

6. A client visits the clinic and tells the nurse that he is depressed because of a recent job loss. He complains of dull, aching, tight, and diffuse headaches that have lasted for several days. The nurse should document the client's

    **a.** cluster headaches.

    **b.** tumor-related headaches.

    **c.** migraine headaches.

    **d.** tension headaches.

7. An older client visits the clinic accompanied by his daughter. The daughter tells the nurse that her father has been experiencing severe headaches that usually begin in the morning and become worse when he coughs. The client tells the nurse that he feels dizzy when he has the headaches. The nurse refers the client for further evaluation because these symptoms are characteristic of a

    **a.** migraine headache.

    **b.** cluster headache.

    **c.** tension headache.

    **d.** tumor-related headache.

8. The nurse is preparing to perform a head and neck assessment of an adult client who has immigrated to the United States from Cambodia. The nurse should first

    **a.** explain to the client why the assessment is necessary.

    **b.** ask the client if touching the head is permissible.

    **c.** determine whether the client desires a family member present.

    **d.** examine the lymph nodes of the neck before examining the head.

9. While assessing an adult client's skull, the nurse observes that the client's skull and facial bones are larger and thicker than usual. The nurse should assess the client for

    **a.** parotid gland enlargement.

    **b.** acromegaly.

    **c.** Paget's disease.

    **d.** Cushing's syndrome.

10. While assessing an adult client's skull, the nurse observes that the client's skull bones are acorn shaped and enlarged. The nurse should refer the client to a physician for possible

    **a.** Cushing's syndrome.

    **b.** scleroderma.

    **c.** Paget's disease.

    **d.** Parkinson's disease.

*d* 11. While assessing an adult client's head and neck, the nurse observes asymmetry in front of the client's earlobes. The nurse refers the client to the physician because the nurse suspects the client is most likely experiencing a/an

　　**a.** enlarged thyroid.

　　**b.** lymph node abscess.

　　**c.** neurologic disorder.

　　**d.** parotid gland enlargement.

*b* 12. The nurse is preparing to assess the neck of an adult client. To inspect movement of the client's thyroid gland, the nurse should ask the client to

　　**a.** inhale deeply.

　　**b.** swallow a small sip of water.

　　**c.** cough deeply.

　　**d.** flex the neck to each side.

*c* 13. While assessing an older adult client's neck, the nurse observes that the client's trachea is pulled to the left side. The nurse should

　　**a.** ask the client to flex his neck to the left side.

　　**b.** observe whether the client has difficulty swallowing water.

　　**c.** refer the client to a physician for further evaluation.

　　**d.** palpate the cricoid cartilage for smoothness.

*b* 14. The nurse is planning to assess an adult client's thyroid gland. The nurse should plan to

　　**a.** ask the client to raise the chin.

　　**b.** approach the client posteriorly.

　　**c.** turn the client's neck slightly backward.

　　**d.** place the fingers above the cricoid cartilage.

*d* 15. The nurse is preparing to assess the lymph nodes of an adult client. The nurse should instruct the client to

　　**a.** lie in a supine position.

　　**b.** lie in a side-lying position.

　　**c.** stand upright in front of the nurse.

　　**d.** sit in an upright position.

*c* 16. A female client visits the clinic and tells the nurse that she wants to "stay healthy." The nurse observes that the client has diffuse neck enlargement, is perspiring, and is quite fidgety. The client tells the nurse that she is "hungry all the time, but I have lost weight." A priority nursing diagnosis for the client is

　　**a.** imbalanced nutrition: less than body requirements related to energy level.

　　**b.** ineffective health maintenance related to increased metabolism and hunger.

　　**c.** health-seeking behaviors related to verbalization of wanting to stay healthy.

　　**d.** thyroid dysfunction related to neck swelling, perspiration, and fidgeting.

**Activity G** **CRITICAL THINKING AND CASE STUDIES**

**1.** Explain how head sizes and shapes vary among different cultures.

**2.** Ask students to discuss the significance of abnormal facial features described as asymmetric, moon-shaped, mask-like, tightened-hard, sunken, or pale and edematous.

**3.** Read the following case study:

Marie Lawsome is a 26-year-old woman who is having frequent headaches in the frontal region of her head. She states that the headaches are dull and aching and have lasted days and occasionally weeks at a time. Ms. Lawsome reports using a warm cloth on her forehead and taking over-the-counter analgesics to help the pain, though the headaches are not always completely relieved.

**a.** Describe the type of headache the client is most likely experiencing.

**b.** Analyze what type of precipitating factors are likely to be revealed from your interview with Ms. Lawsome.

**4.** Based on the following case study assessment information, work through the steps of analyzing the data. Identify abnormal data and strengths in **subjective and objective findings**, assemble **cue clusters**, draw **inferences**, make possible **nursing diagnoses**, identify **defining characteristics**, **confirm or rule out** the diagnoses, and **document** your conclusions. Use the blank diagnostic analysis charts provided at the end of this book to guide your thinking. You may want to write on the chart or use separate paper. In either case, propose nursing diagnoses that are specific to the client in the case study. Identify collaborative problems, if any, for this client. Finally, identify data, if any, that point toward a medical problem requiring a referral.

Dorothy Grant is a married, 38-year-old, white woman who has come to the office of the school nurse with what she describes as a migraine headache. She is employed by the school system as a music teacher for grades K through 8. She has had a long history of migraine headaches and experienced her first episode at the age of 16. Her father also had migraine headaches until his mid-50s. She is employed full time and is the mother of two school-aged children. She states that she is 5 feet 4 inches tall and weighs 140 pounds.

Dorothy relates that she has severe throbbing pain in the right temporal region. On a scale of 0 to 5 (with 5 being the worst), she rates her pain as a 4.5. She says she feels nauseated but denies vomiting. Although she is not currently experiencing visual disturbances, she did experience some about 2 hours ago. She describes them as beginning with loss of her central field of vision, followed by flashing lights and then "orange and blue triangles moving from left to right" across her visual field. About an hour later, she experienced the pain. She also reports feeling "a little light-headed."

She took 600 mg of ibuprofen about 20 minutes ago. She states that sleeping for several hours is the best remedy. Although she usually sleeps well for 7 hours a night, lately she has not been getting adequate sleep and has been "eating cheeseburgers on the run." This is a departure from her usual habit of eating three healthy meals a day with a snack of fruit or popcorn. Dorothy routinely attends a step aerobics class four to five times a week, although she has not attended any classes for the past 2 weeks because of late practices for the annual Christmas program. There is no other history of head or neck problems.

Physical assessment reveals that her skin is warm, pale, and dry to touch. Her voice trembles slightly when she is speaking. Her pulse is 78 beats/minute, her respirations are 24 breaths/minute, her blood pressure is 128/74 mm Hg, and her temperature is 98.8°F. Her head and face are round and symmetric, with her head in a central position; no masses are noted. The client demonstrates normal range of motion of the head and neck, with no abnormal movements. The trachea is in the midline; the thyroid gland is nonpalpable. The cervical and supraclavicular lymph nodes are nonpalpable and nontender. The temporal area is tender to touch; the temporal artery is palpated. Test results of cranial nerves V, VII, and XI are normal. Her posture is erect, but she is holding her head with her hand.

# SELF-REFLECTION AND EVALUATION OF LEARNER OBJECTIVES

After you have read Chapter 14 and completed the above quizzes and activities, please identify to what degree you have met each of the following chapter learning objectives. For those objectives that you have met partially or not at all, you will want to review the chapter content for that learning objective.

| Objective | Very Much | Somewhat | Not At All |
|---|---|---|---|
| 1. Describe the structures and functions of the head and neck. | | | |
| 2. Obtain an accurate nursing history of the client's head and neck. | | | |
| 3. Differentiate between the four major types of headaches. | | | |
| 4. Obtain the necessary equipment and prepare the client for an examination of the head and neck. | | | |
| 5. Assess the head for size, shape, configuration, and consistency (hard and smooth). | | | |
| 6. Assess the face for symmetry, features, movement, expression, and condition of the skin. | | | |
| 7. Assess the temporal arteries for tenderness and elasticity. | | | |
| 8. Describe age-related changes of the face and temporal arteries. | | | |
| 9. Assess the temporomandibular joint for full range of motion, swelling, tenderness, and crepitation. | | | |
| 10. Assess the neck for symmetry and range of motion. | | | |
| 11. Assess the thyroid gland. | | | |
| 12. Assess the trachea for position and discuss its significance. | | | |
| 13. Assess the lymph nodes in the head and neck for size, shape, delineation, mobility, consistency, and tenderness. | | | |
| 14. Discuss various nursing diagnoses and collaborative problems commonly seen with assessment of the head and neck. | | | |
| For additional information on this book, be sure to visit http://connection.lww.com. | | | |

# 15

# Eyes

## Chapter Overview

Healthy eyes are essential for vision. Vision informs our lives, permits mobility, and assists learning. People without vision are handicapped indeed. This chapter reviews the structures and functions of the eye and the tests and techniques used by nurses to evaluate a client's visual acuity.

## CHAPTER PRETEST

### Activity A MULTIPLE CHOICE

*Choose the one best answer for each of the following multiple-choice questions.*

1. The bony orbit and fat cushion of the eye serves as a
   a. caruncle.
   b. channel.
   c. protector.
   d. filter.

2. The tarsal plates of the upper eyelid contain
   a. meibomian glands.
   b. sebaceous glands.
   c. tear ducts.
   d. ocular muscles.

3. The conjunctiva of the eye is divided into the palpebral portion and the
   a. canthus portion.
   b. intraocular portion.
   c. nasolacrimal portion.
   d. bulbar portion.

4. Straight movements of the eye are controlled by the
   a. lacrimal muscles.
   b. oblique muscles.
   c. corneal muscles.
   d. rectus muscles.

a **5.** The middle layer of the eye is known as the
  **a.** choroid layer.
  **b.** scleral layer.
  **c.** retinal layer.
  **d.** optic layer.

c **6.** Photoreceptors of the eye are located in the eye's
  **a.** ciliary body.
  **b.** lens.
  **c.** retina.
  **d.** pupil.

a **7.** The meibomian glands secrete
  **a.** an oily substance to lubricate the eyes.
  **b.** sweat.
  **c.** hormones.
  **d.** clear liquid tears.

d **8.** The chambers of the eye contain aqueous humor, which helps to maintain intraocular pressure and
  **a.** transmit light rays.
  **b.** maintain the retinal vessels.
  **c.** change refractory of the lens.
  **d.** cleanse the cornea and the lens.

a **9.** The optic nerves from each eyeball cross at the
  **a.** optic chiasma.
  **b.** vitreous humor.
  **c.** optic disc.
  **d.** visual cortex.

b **10.** The functional reflex that allows the eyes to focus on near objects is termed
  **a.** pupillary reflex.
  **b.** accommodation.
  **c.** refraction.
  **d.** indirect reflex.

## Activity B LABELING ACTIVITIES

*Label the external structures of the eye in the following figure.*

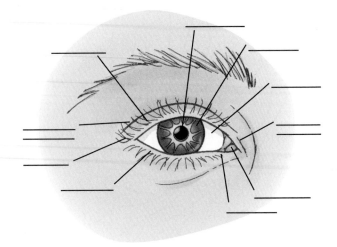

External structures of the eye.

*Label the structure indicated by the line; then match your answer with the label on the matching figure in Chapter 15 of your textbook.*

*Label the structures of the lacrimal apparatus in the following figure.*

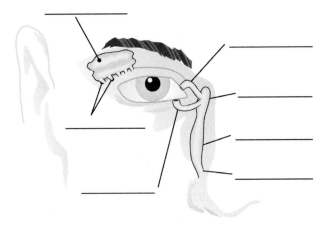

Lacrimal apparatus.

*Label the structure indicated by the line; then match your answer with the label on the matching figure in Chapter 15 of your textbook.*

*Label the structures of the eye in the following figure.*

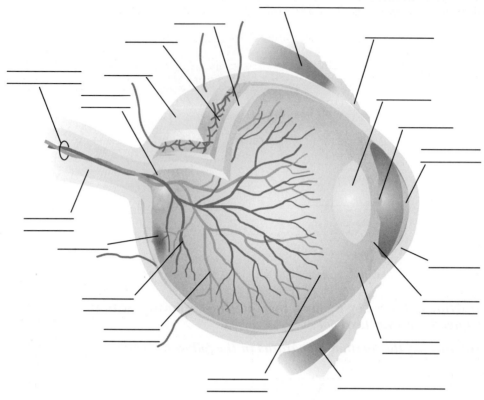

Anatomy of the eye.

*Label the structure indicated by the line; then match your answer with the label on the matching figure in Chapter 15 of your textbook.*

**Activity C** LEARNER ACTIVITIES

*Working with peers in learning lab*

*After reading Chapter 15, participate in the following learning activities.*

1. Review the information in "Promote Health: Cataracts, Glaucoma, and Macular Degeneration" in Chapter 15 and determine your lab partner's risk for cataracts. Discuss ways to reduce these risks.

2. Prepare your lab partner for an eye exam (include positioning, explanation, and gathering of necessary equipment).

3. Interview your lab partner, using the questions in Chapter 15 under "Collecting Subjective Data, Nursing History."

4. Obtain an ophthalmoscope and discuss how to use it, following the directions in Chapter 15.

5. Assess your lab partner's vision, using the Snellen chart. Interpret the results.

6. Assess your lab partner's visual fields. Describe your findings.

7. Inspect your lab partner's external eye structures. Describe the eyelids, lashes, position of eyeballs, bulbar conjunctiva and sclera, palpebral conjunctiva, and lacrimal apparatus.

8. Assess your lab partner's pupillary reaction to light and accommodation.

9. Use the ophthalmoscope to examine your lab partner's internal eye structures. Describe the red reflex, optic disc, retinal vessels, retinal background, fovea and macula, and anterior chamber.

**Activity D**  **INTERVIEWING AND RECORDING ASSESSMENT FINDINGS**

Use the following Nursing History Checklist as your guide to interviewing and recording your findings in a vision and eye assessment of a peer, friend, or family member.

### Nursing History Checklist

| Questions | Satisfactory Data | Needs Additional Data | Data Missing |
|---|---|---|---|
| *Current Symptoms* | | | |
| 1. Recent changes in vision? | | | |
| 2. Spots or floaters in front of eyes? | | | |
| 3. Blind spots, halos, or rings around lights? | | | |
| 4. Trouble seeing at night? | | | |
| 5. Double vision? | | | |
| 6. Eye pain? | | | |
| 7. Redness or swelling in eyes? | | | |
| 8. Excessive watering or tearing or other discharge from eyes? | | | |
| *Past History* | | | |
| 1. Previous eye or vision problems (medication, surgery, laser treatments, corrective lenses)? | | | |
| Family History | | | |
| 1. Family history of eye problems or vision loss? | | | |
| *Lifestyle and Health Practices* | | | |
| 1. Exposure to chemicals, fumes, smoke, dust, flying sparks, etc.? | | | |
| 2. Use of safety glasses? | | | |
| 3. Use of sunglasses? | | | |
| 4. Medications (corticosteroids, lovstatin, pyridostigmine, quinidine, risperadol, and rifampin) may have ocular side effects? | | | |
| 5. Has vision loss affected ability to work or care for self or others? | | | |
| 6. Date of last eye examination? | | | |
| 7. Have glasses or contacts? Are they worn regularly? | | | |
| 8. Live or work around frequent or continuous loud noise? | | | |
| 9. Use of ear protection from noise or while in water? | | | |

**Activity E** PERFORMING PHYSICAL ASSESSMENT

Use the following Physical Assessment Checklist to examine the eye of a peer, friend, or family member. Column 1 can be used by you to guide your physical assessment. Column 2 may be used by your instructor to evaluate your skills as necessary.

### Physical Assessment Checklist

| Assessment Skill | Findings (Normal or Abnormal) and Notes | | Performance (Satisfactory, Needs Improvement, Unsatisfactory) | | |
|---|---|---|---|---|---|
| | N | A | S | N | U |
| 1. Gather equipment (Snellen chart, handheld Snellen chart or near-vision screener, penlight, opaque card, and ophthalmoscope). | ☐ | ☐ | ☐ | ☐ | ☐ |
| 2. Explain procedures to client. | ☐ | ☐ | ☐ | ☐ | ☐ |
| *Perform Vision Tests* | | | | | |
| 1. Distant visual acuity (with Snellen chart, normal acuity is 20/20 with or without corrective lenses). | ☐ | ☐ | ☐ | ☐ | ☐ |
| 2. Near visual acuity (with a handheld vision chart, normal acuity is 14/14 with or without corrective lenses). | ☐ | ☐ | ☐ | ☐ | ☐ |
| 3. Visual fields (use procedure discussed in text to test peripheral vision). | ☐ | ☐ | ☐ | ☐ | ☐ |
| *Perform Extraocular Muscle Function Tests* | | | | | |
| 1. Corneal light reflex (using a penlight to observe parallel alignment of light reflection on corneas). | ☐ | ☐ | ☐ | ☐ | ☐ |
| 2. Cover test (using an opaque card to cover an eye to observe for eye movement). | ☐ | ☐ | ☐ | ☐ | ☐ |
| 3. Positions test (observing for eye movement). | ☐ | ☐ | ☐ | ☐ | ☐ |
| *External Eye Structures* | | | | | |
| 1. Inspect eyelids and lashes (width and position of palpebral fissures, ability to close eyelids, direction of eyelids in comparison with eyeballs, color, swelling, lesions, or discharge). | ☐ | ☐ | ☐ | ☐ | ☐ |
| 2. Inspect positioning of eyeballs (alignment in sockets, protruding or sunken). | ☐ | ☐ | ☐ | ☐ | ☐ |
| 3. Inspect bulbar conjunctiva and sclera (clarity, color, and texture). | ☐ | ☐ | ☐ | ☐ | ☐ |
| 4. Inspect the palpebral conjunctive (eversion of upper eyelid is usually performed only with complaints of eye pain or sensation of something in eye). | ☐ | ☐ | ☐ | ☐ | ☐ |
| 5. Inspect the lacrimal apparatus over the lacrimal glands (lateral aspect of upper eyelid) and the puncta (medial aspect of lower eyelid). Observe for swelling, redness, or drainage. | ☐ | ☐ | ☐ | ☐ | ☐ |
| 6. Palpate the lacrimal apparatus, noting drainage from the puncta when palpating the nasolacrimal duct. | ☐ | ☐ | ☐ | ☐ | ☐ |
| 7. Inspect the cornea and lens by shining a light to determine transparency. | ☐ | ☐ | ☐ | ☐ | ☐ |

| Assessment Skill | Findings (Normal or Abnormal) and Notes | | Performance (Satisfactory, Needs Improvement, Unsatisfactory) | | |
|---|---|---|---|---|---|
| | N | A | S | N | U |
| 8. Inspect the iris and pupil for shape and color of the iris and size and shape of the pupil. | ☐ | ☐ | ☐ | ☐ | ☐ |
| 9. Test pupillary reaction to light (in a darkened room, have client focus on a distant object, shine a light obliquely into the pupil, and observe the pupil's reaction to light—normally, pupils constrict). | ☐ | ☐ | ☐ | ☐ | ☐ |
| 10. Test accommodation of pupils by shifting gaze from far to near (normally, pupils constrict). | ☐ | ☐ | ☐ | ☐ | ☐ |
| *Internal Eye Structure* | | | | | |
| 1. Inspect the red reflex by using an ophthalmoscope to shine the light beam toward the client's pupil (normally, a red reflex is easily seen and should appear round with regular borders). | ☐ | ☐ | ☐ | ☐ | ☐ |
| 2. Inspect the optic disc by using the ophthalmoscope focused on the pupil and moving very close to the eye. Rotate the diopter setting until the retinal structures are in sharp focus (observe disc for shape, color, size, and physiologic cup). | ☐ | ☐ | ☐ | ☐ | ☐ |
| 3. Inspect the retinal vessels using the above technique (observe vessels for numbers of sets, color, diameter, arteriovenous ratio, and arteriovenous crossings). | ☐ | ☐ | ☐ | ☐ | ☐ |
| 4. Inspect retinal background for color and the presence of lesions. | ☐ | ☐ | ☐ | ☐ | ☐ |
| 5. Inspect the fovea and macula for lesions. | ☐ | ☐ | ☐ | ☐ | ☐ |
| 6. Inspect the anterior chamber for transparency. | ☐ | ☐ | ☐ | ☐ | ☐ |
| *Analysis of Data* | | | | | |
| 1. Formulate nursing diagnoses (wellness, risk, actual). | ☐ | ☐ | ☐ | ☐ | ☐ |
| 2. Formulate collaborative problems. | ☐ | ☐ | ☐ | ☐ | ☐ |
| 3. Make necessary referrals. | ☐ | ☐ | ☐ | ☐ | ☐ |

# CHAPTER POSTTEST

**Activity F** **MULTIPLE CHOICE**

*Choose the one best answer for each of the following multiple-choice questions.*

1. While assessing the eyes of an adult client, the nurse uses a wisp of cotton to stimulate the client's
   a. eyelid reflexes.
   b. refractory mechanism.
   c. lacrimal reflexes.
   d. corneal reflexes.

d 2. An adult client visits the clinic and tells the nurse that she has had a sudden change in her vision. The nurse should explain to the client that sudden changes in vision are often associated with

   a. diabetes.

   b. the aging process.

   c. hypertension.

   d. head trauma.

c 3. An adult client tells the nurse that he has been experiencing gradual vision loss. The nurse should

   a. ask about the client's diet.

   b. determine whether there is a history of glaucoma.

   c. check the client's blood pressure.

   d. ask the client if he has any known allergies.

a 4. A 45-year-old client tells the nurse that he occasionally sees spots in front of his eyes. The nurse should

   a. tell the client that these often occur with aging.

   b. refer the client to an ophthalmologist.

   c. re-examine the client in 2 weeks.

   d. assess the client for signs of diabetes.

a 5. An adult client tells the nurse that her peripheral vision is not what it used to be and she has a blind spot in her left eye. The nurse should refer the client for evaluation of possible

   a. glaucoma.

   b. increased intracranial pressure.

   c. bacterial infection.

   d. migraine headaches.

b 6. A client visits the local clinic after experiencing head trauma. The client tells the nurse that he has a consistent blind spot in his right eye. The nurse should

   a. examine the area of head trauma.

   b. refer the client to an ophthalmologist.

   c. assess the client for double vision.

   d. ask the client if he sees "halos."

d 7. A client tells the nurse that she has difficulty seeing while driving at night. The nurse should explain to the client that night blindness is often associated with

   a. retinal deterioration.

   b. head trauma.

   c. migraine headaches.

   d. vitamin A deficiency.

b 8. An adult client visits the clinic and tells the nurse that he has been experiencing double vision for the past few days. The nurse refers the client to a physician for evaluation of possible

   a. glaucoma.

   b. increased intracranial pressure.

   c. hypertension.

   d. ophthalmic migraine.

*d*  9. An adult client tells the nurse that she frequently experiences burning and itching of both eyes. The nurse should assess the client for

   **a.** a foreign body.

   **b.** recent trauma.

   **c.** blind spots.

   **d.** allergies.

*d*  10. An adult client visits the outpatient clinic and tells the nurse that he has a throbbing aching pain in his right eye. The nurse should assess the client for

   **a.** recent exposure to irritants.

   **b.** increased intracranial pressure.

   **c.** excessive tearing.

   **d.** a foreign body in the eye.

*d*  11. An adult client visits the clinic and tells the nurse that he has had excessive tearing in his left eye. The nurse should assess the client's eye for

   **a.** viral infection.

   **b.** double vision.

   **c.** allergic reactions.

   **d.** lacrimal obstruction.

*b*  12. The nurse is caring for a healthy adult client with no history of vision problems. The nurse should tell the client that a thorough eye examination is recommended every

   **a.** year.

   **b.** 2 years.

   **c.** 3 years.

   **d.** 4 years.

*d*  13. An adult client tells the nurse that his eyes are painful because he left his contact lenses in too long the day before yesterday. The nurse should instruct the client that prolonged wearing of contact lenses can lead to

   **a.** retinal damage.

   **b.** cataracts.

   **c.** myopia.

   **d.** corneal damage.

*b*  14. An adult client tells the nurse that his father had cataracts. He asks the nurse about risk factors for cataracts. The nurse should instruct the client that a potential risk factor is

   **a.** lack of vitamin C in the diet.

   **b.** ultraviolet light exposure.

   **c.** obesity.

   **d.** use of antibiotics.

*a*  15. The nurse is preparing to examine an adult client's eyes, using a Snellen chart. The nurse should

   **a.** position the client 20 feet away from the chart.

   **b.** ask the client to remove his glasses.

   **c.** ask the client to read each line with both eyes open.

   **d.** instruct the client to begin reading from the bottom of the chart.

*a* **16.** A client has tested 20/40 on the distant visual acuity test using a Snellen chart. The nurse should
   **a.** document the results in the client's record.
   **b.** ask the client to read a handheld vision chart.
   **c.** ask the client to return in 2 weeks for another examination.
   **d.** refer the client to an optometrist.

*d* **17.** The nurse has tested an adult client's visual fields and determined that the temporal field is 90 degrees in both eyes. The nurse should
   **a.** refer the client for further evaluation.
   **b.** examine the client for other signs of glaucoma.
   **c.** ask the client if there is a genetic history of blindness.
   **d.** document the findings in the client's records.

*b* **18.** The nurse has tested the near visual acuity of a 45-year-old client. The nurse explains to the client that the client has impaired near vision and discusses a possible reason for the condition. The nurse determines that the client has understood the instructions when the client says that presbyopia is usually due to
   **a.** congenital cataracts.
   **b.** decreased accommodation.
   **c.** muscle weakness.
   **d.** constant misalignment of the eyes.

*a* **19.** While assessing the eye of an adult client, the nurse observes an inward turning of the client's left eye. The nurse should document the client's
   **a.** esotropia.
   **b.** strabismus.
   **c.** phoria.
   **d.** exotropia.

*c* **20.** The nurse is examining an adult client's eyes. The nurse has explained the positions test to the client. The nurse determines that the client needs further instructions when the client says that the positions test
   **a.** assesses the muscle strength of the eye.
   **b.** assesses the functioning of the cranial nerves innervating the eye muscles.
   **c.** requires the covering of each eye separately.
   **d.** requires the client to focus on an object.

## Activity G CRITICAL THINKING AND CASE STUDIES

**1.** A 62-year-old woman arrives for an eye examination complaining of blurred vision. You find out from the nursing history that she has smoked a half pack of cigarettes a day for 30 years and spends a lot of time at the beach. She also tells you that she is taking medication for high blood pressure but often forgets to take it. Describe what areas you will focus on during her eye examination, and analyze her possible risk factors for eye disorders.

**2.** On the basis of the following case study assessment information, work through the steps of analyzing the data. Identify abnormal data and strengths in **subjective and objective findings**, assemble **cue clusters**, draw **inferences**, make possible **nursing diagnoses**, identify **defining characteristics**, **confirm or rule out** the diagnoses, and **document** your conclusions. Use the blank diagnostic analysis charts provided at the end of this book to guide your thinking. You may want to write on the chart or use separate paper. In either case, propose nursing diagnoses that are specific to the client in the case study. Identify collaborative problems, if any, for this client. Finally, identify data, if any, that point toward a medical problem requiring a referral.

Mrs. Hira is a 68-year-old woman of Indian descent who comes to the community outpatient clinic for evaluation because she states that she "can't see as well as I used to." She has been retired from the telephone company for 3 years. Her 71-year-old husband had a major stroke 1 year ago, and she is solely responsible for his care. They live in a small one-story house and have a car, which Mrs. Hira uses for grocery shopping and to go to church. Their daughter and her family live 200 miles away.

When interviewed, Mrs. Hira reports progressive changes in her vision over the past 5 months. She reports changes in her vision as "blurring that seems to be getting worse" and reports a halo effect at night when looking at lights. She said that she does not drive much at night any more because of this. She has worn glasses for reading for the past 20 years. She denies eye pain, swelling, excessive tearing, or discharge. Mrs. Hira says that she had an eye examination 4 years ago. She states that she has never experienced any trauma to her eyes or head and has never had any serious eye problems or surgery. She does not know of any family history of eye problems.

Your physical assessment reveals distant visual acuity in the right eye (OD) 20/40, in the left eye (OS) 20/40. No lid lag is noted. The extraocular muscles are intact. The visual fields are equal to the examiner's. No excessive tearing or blinking is noted. The conjunctivae are smooth and without redness. The pupils are bilaterally round, equal in size, and reactive to light and accommodation. No nystagmus is noted. You are unable to assess the red reflex or perform an ophthalmic examination because of bilateral opacities of the lens.

## SELF-REFLECTION AND EVALUATION OF LEARNER OBJECTIVES

After you have read Chapter 15 and completed the above quizzes and activities, please identify to what degree you have met each of the following chapter learning objectives. For those objectives that you have met partially or not at all, you will want to review the chapter content for that learning objective.

| Objective | Very Much | Somewhat | Not At All |
|---|---|---|---|
| 1. Describe the structures and function of the eye. | | | |
| 2. Discuss the risk factors for cataracts and ways to reduce those risk factors. | | | |
| 3. Describe the equipment and client preparation necessary for an eye exam. | | | |
| 4. Demonstrate the proper method for testing a client's distal and near vision. | | | |
| 5. Demonstrate the testing of visual fields. | | | |
| 6. Demonstrate assessment of the client's extraocular muscle function. | | | |
| 7. Demonstrate assessment of the client's external eye structures. | | | |
| 8. Demonstrate examination of the client's pupillary reaction to light and accommodation. | | | |
| 9. Use the ophthalmoscope to inspect the client's<br>a. red reflex<br>b. optic disc<br>c. retinal vessels<br>d. retinal background<br>e. fovea and macula<br>f. anterior chamber | | | |

# Ears

## Chapter Overview

The sense organ of hearing and equilibrium is the ear, which has many parts, in particular the external ear, the middle ear, and the inner ear. Healthy ears are essential to effective communication and balance. This chapter reviews the structure and functions connected with hearing and balance as well as the techniques used in physical assessment of hearing acuity and sound conduction.

## CHAPTER PRETEST

### Activity A  MULTIPLE CHOICE

*Choose one best answer for each of the following multiple-choice questions.*

 1. The cone of light is located in the

 a. inner ear.

 b. middle ear.

 c. external ear.

 d. semicircular canal.

 2. The ossicles contained in the middle ear include the malleus, the incus, and the

 a. pars tensa.

 b. pars flaccida.

 c. umbo.

 d. stapes.

 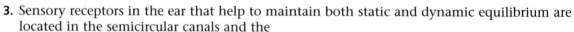 3. Sensory receptors in the ear that help to maintain both static and dynamic equilibrium are located in the semicircular canals and the

 a. vestibule.

 b. tympanic membrane.

 c. cone of light.

 d. eustachian tube.

**4.** In the hearing pathway, hair cells of the spiral organ of Corti are stimulated by movement of

   **a.** fluid.

   **b.** sound.

   **c.** air.

   **d.** bone.

**5.** The transmission of sound waves through the external ear and the middle ear is known as

   **a.** perceptive hearing.

   **b.** conductive hearing.

   **c.** external hearing.

   **d.** connective hearing.

**6.** Transmission of sound waves in the inner ear is known as

   **a.** conducive hearing.

   **b.** tympanic hearing.

   **c.** neuromotor hearing.

   **d.** perceptive hearing.

**Activity B** **LABELING ACTIVITIES**

*Label the structures of the ear in the following figure.*

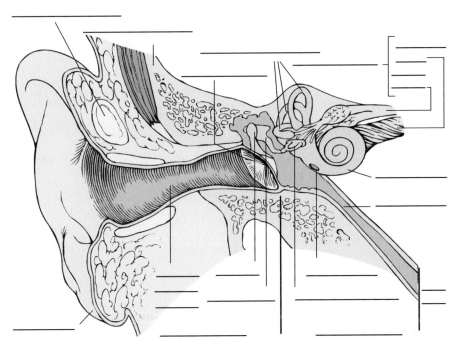

External, middle, and inner ear.

*Label the structure indicated by the line; then match your answer with the label on the matching figure in Chapter 16 of your textbook.*

*Label the structures of the tympanic membrane in the following figure.*

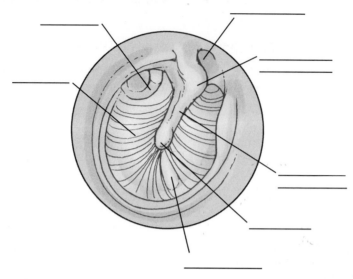

Right tympanic membrane.

*Label the structure indicated by the line; then match your answer with the label on the matching figure in Chapter 16 of your textbook.*

*Label the pathways of hearing in the following figure.*

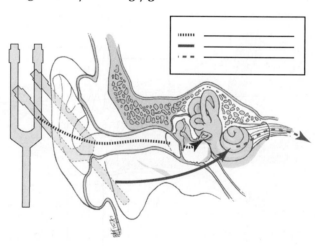

Pathways of hearing.

*Label the pathway of sound transmission indicated by each line; then match your answer with the label on the matching figure in Chapter 16 of your textbook.*

### Activity C  LEARNER ACTIVITIES

**Working with peers in learning lab**

*After reading Chapter 16, participate in the following learning activities.*

1. Obtain an otoscope. Read "How to Use an Otoscope" (Equipment Spotlight 16.1) in Chapter 16 of your textbook. Practice handling and operating the otoscope before using it to inspect the eardrum of your lab partner. Report your findings.

2. Examine the ears of an elderly client, friend, or relative, and report your findings. Compare your findings with the variation of findings in the elderly discussed in the text.

3. Obtain a tuning fork. Practice using it after reading the instructions in your textbook. Explain how to perform both the Weber test and the Rinne test, and discuss the significance of each. Perform the Weber and Rinne tests on your lab partner and report your findings.

### Activity D INTERVIEWING AND RECORDING ASSESSMENT FINDINGS

Use the following Nursing History Checklist to interview a peer friend or family member regarding hearing and ear health.

**Nursing History Checklist**

| Questions | Satisfactory Data | Needs Additional Data | Data Missing |
|---|---|---|---|
| *Current Symptoms* | | | |
| 1. Recent changes in hearing (if yes, were all or just some sounds affected)? | | | |
| 2. Ear discharge (if yes, amount/odor)? | | | |
| 3. Ear pain (if yes, is there accompanying sore throat, sinus infection, or problem with teeth or gums)? | | | |
| 4. Ringing or crackling in ears? | | | |
| *Past History* | | | |
| 1. Previous ear or hearing problems such as infections, trauma, or earaches (medications, surgery, hearing aids)? | | | |
| *Family History* | | | |
| 1. Family history of ear problems or hearing loss? | | | |
| *Lifestyle and Health Practices* | | | |
| 1. Live or work around frequent or continuous loud noise? | | | |
| 2. Use of ear protection from noise or while in water? | | | |
| 3. Has hearing loss affected ability to work or care for self or others? | | | |

### Activity E PERFORMING PHYSICAL ASSESSMENT

Use the following Physical Assessment Checklist as your guide to performing a hearing and ear assessment for a peer, friend, or family member. Column 1 can be used by you to guide your physical assessment. Column 2 may be used by your instructor to evaluate your skills as necessary.

## Physical Assessment Checklist

| Assessment Skill | Findings (Normal or Abnormal) and Notes | | Performance (Satisfactory, Needs Improvement, Unsatisfactory) | | |
|---|---|---|---|---|---|
| | **N** | **A** | **S** | **N** | **U** |
| *External Ear Structures* | | | | | |
| 1. Inspect the auricle, tragus, and lobule for size and shape, position, lesions/discoloration, and discharge. | ☐ | ☐ | ☐ | ☐ | ☐ |
| 2. Palpate the auricle and mastoid process for tenderness. | ☐ | ☐ | ☐ | ☐ | ☐ |
| *Otoscopic Examination* | | | | | |
| 1. Inspect the external auditory canal with the otoscope for discharge, color and consistency of cerumen, color and consistency of canal walls, and nodules. | ☐ | ☐ | ☐ | ☐ | ☐ |
| 2. Inspect the tympanic membrane, using the otoscope, for color and shape, consistency, and landmarks. | ☐ | ☐ | ☐ | ☐ | ☐ |
| 3. Have the client perform the Valsalva maneuver, and observe the center of the tympanic membrane for a flutter. (Do not do this procedure on an older client, as it may interfere with equilibrium and cause dizziness.) | ☐ | ☐ | ☐ | ☐ | ☐ |
| *Hearing and Equilibrium Tests* | | | | | |
| 1. Perform the whisper test by having the client place a finger on the tragus of one ear. Whisper a two-syllable word 1 to 2 feet behind the client. Repeat on the other ear. | ☐ | ☐ | ☐ | ☐ | ☐ |
| 2. Perform the Weber test by using a tuning fork placed on the center of the head or forehead and asking whether the client hears the sound better in one ear or the same in both ears. | ☐ | ☐ | ☐ | ☐ | ☐ |
| 3. Perform the Rinne test by using a tuning fork and placing the base on the client's mastoid process. When the client no longer hears the sound, note the time interval, and move it in front of the external ear. When the client no longer hears a sound, note the time interval. | ☐ | ☐ | ☐ | ☐ | ☐ |
| 4. Perform the Romberg test to evaluate equilibrium. With feet together and arms at the side, close eyes for 20 seconds. Observe for swaying. (Refer to text, Chapters 16 and 26.) | ☐ | ☐ | ☐ | ☐ | ☐ |
| *Analysis of Data* | | | | | |
| 1. Formulate nursing diagnoses (wellness, risk, actual). | ☐ | ☐ | ☐ | ☐ | ☐ |
| 2. Formulate collaborative problems. | ☐ | ☐ | ☐ | ☐ | ☐ |
| 3. Make necessary referrals. | ☐ | ☐ | ☐ | ☐ | ☐ |

# CHAPTER POSTTEST

**Activity F** **MULTIPLE CHOICE**

*Choose the one best answer for each of the following multiple-choice questions.*

**1.** An adult client visits the clinic and complains of tinnitus. The nurse should ask the client if she has been

   **a.** dizzy.

   **b.** hypotensive.

   **c.** taking antibiotics.

   **d.** experiencing ear drainage.

**2.** An adult client tells the nurse that his 80-year-old father is almost completely deaf. After an explanation to the client about risk factors for hearing loss, the nurse determines that the client needs further instruction when the client says

   **a.** "There is a genetic predisposition to hearing loss."

   **b.** "Certain cultural groups have a higher rate of hearing loss."

   **c.** "It is difficult to prevent hearing loss or worsening of hearing."

   **d.** "Chronic otitis media has been associated with hearing loss."

**3.** The nurse is planning to perform an eye and ear examination on an adult client. After explaining the procedures to the client, the nurse should

   **a.** ask the client to remain standing.

   **b.** show the client the otoscope.

   **c.** ask the client to remove his contact lenses.

   **d.** observe the client's response to the explanations.

**4.** The nurse is preparing to examine the ears of an adult client with an otoscope. The nurse should plan to

   **a.** ask the client to tilt the head slightly forward.

   **b.** release the auricle during the examination.

   **c.** use a speculum that measures 10 mm in diameter.

   **d.** firmly pull the auricle out, up, and back.

**5.** While assessing the ears of an adult client, the nurse observes bloody drainage in the client's ear. The nurse should

   **a.** document the finding in the client's chart.

   **b.** determine whether a foreign body is present in the ear.

   **c.** assess the client for further signs of otitis media.

   **d.** refer the client to a physician.

**6.** While assessing the ears of an adult client, the nurse observes that the tympanic membrane is completely immobile. The nurse should further assess the client for signs and symptoms of

   **a.** infection.

   **b.** skull injury.

   **c.** vestibular disorders.

   **d.** healed perforations.

A   7. The nurse is planning to conduct the Weber test on an adult male client. To perform this test, the nurse should plan to

   a. strike a tuning fork and place it at the base of the client's mastoid process.

   b. whisper a word with two distinct syllables to the client.

   c. ask the client to close his eyes while standing with feet together.

   d. strike a tuning fork and place it on the center of the client's head or forehead.

C   8. The nurse has performed the Rinne test on an older adult client. After the test, the client reports that her bone conduction sound was heard longer than the air conduction sound. The nurse determines that the client is most likely experiencing

   a. normal hearing.

   b. sensorineural hearing loss.

   c. conductive hearing loss.

   d. central hearing loss.

*[handwritten: BC > AC = conductive hearing loss; AC > BC = normal]*

## Activity G  MATCHING

*Match the terms in the left column with the correct descriptions in the right column.*

**Term**

____ 1. Conductive hearing

____ 2. Perceptive or sensorineural hearing

____ 3. Presbycusis

____ 4. Otorrhea

____ 5. Otalgia

____ 6. Tinnitus

____ 7. Vertigo

____ 8. Swimmer's ear

____ 9. Cerumen

**Description**

a. Gradual hearing loss

b. Infection of the ear canal

c. Drainage from the ear

d. Ringing in the ears

e. Earache

f. Ear wax

g. Transmission of sound waves through the external and middle ear

h. True spinning motion

i. Transmission of sound waves in the inner ear

## Activity H  CRITICAL THINKING AND CASE STUDIES

1. Discuss normal findings and what may be occurring if tenderness is present during the ear exam.

2. Discuss ethnic variations that may be found during the ear exam.

3. Discuss the differences between conductive and sensorineural hearing.

4. Explain the meaning of the findings identified during a Weber test and a Rinne test.

5. On the basis of the following case study assessment information, work through the steps of analyzing the data. Identify abnormal data and strengths in **subjective and objective findings**, assemble **cue clusters**, draw **inferences**, make possible **nursing diagnoses**, identify **defining characteristics**, **confirm or rule out** the diagnoses, and **document** your conclusions. Use the blank diagnostic analysis charts provided at the end of this book to guide your thinking. You may want to write on the chart or use separate paper. In either case, propose nursing diagnoses that are specific to the client in the case study. Identify collaborative problems, if any, for this client. Finally, identify data, if any, that point toward a medical problem requiring a referral.

Jack Jones, a 28-year-old man, currently works in an industrial plant as a supervisor. He has noticed lately that he is having trouble hearing conversations with his friends, but of even more concern is that he misunderstands his workers when they are giving him information about the projects they are working on. He denies any major current or past illnesses—"just the kid stuff, you know, colds and fevers. I do have trouble with ringing in my ears." He admits that when he was in his teens he frequently attended music concerts that were often loud, and he still goes occasionally. He tells you that he likes to listen to loud—"the louder the better"—rock music, using tight earphones. When he watches TV in the evening, he has to turn up the volume to hear clearly.

## SELF-REFLECTION AND EVALUATION OF LEARNER OBJECTIVES

After you have read Chapter 16 and completed the above quizzes and activities, please identify to what extent you have met each of the following chapter learning objectives. For those that you have met partially or not at all, you will want to review the chapter content for that learning objective.

| Objective | Very Much | Somewhat | Not At All |
| --- | --- | --- | --- |
| 1. Describe the functions and the structures of an ear. | | | |
| 2. Describe the equipment necessary to perform an ear assessment. | | | |
| 3. Assess the external ear structures by inspecting the auricle, tragus, and lobule and by palpating the auricle and mastoid process. | | | |
| 4. Describe the expected changes with aging of an ear. | | | |
| 5. Use the otoscope to inspect the auditory canal and the tympanic membrane. | | | |
| 6. Perform three tests—the whisper, Weber, and Rinne tests—to assess the client's hearing. | | | |
| 7. Perform the Romberg test to assess the client's equilibrium. | | | |
| 8. Discuss various nursing diagnoses and collaborative problems related to assessment of the ears. | | | |

# Mouth, Throat, Nose, and Sinuses

The mouth, throat, nose, and sinuses are the structures associated with eating, smell and taste, swallowing, speech, and purifying and warming the air that is transported to the lungs. Use the following activities and quizzes to review the structure and function of these very important tissues.

## CHAPTER PRETEST

**Activity A** **MULTIPLE CHOICE**

*Choose the one best answer for each of the following multiple-choice questions.*

____ **1.** The roof of the oral cavity of the mouth is formed by the anterior hard palate and the

　**a.** teeth.

　**b.** gums.

　**c.** muscles.

　**d.** soft palate.

____ **2.** An extension of the soft palate of the mouth, which hangs in the posterior midline of the oropharynx, is the

　**a.** uvula.

　**b.** frenulum.

　**c.** taste buds.

　**d.** sublingual fold.

____ **3.** The tongue is attached to the hyoid bone and styloid process of the temporal bone and is connected to the floor of the mouth by the

　**a.** mandible.

　**b.** frenulum.

　**c.** gums.

　**d.** soft palate.

____ **4.** The submandibular glands open under the tongue through openings called
- **a.** parasinal ducts.
- **b.** Stensen's ducts.
- **c.** Wharton's ducts.
- **d.** lacrimonasal ducts.

____ **5.** The rich blood supply of the nose serves to
- **a.** help propel moist air to the body.
- **b.** propel debris to the throat.
- **c.** filter large particles from the air.
- **d.** warm the inspired air.

## Activity B  LABELING ACTIVITIES

*Label the following structures of the mouth.*

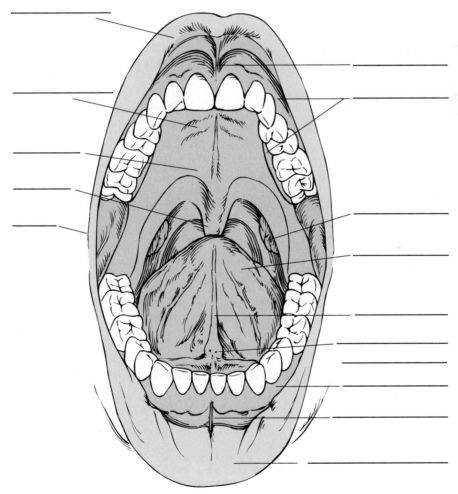

Structures of the mouth.

*Label the structure indicated by the line; then match your answer with the label on the matching figure in Chapter 17 of your textbook.*

*Label the following teeth.*

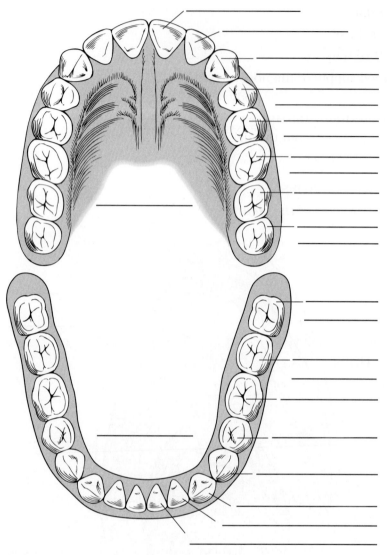

Teeth.

*Label the structure indicated by the line; then match your answer with the label on the matching figure in Chapter 17 of your textbook.*

*Label the structures of the salivary glands.*

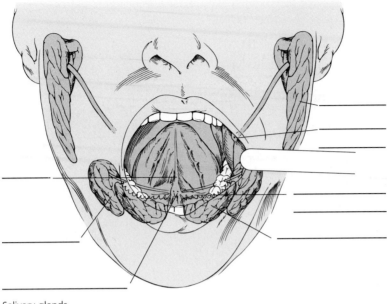

Salivary glands.

*Label the structure indicated by the line; then match your answer with the label on the matching figure in Chapter 17 of your textbook.*

*Label the structures of the nasal cavity and throat.*

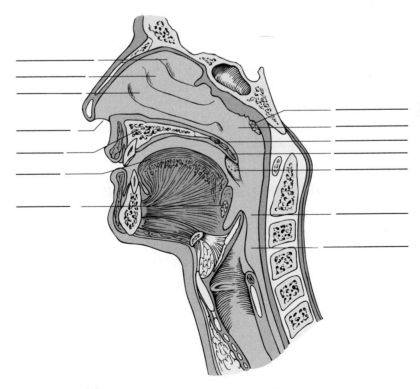

Nasal cavity and throat.

*Label the structure indicated by the line; then match your answer with the label on the matching figure in Chapter 17 of your textbook.*

*Label the structures of the paranasal sinuses.*

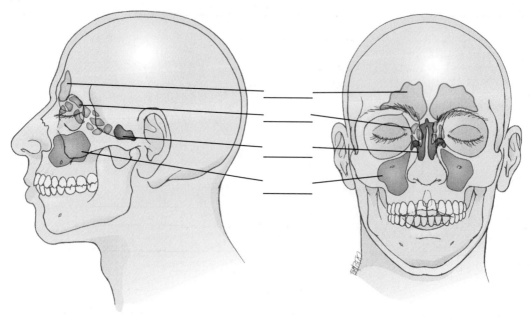

Paranasal sinuses.

*Label the structure indicated by the line; then match your answer with the label on the matching figure in Chapter 17 of your textbook.*

## Activity C  LEARNER ACTIVITIES

### Working with peers in learning lab

*After reading Chapter 17, participate in the following learning activities.*

1. Review the information in "Promote Health: Cancer of the Oral Cavity" in Chapter 17. Determine your own risk for oral cancer. Next, discuss various behaviors—cultural and otherwise—that contribute to oral cancer.

2. Find an elderly client, friend, or relative whose mouth, throat, nose, and sinuses you can examine. Discuss with peers your findings as they compare with those of a younger person's mouth, throat, nose, and sinuses.

## Activity D  INTERVIEWING AND RECORDING ASSESSMENT FINDINGS

Use the following Nursing History Checklist to interview and record your findings from a mouth, throat, nose, and sinus assessment of a peer, friend, or family member.

### Nursing History Checklist

| Questions | Satisfactory Data | Needs Additional Data | Data Missing |
|---|---|---|---|
| *Current Symptoms* | | | |
| 1. Mouth problems (tongue or mouth sores or lesions, gum or mouth redness, swelling, bleeding, or pain)? | | | |
| 2. Sinus problems (pain over sinuses, postnasal drip)? | | | |
| 3. Nose problems (nosebleeds, stuffy nose, cannot breath through one or both nostrils, change in ability to smell or taste)? | | | |

| Questions | Satisfactory Data | Needs Additional Data | Data Missing |
|---|---|---|---|
| *Past History* | | | |
| 1. Previous problems with mouth, throat, nose, or sinuses (surgeries or treatment; how much and how often)? | | | |
| 2. Use of nasal sprays? | | | |
| 3. History of tooth grinding? | | | |
| 4. Last dental exam? Fit of dentures? | | | |
| *Family History* | | | |
| 1. Family history of oral, nasal, or sinus cancer or chronic problems? | | | |
| *Lifestyle and Health Practices* | | | |
| 1. Daily practice of oral care, tooth care, or denture care? | | | |
| 2. Usual diet? | | | |
| 3. History of smoking, use of, how much, and how often? | | | |
| 4. Use of alcohol (how much and how often)? | | | |

## Activity E   PERFORMING PHYSICAL ASSESSMENT

Use the following Physical Assessment Checklist to guide your mouth, throat, nose, and sinus examination of a peer, friend, or family member. Column 1 can be used by you to guide your physical assessment. Column 2 may be used by your instructor to evaluate your skills as necessary.

### Physical Assessment Checklist

| Assessment Skill | Findings (Normal or Abnormal) and Notes | | Performance (Satisfactory, Needs Improvement, Unsatisfactory) | | |
|---|---|---|---|---|---|
| | N | A | S | N | U |
| 1. Gather equipment (gloves, cotton gauze pads, penlight, speculum attached to otoscope, tongue blade). | ☐ | ☐ | ☐ | ☐ | ☐ |
| 2. Explain procedure to client. | ☐ | ☐ | ☐ | ☐ | ☐ |
| *Mouth* | | | | | |
| 1. Note any distinctive odors. | ☐ | ☐ | ☐ | ☐ | ☐ |
| 2. Inspect and palpate lips, buccal mucosa, gums, and tongue for color variations (pallor, redness, white patches, bluish hue), moisture, tissue consistency, or lesions (induration, roughness, vesicles, crusts, plaques, nodules, ulcers, cracking, patches, bleeding, Koplik's spots, cancer sores), Stensen's and Wharton's ducts. | ☐ | ☐ | ☐ | ☐ | ☐ |
| 3. Inspect gums for hyperplasia, blue-black line. | ☐ | ☐ | ☐ | ☐ | ☐ |

| Assessment Skill | Findings (Normal or Abnormal) and Notes | | Performance (Satisfactory, Needs Improvement, Unsatisfactory) | | |
|---|---|---|---|---|---|
| | N | A | S | N | U |
| 4. Inspect teeth for number and shape, color (white, brown, yellow, chalky white areas), occlusion. | ☐ | ☐ | ☐ | ☐ | ☐ |
| 5. Inspect and palpate tongue for color, texture and consistency (black, hairy, white patches, smooth, reddish, shiny without papillae), moisture, and size (enlarged or very small). | ☐ | ☐ | ☐ | ☐ | ☐ |
| *Throat* | | | | | |
| 1. Inspect the throat for color, consistency, torus palatinus, uvula (singular). | ☐ | ☐ | ☐ | ☐ | ☐ |
| 2. Inspect the tonsils for color and consistency; grading scale (1+, 2+, 3+, 4+). | ☐ | ☐ | ☐ | ☐ | ☐ |
| *Nose* | | | | | |
| 1. Inspect and palpate the external nose for color, shape, consistency, tenderness, and patency of airflow. | ☐ | ☐ | ☐ | ☐ | ☐ |
| 2. Inspect the internal nose for color, swelling, exudate, bleeding, ulcers, perforated septum, or polyps. | ☐ | ☐ | ☐ | ☐ | ☐ |
| *Sinuses* | | | | | |
| 1. Palpate the sinuses for tenderness. | ☐ | ☐ | ☐ | ☐ | ☐ |
| 2. Percuss and transilluminate the sinuses for air versus fluid or pus. | ☐ | ☐ | ☐ | ☐ | ☐ |
| *Analysis of Data* | | | | | |
| 1. Formulate nursing diagnoses (wellness, risk, actual). | ☐ | ☐ | ☐ | ☐ | ☐ |
| 2. Formulate collaborative problems. | ☐ | ☐ | ☐ | ☐ | ☐ |
| 3. Make necessary referrals. | ☐ | ☐ | ☐ | ☐ | ☐ |

# CHAPTER POSTTEST

### Activity F   MULTIPLE CHOICE

*Choose the one best answer for each of the following multiple-choice questions.*

_____ **1.** The nurse is preparing to examine the sinuses of an adult client. After examining the frontal sinuses, the nurse should proceed to examine the

   **a.** ethmoidal sinuses.

   **b.** laryngeal sinuses.

   **c.** maxillary sinuses.

   **d.** sphenoidal sinuses.

____ **2.** An adult client visits the clinic complaining of recurrent ulcers in the mouth. The nurse assesses the client's mouth and observes a painful ulcer. The nurse should document the presence of

    **a.** a cancerous lesion.

    **b.** *Candida albicans* infection.

    **c.** an oral ulceration.

    **d.** aphthous stomatitis.

____ **3.** A nurse assesses the mouth of an adult male client and observes a rough, crusty, eroded area. The nurse should

    **a.** refer the client for further evaluation.

    **b.** document the presence of herpes simplex.

    **c.** ask the client if his gums bleed.

    **d.** document the presence of a canker sore.

____ **4.** An adult client visits the clinic and tells the nurse that she has been experiencing frequent nosebleeds for the past month. The nurse should

    **a.** ask the client if she has had recent oral surgery.

    **b.** assess the client's nasal passages for blockage.

    **c.** ask the client if she is a smoker.

    **d.** refer the client for further evaluation.

____ **5.** The nurse is assessing the mouth of an older adult and observes that the client appears to have poorly fitting dentures. The nurse should instruct the client that she may be at greater risk for

    **a.** aspiration.

    **b.** malocclusion.

    **c.** gingivitis.

    **d.** throat soreness.

____ **6.** An adolescent client tells the nurse that her mother says she grinds her teeth when she sleeps. The nurse should explain to the client that grinding the teeth may be a sign of

    **a.** precancerous lesions.

    **b.** poor oral hygiene.

    **c.** malabsorption.

    **d.** stress and anxiety.

____ **7.** The nurse is planning a presentation to a group of high school students about the risk factors for oral cancer. Which of the following should be included in the nurse's plan?

    **a.** Diets low in fruits and vegetables are a possible risk factor for oral cancer.

    **b.** About 40% of all cancers occur in the lips, mouth, and tongue.

    **c.** The incidence of oral cancers is higher in women than in men.

    **d.** Most oral cancers are detected in people in their 70s.

____ **8.** Before examining the mouth of an adult client, the nurse should first

    **a.** ask the client to leave dentures in place.

    **b.** don sterile gloves for the procedure.

    **c.** offer the client mouthwash.

    **d.** don clean gloves for the procedure.

____ **9.** A client visits the clinic and tells the nurse that she has painful cracking in the corners of her lips. The nurse should assess the client's diet for a deficiency of

    **a.** vitamin C.

    **b.** fluoride.

    **c.** vitamin A.

    **d.** riboflavin.

____ **10.** The nurse is assessing a client who has been taking antibiotics for an infection for 10 days. The nurse observes whitish curd-like patches in the client's mouth. The nurse should explain to the client that these spots are most likely

    **a.** *Candida albicans* infection.

    **b.** Koplik's spots.

    **c.** leukoplakia.

    **d.** Fordyce spots.

____ **11.** The nurse is assessing an adult client's oral cavity for possible oral cancer. The nurse should explain to the client that the most common site of oral cancer is the

    **a.** area on top of the tongue.

    **b.** area underneath the tongue.

    **c.** inside of the cheeks.

    **d.** area near the salivary glands.

____ **12.** The nurse is planning to inspect an adult client's mouth, using a tongue depressor. The nurse should plan to

    **a.** depress the tongue blade slightly off center.

    **b.** depress the tongue blade as close to the center as possible.

    **c.** ask the client to keep the mouth partially open.

    **d.** insert the tongue blade at the back of the client's tongue.

____ **13.** An adult client visits the clinic complaining of a sore throat. After assessing the throat, the nurse documents the client's tonsils as 4+. The nurse should explain to the client that 4+ tonsils are present when the nurse observes tonsils that are

    **a.** touching the uvula.

    **b.** visible upon inspection.

    **c.** touching each other.

    **d.** midway between the tonsillar pillars and uvula.

____ **14.** The nurse is preparing to inspect the nose of an adult client with an otoscope. The nurse plans to

    **a.** position the handle of the otoscope to one side.

    **b.** tip the client's head as far back as possible.

    **c.** direct the otoscope tip quickly back and down the nostril.

    **d.** position the handle of the otoscope straight and up.

____ **15.** The nurse has assessed the nose of an adult client and has explained to the client about her thick yellowish nasal discharge. The nurse determines that the client understands the instructions when the client says that the yellowish discharge is most likely due to

    **a.** too much smoking.

    **b.** chronic allergies.

    **c.** trauma to the nasal passages.

    **d.** an upper respiratory infection.

**Activity G** MATCHING

*Match the terms in the left column with correct descriptions in the right column.*

**Term**

_____ **1.** Transillumination

_____ **2.** Palpation and percussion

_____ **3.** Kiesselbach's area

_____ **4.** Stensen's ducts

_____ **5.** Wharton's ducts

_____ **6.** Side of tongue

_____ **7.** Torus palatinus

_____ **8.** Bifid uvula

_____ **9.** Grade 3+ tonsils

_____ **10.** Method for assessing the internal nose

_____ **11.** Method used to palpate frontal sinuses

_____ **12.** Method used to palpate maxillary sinuses

_____ **13.** Significance of a red glow with transillumination

_____ **14.** Absence of a red glow with transillumination

_____ **15.** Cheilosis

_____ **16.** Lip pits

**Description**

**a.** Press up with thumbs on sinuses

**b.** Touch the uvula

**c.** Most common site of tongue cancer

**d.** Cracking at the corner of the lips seen in riboflavin deficiency

**e.** Method used to test for fluid in the sinuses

**f.** Sinus filled with air

**g.** Inspection using otoscope with short wide tip attachment

**h.** Methods used to test for sinus tenderness

**i.** Press up on brow on each side of nose

**j.** Openings found on buccal mucosa across from second upper molars

**k.** Bony protuberance in the midline of the hard palate

**l.** Sinus filled with fluid or pus

**m.** Common site of nasal bleeding

**n.** A variation that looks split or partially severed and may be associated with a submucous cleft palate

**o.** Normal variation that occurs in the crease between the upper and lower lip

**p.** Openings found on either side of the frenulum of the floor of the mouth

**Activity H** CRITICAL THINKING AND CASE STUDIES

**1.** Discuss how would you differentiate allergic conditions from infections.

**2.** Read the following case study. Analyze the client's risk factors for oral cancer.

Clara Burton is a 25-year-old college student with chronic rhinitis. She says that she has a history of sinus infections about twice a year. She smokes two packs of cigarettes a day, drinks beer every weekend and occasionally during the week, and eats a poorly balanced diet on the run. Her father smoked a pipe and had lip cancer.

**3.** On the basis of the following case study assessment information, work through the steps of analyzing the data. Identify abnormal data and strengths in **subjective and objective findings**, assemble **cue clusters**, draw **inferences**, make possible **nursing diagnoses**, identify **defining characteristics**, **confirm or rule out** the diagnoses, and **document** your conclusions.

Use the blank diagnostic analysis charts provided at the end of this book to guide your thinking. You may want to write on the chart or use separate paper. In either case, propose nursing diagnoses that are specific to the client in the case study. Identify collaborative problems, if any, for this client. Finally, identify data, if any, that point toward a medical problem requiring a referral.

Alice Kennedy is a 50-year-old divorced woman with a medical diagnosis of carcinoma of the sphenoid sinus and nasal pharynx. She has been referred by the physician to the hospital's home health service for weekly skilled nursing visits by an R.N. She lives in her own home and is currently being cared for by her younger sister. Alice has two grown sons. One son lives close by; the other lives in another state.

Ms. Kennedy is currently being treated with radiation therapy, which she receives three times weekly. She states that she is experiencing some pain across the bridge of her nose (2 on a scale of 0 to 5, with 5 being the worst). She uses cold compresses to help relieve the pain. Three small oral ulcers approximately 3 to 5 cm wide are noted on the left buccal mucosa. Ms. Kennedy reports that she has no difficulty swallowing, but the sores are painful when she eats, especially when she eats citrus fruits. She uses a soft-bristled toothbrush and brushes her teeth gently after eating, and she tries to avoid irritating food. The findings in the rest of the oral examination are within normal limits.

The nasal examination reveals a slightly reddened color of the nose, with some tenderness noted across the bridge of the nose. There is no occlusion of either nostril. The nasal septum is intact, with no ulcers or perforations. The nasal mucosa is red and slightly swollen. Both frontal and maxillary sinuses transilluminate; the frontal sinus area is slightly tender to palpation.

Ms. Kennedy's sister has taken over most of the housekeeping responsibilities. She says that she is currently able to keep up with everything but is concerned about whether she will be able to continue to care for her sister as her condition worsens.

# SELF-REFLECTION AND EVALUATION
# OF LEARNER OBJECTIVES

After you have read Chapter 17 and completed the above quizzes and activities, please identify to what degree you have met each of the following chapter learning objectives. For those objectives that you have met partially or not at all, you will want to review the chapter content for that learning objective.

| Objective | Very Much | Somewhat | Not At All |
|---|---|---|---|
| 1. Describe the structure and functions of the mouth, throat, nose, and sinuses. | | | |
| 2. Discuss risk factors for cancer of the oral cavity and ways to reduce these factors. | | | |
| 3. Discuss the prevalence of oral cavity cancer across cultures. | | | |
| 4. Obtain an accurate nursing history of the client's mouth, throat, nose, and sinuses. | | | |
| 5. Explain how to prepare the client for an examination of the mouth, throat, nose, and sinuses. | | | |
| 6. Describe the equipment necessary to perform this assessment. | | | |
| 7. Describe the two physical exam techniques (inspection and palpation) used for this assessment. | | | |
| 8. Inspect the lips, buccal mucosa, gums, and tongue for color and consistency, lesions, ulcers, or induration, noting Stensen's ducts, Wharton's ducts, and breath odor. | | | |
| 9. Inspect the teeth for number, color, condition, and alignment. | | | |

| Objective | Very Much | Somewhat | Not At All |
|---|---|---|---|
| 10. Inspect the throat for characteristics and position of the uvula, presence of gag reflex, grading of the tonsils, and tonsils and palate for color, size, condition, exudates, or lesions. | | | |
| 11. Assess the nose for internal and external color, shape, consistence, tenderness, smell, and patency of airflow. | | | |
| 12. Inspect the turbinates for color, moisture, and lesions. | | | |
| 13. Describe the three physical exam techniques (palpation, percussion, and transillumination) used to assess the sinuses. | | | |
| 14. Inspect the sinuses for tenderness, air versus fluid, or pus filling. | | | |
| 15. Describe cultural variations of the mouth and throat. | | | |
| 16. Describe expected changes with aging of the mouth, throat, nose, and sinuses. | | | |

# 18

# Thorax and Lungs

## Chapter Overview

Respiration is a life-sustaining function, which makes precise assessment of the chest and breathing structures an essential nursing skill. Use the following exercises and quizzes as a guide to effective physical assessment of the thorax and lungs.

## CHAPTER PRETEST

### Activity A MULTIPLE CHOICE

*Choose one best answer for each of the following multiple-choice questions.*

_____ 1. The clavicles extend from the acromion of the scapula to the part of the sternum termed the
   a. body.
   b. xiphoid process.
   c. angle.
   d. manubrium.

_____ 2. A bony ridge located at the point where the manubrium articulates with the body of the sternum is termed the sternal
   a. angle.
   b. notch.
   c. space.
   d. prominens.

_____ 3. The spinous process termed the vertebra prominens is in which cervical vertebra?
   a. fifth.
   b. sixth.
   c. seventh.
   d. eighth.

_____ 4. The apex of each lung is located at the
   a. level of the diaphragm.
   b. area slightly above the clavicle.
   c. level of the sixth rib.
   d. left oblique fissure.

____ **5.** The thin double-layered serous membrane that lines the chest cavity is termed

    **a.** parietal pleura.

    **b.** pulmonary pleura.

    **c.** visceral pleura.

    **d.** thoracic pleura.

____ **6.** The lining of the trachea and bronchi, which serves to remove dust, foreign bodies, and bacteria, is termed the

    **a.** bronchioles.

    **b.** alveolar sacs.

    **c.** alveolar ducts.

    **d.** cilia.

____ **7.** Under normal circumstances, the strongest stimulus in a human being to breathe is

    **a.** hypoxemia.

    **b.** hypocapnia.

    **c.** pH changes.

    **d.** hypercapnia.

### Activity B  LABELING ACTIVITIES

*Label the following structures of the anterior thoracic cage.*

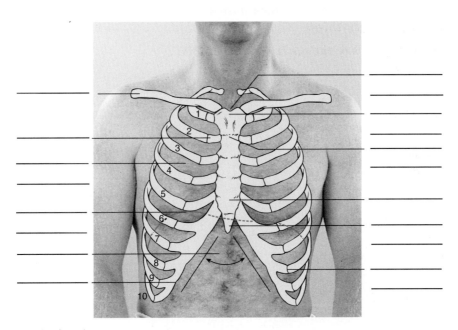

Anterior thoracic cage.

*Label the structure indicated by the line; then match your answer with the label on the matching figure in Chapter 18 of your textbook.*

*Label the following structures of the posterior thoracic cage.*

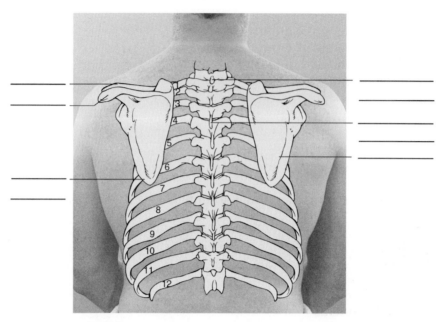

Posterior thoracic cage.

*Label the structure indicated by the line; then match your answer with the label on the matching figure in Chapter 18 of your textbook.*

*Label the following structures of the anterior vertical lines.*

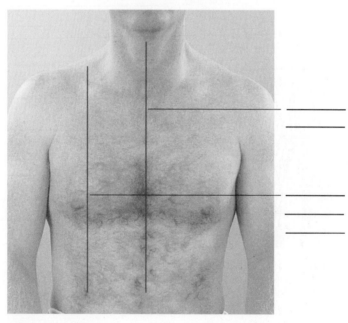

Anterior vertical lines.

*Label the structure indicated by the line; then match your answer with the label on the matching figure in Chapter 18 of your textbook.*

*Label the following structures of the posterior vertical lines.*

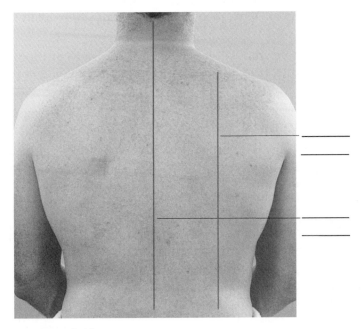

Posterior vertical lines.

*Label the structure indicated by the line; then match your answer with the label on the matching figure in Chapter 18 of your textbook.*

*Label the following structures of the lateral vertical lines.*

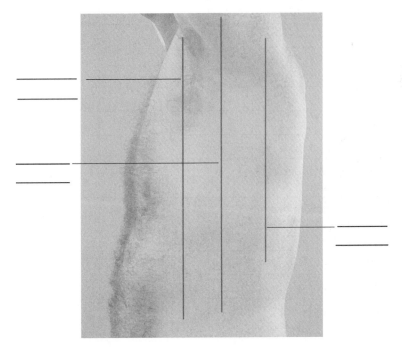

Lateral vertical lines.

*Label the structure indicated by the line; then match your answer with the label on the matching figure in Chapter 18 of your textbook.*

**Activity C** **LEARNER ACTIVITIES**

1. Review the information in "Promote Health: Lung Cancer" in Chapter 18 of your textbook. Determine your own risk for lung cancer. Next, identify ethnic groups that are at highest risk for lung cancer.

2. Find an elderly client, friend, or relative who will let you examine his or her thorax and lungs. Discuss with peers your findings as they compare with the findings in a younger person's thorax and lungs.

**Activity D** **INTERVIEWING AND RECORDING ASSESSMENT FINDINGS**

Use the following Nursing History Checklist as your guide to interviewing and recording your findings in thoracic and lung assessment.

### Nursing History Checklist

| Questions | Satisfactory Data | Needs Additional Data | Data Missing |
|---|---|---|---|
| *Current Symptoms* | | | |
| 1. Difficulty breathing (at rest, with specific activities, while sleeping, other symptoms when having trouble breathing)? | | | |
| 2. Chest pain associated with a cold, a fever, or deep breathing? | | | |
| 3. Cough, with or without sputum? | | | |
| *Past History* | | | |
| 1. Prior respiratory problems? | | | |
| 2. Previous thoracic surgery, biopsy, or trauma? | | | |
| 3. Allergies, symptoms/treatments? | | | |
| 4. Pulmonary studies/tests: chest x-ray, TB skin test, or influenza immunization? | | | |
| *Family History* | | | |
| 1. Family history of lung disease? | | | |
| *Lifestyle and Health Practices* | | | |
| 1. Use of tobacco products, cigarettes or cigars (number of years, number per day)? | | | |
| 2. Exposure to environmental conditions that affect breathing at work or at home, including secondhand smoke? | | | |
| 3. Difficulty performing usual daily activities? | | | |
| 4. Degree of stress, effect on breathing? | | | |
| 5. Medications for breathing (prescribed or OTC), other breathing treatments? | | | |

**Activity E** **PERFORMING PHYSICAL ASSESSMENT**

Use the following Physical Assessment Checklist as your guide to performing a thoracic and lung assessment. Column 1 can be used by you to guide your physical assessment. Column 2 may be used by your instructor to evaluate your skills as necessary.

**Physical Assessment Checklist**

| Assessment Skill | Findings (Normal or Abnormal) and Notes | | Performance (Satisfactory, Needs Improvement, Unsatisfactory) | | |
|---|---|---|---|---|---|
| | N | A | S | N | U |
| 1. Gather equipment (gown and drape, gloves, stethoscope, exam light, mask, skin marker, metric ruler). | ☐ | ☐ | ☐ | ☐ | ☐ |
| 2. Explain procedure to client. | ☐ | ☐ | ☐ | ☐ | ☐ |
| 3. Ask client to put on a gown. | ☐ | ☐ | ☐ | ☐ | ☐ |
| *Posterior Thorax* | | | | | |
| 1. Inspect for shape and configuration of the chest wall and position of scapulae. | ☐ | ☐ | ☐ | ☐ | ☐ |
| 2. Inspect for use of accessory muscles. | ☐ | ☐ | ☐ | ☐ | ☐ |
| 3. Inspect client's positioning noting posture and ability to support weight while breathing. | ☐ | ☐ | ☐ | ☐ | ☐ |
| 4. Palpate for tenderness and sensation with gloved fingers. | ☐ | ☐ | ☐ | ☐ | ☐ |
| 5. Palpate for surface characteristics such as lesions or masses with gloved fingers. | ☐ | ☐ | ☐ | ☐ | ☐ |
| 6. Palpate for fremitus, using the ball or ulnar edge of one hand while client says "ninety-nine." Assess for symmetry and intensity of vibration. | ☐ | ☐ | ☐ | ☐ | ☐ |
| 7. Palpate for chest expansion. Place hands on the posterior chest wall with your thumbs at the level of T9 or T10, and observe the movement of your thumbs as the client takes a deep breath. | ☐ | ☐ | ☐ | ☐ | ☐ |
| 8. Percuss for tone, starting at the apices above the scapulae and across the tops of both shoulders. | ☐ | ☐ | ☐ | ☐ | ☐ |
| 9. Percuss intercostal spaces across and down, comparing sides. | ☐ | ☐ | ☐ | ☐ | ☐ |
| 10. Percuss to the lateral aspects at the bases of the lungs, and compare sides. | ☐ | ☐ | ☐ | ☐ | ☐ |
| 11. Percuss for diaphragmatic excursion, using the procedure in Chapter 18 of the text. | ☐ | ☐ | ☐ | ☐ | ☐ |
| 12. Auscultate for breath sounds (normal: bronchial, bronchiovesicular, and vesicular), noting location. | ☐ | ☐ | ☐ | ☐ | ☐ |
| 13. Auscultate for adventitious sounds (crackles, fine or coarse, pleural friction rub, wheeze, sibilant, or sonorous). | ☐ | ☐ | ☐ | ☐ | ☐ |

| Assessment Skill | Findings (Normal or Abnormal) and Notes | | Performance (Satisfactory, Needs Improvement, Unsatisfactory) | | |
|---|---|---|---|---|---|
| | N | A | S | N | U |
| 14. Auscultate for voice sounds over the chest wall: Bronchophony—ask client to repeat the phrase "ninety-nine." Egophony—ask the client to repeat the letter "E." Whispered pectoriloquy—ask the client to whisper the phrase "one-two-three." | ☐ | ☐ | ☐ | ☐ | ☐ |
| *Anterior Thorax* | | | | | |
| 1. Inspect for shape and configuration to determine the ratio of anteroposterior diameter to transverse diameter (normally 1:2). | ☐ | ☐ | ☐ | ☐ | ☐ |
| 2. Inspect for position of sternum from anterior and lateral viewpoints. | ☐ | ☐ | ☐ | ☐ | ☐ |
| 3. Inspect for slope of the ribs from anterior and lateral viewpoints. | ☐ | ☐ | ☐ | ☐ | ☐ |
| 4. Inspect for quality and pattern of respiration, noting breathing characteristics, rate, rhythm, and depth. | ☐ | ☐ | ☐ | ☐ | ☐ |
| 5. Inspect intercostal spaces while client breathes normally. | ☐ | ☐ | ☐ | ☐ | ☐ |
| 6. Inspect for use of accessory muscles. | ☐ | ☐ | ☐ | ☐ | ☐ |
| 7. Palpate for tenderness and sensation, using fingers. | ☐ | ☐ | ☐ | ☐ | ☐ |
| 8. Palpate surface characteristics such as lesions or masses, using fingers of gloved hand. | ☐ | ☐ | ☐ | ☐ | ☐ |
| 9. Palpate for fremitus while the client says "ninety-nine." | ☐ | ☐ | ☐ | ☐ | ☐ |
| 10. Palpate for chest expansion by placing hands on anterolateral wall with the thumbs along the costal margins and pointing toward the xiphoid process. Observe movement of the thumbs as the client takes a deep breath. | ☐ | ☐ | ☐ | ☐ | ☐ |
| 11. Percuss for tone above the clavicles and then the intercostal spaces across and down, comparing sides. | ☐ | ☐ | ☐ | ☐ | ☐ |
| 12. Auscultate for breath sounds, adventitious sounds, and voice sounds. | ☐ | ☐ | ☐ | ☐ | ☐ |
| *Analysis of Data* | | | | | |
| 1. Formulate nursing diagnoses (wellness, risk, actual). | ☐ | ☐ | ☐ | ☐ | ☐ |
| 2. Formulate collaborative problems. | ☐ | ☐ | ☐ | ☐ | ☐ |
| 3. Make necessary referrals. | ☐ | ☐ | ☐ | ☐ | ☐ |

# CHAPTER POSTTEST

**Activity F** **MULTIPLE CHOICE**

*Choose the one best answer for each of the following multiple-choice questions.*

____ 1. While assessing an adult client, the client tells the nurse that she "has had difficulty catching her breath since yesterday." The nurse should assess the client further for signs and symptoms of
   a. emphysema.
   b. cardiac disease.
   c. trauma to the chest.
   d. infection.

____ 2. An adult client visits the clinic and tells the nurse that he has been "spitting up rust-colored sputum." The nurse should refer the client to the physician for possible
   a. pulmonary edema.
   b. bronchitis.
   c. asthma.
   d. tuberculosis.

____ 3. The nurse is planning a presentation to a group of high school students on the topic of lung cancer. Which of the following should the nurse plan to include in the presentation?
   a. Compared with whites in the United States, African-Americans have a lower incidence of lung cancer.
   b. Lung cancer is the third leading cause of death in the United States.
   c. There is a higher incidence of lung cancer in women than men in the United States.
   d. Studies have indicated that there is a genetic component in the development of lung cancer.

____ 4. While assessing an adult client, the nurse observes decreased chest expansion at the bases of the client's lungs. The nurse should refer the client to a physician for possible
   a. atelectasis.
   b. pneumonia.
   c. chest trauma.
   d. chronic obstructive pulmonary disease.

____ 5. The nurse is planning to percuss the chest of an adult male client for diaphragmatic excursion. The nurse should begin the assessment by
   a. asking the client to take a deep breath and hold it.
   b. percussing upward from the base of the lungs.
   c. percussing downward until the tone changes to resonance.
   d. asking the client to exhale forcefully and hold his breath.

____ 6. The nurse is preparing to auscultate the posterior thorax of an adult female client. The nurse should
   a. place the bell of the stethoscope firmly on the posterior chest wall.
   b. auscultate from the base of the lungs to the apices.
   c. ask the client to breathe deeply through her mouth.
   d. ask the client to breathe normally through her nose.

___ **7.** While assessing the thoracic area of an adult client, the nurse plans to auscultate for voice sounds. To assess bronchophony, the nurse should ask the client to

    **a.** repeat the phrase "ninety-nine."

    **b.** repeat the letter "E."

    **c.** whisper the phrase "one-two-three."

    **d.** repeat the letter "A."

___ **8.** The nurse assesses an adult client's thoracic area and observes a markedly sunken sternum and adjacent cartilages. The nurse should document the client's

    **a.** pectus thorax.

    **b.** pectus excavatum.

    **c.** pectus carinatum.

    **d.** pectus diaphragm.

___ **9.** The nurse assesses an adult client and observes that the client's breathing pattern is very labored and noisy, with occasional coughing. The nurse should refer the client to a physician for possible

    **a.** chronic bronchitis.

    **b.** atelectasis.

    **c.** renal failure.

    **d.** congestive heart failure.

___ **10.** While assessing an adult client's lungs during the postoperative period, the nurse detects coarse crackles. The nurse should refer the client to a physician for possible

    **a.** pneumonia.

    **b.** pleuritis.

    **c.** bronchitis.

    **d.** asthma.

___ **11.** The nurse assesses an adult client's breath sounds and hears sonorous wheezes, primarily during the client's expiration. The nurse should refer the client to a physician for possible

    **a.** asthma.

    **b.** chronic emphysema.

    **c.** pleuritis.

    **d.** bronchitis.

___ **12.** The nurse has assessed the respiratory pattern of an adult client. The nurse determines that the client is exhibiting Kussmaul's respirations with hyperventilation. The nurse should contact the client's physician because this type of respiratory pattern usually indicates

    **a.** diabetic ketoacidosis.

    **b.** central nervous system injury.

    **c.** drug overdose.

    **d.** congestive heart failure.

**Activity G** MATCHING

*Match the terms in the left column with the correct description in the right column.*

**Term**

___ **1.** Promotes the strongest stimulus to breathe

___ **2.** Orthopnea

___ **3.** Crepitus

___ **4.** Pectus excavatum

___ **5.** Pectus carinatum

___ **6.** Pleural friction rub

___ **7.** Wheeze (sibilant)

___ **8.** Wheeze (sonorous)

___ **9.** Crackles (fine)

___ **10.** Crackles (coarse)

**Description**

**a.** High-pitched, short, popping sounds

**b.** Forward protrusion of the sternum

**c.** High-pitched musical sounds

**d.** An increase in carbon dioxide in the blood

**e.** Low-pitched, bubbling, moist sounds

**f.** Low-pitched snoring or moaning sounds

**g.** Difficulty breathing when lying supine

**h.** Markedly sunken sternum and adjacent cartilage

**i.** Low-pitched, dry, grating sounds

**j.** A "crackling" sensation

**Activity H** CRITICAL THINKING AND CASE STUDIES

**1.** Read the following case study. Develop appropriate nursing diagnoses for the client.

Bo Thomson, 61, arrives at the outpatient clinic complaining of shortness of breath. He tells you that he has been employed by an asbestos removal company for the past 15 years. He says he has followed safety precautions "most of the time." He also tells you that on weekends he always relaxes by drinking beer and smoking a little at his favorite bar. He is divorced and has two grown sons, who live about 20 miles away. There is no history of lung cancer in his family that he can remember. He says, "I know I don't live a very healthy life, but I'm too old to change my ways now."

**2.** On the basis of the following assessment information, work through the steps of analyzing the data. Identify abnormal data and strengths in **subjective and objective findings**, assemble **cue clusters**, draw **inferences**, make possible **nursing diagnoses**, identify **defining characteristics**, **confirm or rule out** the nursing diagnosis, and **document** your conclusions.

Use the blank diagnostic analysis charts provided at the end of this book to guide your thinking. You may want to write on the chart or use separate paper. Propose nursing diagnoses that are specific to the client in the case study. Identify collaborative problems, if any, for this client. Finally, identify data, if any, that point toward a medical problem requiring a referral.

Theresa Johnson is a 55-year-old white woman. She is a part-time secretary for a local businessman and is very active in her community. She is married and has two children. T.J. presents at the nursing clinic this morning with a complaint of extreme shortness of breath. When entering the examination room, she appears very anxious and states that she has experienced this problem since yesterday afternoon.

Theresa has no previous diagnosis of asthma, allergies, or respiratory problems, but her brother and father have cases of mild asthma. The client has smoked for 35 years but reports limiting her smoking to a pack every 2 to 3 days for the past 10 years. Before that, she reports having smoked a pack every day. She worked in her office yesterday and reports having felt fine. She met friends at a local park for lunch but denies anything unusual about her daily activity. She states she has experienced "tightness in my chest," increasing in severity since about 5:00 p.m. yesterday. She denies any other associated symptoms such as pain or cough. Her discomfort made sleeping difficult last night, and she states that she has not eaten today because of her shortness of breath.

She currently takes no medications. She reports having no regular exercise program but denies any intolerance to activity until the onset of dyspnea. She reports having tried only rest to alleviate the problem and knows "nothing else to do but go to the doctor."

Her respiratory rate is 26 breaths/minute and appears somewhat labored. The client seems somewhat apprehensive and experiences obvious dyspnea on even mild exertion. Her anteroposterior diameter is within normal limits. The use of accessory muscles is noted, with respiration immediately after exertion. Expiration is somewhat labored and prolonged. Tactile fremitus is decreased, especially in lower lobes. Percussion tones are resonant over all lung fields. Breath sounds are decreased, with prolonged expiration. Voice sounds are also decreased. Expiratory wheeze is noted throughout the lung fields, especially bilaterally in the lower lobes.

# SELF-REFLECTION AND EVALUATION OF LEARNING OBJECTIVES

After you have read Chapter 18 and completed the above quizzes and activities, please identify to what degree you have met each of the following chapter learning objectives. For those objectives that you have met partially or not at all, you will want to review the chapter content for that learning objective.

| Objective | Very Much | Somewhat | Not At All |
|---|---|---|---|
| 1. Describe the structures and functions of the thorax and lungs. | | | |
| 2. Discuss risk factors for lung cancer and ways to reduce these risk factors. | | | |
| 3. Discuss the prevalence of lung cancer across the cultures. | | | |
| 4. Obtain an accurate nursing history of the client's thorax and lungs. | | | |
| 5. Explain how to prepare the client for an examination of the thorax and lungs. | | | |
| 6. Inspect the client's chest for shape and configuration of the chest wall and position of the scapulae. | | | |
| 7. Inspect the client's use of accessory muscles during respirations. | | | |
| 8. Inspect the client's positioning. | | | |
| 9. Palpate the client's thorax for tenderness and sensation, surface characteristics, fremitus, and chest expansion. | | | |
| 10. Percuss the client's thorax for tone and diaphragmatic excursion. | | | |
| 11. Describe expected age-related changes of the thorax and lungs. | | | |
| 12. Assess the client's breath sounds by auscultating the lungs. | | | |
| 13. Distinguish between normal and abnormal breath sounds. | | | |
| 14. Auscultate the client's posterior chest for adventitious sounds. | | | |
| 15. Auscultate the client's posterior chest for voice sounds. | | | |

| Objective | Very Much | Somewhat | Not At All |
|---|---|---|---|
| 16. Inspect the client's anterior chest for shape and configuration, position of the sternum, and slope of the ribs. | | | |
| 17. Inspect the client's respirations for quality and pattern. | | | |
| 18. Inspect the client's intercostal spaces and use of accessory muscles. | | | |
| 19. Palpate the anterior chest for tenderness and sensation and surface characteristics. | | | |
| 20. Palpate the anterior chest for fremitus and chest expansion. | | | |
| 21. Percuss the anterior chest. | | | |
| 22. Auscultate the anterior chest for breath sounds, adventitious sounds, and voice sounds. | | | |
| 23. Auscultate the client's anterior chest for adventitious sounds. | | | |

# Breasts and Lymphatic System

## Chapter Overview

Breast and lymphatic health is an important issue, not only for women during their childbearing years and throughout their lives, but also for men, whose breast development and health may be affected by various factors such as medications and hormonal problems. Use the following exercises and quizzes to guide your physical assessment of the breast and lymphatic structures.

## CHAPTER PRETEST

**Activity A  MULTIPLE CHOICE**

*Choose the best answer for each of the following multiple-choice questions.*

_____ **1.** At puberty, the female breasts enlarge in response to estrogen and
  **a.** progesterone.
  **b.** aldosterone.
  **c.** lactogen.
  **d.** prolactin.

_____ **2.** Elevated sebaceous glands, known as Montgomery's glands, are located in the breast's
  **a.** nipples.
  **b.** hair follicles.
  **c.** lactiferous ducts.
  **d.** areolas.

_____ **3.** The functional part of the breast that allows for milk production consists of tissue termed
  **a.** fibrous.
  **b.** glandular.
  **c.** adipose.
  **d.** lactiferous.

____ **4.** Fibrous tissue that provides support for the glandular tissue of the breasts is termed
    **a.** lateral ligaments.
    **b.** Wharton's ligaments.
    **c.** pectoral ligaments.
    **d.** Cooper's ligaments.

____ **5.** The size and shape of the breasts in females is related to the amount of
    **a.** glandular tissue.
    **b.** fibrous tissue.
    **c.** lactiferous ducts.
    **d.** fatty tissue.

____ **6.** The lymph nodes that are responsible for drainage from the arms are the
    **a.** lateral lymph nodes.
    **b.** central lymph nodes.
    **c.** anterior lymph nodes.
    **d.** posterior lymph nodes.

**Activity B** **LABELING ACTIVITIES**

*Label the following structures of the anterior chest.*

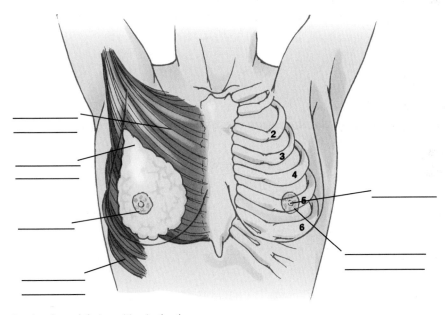

Landmarks and their position in the thorax.

*Label the structure indicated by the line; then match your answer with the label on the matching figure in Chapter 19 of your textbook.*

*Label the following breast quadrants.*

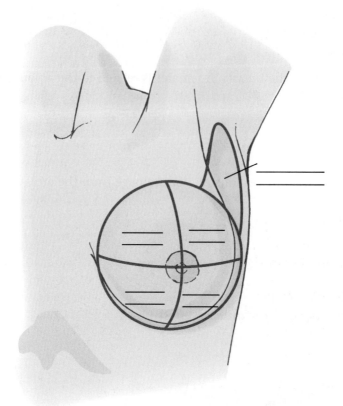

Breast quadrants.

*Label the structure indicated by the line; then match your answer with the label on the matching figure in Chapter 19 of your textbook.*

*Label the internal anatomic structures of the breast.*

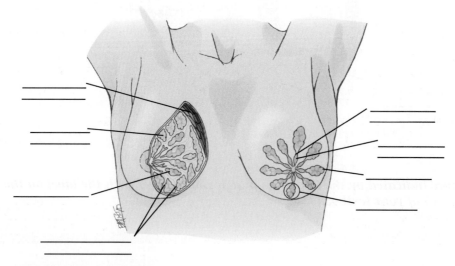

Internal anatomy of the breast.

*Label the structure indicated by the line; then match your answer with the label on the matching figure in Chapter 19 of your textbook.*

*Label the following major axillary lymph nodes.*

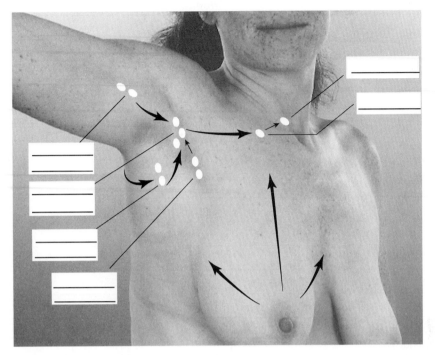

The major axillary lymph nodes.

*Label the structure indicated by the line; then match your answer with the label on the matching figure in Chapter 19 of your textbook.*

**LEARNER ACTIVITIES**

*Working with peers in learning lab*

*After reading Chapter 19, participate in the following learning activities.*

**1.** Review the information in "Promote Health: Breast Cancer" in Chapter 19 in your textbook. Determine your own risk of breast cancer. Next, identify ethnic groups that are at higher risk for breast cancer.

**2.** Use a breast model to review the anatomy and function of each anatomic structure. Discuss the changes of the breast and surrounding tissue that occur with aging.

**3.** Obtain an information packet from a local agency that performs mammograms. Review the material with a lab partner, and discuss how you would teach a client to do a breast self-examination.

**Activity D** **INTERVIEWING AND RECORDING ASSESSMENT FINDINGS**

Use the following Nursing History Checklist as your guide to interviewing and recording your findings in a breast assessment.

**Nursing History Checklist**

| Questions | Satisfactory Data | Needs Additional Data | Data Missing |
|---|---|---|---|
| *Current Symptoms* | | | |
| 1. Changes in breasts (lumps, swelling, redness, warmth, dimpling, size, firmness, pain, discharge)? | | | |

| Questions | Satisfactory Data | Needs Additional Data | Data Missing |
|---|---|---|---|
| *Past History* | | | |
| 1. Previous problems with breasts (treatment and surgery)? | | | |
| 2. Age at menses? | | | |
| 3. Age at menopause? | | | |
| 4. Given birth? | | | |
| 5. Age at first birth? | | | |
| 6. First and last day of menstrual cycle? | | | |
| *Family History* | | | |
| 1. Family history of breast cancer? | | | |
| *Lifestyle and Health Practices* | | | |
| 1. Use of hormones, contraceptives, or antidepressants? | | | |
| 2. Exposure to radiation, benzene, or asbestos? | | | |
| 3. Usual diet, including intake of alcohol, coffee, tea, soft drinks, and chocolate? | | | |
| 4. Usual exercise patterns? | | | |
| 5. Type of bra worn during exercise? | | | |
| 6. Examine own breasts/frequency? | | | |
| 7. Last breast exam by physician? | | | |
| 8. Last mammogram? | | | |

## Activity E  PERFORMING PHYSICAL ASSESSMENT

Use the following Physical Assessment Checklist as your guide to performing a breast assessment. Column 1 can be used by you to guide your physical assessment. Column 2 may be used by your instructor to evaluate your skills as necessary.

### Physical Assessment Checklist

| Assessment Skill | Findings (Normal or Abnormal) and Notes | | Performance (Satisfactory, Needs Improvement, Unsatisfactory) | | |
|---|---|---|---|---|---|
| | N | A | S | N | U |
| 1. Gather equipment (centimeter ruler, small pillow, gloves, client handout on breast self-examination, slide for specimen). | ☐ | ☐ | ☐ | ☐ | ☐ |
| 2. Explain procedure to client. | ☐ | ☐ | ☐ | ☐ | ☐ |
| 3. Ask client to put on a gown. | ☐ | ☐ | ☐ | ☐ | ☐ |

| Assessment Skill | Findings (Normal or Abnormal) and Notes | | Performance (Satisfactory, Needs Improvement, Unsatisfactory) | | |
|---|---|---|---|---|---|
| | N | A | S | N | U |
| *Female Breasts* | | | | | |
| 1. *Inspect breasts*<br>  a. Size and symmetry<br>  b. Color and texture<br>  c. Superficial venous patterns<br>  d. Retraction and dimpling<br>  e. Bilaterally, note color, size, shape, and texture of areolas<br>  f. Bilaterally, note size and direction of nipples | ☐<br>☐<br>☐<br>☐<br>☐<br>☐ | ☐<br>☐<br>☐<br>☐<br>☐<br>☐ | ☐<br>☐<br>☐<br>☐<br>☐<br>☐ | ☐<br>☐<br>☐<br>☐<br>☐<br>☐ | ☐<br>☐<br>☐<br>☐<br>☐<br>☐ |
| 2. *Palpate breasts*<br>  a. Texture and elasticity<br>  b. Tenderness and temperature<br>  c. Masses: noting location, size in centimeters, shape, mobility, consistency, and tenderness<br>  d. Palpate nipples by compressing nipple gently between thumb and index finger; observe for discharge<br>  e. Palpate mastectomy site, if applicable, observing the scar and any remaining breast or axillary tissue for redness, lesions, lumps, swelling, or tenderness | ☐<br>☐<br>☐<br><br>☐<br><br>☐ | ☐<br>☐<br>☐<br><br>☐<br><br>☐ | ☐<br>☐<br>☐<br><br>☐<br><br>☐ | ☐<br>☐<br>☐<br><br>☐<br><br>☐ | ☐<br>☐<br>☐<br><br>☐<br><br>☐ |
| *Male Breasts* | | | | | |
| 1. Inspect and palpate the breasts, areolas, and nipples for swelling, nodules, or ulcerations. | ☐ | ☐ | ☐ | ☐ | ☐ |
| *Axillae* | | | | | |
| 1. Inspect for rashes or infection. | ☐ | ☐ | ☐ | ☐ | ☐ |
| 2. Hold the elbow with one hand and use the three fingerpads of your other hand to palpate firmly the axillary lymph nodes. | ☐ | ☐ | ☐ | ☐ | ☐ |
| 3. Palpate high into the axillae, moving downward against the ribs to feel for the central nodes. Continue down the posterior axillae to feel for the posterior nodes. | ☐ | ☐ | ☐ | ☐ | ☐ |
| 4. Use bimanual palpation to feel for the anterior axillary nodes. | ☐ | ☐ | ☐ | ☐ | ☐ |
| 5. Palpate down the inner aspect of the upper arm. | ☐ | ☐ | ☐ | ☐ | ☐ |
| *Analysis of Data* | | | | | |
| 1. Formulate nursing diagnoses (wellness, risk, actual). | ☐ | ☐ | ☐ | ☐ | ☐ |
| 2. Formulate collaborative problems. | ☐ | ☐ | ☐ | ☐ | ☐ |
| 3. Make necessary referrals. | ☐ | ☐ | ☐ | ☐ | ☐ |

# CHAPTER POSTTEST

## Activity F MULTIPLE CHOICE

*Choose the one best answer for each of the following multiple-choice questions.*

_____ 1. After assessing the breasts of a female client, the nurse should explain to the client that most breast tumors occur in the

 a. upper inner quadrant.

 b. lower inner quadrant.

 c. upper outer quadrant.

 d. lower outer quadrant.

_____ 2. A female client tells the nurse that her breasts become lumpy and sore before menstruation but get better at the end of the menstrual cycle. The nurse should explain to the client that these symptoms are often associated with

 a. malignant tumors.

 b. fibroadenoma.

 c. fibrocystic breast disease.

 d. increased estrogen production.

_____ 3. The nurse has discussed the risks for breast cancer with a group of high school seniors. The nurse determines that one of the students needs further instructions when the student says that one risk factor is

 a. having a baby before the age of 20 years.

 b. a family history of breast cancer.

 c. consumption of a high-fat diet.

 d. late menopause.

_____ 4. Cultural beliefs about the causes of breast cancer do not always agree with medical findings. Hispanic Americans often associate breast cancer with

 a. improper diet.

 b. punishment from God.

 c. physical stress.

 d. evil thoughts.

_____ 5. The nurse is working with a community group to set up teaching programs to increase awareness among African-American women about preventive screening techniques for breast cancer. In the teaching program, the nurse should plan to include

 a. local female physicians who work with cancer clients.

 b. hospital clinic workers from various racial backgrounds.

 c. nurses who work in outpatient centers.

 d. breast cancer patients of the same race.

_____ 6. The nurse is caring for an adult female client when the client tells the nurse that she has had a clear discharge from her nipples for the past month. The nurse should ask the client if she has been taking

 a. antidepressants.

 b. antibiotics.

 c. insulin.

 d. contraceptives.

_____ **7.** The nurse is assessing an adult male client when the nurse observes gynecomastia in the client. The nurse should ask the client if he is taking any medications for

   **a.** inflammation.

   **b.** depression.

   **c.** infection.

   **d.** ulcers.

_____ **8.** The nurse is caring for a female client who has received a diagnosis of fibrocystic breast disease. The nurse has instructed the client about the disease. The nurse determines that the client needs further instructions when the client says she should avoid drinking

   **a.** regular coffee.

   **b.** regular tea.

   **c.** diet colas.

   **d.** grapefruit juice.

_____ **9.** The nurse plans to instruct an adult female client with regular menstrual cycles, who is not taking oral contraceptives, about breast self-examination. The nurse should plan to instruct the client to perform breast self-examination

   **a.** during menstruation.

   **b.** on the same day every month.

   **c.** midway between the cycles.

   **d.** right after menstruation.

_____ **10.** The nurse observes an orange-peel appearance, or peau d'orange, of the areolae of a client's breasts. The nurse should explain to the client that this is most likely due to

   **a.** blocked lymphatic drainage.

   **b.** fibrocystic breast disease.

   **c.** fibroadenomas.

   **d.** radiation therapy.

_____ **11.** The nurse is assessing a 50-year-old client's breasts and observes a spontaneous discharge of fluid from the left nipple. The nurse should

   **a.** document this as a normal finding.

   **b.** ask the client if she has had retracted nipples.

   **c.** refer the client for a cytology examination.

   **d.** determine whether the client wears a supportive bra.

_____ **12.** The nurse observes dimpling in an adult female client's breasts. The nurse should explain to the client that dimpling of the breast may indicate a

   **a.** fibroadenoma.

   **b.** tumor.

   **c.** genetic deviation.

   **d.** fibrocystic breast.

_____ **13.** The nurse is preparing to examine the breasts of a female client who had a left radical mastectomy 3 years ago. When examining the client, the nurse observes redness at the scar area. The nurse should explain to the client that this may be indicative of

   **a.** additional tumors.

   **b.** poor lymphatic drainage.

   **c.** an infectious process.

   **d.** metastasis to the right breast.

_____ **14.** A client has had a recent mastectomy and visits the clinic for postoperative evaluation. The client tells the nurse that she has been depressed and feels as if she is no longer a woman. The most appropriate nursing diagnosis for this client is

    **a.** ineffective individual coping related to mastectomy.

    **b.** fear of additional breast cancer related to presence of risk factors.

    **c.** PC: hematoma after mastectomy.

    **d.** disturbed body image related to mastectomy.

### Activity G   MATCHING

*Match the terms in the left column with the correct descriptions in the right column.*

**Term**

_____ **1.** Axillary lymph nodes

_____ **2.** Mammary gland

_____ **3.** Mastectomy

_____ **4.** Lactiferous duct

_____ **5.** Lactiferous sinus

_____ **6.** Cooper's ligaments

_____ **7.** Tail of Spence

_____ **8.** Areola

_____ **9.** Nipple

_____ **10.** Paget's disease

_____ **11.** Peau d'orange

_____ **12.** Mastitis

_____ **13.** Mammography

_____ **14.** Gynecomastia

**Description**

**a.** Lymphatic obstruction, causing edema, which thickens the skin, exaggerates the hair follicles, and gives the breast an orange-peel or pigskin look

**b.** Darkly pigmented area surrounding the nipple of the mammary gland

**c.** Enlargement of one or both male breasts, seen more frequently in adolescent boys and elderly men

**d.** Reservoirs for storing milk, located behind the nipple

**e.** Pigmented projection at the tip of each breast, which allows passage of milk from the breast

**f.** Specialized gland of the skin of females, which secretes milk for nourishment of the young

**g.** Roentgenography of the breast to detect any underlying mass

**h.** Ducts conveying the milk secreted by the lobes of the breast to and through the nipples

**i.** Groups of lymph nodes located under the arm (the axilla)

**j.** Inflammation of the breast

**k.** Cone-shaped breast tissue that projects up into the axillae

**l.** Surgical removal of breast tissue

**m.** Fibrous glands extending vertically from the breast surface to attach on the chest wall muscles

**n.** Erythematous scaling lesion of the breast, involving the nipple and areola unilaterally, and associated with an underlying malignancy

### Activity H   CRITICAL THINKING AND CASE STUDIES

**1.** Read the following case study and analyze the client's risk factors for the development of breast cancer.

Julia Hershey is a 67-year-old retired secretary. Her mother and a sister have been treated for breast cancer, but Ms. Hershey has no personal history of cancer. She gave birth to her only child when she was 37 years of age. She states that her daughter was a "bottle baby" and that breast-feeding was not "proper" back when her daughter was a baby. Ms. Hershey states that she went through the "change" (menopause) in her late 40s. Although she understands how to perform breast self-examinations, Ms. Hershey states that she does not do them on a regular basis. Her chart indicates that her last mammogram was 6 years ago.

2. Explain how you would assess the male breast and surrounding tissue. What would you explain to the male client about this part of the examination?

3. On the basis of the following assessment information, work through the steps of analyzing the data. Identify abnormal data and strengths in **subjective and objective findings**. Assemble **cue clusters**, draw **inferences**, make possible **nursing diagnoses**, identify **defining characteristics**, **confirm or rule out** the nursing diagnosis, and **document** your conclusions. Use the blank diagnostic analysis charts provided at the end of this book to guide your thinking. You may want to write on the chart or use separate paper. Propose nursing diagnoses that are specific to the client in the case study. Identify collaborative problems, if any, for this client. Finally, identify data, if any, that point toward a medical problem requiring a referral.

Carol Lawrence, a teacher, is a 42-year-old white woman. She is married and has three children. She has a history of fibrocystic breast disease. She felt a distinct tender lump in her left breast while taking a shower 2 days ago. At age 56, the client's mother died of breast cancer. Carol had one breast biopsy years ago, and the results were negative for cancer. At that time her mammography revealed fibrocystic breast disease. Carol has one natural child, aged 4 years, and two adopted children, aged 10 and 12 years. She states, "I'm so afraid that this might be cancer."

Physical examination reveals symmetric, round, smooth, pink breasts. The areolae are dark brown, and the nipples are everted. No rashes, lesions, dimpling, or retraction of breast tissue are noted while the client is in various positions. The client has tears in her eyes and a quavering voice. Palpation reveals generalized bilateral breast tenderness. Clear discharge is excreted from the left nipple. Bilateral, multiple, scattered, small, rubbery nodules are palpated bilaterally. No enlarged lumps or masses are palpated in the right breast. A 3 cm × 2 cm × 1 cm firm, oval, nonmobile, tender lump is palpated in left breast. No lymph nodes are palpable. Demonstrates appropriate technique for breast self-examination.

# SELF-REFLECTION AND EVALUATION OF LEARNING OBJECTIVES

After you have read Chapter 19 and completed the above quizzes and activities, please identify to what degree you have met each of the following chapter learning objectives. For those objectives that you have met partially or not at all, you will want to review the chapter content for that learning objective.

| Objective | Very Much | Somewhat | Not At All |
|---|---|---|---|
| 1. Describe the structure and functions of the breast and major axillary lymph nodes. | | | |
| 2. Discuss risk factors for breast cancer and ways to reduce these risk factors. | | | |
| 3. Discuss the prevalence of breast cancer across cultures. | | | |
| 4. Obtain an accurate nursing history of the client's breast and axillary region. | | | |
| 5. Explain how to prepare the client for an examination of the breasts and axillary region. | | | |
| 6. Describe the equipment necessary to perform a breast and axillary assessment. | | | |
| 7. Describe the two physical examination techniques (inspection and palpation) used to assess the breasts and axillae. | | | |

| Objective | Very Much | Somewhat | Not At All |
|---|---|---|---|
| 8. Assess the female breasts for size, symmetry, color, texture, and venous patterns. | | | |
| 9. Describe expected changes with aging of the female breasts. | | | |
| 10. Assess the areolas for color, size, shape, and texture. Assess the size and direction of the nipples. | | | |
| 11. Assess breasts for retraction and dimpling. | | | |
| 12. Palpate the breasts for texture, elasticity, temperature, and masses. | | | |
| 13. Describe the procedure for palpating the nipples and collecting a specimen. | | | |
| 14. Inspect and palpate the male breasts, areolas, and nipples. | | | |
| 15. Assess the axillae for rashes or infections. | | | |
| 16. Teach clients how to perform breast self-examinations. | | | |

# Heart and Neck Vessels

## Chapter Overview

One of the most complex and important aspects of the physical examination is the assessment of heart function and neck vessel patency. The heart needs to pump blood efficiently, and the neck vessels need to deliver the blood to and from the brain to ensure health, life, and mental and physical function. Use the following quizzes and exercises as a guide to your physical assessment activities.

## CHAPTER PRETEST

### Activity A  MULTIPLE CHOICE

*Choose the one best answer for each of the following multiple-choice questions.*

_____  1. The anterior chest area that overlies the heart and great vessels is called the
   a. precordium.
   b. epicardium.
   c. myocardium.
   d. endocardium.

_____  2. The bicuspid, or mitral, valve is located
   a. between the left atrium and the left ventricle.
   b. between the right atrium and the right ventricle.
   c. at the beginning of the ascending aorta.
   d. at the exit of each ventricle near the great vessels.

_____  3. The semilunar valves are located
   a. at the exit of each ventricle at the beginning of the great vessels.
   b. between the right atrium and the right ventricle.
   c. between the left atrium and the left ventricle.
   d. at the beginning of the ascending aorta.

_____  4. The sinoatrial node of the heart is located on the
   a. posterior wall of the right atrium.
   b. anterior wall of the right atrium.
   c. upper intraventricular system.
   d. anterior wall of the left atrium.

____ **5.** The P-wave phase of an electrocardiogram (ECG) represents

    **a.** conduction of the impulse throughout the atria.

    **b.** conduction of the impulse throughout the ventricles.

    **c.** ventricular repolarization.

    **d.** ventricular polarization.

**Activity B** **LABELING ACTIVITIES**

*Label the following heart positions.*

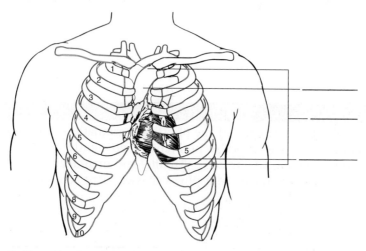

Position of heart.

*Label the structure indicated by the line; then match your answer with the label on the matching figure in Chapter 20 of your textbook.*

*Label the following heart structures.*

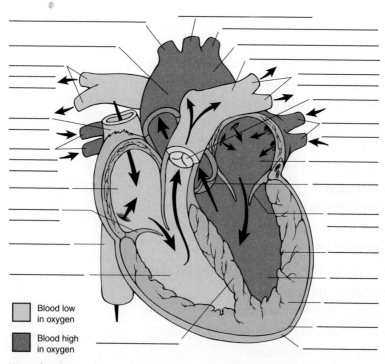

Heart chambers, valves, and circulation.

*Label the structure indicated by the line; then match your answer with the label on the matching figure in Chapter 20 of your textbook.*

*Label the following neck vessels.*

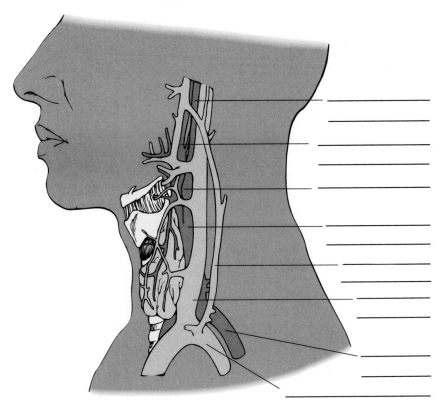

Neck vessels.

*Label the structure indicated by the line; then match your answer with the label on the matching figure in Chapter 20 of your textbook.*

### Activity C LEARNER ACTIVITIES

#### Working with peers in learning lab

*After reading Chapter 20, participate in the following learning activities.*

1. Review the information in "Promote Health: Coronary Heart Disease" in Chapter 20. Determine your own risk for coronary heart disease (CHD). Identify ways to reduce your risk factors. Which ethnic groups are at higher risk for CHD?

2. Find an elderly client, friend, or relative whose heart and neck vessels you can examine. Discuss with your lab partner your assessment findings as they compare with those of a younger person.

3. Discuss with your lab partner what teaching would be appropriate to reduce an individual's risk for CHD.

**Activity D** INTERVIEWING AND RECORDING ASSESSMENT FINDINGS

Use the following Nursing History Checklist as your guide to interviewing and recording your findings in your heart and neck vessels assessment. Column 1 can be used by you to guide your physical assessment. Column 2 may be used by your instructor to evaluate your skills as necessary.

### Nursing History Checklist

| Questions | Satisfactory Data | Needs Additional Data | Data Missing |
|---|---|---|---|
| *Current Symptoms* | | | |
| 1. Chest pain (type, location, radiation, duration, frequency, intensity)? | | | |
| 2. Palpitations? | | | |
| 3. Dizziness? | | | |
| 4. Swollen ankles? | | | |
| *Past History* | | | |
| 1. Previous heart problems: heart defect, murmur, heart attack (MI)? | | | |
| 2. Previous diagnosis of rheumatic fever, hypertension, elevated cholesterol, diabetes mellitus? | | | |
| 3. Heart surgery or cardiac balloon intervention? | | | |
| *Family History* | | | |
| 1. Hypertension? | | | |
| 2. Myocardial infarction? | | | |
| 3. Coronary heart disease? | | | |
| 4. Elevated cholesterol? | | | |
| 5. Diabetes mellitus? | | | |
| *Lifestyle and Health Practices* | | | |
| 1. Cigarette smoking pattern? | | | |
| 2. Life stress—type and amount? | | | |
| 3. Usual diet and exercise patterns? | | | |
| 4. Use of alcohol? | | | |
| 5. Sleep routine (use of extra pillows, up to urinate, feels rested)? | | | |
| 6. Use of medications or treatments for heart disease? | | | |
| 7. Self-monitoring of heart rate or blood pressure? | | | |
| 8. Screenings for blood pressure, cholesterol, ECG? | | | |
| 9. Impact of CHD on sexual activity? | | | |

## Activity E PERFORMING PHYSICAL ASSESSMENT

Use the following Physical Assessment Checklist as your guide to performing a heart and neck vessel assessment. Column 1 can be used by you to guide your physical assessment. Column 2 may be used by your instructor to evaluate your skills as necessary.

### Physical Assessment Checklist

| Assessment Skill | Findings (Normal or Abnormal) and Notes | | Performance (Satisfactory, Needs Improvement, Unsatisfactory) | | |
|---|---|---|---|---|---|
| | N | A | S | N | U |
| 1. Gather equipment (stethoscope with bell diaphragm, small pillow, penlight or movable exam light, watch with second hand, two centimeter rulers). | ☐ | ☐ | ☐ | ☐ | ☐ |
| 2. Explain procedure to client. | ☐ | ☐ | ☐ | ☐ | ☐ |
| 3. Ask client to put on a gown. | ☐ | ☐ | ☐ | ☐ | ☐ |
| *Neck Vessels* | | | | | |
| 1. Auscultate carotid arteries for bruits. | ☐ | ☐ | ☐ | ☐ | ☐ |
| 2. Palpate each carotid artery for amplitude and contour of the pulse, elasticity of the vessel, and thrills. | ☐ | ☐ | ☐ | ☐ | ☐ |
| 3. Inspect for jugular venous pulse. | ☐ | ☐ | ☐ | ☐ | ☐ |
| 4. Measure jugular venous pressure. | ☐ | ☐ | ☐ | ☐ | ☐ |
| *Heart (Precordium)* | | | | | |
| 1. Inspect for visible pulsations (note if apical or other). | ☐ | ☐ | ☐ | ☐ | ☐ |
| 2. Palpate apical pulse for location, size, strength, and duration of pulsation. | ☐ | ☐ | ☐ | ☐ | ☐ |
| 3. Palpate for abnormal pulsations or vibrations at apex, left sternal border, and base. | ☐ | ☐ | ☐ | ☐ | ☐ |
| 4. Auscultate heart sounds for rate and rhythm (apical and radial pulses, pulse rate deficit, $S_1$ and $S_2$). | ☐ | ☐ | ☐ | ☐ | ☐ |
| 5. Auscultate $S_1$ and $S_2$ heart sounds for sound location and strength pattern (louder/softer at locations and with respiration, splitting of $S_2$). | ☐ | ☐ | ☐ | ☐ | ☐ |
| 6. Auscultate for extra heart sounds (clicks, rubs) and murmurs (systolic or diastolic, intensity grade, pitch, quality, shape or pattern, location, transmission, effect of ventilation and position). | ☐ | ☐ | ☐ | ☐ | ☐ |
| 7. Auscultate with the client in the left lateral position and with the client sitting up, leaning forward, and exhaling. | ☐ | ☐ | ☐ | ☐ | ☐ |
| *Analysis of Data* | | | | | |
| 1. Formulate nursing diagnoses (wellness, risk, actual). | ☐ | ☐ | ☐ | ☐ | ☐ |
| 2. Formulate collaborative problems. | ☐ | ☐ | ☐ | ☐ | ☐ |
| 3. Make necessary referrals. | ☐ | ☐ | ☐ | ☐ | ☐ |

# CHAPTER POSTTEST

**Activity F** **MULTIPLE CHOICE**

*Choose the one best answer for each of the following multiple-choice questions.*

____ 1. During a cardiac examination, the nurse can best hear the $S_1$ heart sound by placing the stethoscope at the client's
   a. base of the heart.
   b. pulmonic valve area.
   c. apex of the heart.
   d. second left interspace.

____ 2. The $S_4$ heart sound
   a. can be heard during systole.
   b. is often termed *ventricular gallop*.
   c. is usually due to a heart murmur.
   d. can be heard during diastole.

____ 3. An adult client visits the clinic and tells the nurse that she feels chest pain and pain down her left arm. The nurse should refer the client to a physician for possible
   a. congestive heart failure.
   b. angina.
   c. palpitations.
   d. acute anxiety reaction.

____ 4. An adult client tells the nurse that his father died of a massive coronary attack at the age of 65. The nurse should explain to the client that one of the risk factors for coronary heart disease is
   a. high serum level of low-density lipoproteins.
   b. low-carbohydrate diets.
   c. high serum level of high-density lipoproteins.
   d. diets that are high in antioxidant vitamins.

____ 5. The nurse is planning a presentation about coronary heart disease for a group of middle-aged adults. Which of the following should be included in the nurse's teaching plan?
   a. Hispanic clients have a higher incidence of CHD than black or white Americans.
   b. The incidence of hypertension in the white population of the United States is greater than in the black population.
   c. Women are more likely to have serious stenosis after a heart attack.
   d. Estrogen replacement therapy in postmenopausal women decreases the risk of heart attack.

____ 6. The nurse is preparing to assess the cardiovascular system of an adult client with emphysema. The nurse anticipates that there may be some difficulty palpating the client's
   a. apical pulse.
   b. breath sounds.
   c. jugular veins.
   d. carotid arteries.

_____ **7.** The nurse is planning to auscultate a female adult client's carotid arteries. The nurse should plan to
    **a.** ask the client to hold her breath.
    **b.** palpate the arteries before auscultation.
    **c.** place the diaphragm of the stethoscope over the artery.
    **d.** ask the client to breathe normally.

_____ **8.** While assessing an older adult client, the nurse detects a bruit over the carotid artery. The nurse should explain to the client that a bruit is
    **a.** a normal sound heard in adult clients.
    **b.** a wheezing sound.
    **c.** associated with occlusive arterial disease.
    **d.** heard when the artery is almost totally occluded.

_____ **9.** The nurse assesses a hospitalized adult client and observes that the client's jugular veins are fully extended. The nurse contacts the client's physician because the client's signs are indicative of
    **a.** pulmonary emphysema.
    **b.** diastolic murmurs.
    **c.** patent ductus arteriosus.
    **d.** increased central venous pressure.

_____ **10.** While palpating the apex, left sternal border, and base in an adult client, the nurse detects a thrill. The nurse should further assess the client for
    **a.** cardiac murmur.
    **b.** left-sided heart failure.
    **c.** constrictive pericarditis.
    **d.** congestive heart failure.

_____ **11.** The nurse is auscultating the heart sounds of an adult client. To auscultate Erb's point, the nurse should place the stethoscope at the
    **a.** second intercostal space at the right sternal border.
    **b.** third to fifth intercostal space at the left sternal border.
    **c.** apex of the heart near the midclavicular line (MCL).
    **d.** fourth or fifth intercostal space at the left lower sternal border.

_____ **12.** While auscultating an adult client's heart rate and rhythm, the nurse detects a irregular pattern. The nurse should
    **a.** assess the client for signs and symptoms of pulmonary disease.
    **b.** document this as a normal finding.
    **c.** schedule the client for an ECG.
    **d.** refer the client to a physician.

_____ **13.** The nurse has assessed the heart sounds of an adolescent client and detects the presence of an $S_3$ heart sound at the beginning of the diastolic pause. The nurse should instruct the client that she should
    **a.** be referred to a cardiologist for further evaluation.
    **b.** be examined again in 6 months.
    **c.** restrict exercise and strenuous activities.
    **d.** recognize that this finding is normal in adolescents.

_____ **14.** While assessing an adult client, the nurse detects opening snaps early in diastole during auscultation of the heart. The nurse should refer the client to a physician because this is usually indicative of

    **a.** pulmonary hypertension.

    **b.** aortic stenosis.

    **c.** mitral valve stenosis.

    **d.** pulmonary hypotension.

_____ **15.** The nurse detects paradoxical pulses in an adult client during an examination. The nurse should explain to the client that paradoxical pulses are usually indicative of

    **a.** obstructive lung disease.

    **b.** left-sided heart failure.

    **c.** premature ventricular contractions.

    **d.** aortic stenosis.

_____ **16.** The nurse is assessing an adult client with a diagnosis of sinus arrhythmia. The nurse should explain to the client that this indicates that the

    **a.** heartbeats are followed by a pause.

    **b.** ventricular contraction occurs irregularly.

    **c.** $S_1$ and $S_2$ sounds are both split.

    **d.** heart rate speeds up and slows down during a cycle.

_____ **17.** The fourth heart sound, $S_4$, is a/an

    **a.** low-frequency sound best heard with the bell of the stethoscope.

    **b.** abnormal finding in trained athletes.

    **c.** sound that can be heard in the absence of atrial contraction.

    **d.** sound that may increase during expiration.

**Activity G** **CROSSWORD PUZZLE**

_Complete the following crossword puzzle to become more familiar with the terminology used with assessment of the neck vessels and heart._

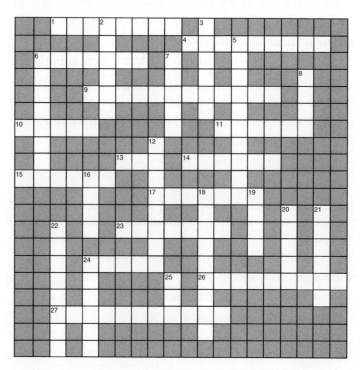

## ACROSS

1. Area of auscultation located at second ICS at left sternal border

4. Part of stethoscope used to auscultate normal heart sounds

6. Localized area of tissue necrosis caused by prolonged anoxia

9. Assessment technique most often associated with evaluation of the cardiovascular system

10. Dorsalis _____: peripheral pulse located on dorsum of foot just lateral to tendon of great toe

11. Palpable murmur described as feeling like the throat of a purring cat

13. Abbreviation for specific area of the chest where the heartbeat is palpated most clearly

14. Area of auscultation located at the apex and assessing the left ventricle; fourth to fifth ICS at left midclavicular line (MCL)

15. Peripheral pulse felt most often because of its accessibility

17. Event of the heart when contraction of the ventricles forces blood into major vessels

23. Area of auscultation at second ICS and right sternal border

24. Palpable, diffuse, sustained lift of the chest wall or a portion of the wall

26. Audible variation between closure of two valves

27. An abnormally slowed heart rate, usually under 50 beats/minute

## DOWN

2. Results of turbulent blood flow produced by pathologic condition of valvular or septal wall

3. Posterior _____: peripheral noted just behind the medial malleolus (ankle bone)

5. Classification of pulses detectable by feeling

6. Diminished blood supply to an organ or body part

7. Pressure waves that temporarily expand the wall of the artery from the propulsion of blood

8. The portion of the stethoscope used to assess for murmurs

12. Event in the heart cycle that involves relaxation of the ventricles

16. Most frequent location of $S_3$ and $S_4$ heart sounds; "point of the heart"

18. Area of auscultation located at the fourth to fifth ICS at the left sternal border; evaluates right ventricle

19. "Point" located at the third ICS at left sternal border; murmurs most often heard here

20. Audible murmur (a blowing sound heard in auscultating over a peripheral vessel or organ)

21. Paroxysmal pain in chest, often associated with myocardial ischemia

22. Blood clot attached to the inner wall of a vessel; usually causes some degree of occlusion

24. Calf pain associated with rapid dorsiflexion of the foot: sign

25. Abbreviation for the heart rate that originates within the SA node in right atrium

---

**Activity H** **CRITICAL THINKING AND CASE STUDIES**

1. Your client states that his physician informed him that he has a new grade 3 heart murmur. He asks you to explain the following to him in layman's terms:

   a. What is a heart murmur?

   b. What does grade 3 mean?

   c. What causes a heart murmur?

   d. What does my murmur sound like?

**2.** On the basis of the following assessment information, work through the steps of analyzing the data. Identify abnormal data and strengths in **subjective and objective findings**. Assemble **cue clusters**, draw **inferences**, make possible **nursing diagnoses**, identify **defining characteristics**, **confirm or rule out** the nursing diagnosis, and **document** your conclusions. Use the blank diagnostic analysis charts provided at the end of this book to guide your thinking. You may want to write on the chart or use separate paper. Propose nursing diagnoses that are specific to the client in the case study. Identify collaborative problems, if any, for this client. Finally, identify data, if any, that point toward a medical problem requiring a referral.

Larry Manning is a 37-year-old African-American male client. He is a registered nurse and works 12-hour night shifts (7 p.m. to 7 a.m.) in an intensive care unit. He is married and has two daughters, aged 9 and 6. He has come to a local nurse practitioner for an annual physical examination. He is particularly worried about his risk for cardiac problems.

When interviewed, Larry describes his general health as good. He denies any history of heart problems, surgery, or rheumatic fever and is not currently taking any medications. No previous lipid screening results are available. Larry states that he believes his father has high blood pressure. He states that he drinks socially: one to two beers two to three times per week. He smokes about a half pack of cigarettes per day. He says, "I try to quit, but my job is so stressful, and smoking relaxes me." He states that he does not follow any specific diet, and he admits a weakness for sweets and chocolate. He denies any cough, dyspnea, chest pain, dizziness, palpitations, or swelling in his feet or legs. He states that he exercises sporadically, mainly playing tennis and basketball. He relates that he sometimes has difficulty sleeping during the day and then uses that time to get some chores done.

Physical examination reveals a blood pressure of 160/84 mm Hg. The carotid pulses are equal bilaterally, 2+, elastic; no bruits are auscultated. Jugular venous pulsation disappears when the client is upright. Jugular venous pressure is 2 cm. The precordium is intact, with uniform color and no visible pulsations, heaves, or lifts. The apical impulse palpated in the fifth intercostal space (ICS) at the left MCL and is approximately the size of a nickel, with no thrill. The apical heart rate is auscultated at 88 beats/minute, with regular rhythm; $S_1$ is heard best at the apex, $S_2$ is heard best at the base. No splitting, snaps, clicks, or murmurs are noted.

# SELF-REFLECTION AND EVALUATION OF LEARNER OBJECTIVES

After you have read Chapter 20 and completed the above quizzes and activities, please identify to what degree you have met each of the following chapter learning objectives. For those objectives that you have met partially or not at all, you will want to review the chapter content for that learning objective.

| Objective | Very Much | Somewhat | Not At All |
|---|---|---|---|
| 1. Describe the structure and functions of the heart and neck vessels. | | | |
| 2. Describe the electrical conduction system of the heart. | | | |
| 3. Describe each phase of the ECG. | | | |
| 4. Discuss the two phases of the cardiac cycle. | | | |
| 5. Describe normal heart sounds and extra heart sounds. | | | |
| 6. Discuss possible conditions that contribute to extra heart sounds or heart murmurs. | | | |
| 7. Discuss the components of the jugular venous pulse wave. | | | |

| Objective | Very Much | Somewhat | Not At All |
|---|---|---|---|
| 8. Discuss risk factors for coronary heart disease (CHD) and ways to reduce these risk factors. | | | |
| 9. Obtain an accurate nursing history of the client's heart and neck vessels. | | | |
| 10. Prepare the client for an examination of the heart and neck vessels. | | | |
| 11. Describe the equipment necessary to perform a heart and neck vessel assessment. | | | |
| 12. Describe the two physical examination techniques (auscultation and palpation) used to assess the neck vessels and the three techniques (auscultation, palpation, and inspection) used to assess the precordium and heart sounds. | | | |
| 13. Auscultate and palpate the carotid arteries for bruits, amplitude, regularity, and contour of the pulse, vessel elasticity, or presence of thrills. Inspect the jugular for visibility of pulse, and measure jugular venous pressure. | | | |
| 14. Assess the heart and precordium for pulsations, heart sounds, heart rate, and rhythm. | | | |
| 15. Identify appropriate nursing diagnoses and collaborative problems commonly seen with assessment of the heart and neck vessels. | | | |

# Peripheral Vascular System

The arteries and veins of the arms and legs, the lymphatic system, and the capillaries are the vessels of peripheral vascular circulation. They deliver and exchange blood and fluids to and from the arms, legs, hands, and feet. As such, their function is a key factor in mobility and health. Use the following exercises and quizzes to help you review and master basic techniques and skills for peripheral vascular assessment.

## CHAPTER PRETEST

**Activity A  MULTIPLE CHOICE**

*Choose the one best answer for each of the following multiple-choice questions.*

_____ **1.** The major artery that supplies blood to the arm is the

    **a.** radial artery.

    **b.** ulnar artery.

    **c.** posterior artery.

    **d.** brachial artery.

_____ **2.** The popliteal artery can be palpated at the

    **a.** knee.

    **b.** great toe.

    **c.** ankle.

    **d.** inguinal ligament.

_____ **3.** The posterior tibial pulse can be palpated at the

    **a.** great toe.

    **b.** knee.

    **c.** top of the foot.

    **d.** ankle.

_____ **4.** Blood from the lower trunk and legs drains upward into the inferior vena cava. The percentage of the body's blood volume that is contained in the veins is nearly

   **a.** 50%.

   **b.** 60%.

   **c.** 70%.

   **d.** 80%.

**Activity B** **LABELING ACTIVITIES**

*Label the following major arteries of the arms and legs.*

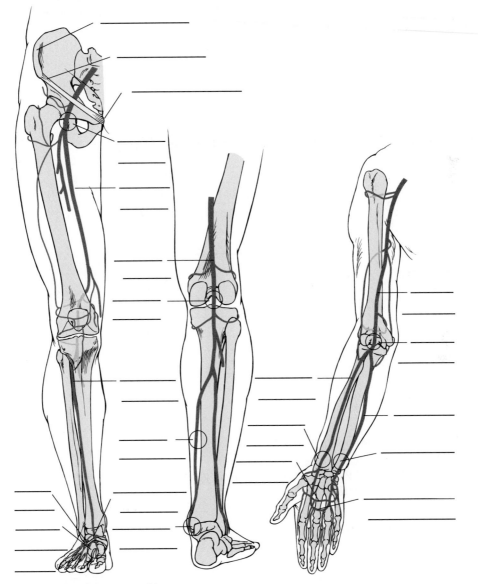

Major arteries of the arms and legs.

*Label the structure indicated by the line; then match your answer with the label on the matching figure in Chapter 21 of your textbook.*

*Label the following major leg veins.*

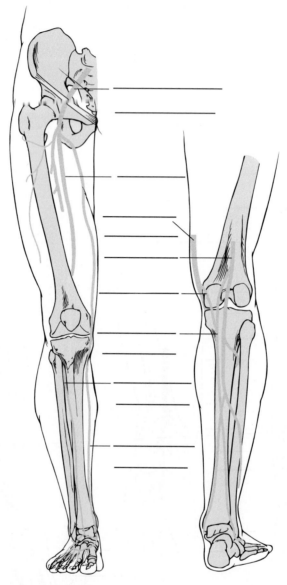

Major veins of the legs.

*Label the structure indicated by the line; then match your answer with the label on the matching figure in Chapter 21 of your textbook.*

*Label the following superficial lymph nodes of the arms and legs.*

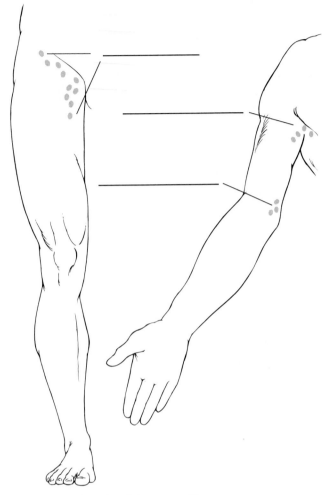

Superficial lymph nodes of the arms and legs.

*Label the structure indicated by the line; then match your answer with the label on the matching figure in Chapter 21 of your textbook.*

### Activity C LEARNER ACTIVITIES

#### Working with peers in learning lab

*After reading Chapter 21, participate in the following learning activities.*

1. Review the information in "Promote Health: Deep Vein Thrombosis" in Chapter 21. Determine your own risk for deep vein thrombosis. Identify ways to reduce your risk factors.

2. Find an elderly client, friend, or relative who will let you examine his or her peripheral vascular system. Discuss your assessment findings with your lab partner as they compare with those of a younger person.

3. Discuss with your lab partner what teaching would be appropriate to reduce an individual's risk of peripheral vascular disease.

**Activity D** INTERVIEWING AND RECORDING ASSESSMENT FINDINGS

Use the following Nursing History Checklist to interview a peer, friend, or family member regarding peripheral vascular status.

**Nursing History Checklist**

| Questions | Satisfactory Data | Needs Additional Data | Data Missing |
|---|---|---|---|
| Current Symptoms | | | |
| 1. Skin changes (color, temperature, or texture)? | | | |
| 2. Leg pain, heaviness, or aching? Does it awaken you at night? | | | |
| 3. Leg veins (rope-like, bulging, or contorted)? | | | |
| 4. Leg sores or open wounds (location, pain)? | | | |
| 5. Swelling in legs or feet? | | | |
| 6. Men: sexual activity changes? | | | |
| 7. Swollen glands or nodules (pain)? | | | |
| Past History | | | |
| 1. Previous problems with circulation in arms or legs (blood clots, ulcers, coldness, hair loss, numbness, swelling, or poor healing)? | | | |
| 2. Heart or blood vessel surgeries or treatments (coronary artery bypass, repair of an aneurysm, or vein stripping)? | | | |
| Family History | | | |
| 1. Family history of varicose veins, diabetes, hypertension, coronary heart disease, or elevated cholesterol or triglyceride levels? | | | |
| Lifestyle and Health Practices | | | |
| 1. Cigarettes or other forms of tobacco, past or present use (explain: quantity and length of time)? | | | |
| 2. Regular exercise? | | | |
| 3. Women: use of oral contraceptives? | | | |
| 4. Degree of stress? | | | |
| 5. Peripheral vascular problems that interfere with ADLs? | | | |
| 6. Use of medications to improve circulation or control blood pressure? | | | |
| 7. Use of support hose? | | | |

**Activity E** PERFORMING PHYSICAL ASSESSMENT

Use the following Physical Assessment Checklist as your guide to performing a peripheral vascular assessment. Column 1 can be used by you to guide your physical assessment. Column 2 may be used by your instructor to evaluate your skills as necessary.

## Physical Assessment Checklist

| Assessment Skill | Findings (Normal or Abnormal) and Notes | | Performance (Satisfactory, Needs Improvement, Unsatisfactory) | | |
|---|---|---|---|---|---|
| | N | A | S | N | U |
| 1. Gather equipment (gloves, centimeter tape, stethoscope, Doppler ultrasound probe, tourniquet). | ☐ | ☐ | ☐ | ☐ | ☐ |
| 2. Explain procedure to client. | ☐ | ☐ | ☐ | ☐ | ☐ |
| 3. Ask client to put on a gown. | ☐ | ☐ | ☐ | ☐ | ☐ |
| *Arms* | | | | | |
| 1. Inspect bilaterally for size, presence of edema, and venous patterning. | ☐ | ☐ | ☐ | ☐ | ☐ |
| 2. Inspect bilaterally for skin color. | ☐ | ☐ | ☐ | ☐ | ☐ |
| 3. Inspect fingertips for clubbing. | | | | | |
| 4. Palpate fingers, hands, and arms for temperature, using dorsal surface of your fingers. | ☐ | ☐ | ☐ | ☐ | ☐ |
| 5. Determine capillary refill time. | ☐ | ☐ | ☐ | ☐ | ☐ |
| 6. Palpate radial, ulnar, and brachial pulses. | ☐ | ☐ | ☐ | ☐ | ☐ |
| 7. Palpate epitrochlear lymph nodes behind the elbow in the groove between the biceps and triceps muscles. | ☐ | ☐ | ☐ | ☐ | ☐ |
| 8. Perform Allen's test by occluding the radial and ulnar arteries and observing for palm pallor. Then, release the ulnar artery and watch for color to return to hand. | ☐ | ☐ | ☐ | ☐ | ☐ |
| *Legs* | | | | | |
| 1. Inspect bilaterally for skin color (client in supine position). | ☐ | ☐ | ☐ | ☐ | ☐ |
| 2. Inspect bilaterally for distribution of hair. | ☐ | ☐ | ☐ | ☐ | ☐ |
| 3. Inspect for lesions or ulcers (note whether margins are smooth and even, location such as at pressure points, size, depth, drainage, odor). | ☐ | ☐ | ☐ | ☐ | ☐ |
| 4. Inspect for edema, unilateral or bilateral (if calves are asymmetric, measure calf circumference). | ☐ | ☐ | ☐ | ☐ | ☐ |
| 5. If client has edema, determine whether it is pitting or nonpitting. If client has pitting edema, rate on a 1+ to 4+ scale. | ☐ | ☐ | ☐ | ☐ | ☐ |
| 6. Palpate skin temperature (cool, warm, hot). Use dorsal surface of hands. | ☐ | ☐ | ☐ | ☐ | ☐ |
| 7. Palpate the superficial inguinal lymph nodes while keeping the genitals draped. If detected, note size, mobility, or tenderness. | ☐ | ☐ | ☐ | ☐ | ☐ |
| 8. Palpate and auscultate femoral pulses over artery. Listen for bruits. | ☐ | ☐ | ☐ | ☐ | ☐ |
| 9. Palpate popliteal, dorsalis pedis, and posterior tibial pulses. | ☐ | ☐ | ☐ | ☐ | ☐ |
| 10. Inspect for varicosities and thrombophlebitis by asking client to stand. | ☐ | ☐ | ☐ | ☐ | ☐ |

| Assessment Skill | Findings (Normal or Abnormal) and Notes | | Performance (Satisfactory, Needs Improvement, Unsatisfactory) | | |
|---|---|---|---|---|---|
| | N | A | S | N | U |
| 11. Assess for arterial or venous insufficiency by eliciting bilaterally for Homans' sign by having client in supine position and | ☐ | ☐ | ☐ | ☐ | ☐ |
| a. flexing knee 5 degrees and quickly squeezing the muscle against the tibia | ☐ | ☐ | ☐ | ☐ | ☐ |
| OR | | | | | |
| b. with hand under slightly flexed knee, sharply dorsiflex the foot—performing position change test for arterial insufficiency while client is in the supine position. Place hands under both of the client's ankles. Raise legs 12 inches above heart level, and ask client to pump feet up and down for 1 minute. Have client sit up and dangle legs. Note color of feet. Time the interval for color to return. | ☐ | ☐ | ☐ | ☐ | ☐ |
| 12. If varicosities present, perform the manual compression test by having client stand. Firmly compress the lower portion of the varicose vein with one hand. Place other hand 6 to 8 inches above hand. Feel for pulsation in the upper hand. | ☐ | ☐ | ☐ | ☐ | ☐ |
| 13. If varicosities are present, perform the Trendelenburg test with client in supine position. Elevate leg 90 degrees for 15 seconds. With legs elevated, apply a tourniquet to the upper thigh. Assist client to a standing position, and observe for venous filling. Remove tourniquet after 30 seconds, and watch for sudden filling of the varicose veins from above. | ☐ | ☐ | ☐ | ☐ | ☐ |
| *Analysis of Data* | | | | | |
| 1. Formulate nursing diagnoses (wellness, risk, actual). | ☐ | ☐ | ☐ | ☐ | ☐ |
| 2. Formulate collaborative problems. | ☐ | ☐ | ☐ | ☐ | ☐ |
| 3. Make necessary referrals. | ☐ | ☐ | ☐ | ☐ | ☐ |

# CHAPTER POSTTEST

## Activity F MULTIPLE CHOICE

*Choose the one best answer for each of the following multiple-choice questions.*

——— **1.** While assessing the peripheral vascular system of an adult client, the nurse detects cold clammy skin and loss of hair on the client's legs. The nurse suspects that the client may be experiencing

    **a.** venous stasis.

    **b.** varicose veins.

    **c.** thrombophlebitis.

    **d.** arterial insufficiency.

——— **2.** During a physical examination, the nurse detects warm skin and brown pigmentation around an adult client's ankles. The nurse suspects that the client may be experiencing

    **a.** venous insufficiency.

    **b.** arterial occlusive disease.

    **c.** venous ulcers.

    **d.** ankle edema.

_____ 3. The nurse is assessing the peripheral vascular system of an older adult client. The client tells the nurse that her legs "seem cold all the time and sometimes feel tingly." The nurse suspects that the client may be experiencing

    **a.** varicose veins.

    **b.** intermittent claudication.

    **c.** edema.

    **d.** thrombophlebitis.

_____ 4. The nurse is caring for a client who is employed as a typist and has a family history of peripheral vascular disease. The nurse should instruct the client to reduce her risk factors by

    **a.** eating a high-protein diet.

    **b.** resting frequently.

    **c.** drinking large quantities of milk.

    **d.** getting regular exercise.

_____ 5. The nurse is preparing to use a Doppler ultrasound probe to detect blood flow in the femoral artery of an adult client. The nurse should

    **a.** apply K-Y jelly to the client's skin.

    **b.** place the client in a supine position with the head flat.

    **c.** place the tip of the probe in a 30-degree angle to the artery.

    **d.** apply gel used for ECG to the client's skin.

_____ 6. A client visits the clinic and tells the nurse that she had a mastectomy 2 years ago. The nurse should assess the client for

    **a.** lymphedema.

    **b.** Raynaud's disease.

    **c.** poor peripheral pulses.

    **d.** bruits over the radial artery.

_____ 7. After palpating the radial pulse of an adult client, the nurse suspects arterial insufficiency. The nurse should next assess the client's

    **a.** femoral pulse.

    **b.** popliteal pulse.

    **c.** brachial pulse.

    **d.** tibial pulse.

_____ 8. The nurse is preparing to palpate the epitrochlear lymph nodes of an adult male client. The nurse should instruct the client to

    **a.** assume a supine position.

    **b.** rest his arm on the examination table.

    **c.** flex his elbow about 90 degrees.

    **d.** make a fist with his left hand.

_____ 9. While inspecting the skin color of a male client's legs, the nurse observes that the client's legs are slightly cyanotic while he is sitting on the edge of the examination table. The nurse should refer the client to a physician for possible

    **a.** arterial insufficiency.

    **b.** congestive heart failure.

    **c.** Raynaud's disease.

    **d.** venous insufficiency.

_____ **10.** While assessing the inguinal lymph nodes in an older adult client, the nurse detects that the lymph nodes are approximately 3 cm in diameter, nontender, and fixed. The nurse should refer the client to a physician because these findings are generally associated with

   **a.** localized infection.

   **b.** systemic infection.

   **c.** arterial insufficiency.

   **d.** malignancy.

_____ **11.** The nurse plans to assess an adult client for Homans' sign. The nurse should

   **a.** ask the client to remain standing for the procedure.

   **b.** place the hands on the client's thigh muscle.

   **c.** place the hands near the client's ankle.

   **d.** flex the client's knee, then dorsiflex the foot.

_____ **12.** The nurse is planning to perform the Trendelenburg test on an adult client. The nurse should explain to the client that this test is used to determine the

   **a.** degree of arterial occlusion that exists.

   **b.** pulse of a client with poor elasticity.

   **c.** competence of the saphenous vein valves.

   **d.** severity of thrombophlebitis.

**Activity G** **MATCHING**

*Match the terms in the left column with the correct descriptions in the right column.*

**Term**

_____ **1.** Doppler ultrasound probe

_____ **2.** Edema

_____ **3.** Clubbing

_____ **4.** Raynaud's disease

_____ **5.** Capillary refill time

_____ **6.** Allen's test

_____ **7.** Varicose veins

_____ **8.** Thrombophlebitis

_____ **9.** Homans' sign (positive)

_____ **10.** Arterial ulcer

_____ **11.** Venous ulcer

_____ **12.** Ischemia

_____ **13.** Arteriosclerosis

**Description**

**a.** Deficient supply of oxygenated arterial blood to a tissue; caused by obstruction of a blood vessel

**b.** Swollen, distended, and knotted veins; occur most commonly in the legs

**c.** Usually occur on tips of toes, metatarsal heads, and lateral malleoli; ulcers have pale ischemic base, well-defined edges, and no bleeding

**d.** Swelling caused by excess fluid

**e.** Usually occur on medial malleoli; ulcers have bleeding uneven edges

**f.** Calf pain elicited when the calf muscle is compressed against the tibia or when the foot is sharply dorsiflexed against the calf

**g.** The time it takes for color to return to the nail beds after they have been blanched by pressure; a good measure of peripheral perfusion and cardiac output

**h.** Rigid peripheral blood vessels; occurs more commonly in older adults

**i.** Used to detect a weak peripheral pulse to monitor blood pressure in infants or children and to measure blood pressure in a lower extremity; it magnifies pulse sounds from the heart and blood vessels

**j.** Inflammation of a vein associated with thrombus formation

**k.** Diffuse enlargement of terminal phalanges

**l.** Determines the patency of the radial and ulnar arteries

**m.** A vasospastic disorder, primarily affects the hands, characterized by color change from pallor, to cyanosis, to rubor; attacks precipitated by cold or emotional upset and relieved by warmth

**Activity H** **CRITICAL THINKING AND CASE STUDIES**

1. Explain how to differentiate between arterial and venous insufficiency.

2. Explain how to differentiate between edema associated with lymphedema versus edema associated with chronic venous insufficiency.

3. On the basis of the following assessment information, work through the steps of analyzing the data. Identify abnormal data and strengths in **subjective and objective findings**. Assemble **cue clusters**, draw **inferences**, make possible **nursing diagnoses**, identify **defining characteristics**, **confirm or rule out** the nursing diagnosis, and **document** your conclusions. Use the blank diagnostic analysis charts provided at the end of this book to guide your thinking. You may want to write on the chart or use separate paper. Propose nursing diagnoses that are specific to the client in the case study. Identify collaborative problems, if any, for this client. Finally, identify data, if any, that point toward a medical problem requiring a referral.

Fran Hensley is an 84-year-old white widow with a medical diagnosis of venous (stasis) ulcers on the medial surface of her right lower leg. She is 4 feet 11 inches tall and weighs 100 pounds. She has been referred by her physician to the Visiting Nurse Association (VNA) for skilled visits three times a week by an R.N. She lives in a small rural community in her own home. She lives alone, but her older sister, aged 87 years, lives across the street and looks after her. Fran has one adult daughter, who is married and lives out of state.

When interviewed, Fran says she has had a history of venous ulcers for the past 10 years and has been seen in the past by the VNA for treatment of these ulcers. The last time she was seen for this was approximately 8 months ago, when she had venous ulcers on the medial aspects of both legs. Both areas were well healed at the time of discharge.

Although communication with Fran is difficult because of a hearing loss, she denies any pain from the ulcers. However, she does cry out at times during the dressing changes. Her sister provides most of the information for the nurses and states that Fran has been up more than usual during the past few weeks and does not rest with her legs elevated as much as she should. Fran can ambulate with the aid of a walker. Her sister checks on Fran several times during the day and prepares meals for her.

Physical assessment reveals the following findings on the upper extremities: no edema, pink, and no areas of discoloration observed bilaterally. The nail beds have no signs of clubbing. The upper and lower arms are warm to touch; however, the hands are slightly cool to touch. Capillary refill time is normal. The radial and brachial pulses are strong bilaterally. The epitrochlear lymph nodes are nonpalpable. The ulnar pulses are nonpalpable. Results of Allen's test are normal.

Physical assessment of lower extremities reveals areas of brownish pigmentation at the ankles. The legs are warm to the touch. An area of ulceration approximately 4 cm × 7 cm is present on the medial aspect of the left ankle. The medial aspect of the right lower leg has an area of scar tissue approximately 3 cm × 8 cm. Both lower legs are thin, but the left leg is slightly swollen, with 1+ pitting edema. No varicosities are noted. The inguinal lymph nodes are nonpalpable, and the femoral pulses are strong and equal bilaterally. The popliteal pulses are absent, and the dorsalis pedal pulses are weak in both feet. The posterior tibial pulses are present but weak. Homans' sign is negative bilaterally. The client is unable to complete testing for arterial insufficiency.

# SELF-REFLECTION AND EVALUATION OF LEARNER OBJECTIVES

After you have read Chapter 21 and completed the above review items, please identify to what degree you have met each of the following chapter learning objectives. For those objectives that you have met partially or not at all, you will want to review the chapter content for that learning objective(s).

| Objective | Very Much | Somewhat | Not At All |
|---|---|---|---|
| 1. Describe the structure and functions of the blood vessel walls. | | | |
| 2. Describe capillary and lymphatic circulation. | | | |
| 3. Discuss risk factors for peripheral vascular disease and ways to reduce these risk factors. | | | |
| 4. Discuss the incidence of peripheral vascular disease across cultures. | | | |
| 5. Obtain an accurate nursing history of the client's peripheral vascular system. | | | |
| 6. Explain how to prepare the client for an examination of the peripheral vascular system. | | | |
| 7. Describe the equipment necessary to perform an examination of the peripheral vascular system. | | | |
| 8. Inspect the size, presence of edema, venous patterning, color, and clubbing of fingertips. | | | |
| 9. Palpate the temperature of the client's fingers, hands, and arms. | | | |
| 10. Assess the client's capillary refill time. | | | |
| 11. Palpate the client's radial, ulnar, and brachial pulses. | | | |
| 12. Assess the client for epitrochlear lymph nodes. | | | |
| 13. Perform the Allen's test on a client. | | | |
| 14. Inspect and palpate the client's legs for color, hair distribution, lesions or ulcers, edema, and skin temperature. | | | |
| 15. Palpate the client's inguinal area for the superficial inguinal lymph nodes. | | | |
| 16. Palpate the client's femoral, popliteal, dorsalis pedis, and posterior tibial pulses. | | | |
| 17. Inspect the client's legs for varicosities and thrombophlebitis. | | | |
| 18. Assess the client for arterial and venous insufficiency of the legs. | | | |

# Abdomen

## Chapter Overview

The abdomen houses the structures of several different body systems—gastrointestinal, reproductive (female), lymphatic, and urinary. Known as the solid or hollow abdominal viscera, these structures include the liver, pancreas, spleen, adrenal glands, kidneys, ovaries, and uterus (solid viscera) and the stomach, gallbladder, small intestine, colon, and bladder (hollow viscera). Abdominal assessment is complex, largely because of the many vital organs and blood vessels within the abdominal cavity and the life-sustaining functions, such as digestion and elimination that are performed there.

## CHAPTER PRETEST

### Activity A  MULTIPLE CHOICE

*Choose the one best answer for each of the following multiple-choice questions.*

_____ 1. The abdominal contents are enclosed externally by the abdominal wall musculature—three layers of muscle extending from the back, around the flanks, to the front. The outer muscle layer is the external

    **a.** rectal abdominis.

    **b.** transverse abdominis.

    **c.** abdominal oblique.

    **d.** umbilical oblique.

_____ 2. The sigmoid colon is located in this area of the abdomen: the

    **a.** left upper quadrant.

    **b.** left lower quadrant.

    **c.** right upper quadrant.

    **d.** right lower quadrant.

_____ 3. The pancreas of an adult client is located

    **a.** below the diaphragm and extending below the right costal margin.

    **b.** posterior to the left midaxillary line and posterior to the stomach.

    **c.** high and deep under the diaphragm and can be palpated.

    **d.** deep in the upper abdomen and is not normally palpable.

___ **4.** The primary function of the gallbladder is to
    **a.** store and excrete bile.
    **b.** aid in the digestion of protein.
    **c.** produce alkaline mucus.
    **d.** produce hormones.

___ **5.** The colon originates in this abdominal area: the
    **a.** right lower quadrant.
    **b.** right upper quadrant.
    **c.** left lower quadrant.
    **d.** left upper quadrant.

### Activity B   LABELING ACTIVITIES

*Label the landmarks of the abdomen in the following figure.*

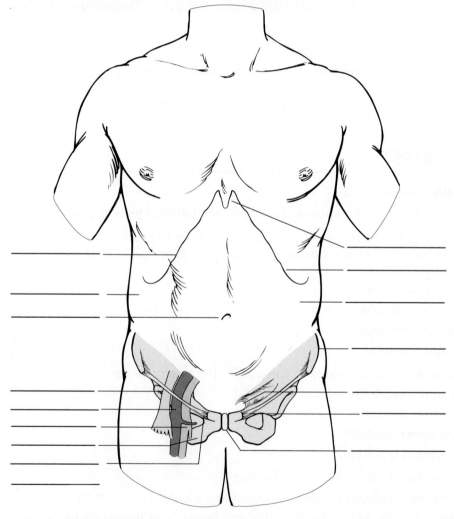

Landmarks of the abdomen.

*Label the structure indicated by the line; then match your answer with the label on the matching figure in Chapter 22 of your textbook.*

*Label the structures of the four quadrants and the nine regions of the abdomen in the following two figures.*

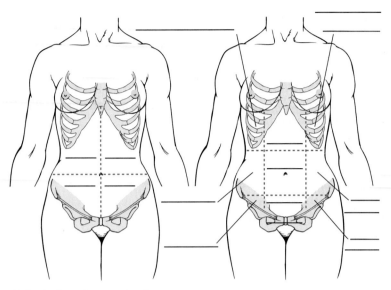

Abdominal quadrants and regions.

*Label the structure indicated by the line; then match your answer with the label on the matching figure in Chapter 22 of your textbook.*

*Label the organs of the abdomen in the following figure.*

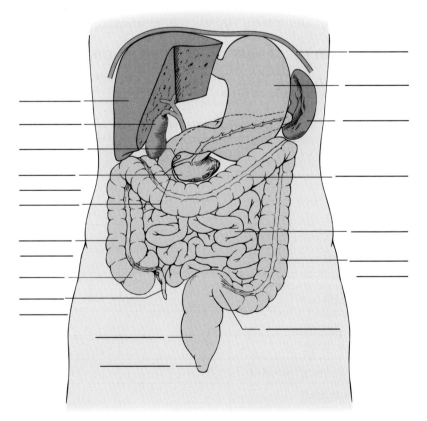

Abdominal viscera.

*Label the structure indicated by the line; then match your answer with the label on the matching figure in Chapter 22 of your textbook.*

**Activity C** LEARNER ACTIVITIES

### Working with peers in learning lab

*After reading Chapter 22, participate in the following learning activities.*

1. Practice preparing your lab partner for an abdominal exam. Discuss the purpose of emptying the bladder and positioning. Obtain the necessary equipment.

2. Use a washable marker to mark off the four quadrants of the abdomen on your lab partner. Identify the organs found in each quadrant. Now have your partner mark with a washable marker the nine regions on your abdomen. Identify the organs found in each of the nine regions.

3. Inspect the skin and umbilicus of your lab partner. Discuss the differences between a deviated umbilicus and an everted umbilicus. Differentiate between abdominal respiratory movements, aortic pulsations, and peristaltic waves.

4. Measure the abdominal girth of your lab partner, and discuss the various causes of abdominal distention and asymmetry.

5. Auscultate bowel sounds; record their intensity, pitch, and frequency; and discuss the significance of bowel sounds, including the absence of bowel sounds. Also note where vascular sounds or friction rubs may occur and the significance of each.

6. Percuss the abdomen, and note the significance of the sounds heard.

7. Palpate the span of your partner's liver, documenting the size. Perform the scratch test.

8. Percuss your lab partner's spleen.

9. Perform light and deep palpation of your lab partner's abdomen.

10. Palpate your lab partner's liver and spleen. Discuss the significance of enlargement.

**Activity D** INTERVIEWING AND RECORDING ASSESSMENT FINDINGS

Use the following Nursing History Checklist as your guide to interviewing and recording findings in abdominal assessment.

### Nursing History Checklist

| Questions | Satisfactory Data | Needs Additional Data | Data Missing |
|---|---|---|---|
| *Current Symptoms* | | | |
| 1. Abdominal pain present? | | | |
| 2. What factors precipitate the pain or make it worse? | | | |
| 3. Description and location of the pain? | | | |
| 4. Other symptoms present, such as nausea, vomiting, diarrhea, appetite changes, constipation? | | | |
| 5. Recent weight gain or loss? | | | |
| *Past History* | | | |
| 1. Previous abdominal surgery/trauma/injury/medications? | | | |
| 2. Previous abdominal pain and treatment? | | | |
| 3. Results of any lab work or gastrointestinal studies? | | | |

| Questions | Satisfactory Data | Needs Additional Data | Data Missing |
|---|---|---|---|
| *Family History* | | | |
| 1. Stomach, colon, or liver cancer? | | | |
| 2. Abdominal pain, appendicitis, colitis, bleeding, or hemorrhoids? | | | |
| 3. Person responsible for nutrition in family? | | | |
| *Lifestyle and Health Practices* | | | |
| 1. Smoking, amount? | | | |
| 2. Alcohol use, amount? | | | |
| 3. Diet (food and drink), past 24 hours? | | | |
| 4. Antacid use, amount? | | | |
| 5. Medication use? | | | |
| 6. Fluid intake? | | | |
| 7. Exercise, amount? | | | |
| 8. Cause of stress in life; effect on eating and elimination patterns? | | | |
| 9. Past actions with abdominal pain or problems? | | | |

## Activity E  PERFORMING PHYSICAL ASSESSMENT

Use the following Physical Assessment Checklist as your guide to performing an abdominal assessment. Column 1 can be used by you to guide your physical assessment. Column 2 may be used by your instructor to evaluate your skills as necessary.

### Physical Assessment Checklist

| Assessment Skill | Findings (Normal or Abnormal) and Notes | | Performance (Satisfactory, Needs Improvement, Unsatisfactory) | | |
|---|---|---|---|---|---|
| | N | A | S | N | U |
| 1. Gather equipment (pillow/towel, centimeter ruler, stethoscope, marking pen). | ☐ | ☐ | ☐ | ☐ | ☐ |
| 2. Explain procedure to client. | ☐ | ☐ | ☐ | ☐ | ☐ |
| 3. Ask client to put on a gown. | ☐ | ☐ | ☐ | ☐ | ☐ |
| *Abdomen* | | | | | |
| 1. Inspect the skin, noting color, vascularity, striae, scars, and lesions (wear gloves to inspect lesions). | ☐ | ☐ | ☐ | ☐ | ☐ |
| 2. Inspect the umbilicus, noting color, location, and contour. | ☐ | ☐ | ☐ | ☐ | ☐ |
| 3. Inspect the contour of the abdomen. | ☐ | ☐ | ☐ | ☐ | ☐ |
| 4. Inspect the symmetry of the abdomen. | ☐ | ☐ | ☐ | ☐ | ☐ |

| Assessment Skill | Findings (Normal or Abnormal) and Notes | | Performance (Satisfactory, Needs Improvement, Unsatisfactory) | | |
|---|---|---|---|---|---|
| | N | A | S | N | U |
| 5. Inspect abdominal movement, noting respiratory movement, aortic pulsations, and/or peristaltic waves. | ☐ | ☐ | ☐ | ☐ | ☐ |
| 6. Auscultate for bowel sounds, noting intensity, pitch, and frequency. | ☐ | ☐ | ☐ | ☐ | ☐ |
| 7. Auscultate for vascular sounds and friction rubs. | ☐ | ☐ | ☐ | ☐ | ☐ |
| 8. Percuss the abdomen for tone. | ☐ | ☐ | ☐ | ☐ | ☐ |
| 9. Percuss the liver. | ☐ | ☐ | ☐ | ☐ | ☐ |
| 10. Perform the scratch test. | ☐ | ☐ | ☐ | ☐ | ☐ |
| 11. Percuss the spleen. | ☐ | ☐ | ☐ | ☐ | ☐ |
| 12. Perform blunt percussion on the liver and the kidneys. | ☐ | ☐ | ☐ | ☐ | ☐ |
| 13. Perform light palpation, noting tenderness or guarding in all quadrants. | ☐ | ☐ | ☐ | ☐ | ☐ |
| 14. Perform deep palpation, noting tenderness or masses in all quadrants. | ☐ | ☐ | ☐ | ☐ | ☐ |
| 15. Palpate the umbilicus. | ☐ | ☐ | ☐ | ☐ | ☐ |
| 16. Palpate the aorta. | ☐ | ☐ | ☐ | ☐ | ☐ |
| 17. Palpate the liver, noting consistency and tenderness. | ☐ | ☐ | ☐ | ☐ | ☐ |
| 18. Palpate the spleen, noting consistency and tenderness. | ☐ | ☐ | ☐ | ☐ | ☐ |
| 19. Palpate the kidneys. | ☐ | ☐ | ☐ | ☐ | ☐ |
| 20. Palpate the urinary bladder. | ☐ | ☐ | ☐ | ☐ | ☐ |
| 21. Perform the test for shifting dullness. | ☐ | ☐ | ☐ | ☐ | ☐ |
| 22. Perform the fluid wave test. | ☐ | ☐ | ☐ | ☐ | ☐ |
| 23. Perform the ballottement test. | ☐ | ☐ | ☐ | ☐ | ☐ |
| 24. Perform tests for appendicitis: | ☐ | ☐ | ☐ | ☐ | ☐ |
| Rebound tenderness | ☐ | ☐ | ☐ | ☐ | ☐ |
| Rovsing's sign | ☐ | ☐ | ☐ | ☐ | ☐ |
| Referred rebound tenderness | ☐ | ☐ | ☐ | ☐ | ☐ |
| Psoas sign | ☐ | ☐ | ☐ | ☐ | ☐ |
| Obturator sign | ☐ | ☐ | ☐ | ☐ | ☐ |
| Hypersensitivity test | ☐ | ☐ | ☐ | ☐ | ☐ |
| 25. Perform test for cholecystitis (Murphy's sign). | ☐ | ☐ | ☐ | ☐ | ☐ |
| *Analysis of Data* | | | | | |
| 1. Formulate nursing diagnoses (wellness, risk, actual). | ☐ | ☐ | ☐ | ☐ | ☐ |
| 2. Formulate collaborative problems. | ☐ | ☐ | ☐ | ☐ | ☐ |
| 3. Make necessary referrals. | ☐ | ☐ | ☐ | ☐ | ☐ |

# CHAPTER POSTTEST

**Activity F** MULTIPLE CHOICE

*Choose the one best answer for each of the following multiple-choice questions.*

____ 1. To percuss the liver of an adult client, the nurse should begin the abdominal assessment at the client's
   a. right upper quadrant.
   b. right lower quadrant.
   c. left upper quadrant.
   d. left lower quadrant.

____ 2. To palpate for tenderness of an adult client's appendix, the nurse should begin the abdominal assessment at the client's
   a. left upper quadrant.
   b. left lower quadrant.
   c. right upper quadrant.
   d. right lower quadrant.

____ 3. To palpate the spleen of an adult client, the nurse should begin the abdominal assessment of the client at the
   a. left lower quadrant.
   b. left upper quadrant.
   c. right upper quadrant.
   d. right lower quadrant.

____ 4. The nurse plans to assess an adult client's kidneys for tenderness. The nurse should assess the area at the
   a. right upper quadrant.
   b. left upper quadrant.
   c. external oblique angle.
   d. costovertebral angle.

____ 5. A client visits the clinic because she experienced bright hematemesis yesterday. The nurse should refer the client to a physician because this symptom is indicative of
   a. stomach ulcers.
   b. pancreatic cancer.
   c. decreased gastric motility.
   d. abdominal tumors.

____ 6. The nurse is assessing an older adult client who has lost 5 pounds since her last visit 1 year ago. The client tells the nurse that her husband died 2 months ago. The nurse should further assess the client for
   a. peptic ulcer.
   b. bulimia.
   c. appetite changes.
   d. pancreatic disorders.

____ **7.** A client visits the clinic for a routine examination. The client tells the nurse that she has become constipated because she is taking iron tablets prescribed for anemia. The nurse has instructed the client about the use of iron preparations and possible constipation. The nurse determines that the client has understood the instructions when she says

    **a.** "I can decrease the constipation if I eat foods high in fiber and drink water."

    **b.** "I should cut down on the number of iron tablets I am taking each day."

    **c.** "Constipation should decrease if I take the iron tablets with milk."

    **d.** "I should discontinue the iron tablets and eat foods that are high in iron."

____ **8.** The nurse is caring for a female client during her first postoperative day after a temporary colostomy. The client refuses to look at the colostomy bag or the area. A priority nursing diagnosis for this client is

    **a.** denial related to temporary colostomy.

    **b.** fear related to potential outcome of surgery.

    **c.** disturbed body image related to temporary colostomy.

    **d.** altered role functioning related to frequent colostomy bag changes.

____ **9.** The nurse is preparing to assess the abdomen of a hospitalized client 2 days after abdominal surgery. The nurse should first

    **a.** palpate the incision site.

    **b.** auscultate for bowel sounds.

    **c.** percuss for tympany.

    **d.** inspect the abdominal area.

____ **10.** The nurse is planning to assess the abdomen of an adult male client. Before the nurse begins the assessment, the nurse should

    **a.** ask the client to empty his bladder.

    **b.** place the client in a side-lying position.

    **c.** ask the client to hold his breath for a few seconds.

    **d.** tell the client to raise his arms above his head.

____ **11.** The nurse is assessing the abdomen of an adult client and observes a purple discoloration at the flanks. The nurse should refer the client to a physician for possible

    **a.** liver disease.

    **b.** abdominal distention.

    **c.** Cushing's syndrome.

    **d.** internal bleeding.

____ **12.** While assessing an adult client's abdomen, the nurse observes that the client's umbilicus is deviated to the left. The nurse should refer the client to a physician for possible

    **a.** gallbladder disease.

    **b.** cachexia.

    **c.** kidney trauma.

    **d.** masses.

____ **13.** While assessing an adult client's abdomen, the nurse observes that the client's umbilicus is enlarged and everted. The nurse should refer the client to a physician for possible

    **a.** umbilical hernia.

    **b.** ascites.

    **c.** intraabdominal bleeding.

    **d.** pancreatitis.

____ **14.** The nurse assesses an adult male client's abdomen and observes diminished abdominal respiration. The nurse determines that the client should be further assessed for

   **a.** liver disease.

   **b.** umbilical hernia.

   **c.** intestinal obstruction.

   **d.** peritoneal irritation.

____ **15.** The nurse is assessing the bowel sounds of an adult client. After listening to each quadrant, the nurse determines that bowel sounds are not present. The nurse should refer the client to a physician for possible

   **a.** aortic aneurysm.

   **b.** paralytic ileus.

   **c.** gastroenteritis.

   **d.** fluid and electrolyte imbalances.

____ **16.** While assessing the abdominal sounds of an adult client, the nurse hears high-pitched tingling sounds throughout the distended abdomen. The nurse should refer the client to a physician for possible

   **a.** intestinal obstruction.

   **b.** gastroenteritis.

   **c.** inflamed appendix.

   **d.** cirrhosis of the liver.

____ **17.** During a physical examination of an adult client, the nurse is preparing to auscultate the client's abdomen. The nurse should

   **a.** palpate the abdomen before auscultation.

   **b.** listen in each quadrant for 15 seconds.

   **c.** use the diaphragm of the stethoscope.

   **d.** begin auscultation in the left upper quadrant.

____ **18.** To palpate the spleen of an adult client, the nurse should

   **a.** ask the client to exhale deeply.

   **b.** place the right hand below the left costal margin.

   **c.** point the fingers of the left hand downward.

   **d.** ask the client to remain in a supine position.

____ **19.** The nurse is planning to assess a client's abdomen for rebound tenderness. The nurse should

   **a.** perform this abdominal assessment first.

   **b.** ask the client to assume a side-lying position.

   **c.** palpate lightly while slowly releasing pressure.

   **d.** palpate deeply while quickly releasing pressure.

____ **20.** To assess an adult client for possible appendicitis and a positive psoas sign, the nurse should

   **a.** rotate the client's knee internally.

   **b.** palpate at the lower right quadrant.

   **c.** raise the client's right leg from the hip.

   **d.** support the client's right knee and ankle.

**Activity G** **CRITICAL THINKING AND CASE STUDIES**

1. Suppose you find that a client's abdomen is distended, pale, and taut. Describe the tests you might perform, differentiating between the fluid wave test and the test for shifting dullness.

2. You suspect that a client may have appendicitis. Identify and describe a variety of tests that can be used to detect appendicitis.

3. You suspect that a client may have cholecystitis. Identify and describe the test used to detect cholecystitis.

4. Janet Smith is 63 years old. She has a diagnosis of rheumatoid arthritis, for which she takes 8 to 10 aspirins daily to relieve pain. She states that for the past couple of days her stools have been dark and tarry-looking and her stomach has been upset and "queasy." Hoping to settle her stomach, she changed her diet in the past 2 days to include only soups and fluids. She tells you that the only other medication she takes is a calcium supplement.

   a. Describe the most likely cause for the client's upset stomach.

   b. Describe the type of precipitating factors you would expect to find during an interview with Ms. Smith.

5. On the basis of the following assessment information, work through the steps of analyzing the data. Identify abnormal data and strengths in **subjective and objective findings**, assemble **cue clusters**, draw **inferences**, make possible **nursing diagnoses**, identify **defining characteristics**, **confirm or rule out** the nursing diagnosis, and **document** your conclusions. Use the blank diagnostic analysis charts provided at the end of this book to guide your thinking. You may want to write on the chart or use separate paper. Propose nursing diagnoses that are specific to the client in the case study. Identify collaborative problems, if any, for this client. Finally, identify data, if any, that point toward a medical problem requiring a referral.

Mrs. Vera Wagner is a 60-year-old white woman who emigrated from Germany to the United States at the age of 18. She has come to her primary care physician's office with her daughter. She tells you, "My daughter made me come here because I have had bad stomach pains for about 6 weeks." After you ask about the character, onset, location, duration, severity, and pattern of the pain as well as associated symptoms (COLDSPA), such as what relieves the pain and what functions are affected by pain, you learn the following information. The pain is aching epigastric pain, fairly continuous, and worse at night. It radiates to her back when she lies down. The pain gets progressively worse, is not affected by eating, and interferes with her daily function (it prevented her from attending her grandson's birthday party; it also wakes her up at night). Additionally, Mrs. Wagner admits to loss of appetite, mild nausea, heartburn, and fatigue. For the past several months she has felt full soon after beginning a meal. She tells you that she was afraid to tell her doctor this because "He always says I worry too much."

A review of Mrs. Wagner's chart discloses that she had four normal vaginal deliveries, several bladder and kidney infections, a total abdominal hysterectomy at age 50 for uterine fibroids, cholecystectomy at age 55, two episodes of deep vein thrombosis in the past few years, allergy to penicillin, and stomach sensitivity to medicines (e.g., aspirin). Four years ago she had gastric endoscopy and upper gastrointestinal (GI) barium swallow studies for complaints of heartburn and difficulty swallowing. The results revealed delayed esophageal peristalsis.

Mrs. Wagner takes estrogen and calcium daily (in the form of Tums) as recommended by her physician as a source of hormone and calcium after surgical menopause. She tells you that she has recently started to take acetaminophen once—sometimes twice—daily in the hope that this will relieve her pain. She has had mild temporary relief as a result.

Mrs. Wagner's family history reveals that her mother died at age 58 from "liver problems after having half her stomach removed." Mrs. Wagner says she does not smoke, drink, or use drugs. She says that she has eaten the same diet all her life. "I eat good German food, a lot of potatoes and meats. My children tell me I should eat more vegetables and drink more water, but I don't like fruits and vegetables and I'd rather drink coffee." In response to your question about exercise, you learn that Mrs. Wagner walks to the post office every day, and "I pick up after my husband around the house—does that count?" You comment that Mrs. Wagner looks upset, and she tells you that she is very concerned about her pain. "I have always been strong and healthy, and now I am getting old and sick. It is depressing."

Your physical assessment reveals a firmly palpable left supraclavicular node, approximately 2 cm in diameter, nonmobile, and nontender, as well as the following abdominal findings: abdomen round and symmetric, hysterectomy scar, striae, umbilicus in the midline without inflammation or herniation, slight midline pulsation in the epigastrium. Soft bowel sounds are heard in all four quadrants; no audible bruits. Generalized tympany percussed throughout; span of liver dullness is 13 cm over the MCL, splenic dullness at the 10th intercostal space (ICS), MAL. The abdomen is soft and tender to palpation in the epigastrium; the liver edge descends 2 cm below the right costal margin (RCM) on deep inspiration; no splenomegaly is noted.

## SELF-REFLECTION AND EVALUATION OF LEARNER OBJECTIVES

After you have read Chapter 22 and completed the above review items, please identify to what extent you have met each of the following chapter learning objectives. For those you have met partially or not at all, you will want to review the chapter content for that learning objective.

| Objective | Very Much | Somewhat | Not At All |
|---|---|---|---|
| 1. Describe the structures and the functions of the abdomen. | | | |
| 2. Identify the organs located in each of the quadrants and the nine regions of the abdomen. | | | |
| 3. Obtain an accurate nursing history of the client's abdomen and functions. | | | |
| 4. Differentiate between the three major types of abdominal pain. | | | |
| 5. Describe how to prepare a client for an abdominal exam, and identify the equipment needed. | | | |
| 6. Auscultate the abdomen for bowel sounds, vascular sounds, and friction rubs. | | | |
| 7. Percuss the quadrants of the abdomen, noting the underlying structures, and liver and spleen spans. | | | |
| 8. Perform light and deep palpation of the abdomen, noting any abnormalities. | | | |
| 9. Describe the tests for ballottement and shifting dullness. | | | |
| 10. Describe the five different tests used to detect appendicitis. | | | |
| 11. Describe the test used to detect cholecystitis. | | | |

## CHAPTER 23

# Female Genitalia

## Chapter Overview

The female genitalia consists of internal and external structures, and assessment requires the nurse's tact and sensitivity. The key goals of the assessment are screening and detection of serious or life-threatening problems, such as cervical cancer, and patient education and health promotion. Use the following exercises and quizzes to help you review basic techniques and skills.

## CHAPTER PRETEST

### Activity A MULTIPLE CHOICE

*Choose the one best answer for each of the following multiple-choice questions.*

_____ 1. The skin folds of the labia majora are composed of adipose tissue, sebaceous glands, and
   a. Skene's ducts.
   b. vestibular glands.
   c. sweat glands.
   d. Bartholin's glands.

_____ 2. The visible portion of the clitoris is termed the
   a. corpus.
   b. crura.
   c. vestibule.
   d. glans.

_____ 3. The skin folds of the labia majora and the labia minora form a boat-shaped area termed the
   a. vestibule.
   b. corpus.
   c. Skene's glands.
   d. urethral meatus.

_____ 4. The outermost layer of the vaginal wall is composed of
   a. pink squamous epithelium and connective tissue.
   b. the vascular supply, nerves, and lymphatic channels.
   c. smooth muscle and connective tissue.
   d. connective tissue and the vascular network.

____ **5.** The outer layer of the vaginal wall is under the direct influence of

   **a.** androgen.

   **b.** progesterone.

   **c.** aldosterone.

   **d.** estrogen.

**Activity B** **LABELING ACTIVITIES**

*Label the following structures of the external female genitalia.*

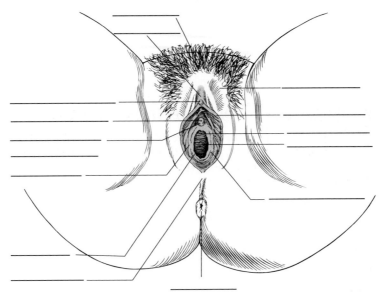

External genitalia.

*Label the structure indicated by the line; then match your answer with the label on the matching figure in Chapter 23 of your textbook.*

*Label the following structures of the internal female genitalia.*

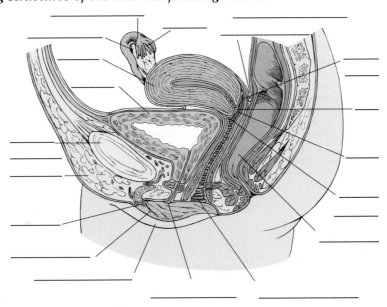

Internal genitalia.

*Label the structure indicated by the line; then match your answer with the label on the matching figure in Chapter 23 of your textbook.*

## Activity C LEARNER ACTIVITIES

### Working with peers in learning lab

*After reading Chapter 23 participate in the following learning activities.*

1. Review the information in "Promote Health: Cervical Cancer" in Chapter 23. Discuss ways to reduce a woman's risk factors for cervical cancer. Next, identify and discuss ethnic groups that are at high risk for cervical cancer.

2. Obtain brochures and literature on cervical cancer and Pap smear testing from the county health department, your campus student health center, or the American Cancer Society. Discuss with your lab partner how to best give a presentation on this topic to teenagers and then to a college-aged group.

3. Using a model of the female genitalia, review the anatomy and function of each anatomic structure. Discuss the assessment findings with your lab partner as they compare with those of an elderly woman.

## Activity D INTERVIEWING AND RECORDING ASSESSMENT FINDINGS

Because of the sensitive nature of completing a female genitalia assessment, you will want to conduct a nursing history either by using a case study provided by your instructor or by having your lab partner assume the role of a fictitious client to answer the questions. Use the following Nursing History Checklist for your interview.

### Nursing History Checklist

| Questions | Normal Findings | Abnormal Findings | Data Missing |
|---|---|---|---|
| *Current Symptoms* | | | |
| 1. Menstrual cycles (date of last period, regular cycles, length, describe typical amount of blood flow, symptoms experienced before or during period)? | | | |
| 2. Age at time of first menstrual period? | | | |
| 3. Menopause: Stopped menstruating (if yes, at what age?) or having irregular periods? What symptoms experienced? | | | |
| 4. Vaginal discharge (unusual in color, amount, or odor)? | | | |
| 5. Pain or itching in genitalia or groin? | | | |
| 6. Lumps, swelling, or masses in genital area? | | | |
| 7. Urinating difficulty, change in urine color, or developed an odor? Difficulty controlling urine? | | | |
| 8. Problems with sexual performance? | | | |
| 9. Recent change in sexual activity pattern or libido? | | | |
| 10. Fertility problems now or in the past? | | | |

| Questions | Normal Findings | Abnormal Findings | Data Missing |
|---|---|---|---|
| *Past History* | | | |
| 1. Previous gynecologic problems and results of any treatment? | | | |
| 2. Date of last pelvic exam by a physician? Date of last Pap smear? Results? | | | |
| 3. Ever diagnosed with a sexually transmitted disease (STD)? How treated? | | | |
| 4. Past pregnancies? Number of pregnancies? Number of children? Possibility of being pregnant now? | | | |
| *Family History* | | | |
| 1. Family history of reproductive or genital cancer? Type? How is the family member related to you? | | | |
| *Lifestyle and Health Practices* | | | |
| 1. Do you smoke, or have you smoked in the past? Amount and length of time? | | | |
| 2. Number of sexual partners? | | | |
| 3. Use of contraceptives? Type? Frequency? | | | |
| 4. Problems with your genitalia that affect your functioning? | | | |
| 5. What is your sexual preference? | | | |
| 6. Comfort level communicating with your partner your sexual likes and dislikes? | | | |
| 7. Fears related to sex? Do you have stress related to sex? | | | |
| 8. Fertility concerns? If so, has this affected your relationship with partner or family? | | | |
| 9. Feelings about going through menopause? | | | |
| 10. Do you perform monthly genital self-exams? | | | |
| 11. Tested for HIV? Results? Why tested? | | | |
| 12. Taking estrogen replacement? Length of treatment? Dosage? | | | |
| 13. Knowledge of toxic shock syndrome? | | | |
| 14. Knowledge of sexually transmitted diseases and their prevention? | | | |

## Activity E  PERFORMING PHYSICAL ASSESSMENT

Obtain a model of the female reproductive system. Use the following Physical Assessment Checklist as your guide to performing a genital assessment. Column 1 can be used by you to guide your physical assessment. Column 2 may be used by your instructor to evaluate your skills as necessary.

### Physical Assessment Checklist

| Assessment Skill | Findings (Normal or Abnormal) and Notes | | Performance (Satisfactory, Needs Improvement, Unsatisfactory) | | |
|---|---|---|---|---|---|
| | N | A | S | N | U |
| 1. Gather equipment (stool, light, speculum, emesis basin filled with warm tap water, Surgilube, cotton-tipped applicators, *Chlamydia* culture tube, culturette, test tube with water, sterile gloves, Ayre spatula (wood stick), and feminine napkins). | ☐ | ☐ | ☐ | ☐ | ☐ |
| 2. Explain procedure to client. | ☐ | ☐ | ☐ | ☐ | ☐ |
| 3. Ask client to put on a gown. | ☐ | ☐ | ☐ | ☐ | ☐ |
| *External Genitalia* | | | | | |
| 1. Inspect the mons pubis. Note pubic hair distribution, signs of infestation. | ☐ | ☐ | ☐ | ☐ | ☐ |
| 2. Inspect the labia majora and perineum. Note lesions, swelling, excoriation. | ☐ | ☐ | ☐ | ☐ | ☐ |
| 3. Inspect the labia minora, clitoris, urethral meatus, and vaginal opening. Note lesions, excoriation, swelling, discharge. | ☐ | ☐ | ☐ | ☐ | ☐ |
| 4. Palpate the Bartholin's glands (if history of swelling or current swelling noted). Note swelling, tenderness, discharge. | ☐ | ☐ | ☐ | ☐ | ☐ |
| 5. Palpate the urethra (if client complains of urethral symptoms or urethritis, or inflammation of Skene's glands is suspected) by inserting gloved index finger into the superior portion of the vagina and milking the urethra from the inside, pushing up and out. Observe for drainage. | ☐ | ☐ | ☐ | ☐ | ☐ |
| *Internal Genitalia* | | | | | |
| 1. Inspect the size of the vaginal opening and the angle of the vagina by moistening gloved index finger with warm water and gently inserting the finger into the vagina. | ☐ | ☐ | ☐ | ☐ | ☐ |
| 2. Assess the vaginal musculature by keeping index finger inserted in the vaginal opening and asking client to squeeze around your finger. Using middle and index fingers to separate the labia minora, ask client to bear down. Observe for bulging or discharge of urine. | ☐ | ☐ | ☐ | ☐ | ☐ |
| 3. Perform the speculum examination:<br>a. Inspect the cervix for color, size, position, surface, os, discharge, or lesions. | ☐ | ☐ | ☐ | ☐ | ☐ |
| b. Obtain specimens for the Pap smear and, if indicated, cultures to test for STDs. | ☐ | ☐ | ☐ | ☐ | ☐ |
| c. Inspect the vagina, unlocking the speculum and inspecting the vagina as the partially open speculum is slowly rotated and removed. Note color, surface, consistency, and discharge. | ☐ | ☐ | ☐ | ☐ | ☐ |

| Assessment Skill | Findings (Normal or Abnormal) and Notes | | Performance (Satisfactory, Needs Improvement, Unsatisfactory) | | |
|---|---|---|---|---|---|
| | N | A | S | N | U |
| 4. Perform the bimanual examination by placing nondominant hand on lower abdomen and inserting gloved lubricated index and middle fingers into the vaginal opening, applying pressure to the posterior wall, and waiting for the opening to relax. Palpate the ovaries by sliding your intravaginal fingers to the right lateral fornix and attempting to palpate the left and then right ovaries. Note size, shape, consistency, mobility, and tenderness. Observe for secretions as fingers are withdrawn. | ☐ | ☐ | ☐ | ☐ | ☐ |
| 5. Perform the rectovaginal examination by changing gloves on dominant hand and lubricating index and middle fingers. Ask client to bear down. Insert index finger into the vagina and middle finger into the rectum. While pushing down on the abdominal wall with the other hand, palpate the internal reproductive structures through the anterior rectal wall, with attention to the area behind the cervix, the rectovaginal septum, the cul-de-sac, and the posterior uterine wall. | ☐ | ☐ | ☐ | ☐ | ☐ |
| *Analysis of Data* | | | | | |
| 1. Formulate nursing diagnoses (wellness, risk, actual). | ☐ | ☐ | ☐ | ☐ | ☐ |
| 2. Formulate collaborative problems. | ☐ | ☐ | ☐ | ☐ | ☐ |
| 3. Make necessary referrals. | ☐ | ☐ | ☐ | ☐ | ☐ |

# CHAPTER POSTTEST

### Activity F MULTIPLE CHOICE

*Choose the one best answer for each of the following multiple-choice questions.*

_____ **1.** A female client tells the nurse that she may be experiencing premenstrual syndrome. An appropriate question for the nurse to ask the client is

    **a.** "How often are your menstrual periods?"

    **b.** "Do you experience mood swings or bloating?"

    **c.** "Are you experiencing regular menstrual cycles?"

    **d.** "How old were you when you began to menstruate?"

_____ **2.** A 53-year-old client tells the nurse that she thinks she is starting the menopausal phase of her life. The nurse should instruct the client that she may experience

    **a.** hot flashes.

    **b.** increased appetite.

    **c.** vaginal discharge.

    **d.** urinary frequency.

_____ **3.** During assessment of the vaginal area of an adult client, the client tells the nurse that she has had pain in her vaginal area. The nurse should further assess the client for

    **a.** trauma.

    **b.** cancer.

    **c.** pregnancy.

    **d.** infection.

_____ **4.** A female client tells the nurse that she has pain while urinating. Besides obtaining a urinalysis, the nurse should assess the client for

    **a.** kidney trauma.

    **b.** sexually transmitted disease.

    **c.** tumors.

    **d.** infestation.

_____ **5.** An older adult client visits the clinic complaining of urinary incontinence. The nurse should explain to the client that this is often due to

    **a.** decreased urethral elasticity.

    **b.** atrophy of the vaginal mucosa.

    **c.** change in the vaginal pH.

    **d.** decreased estrogen production.

_____ **6.** A female client has scheduled a physical examination, including a Pap smear. The nurse should instruct the client to

    **a.** refrain from douching 48 hours before the examination.

    **b.** bring in a urine sample for testing.

    **c.** drink a large volume of fluid before the examination.

    **d.** refrain from using talcum powder after her shower.

_____ **7.** The nurse is preparing to perform a speculum examination on an adult woman. To lubricate the speculum before insertion, the nurse should use

    **a.** sterile water.

    **b.** K-Y jelly.

    **c.** warm tap water.

    **d.** petroleum jelly.

_____ **8.** The nurse is performing a speculum examination on an adult woman. The nurse is having difficulty inserting the speculum because the client is unable to relax. The nurse should ask the client to

    **a.** bear down.

    **b.** hold her breath.

    **c.** use imagery to relax.

    **d.** take a deep breath.

_____ **9.** The nurse is assessing the genitalia of a female client and detects a bulging anterior wall in the vagina. The nurse should plan to refer the client to a physician for

    **a.** stress incontinence.

    **b.** rectocele.

    **c.** tumor of the vagina.

    **d.** cystocele.

____ **10.** An older adult client visits the clinic for a gynecologic examination. The client tells the nurse that she has been told that she has uterine prolapse. The nurse should further assess the client for

    **a.** stress incontinence.

    **b.** cystocele.

    **c.** a retroverted uterus.

    **d.** diastasis recti.

____ **11.** While assessing the cervix of an adult client, the nurse observes a yellowish discharge from the cervix. The nurse should further assess the client for a/an

    **a.** infection.

    **b.** abnormal lesion.

    **c.** positive pregnancy test result.

    **d.** polyp.

____ **12.** While performing a gynecologic examination, the nurse observes small, painful, ulcer-like lesions with red bases on the client's labia. The nurse should refer the client to a physician for possible

    **a.** herpes simplex virus infection.

    **b.** syphilis.

    **c.** lice.

    **d.** herpes zoster virus infection.

____ **13.** While assessing the genitalia of a female client, the nurse observes moist fleshy lesions on the client's labia. The nurse should refer the client to a physician for possible

    **a.** gonorrhea.

    **b.** herpes simplex virus infection.

    **c.** nabothian cysts.

    **d.** genital warts.

____ **14.** During a gynecologic examination, the nurse observes that the client has a yellow-green frothy vaginal discharge. The nurse should plan to test the client for possible

    **a.** *Trichomonas vaginalis* infection.

    **b.** bacterial vaginosis.

    **c.** atrophic vaginitis.

    **d.** *Chlamydia trachomatis* infection.

____ **15.** A client visits the clinic because she has missed one period and suspects she is pregnant. While assessing the client, the nurse detects a solid, mobile, tender, unilateral adnexal mass. The client's cervix is soft. The nurse suspects that the client may be experiencing

    **a.** normal pregnancy.

    **b.** endometriosis.

    **c.** pelvic inflammatory disease.

    **d.** ectopic pregnancy.

## Activity G  MATCHING

*Match the terms in the left column with the correct description in the right column.*

**Term**

_____ **1.** Skene's glands

_____ **2.** Bartholin's glands

_____ **3.** Os

_____ **4.** Libido

_____ **5.** Pediculosis pubis

_____ **6.** Chadwick's sign

_____ **7.** Mons pubis

_____ **8.** Menopause

_____ **9.** Amenorrhea

_____ **10.** Menorrhagia

_____ **11.** Dysmenorrhea

_____ **12.** Dysuria

**Description**

**a.** Painful menstruation

**b.** Cessation of menstruation

**c.** "Crabs"

**d.** Heavy menstruation

**e.** Secrete mucus to aid in lubrication during intercourse

**f.** Desire for sexual activity

**g.** Secrete mucus to lubricate and maintain moist vaginal environment

**h.** Cervix appears blue rather than pink

**i.** Painful urination

**j.** Absence of menstruation

**k.** Opening in center of cervix

**l.** Round firm pad of adipose tissue that covers the symphysis pubis

## Activity H  CRITICAL THINKING AND CASE STUDIES

**1.** Develop a seminar on prevention of sexually transmitted disease (STD) for a group of college freshmen.

**2.** What variations of the cervix are considered normal?

**3.** Compare and contrast how you would focus the nursing history of the female genitalia for an 18-year-old versus that for an 80-year-old.

**4.** Read the following case study. Develop possible nursing diagnoses that are appropriate for this client.

Ann Smith, 37, has made an appointment with the OB/GYN nurse practitioner. You are asked to compile the nursing history. When you ask Mrs. Smith why she is here today, she looks somewhat embarrassed and answers quietly, "I am having trouble with sexual intercourse." She goes on to explain that she has had decreased interest in sex, and her vagina seems drier than usual. When asked whether she has been able to discuss this problem with her husband, she says, "No ... it is embarrassing ... we have always enjoyed sex, and I feel I am not meeting his needs any more. I can tell he is getting very frustrated. He asks me why we never have sex any more, and I just give excuses of having headaches, being tired, or being too busy."

You ask her what is going on in her life right now, and Ann tells you that she is under a lot of stress at her marketing job and that lately she has had to help her two kids, aged 10 and 8, with a lot of school projects. She is also worried about her mother, who is undergoing tests to determine whether she has cancer.

**5.** On the basis of the following assessment information, work through the steps of analyzing the data. Identify abnormal data and strengths in **subjective and objective findings**, assemble **cue clusters**, draw **inferences**, make possible **nursing diagnoses**, identify **defining characteristics**, **confirm or rule out** the nursing diagnosis, and **document** your conclusions. Use the blank diagnostic analysis charts provided at the end of this book to guide your thinking. You may want to write on the chart or use separate paper. Propose nursing diagnoses that are specific to the client in the case study. Identify collaborative problems, if any, for this client. Finally, identify data, if any, that point toward medical problem requiring a referral.

Tina Kehler is a 26-year-old white woman. She is a single mother of two and is employed as a parale-gal in a law firm. She comes to the clinic appearing anxious. She states she is experiencing a brown vaginal discharge that started 2 days ago. When interviewed, she states that her last pelvic examina-tion was 6 months ago. She denies any history of cancer or abnormal Pap smear results. Her last men-strual period was normal and ended 1 week ago today. She has never been tested for HIV. She admits to unprotected sex 3 weeks ago with her boyfriend. A Norplant birth control device was placed in her left arm 1 year ago. Tina denies smoking, states that she does not follow any special diet, and does not exercise on a regular basis. She explains that she is not comfortable discussing this problem with her new boyfriend—"I am afraid he might leave me."

Your physical assessment reveals normal hair distribution and no lesions, masses, or swelling. The labia majora and labia minora are pink, moist, and free of lesions, excoriation, and swelling. A small amount of malodorous brown discharge is noted at the vaginal orifice. There is no bulging at vaginal orifice. The perineum is intact, with a healed episiotomy scar. No discharge is observed on urethral pal-pation. Internal examination reveals cervix to be slightly anterior and pink, with a slit-like os, and free of lesions. A brown discharge is noted on the cervix. The vaginal walls are pink and moist, with streaks of brown discharge. Bimanual examination reveals a mobile, firm, but tender cervix. The fundus is pal-pated at the level of the symphysis pubis. The ovaries are palpated bilaterally without lesions and are approximately 3 cm. The right ovary is very tender on palpation. A routine Pap smear is performed, and culture specimens are taken. A smooth, firm, mobile, nontender posterior uterine wall and a smooth, firm, thin, movable rectovaginal septum are palpated during rectovaginal palpation.

## SELF-REFLECTION AND EVALUATION OF LEARNER OBJECTIVES

After you have read Chapter 23 and completed the above review items, please identify to what degree you have met each of the following chapter learning objectives. For any objective that you have met partially or not at all, you will want to review the chapter content for that learning objective.

| Objective | Very Much | Somewhat | Not At All |
|---|---|---|---|
| 1. Describe the structure and functions of the female genitalia. | | | |
| 2. Discuss risk factors for cervical cancer and ways to reduce these risk factors. | | | |
| 3. Discuss the incidence of cervical cancer across cultures. | | | |
| 4. Obtain an accurate nursing history of the female client's genitalia. | | | |
| 5. Explain how to prepare the client for a genitalia examination. | | | |
| 6. Describe the equipment necessary to perform an examination of the female genitalia. | | | |
| 7. Assess the external genitalia by inspecting the mons pubis for pubic hair distribution and perineum for lesions, swelling, and excoriation. | | | |
| 8. Inspect the labia minora, clitoris, urethral meatus, and vaginal opening for lesions, excoriation, swelling, and discharge. | | | |
| 9. Palpate the Bartholin's glands (if labia swelling noted or a history of swelling) noting swelling, tenderness, and discharge. | | | |

| Objective | Very Much | Somewhat | Not At All |
|---|---|---|---|
| 10. Palpate the urethra if the client has urethral complaints or symptoms. | | | |
| 11. Assess the internal female genitalia by inspecting the size of the vaginal opening, the angle of the vagina, and the vaginal musculature. | | | |
| 12. Assess the internal female genitalia, using the speculum to inspect the vagina for color, size, position, surface, os, consistency, discharge, and lesions. | | | |
| 13. Perform the bimanual examination of the vaginal wall, assessing for texture and tenderness and palpating the cervix for contour, consistency, mobility, and tenderness. | | | |
| 14. Palpate the client's uterus for position, shape, and consistency. | | | |
| 15. Palpate the client's ovaries for size, shape, consistency, mobility, and tenderness. | | | |
| 16. Perform the rectovaginal examination to assess the rectovaginal septum and posterior uterine wall. | | | |

# Male Genitalia

## Chapter Overview

An assessment of male genital structures requires an understanding of both the external and the internal genitalia as well as the inguinal (or groin) structures, because hernias are common in this area. Throughout the assessment, the nurse should keep in mind that Western culture emphasizes the importance of the male sex role and that self-esteem and body image are entwined with the male sex role. Therefore, the assessment may be uncomfortable or embarrassing for the client as well as for the nurse. The key goals of the assessment are screening and detection of serious or life-threatening problems, such as testicular cancer, and patient education and health promotion. Use the following exercises and quizzes to help you review basic techniques and skills.

## CHAPTER PRETEST

### Activity A MULTIPLE CHOICE

*Choose the one best answer for each of the following multiple-choice questions.*

_____ 1. The corpora spongiosum extends distally to form the acorn-shaped
   a. glans.
   b. frenulum.
   c. corona.
   d. scrotum.

_____ 2. If a male client is uncircumcised, the glans of the penis is covered by the
   a. epididymis.
   b. frenulum.
   c. corona.
   d. foreskin.

_____ 3. The testes in the male scrotum are
   a. joined with the ejaculatory duct.
   b. suspended by the spermatic cord.
   c. able to produce progesterone.
   d. the location of the vas deferens.

_____ **4.** The inguinal canal in a male client is located

   **a.** just above and parallel to the inguinal ligament.

   **b.** anteriorly above the symphysis pubis.

   **c.** anterior to the external inguinal ring.

   **d.** posterior to the superior iliac ring.

**Activity B** **LABELING ACTIVITIES**

*Label the following structures of the external and internal genitalia.*

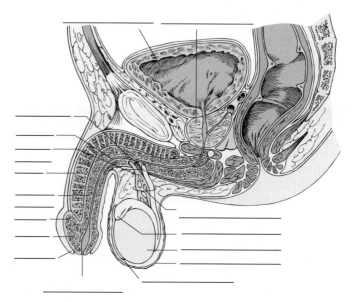

External and internal genitalia.

*Label the structure indicated by the line; then match your answer with the label on the matching figure in Chapter 24 of your textbook.*

*Label the following structures of the inguinal area.*

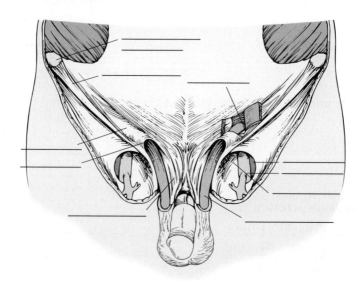

Inguinal area.

*Label the structure indicated by the line; then match your answer with the label on the matching figure in Chapter 24 of your textbook.*

**Activity C** **LEARNER ACTIVITIES**

### Working with peers in the learning lab

### After reading Chapter 24, participate in the following learning activities.

1. Review the information in "Promote Health: HIV/AIDS" in Chapter 24 of the textbook. Determine your own risk for HIV/AIDS. Identify ways to reduce your risk factors. Which groups are at higher risk for contracting HIV/AIDS?

2. Obtain brochures and literature on sexually transmitted diseases (STDs) from the county health department or your campus student health center. Discuss with your lab partner the best way to give a presentation on this topic to teenagers and then to a college-aged group.

3. Review the material from your textbook on testicular cancer and testicular self-examination with a lab partner, and discuss how you would teach a client how to examine himself.

4. Using a model of the male genitalia, review the anatomy and function of each anatomic structure. Discuss the assessment findings with your lab partner, and then compare those findings with what you would find in an elderly man.

**Activity D** **INTERVIEWING AND RECORDING ASSESSMENT FINDINGS**

Because of the sensitive nature of completing a male genitalia assessment, you will want to conduct a nursing history either by using a case study provided by your instructor or by having your lab partner assume the role of a fictitious client to answer the questions. Use the following Nursing History Checklist for your interview.

**Nursing History Checklist**

| Questions | Normal Findings | Abnormal Findings | Data Missing |
|---|---|---|---|
| *Current Symptoms* | | | |
| 1. Pain in penis, scrotum, testes, or groin? | | | |
| 2. Lesions on penis or genital area? | | | |
| 3. Lumps, swelling, or masses in scrotum, genital, or groin area? | | | |
| 4. Heaviness or dragging feeling in scrotum? | | | |
| 5. Difficulty urinating (hesitancy, frequency, or difficulty starting or maintaining a stream)? | | | |
| 6. Changes in color, odor, or amount of urine? | | | |
| 7. Pain or burning when urinating? | | | |
| 8. Incontinence or dribbling of urine? | | | |
| 9. Recent changes in sexual activity pattern or sexual desire? | | | |
| 10. Difficulty attaining or maintaining an erection? Problems with ejaculation? | | | |
| 11. Fertility problems? | | | |

| Questions | Normal Findings | Abnormal Findings | Data Missing |
|---|---|---|---|
| *Past History* | | | |
| 1. Previous problems related to your pelvic area (surgeries, treatments, and results)? | | | |
| 2. Date of last testicular exam by physician or nurse practitioner? Results? | | | |
| 3. Tested for HIV? Why tested? Results? | | | |
| *Family History* | | | |
| 1. Family history of prostate or testicular cancer? What type, and which family member(s)? | | | |
| *Lifestyle and Health Practices* | | | |
| 1. Number of sexual partners? | | | |
| 2. Kind of birth control method? | | | |
| 3. Current or past exposure to chemicals or radiation? | | | |
| 4. Usual daily activity? | | | |
| 5. Heavy lifting? | | | |
| 6. Genital problems that affect daily activities? | | | |
| 7. Fertility concerns? Effect on relationship? | | | |
| 8. Sexual preference? | | | |
| 9. Concerns related to sex? | | | |
| 10. Stress related to sex? | | | |
| 11. Knowledge of sexually transmitted diseases and prevention? | | | |
| 12. Do you perform testicular self-examination? Date last performed? | | | |

## Activity E  PERFORMING PHYSICAL ASSESSMENT

Use the following Physical Assessment Checklist as your guide to performing an assessment of male genitalia. Column 1 can be used by you to guide your physical assessment. Column 2 may be used by your instructor to evaluate your skills as necessary.

### Physical Assessment Checklist

| Assessment Skill | Findings (Normal or Abnormal) and Notes | | Performance (Satisfactory, Needs Improvement, Unsatisfactory) | | |
|---|---|---|---|---|---|
| | N | A | S | N | U |
| 1. Gather equipment (gloves, stool, gown, penlight). | ☐ | ☐ | ☐ | ☐ | ☐ |
| 2. Explain procedure to client. | ☐ | ☐ | ☐ | ☐ | ☐ |
| 3. Ask client to put on gown. | ☐ | ☐ | ☐ | ☐ | ☐ |

| Assessment Skill | Findings (Normal or Abnormal) and Notes | | Performance (Satisfactory, Needs Improvement, Unsatisfactory) | | |
|---|---|---|---|---|---|
| | N | A | S | N | U |
| *Penis* | | | | | |
| 1. Inspect the base of penis and pubic hair for growth pattern and excoriation, erythema, or infestation (client is standing while you sit). | ☐ | ☐ | ☐ | ☐ | ☐ |
| 2. Inspect the skin of the shaft for rashes, lesions, or lumps. | ☐ | ☐ | ☐ | ☐ | ☐ |
| 3. Palpate the shaft for hardened areas or areas of tenderness. | ☐ | ☐ | ☐ | ☐ | ☐ |
| 4. Inspect the foreskin (if present) for color, location, and integrity. | ☐ | ☐ | ☐ | ☐ | ☐ |
| 5. Inspect the glans for size, shape, lesions or redness, and location of the urinary meatus on the glans (if uncircumcised, ask him to retract his foreskin to allow for observation). | ☐ | ☐ | ☐ | ☐ | ☐ |
| 6. Palpate for urethral discharge by gently squeezing the glans between the index finger and thumb. | ☐ | ☐ | ☐ | ☐ | ☐ |
| *Scrotum* | | | | | |
| 1. Inspect the size, shape, and position (penis is held out of the way). | ☐ | ☐ | ☐ | ☐ | ☐ |
| 2. Observe for swelling, lumps, or bulges. | ☐ | ☐ | ☐ | ☐ | ☐ |
| 3. Inspect the skin for color, integrity, and the presence of lesions or rashes. (Spread out the scrotal folds of skin to perform an accurate inspection. Lift the sac to inspect the posterior skin.) | ☐ | ☐ | ☐ | ☐ | ☐ |
| 4. Palpate the scrotal contents (testes and epididymis) between your thumb and first two fingers. Note size, shape, consistency, and presence of tenderness or nodules. Palpate each spermatic cord and vas deferens, noting nodules, swelling, or tenderness. | ☐ | ☐ | ☐ | ☐ | ☐ |
| 5. Transilluminate the scrotal contents (if a mass or swelling was noted). Look for a red glow. | ☐ | ☐ | ☐ | ☐ | ☐ |
| *Inguinal Area* | | | | | |
| 1. Inspect for inguinal and femoral hernia, watching for bulges while the client bears down. | ☐ | ☐ | ☐ | ☐ | ☐ |
| 2. Palpate for inguinal hernia, observing for bulges or masses. Have client shift weight to the left to palpate the right inguinal canal. Place index finger into the right scrotum, and press upward to the slit-like opening of the external inguinal ring. With finger in canal or external inguinal ring, ask him to bear down or cough. Repeat for left side. | ☐ | ☐ | ☐ | ☐ | ☐ |
| 3. Palpate for femoral hernia on the front of the thigh in the femoral canal area. Ask him to bear down or cough while feeling for bulges. Repeat on the other side. | ☐ | ☐ | ☐ | ☐ | ☐ |
| 4. Inspect and palpate for scrotal hernia (if a mass was detected during inspection or palpation of the scrotum). Ask client to lie down, and note whether the bulge disappears. If it remains, auscultate it for bowel sounds. Then gently palpate the mass, and try to push it up into the abdomen unless it is too tender. | ☐ | ☐ | ☐ | ☐ | ☐ |

| Assessment Skill | Findings (Normal or Abnormal) and Notes | | Performance (Satisfactory, Needs Improvement, Unsatisfactory) | | |
|---|---|---|---|---|---|
| | N | A | S | N | U |
| *Analysis of Data* | | | | | |
| 1. Formulate nursing diagnoses (wellness, risk, actual). | ☐ | ☐ | ☐ | ☐ | ☐ |
| 2. Formulate collaborative problems. | ☐ | ☐ | ☐ | ☐ | ☐ |
| 3. Make necessary referrals. | ☐ | ☐ | ☐ | ☐ | ☐ |

# CHAPTER POSTTEST

**Activity F   MULTIPLE CHOICE**

*Choose the one best answer for each of the following multiple-choice questions.*

_____ **1.** During assessment of an elderly male client, the client tells the nurse that he has had difficulty urinating for the past few weeks. The nurse should refer the client to the physician for possible

  **a.** inguinal hernia.

  **b.** sexually transmitted disease.

  **c.** impotence.

  **d.** prostate enlargement.

_____ **2.** A 25-year-old client asks the nurse how often he should have a testicular examination. After instructing the client about the American Cancer Society's guidelines, the nurse determines that the client has understood the instructions when he says he should have a testicular examination every

  **a.** year.

  **b.** 2 years.

  **c.** 3 years.

  **d.** 4 years.

_____ **3.** A 45-year-old male client tells the nurse that he has had problems in having an erection for the last couple of weeks but is "doing better now." The nurse should explain to the client that

  **a.** transient periods of erectile dysfunction are common.

  **b.** impotence in males should be investigated.

  **c.** transient impotence may be indicative of prostate enlargement.

  **d.** inguinal hernias have been associated with transient impotence.

_____ **4.** A male client tells the nurse that his occupation requires heavy lifting and a great deal of strenuous activity. The nurse should assess the client for

  **a.** signs and symptoms of prostate enlargement.

  **b.** erectile dysfunction.

  **c.** inguinal hernia.

  **d.** urinary tract infection.

_____ 5. During assessment of an adult client, which of the following lifestyle practices would indicate to the nurse that the client may be at high risk for HIV/AIDS? A client who

**a.** uses a condom on a regular basis.

**b.** has multiple female partners.

**c.** smokes marijuana occasionally.

**d.** has anal intercourse with other males.

_____ 6. During assessment of the genitalia of an adult male, the client has an erection. The nurse should

**a.** explain to the client that this often happens during an examination.

**b.** cover the client's genitals and discontinue the examination.

**c.** allow the client time to rest before proceeding with the examination.

**d.** continue the examination in an unhurried manner.

_____ 7. Before beginning the examination of the genitalia of an adult male client, the nurse should

**a.** ask the client to empty his bladder.

**b.** tell the client that he will remain in a supine position.

**c.** ask the client to leave his shirt in place.

**d.** tell the client that he may leave his underwear in place.

_____ 8. While assessing an adult male client, the nurse detects pimple-like lesions on the client's glans. The nurse explains the need for a referral to the client. The nurse determines that the client has understood the instructions when the client says he may have

**a.** venereal warts.

**b.** herpes infection.

**c.** syphilis.

**d.** gonorrhea.

_____ 9. While inspecting the genitalia of a male client, the nurse observes a chancre lesion under the foreskin. The nurse has explained this observation to the client. The nurse determines that the client understands the need for a referral when the client says that chancre lesions are associated with

**a.** herpes virus.

**b.** syphilis.

**c.** papilloma virus.

**d.** gonorrhea.

_____ 10. A male client visits the clinic and tells the nurse that he has had a white discharge from his penis for the past few days. The nurse should refer the client to a physician for possible

**a.** urethritis.

**b.** gonorrhea.

**c.** herpes infection.

**d.** syphilis.

_____ 11. The nurse has assessed a male client and determines that one of the testes is absent. The nurse should explain to the client that this condition is termed

**a.** hypospadias.

**b.** hematocele.

**c.** cryptorchidism.

**d.** orchitis.

____ 12. The nurse is assessing the genitalia of an adult male client when he tells the nurse that his testes are swollen and painful. The nurse should refer the client to a physician for possible

    **a.** cancer.

    **b.** hydrocele.

    **c.** epididymitis.

    **d.** hematocele.

____ 13. While transilluminating the scrotal contents in a male adult client, the nurse does not detect a red glow. The nurse should refer the client to a physician for possible

    **a.** spermatocele.

    **b.** orchitis.

    **c.** hydrocele.

    **d.** varicocele.

____ 14. The nurse suspects that a male client may have a hernia. The nurse should further assess the client for

    **a.** bruising at the site.

    **b.** urinary tract infection.

    **c.** cysts at the spermatic cord.

    **d.** bowel sounds at the bulge.

____ 15. A male client tells the nurse that he has received a diagnosis of hernia. He visits the clinic because he is nauseated and has extreme tenderness on the left side. The nurse should

    **a.** refer the client to an emergency room.

    **b.** try to push the mass into the abdomen.

    **c.** assess for a mass on the right side.

    **d.** assess the client's vital signs.

### Activity G   MATCHING

*Match the terms in the left column with the correct descriptions in the right column.*

| Term | Description |
|------|-------------|
| ____ **1.** Corona | **a.** Retracted foreskin that cannot be returned to cover the glans |
| ____ **2.** Hernia | **b.** Displacement of the urinary meatus to the dorsal surface of the penis |
| ____ **3.** Chancres | |
| ____ **4.** Phimosis | **c.** Base of the glans |
| ____ **5.** Paraphimosis | **d.** Undescended testicle |
| ____ **6.** Hypospadias | **e.** Protrusion of bowel through weakened muscles |
| ____ **7.** Epispadias | **f.** A tight foreskin that cannot be retracted |
| ____ **8.** Cryptorchidism | **g.** Red oval ulcerations caused by syphilis |
| | **h.** Displacement of the urinary meatus to the ventral surface of the penis |

### Activity H   CRITICAL THINKING AND CASE STUDIES

**1.** Why would it be necessary to transilluminate the scrotal contents, and what are the possible findings and their significance?

2. During assessment for a hernia, what is the rationale for asking the client to cough or bear down?

3. Compare and contrast how you would focus the nursing history of the male genitalia for an 18-year-old versus that for an 80-year-old.

4. On the basis of the following assessment information, work through the steps of analyzing the data. Identify abnormal data and strengths in **subjective and objective findings**, assemble **cue clusters**, draw **inferences**, make possible **nursing diagnoses**, identify **defining characteristics**, **confirm or rule out** the nursing diagnosis, and **document** your conclusions. Use the blank diagnostic analysis charts provided at the end of this book to guide your thinking. You may want to write on the chart or use separate paper. Propose nursing diagnoses that are specific to the client in the case study. Identify collaborative problems, if any, for this client. Finally, identify data, if any, that point toward a medical problem requiring a referral.

Don Carse is a 32-year-old African-American man who arrives at the clinic for an evaluation by a nurse practitioner. He complains that his right testicle feels heavy or weighted down. He appears very nervous and explains that he has been experiencing this feeling for about 3 months. He explains that he came in today because "my wife is very upset about it and pleaded with me to go to a doctor." When interviewed, the client reports that he does not have trouble becoming erect, but he states, "I feel like it takes longer to ejaculate." He denies past medical problems or a family history of cancer.

He explains that he has not had a genital examination in years—"I really don't like to go to the doctor unless I have a problem." He says he has never done, and does not really know how to do, a testicular self-examination. He tells you that he is afraid he might have cancer.

Your physical examination reveals a normal adult pubic hair pattern and no excoriation or infestation in the pubic hair or at the base of the penis. The penis is circumcised and free of rashes, lesions, and discoloration. No tenderness or nodules are noted on palpation. The urinary meatus is located in the mid-glans, and no discharge is revealed on palpation. Inspection of the scrotum reveals an enlarged right scrotum and redness on the scrotal sac, but no lesions. Palpation of the left testicle, epididymis, and spermatic cord reveal no tenderness, nodules, or swelling. Palpation of the right testicle reveals a 2-cm, nonmobile, nontender nodule on the anterior portion of the testicle. The left epididymis and spermatic cord are free of tenderness, nodules, and swelling. No red glow is seen on transillumination of the scrotal contents on either side. No bulges are noted in the inguinal or femoral canal.

## SELF-REFLECTION AND EVALUATION OF LEARNER OBJECTIVES

After you have read Chapter 24 and completed the above review items, please identify to what degree you have met each of the following chapter learning objectives. For those objectives that you have met partially or not at all, you will want to review the chapter content for that learning objective(s).

| Objective | Very Much | Somewhat | Not At All |
|---|---|---|---|
| 1. Describe the structure and functions of the male genitalia. | | | |
| 2. Discuss risk factors for HIV/AIDS and ways to reduce these risk factors. | | | |
| 3. Discuss the incidence of AIDS across cultures. | | | |
| 4. Obtain an accurate nursing history of the male client's genitalia. | | | |

| Objective | Very Much | Somewhat | Not At All |
|---|---|---|---|
| 5. Explain how to prepare the client for a genitalia examination. | | | |
| 6. Describe the equipment necessary to perform an examination of the male genitalia. | | | |
| 7. Inspect the base of the penis and pubic hair for hair growth pattern and the presence of excoriation, erythema, or infestation. | | | |
| 8. Inspect the skin of the shaft for rashes, lesions, or lumps. | | | |
| 9. Palpate the shaft for hardened areas or tenderness. | | | |
| 10. Inspect the foreskin (if present) for color, location, and integrity. | | | |
| 11. Inspect the glans for size, shape, and presence of lesions or redness. | | | |
| 12. Palpate for urethral discharge. | | | |
| 13. Inspect the client's scrotum for size, shape, and position (observe for swelling, lumps, and bulges) and the skin for color, integrity, and the presence of lesions or rashes. | | | |
| 14. Palpate the client's scrotal sac contents (testes and epididymis) for size, shape, consistency, and presence of tenderness or nodules. Palpate each spermatic cord and vas deferens for nodules, swelling, or tenderness. | | | |
| 15. Transilluminate the scrotal contents if an abnormal mass or swelling is noted. | | | |
| 16. Palpate the client's inguinal area for inguinal and femoral hernias. | | | |
| 17. Palpate for the presence of a scrotal hernia. | | | |
| 18. Describe changes often seen with aging of the male genitalia. | | | |

# Anus, Rectum, and Prostate

The anus and rectum complete the gastrointestinal tract. In men, the prostate gland is integrally entwined with these structures. In both men and women, the colon is also examined during assessment of the rectum and the anus. The assessment is particularly important for detecting signs and symptoms of colon cancer; prostatic conditions, which affect most older men; and other intestinal disorders.

## CHAPTER PRETEST

**Activity A** MULTIPLE CHOICE

*Choose the one best answer for each of the following multiple-choice questions.*

____ **1.** The external sphincter of the anus is

    **a.** composed of smooth muscle.

    **b.** composed of skeletal muscle.

    **c.** composed of striated muscle.

    **d.** under involuntary control.

____ **2.** The external sphincter and internal sphincter of the rectum are divided by the

    **a.** anorectal junction.

    **b.** rectovesical pouch.

    **c.** median sulcus.

    **d.** intersphincteric groove.

____ **3.** The rectum is lined with folds of mucosa, and each fold contains a network of arteries, veins, and visceral nerves. When these veins undergo chronic pressure, the result may be

    **a.** polyps.

    **b.** tumors.

    **c.** fissures.

    **d.** hemorrhoids.

——  **4.** The prostate gland consists of two lobes separated by the

   **a.** median sulcus.

   **b.** rectovesical pouch.

   **c.** anorectal junction.

   **d.** valves of Houston.

——  **5.** The prostate functions to

   **a.** store sperm until ejaculation occurs.

   **b.** secrete a milky substance that neutralizes female acidic secretions.

   **c.** produce the ejaculate that nourishes and protects sperm.

   **d.** produce mucus-like fluid to assist in lubrication.

——  **6.** The Cowper's glands

   **a.** are located inside the rectum.

   **b.** produce a substance to aid in sperm motility.

   **c.** empty into the urethra.

   **d.** can be palpated through the rectum.

**Activity B** **LABELING ACTIVITIES**

*Label the following structures of the anus and rectum.*

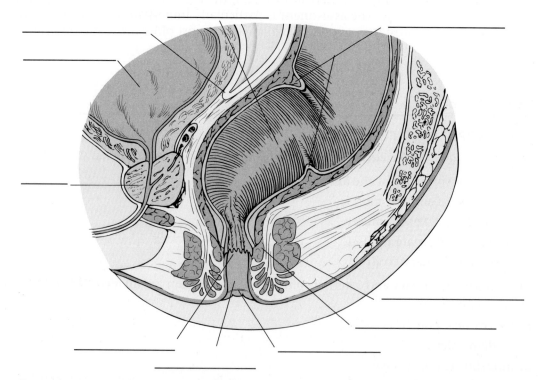

Anus and rectum.

*Label the structure indicated by the line; then match your answer with the label on the matching figure in Chapter 25 of your textbook.*

*Label the following parts of the prostate gland.*

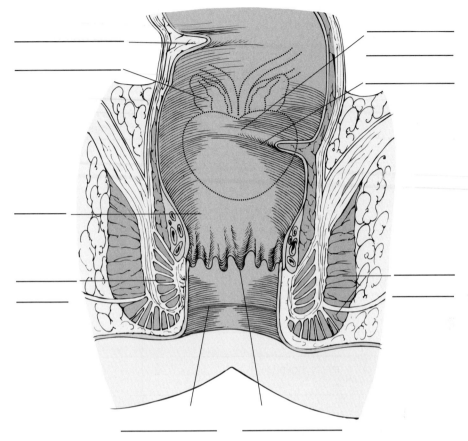

Prostate.

*Label the structure indicated by the line; then match your answer with the label on the matching figure in Chapter 25 of your textbook.*

**Activity C** **LEARNER ACTIVITIES**

### Working with peers in the learning lab

*After reading Chapter 25, participate in the following learning activities.*

1. Review the information in "Promote Health: Colorectal Cancer" in Chapter 25. Determine your own risk for colorectal cancer and ways to reduce these risk factors. Next, identify and discuss the ethnic groups that are at high risk for this type of cancer.

2. Obtain brochures and literature from the county health department, a local health care facility, or the American Cancer Society. Discuss with your lab partner the best way to approach a presentation on this topic to a group of middle-aged men and women.

3. Obtain brochures and literature from the county health department, a local health care facility, or the American Cancer Society about prostate cancer. Discuss with your lab partner how best to present this topic to a group of men. Talk about how you might handle discussing this potentially sensitive topic.

4. Using a model of the anus, rectum, and prostate, review the anatomy and function of each anatomic structure. Discuss the assessment findings with your lab partner as they compare with those of an older person.

## Activity D   INTERVIEWING AND RECORDING ASSESSMENT FINDINGS

Because of the sensitive nature of completing an assessment of the anus, rectum, and prostate, you will want to conduct a nursing history either by using a case study provided by your instructor or by having your lab partner assume the role of a fictitious client to answer the questions. Use the following Nursing History Checklist as a guide to interviewing and recording your findings.

### Nursing History Checklist

| Questions | Normal Findings | Abnormal Findings | Additional Data Needed |
|---|---|---|---|
| *Current Symptoms* | | | |
| 1. Problems with bowels (bowel pattern changes, constipation, diarrhea, bowel control, stool color, blood or mucus in stool, pain or itching in rectal area, hemorrhoids)? | | | |
| 2. Anal and perianal problems (lumps, ulcers, lesions, rashes, redness)? | | | |
| 3. Sacrococcygeal area (pilonidal) swelling, redness, dimpling, or hair? | | | |
| 4. Frequent nighttime urination? | | | |
| *Past History* | | | |
| 1. Previous anal or rectal trauma or surgery, congenital deformities? | | | |
| 2. History of blood in stool? | | | |
| 3. History of prostate enlargement, treatment, or surgery on the prostate? | | | |
| 4. Pattern of health screenings (occult blood, prostate-specific antigen, proctosigmoidoscopy, colonoscopy)? | | | |
| *Lifestyle and Health Practices* | | | |
| 1. Use of laxatives, stool softeners, enemas, or other bowel medications? | | | |
| 2. Practice anal sex? | | | |
| 3. Daily water/fluid intake? | | | |
| 4. Usual diet (high fiber and roughage, saturated fat content)? | | | |
| 5. Usual exercise pattern? | | | |
| 6. Any effect on daily life from anal, rectal, or bowel problems or from prostate problems? | | | |

## Activity E   PERFORMING PHYSICAL ASSESSMENT

Use the following Physical Assessment Checklist as your guide to performing an assessment of the anus, rectum, and prostate gland. Column 1 can be used by you to guide your physical assessment. Column 2 may be used by your instructor to evaluate your skills as necessary.

**Physical Assessment Checklist**

| Assessment Skill | Findings (Normal or Abnormal) and Notes | | Performance (Satisfactory, Needs Improvement, Unsatisfactory) | | |
|---|---|---|---|---|---|
| | N | A | S | N | U |
| 1. Gather equipment (gloves, lubricating gel). | ☐ | ☐ | ☐ | ☐ | ☐ |
| 2. Explain procedure to client. | ☐ | ☐ | ☐ | ☐ | ☐ |
| 3. Ask client to put on a gown. | ☐ | ☐ | ☐ | ☐ | ☐ |
| *Anus and Perianal Area* | | | | | |
| 1. Inspect for lumps, ulcers, lesions, rashes, redness (note size, shape, location, distribution, and configuration). | ☐ | ☐ | ☐ | ☐ | ☐ |
| 2. Inspect sacrococcygeal area for swelling, redness, dimpling, or presence of hair in pilonidal area. | ☐ | ☐ | ☐ | ☐ | ☐ |
| 3. Inspect for rectal prolapse with Valsalva maneuver. | ☐ | ☐ | ☐ | ☐ | ☐ |
| 4. Palpate for anal sphincter tone, tenderness, nodules, or hardness. | ☐ | ☐ | ☐ | ☐ | ☐ |
| *Rectum and Prostate* | | | | | |
| 1. Palpate rectal mucosa for tenderness, irregularities, nodules, and hardness. | ☐ | ☐ | ☐ | ☐ | ☐ |
| 2. Palpate peritoneal cavity for tenderness or nodules, or "rectal shelf." | ☐ | ☐ | ☐ | ☐ | ☐ |
| 3. For males, palpate the prostate gland for tenderness, size, shape, texture, or irregularities. | ☐ | ☐ | ☐ | ☐ | ☐ |
| 4. Inspect the feces for blood, and perform occult blood test. | ☐ | ☐ | ☐ | ☐ | ☐ |
| *Analysis of Data* | | | | | |
| 1. Formulate nursing diagnoses (wellness, risk, actual). | ☐ | ☐ | ☐ | ☐ | ☐ |
| 2. Formulate collaborative problems. | ☐ | ☐ | ☐ | ☐ | ☐ |
| 3. Make necessary referrals. | ☐ | ☐ | ☐ | ☐ | ☐ |

# CHAPTER POSTTEST

**Activity F** **MULTIPLE CHOICE**

*Choose the one best answer for each of the following multiple-choice questions.*

____ **1.** A client visits the clinic and tells the nurse that she has had "runny diarrhea" for 2 days. The nurse should assess the client for

**a.** gastrointestinal infection.

**b.** fecal impaction.

**c.** constipation.

**d.** hemorrhoids.

___ **2.** A client visits the clinic and tells the nurse that his stools have been black for the past 3 days. The nurse should assess the client for

  **a.** gallbladder disease.

  **b.** colitis.

  **c.** polyps.

  **d.** gastrointestinal bleeding.

___ **3.** A client visits the clinic and tells the nurse that his stools have been pale for the past 2 days and his skin has been itching. The nurse should refer the client to a physician for possible

  **a.** biliary disease.

  **b.** cancer.

  **c.** gastrointestinal infection.

  **d.** hemorrhoids.

___ **4.** The nurse has instructed a 55-year-old male client about the need for a stool test for occult blood. The nurse determines that the client understands the instructions when he says the test should be performed every

  **a.** year.

  **b.** 2 years.

  **c.** 3 years.

  **d.** 4 years.

___ **5.** The nurse is planning a presentation on the topic of colorectal cancer to a group of older adults. Which of the following should the nurse plan to include in the presentation?

  **a.** Colorectal cancer rates have steadily fallen over the past 30 years.

  **b.** Eighty percent of those diagnosed with colorectal cancer are younger than 50 years of age.

  **c.** Diets high in fat and low in fiber are associated with colorectal cancer.

  **d.** Colorectal cancer rates are decreasing outside the United States.

___ **6.** A 60-year-old male client asks the nurse about risk factors for prostate cancer. The nurse should explain to the client that one possible risk factor is

  **a.** a high-carbohydrate diet.

  **b.** exposure to sulfur.

  **c.** genetic inheritance.

  **d.** advanced age.

___ **7.** Cultural factors play an important role in the development of prostate cancer in men. Which culture has the highest prostate cancer rate?

  **a.** African-American.

  **b.** White American.

  **c.** Italian.

  **d.** Japanese.

___ **8.** The nurse is planning to assess the anus and rectum of an adult male client. The nurse should position the client in a

  **a.** right lateral position.

  **b.** left lateral position.

  **c.** prone position.

  **d.** knee–chest position.

___ **9.** The nurse is planning to inspect the anal area of an adult male client. To assess for any bulges or lesions, the nurse should ask the client to

   **a.** hold his breath.

   **b.** breathe deeply through his mouth.

   **c.** breathe normally.

   **d.** bear down.

___ **10.** While assessing the anal area of an adult client, the nurse detects redness and excoriation. The nurse determines that this sign is most likely due to

   **a.** internal hemorrhoids.

   **b.** an anorectal fistula.

   **c.** a fungal infection.

   **d.** previous surgery.

___ **11.** While assessing the anal area of an adult client, the nurse observes a reddened swollen area covered by a small tuft of hair located midline on the lower sacrum. The nurse should refer the client to a physician for possible

   **a.** perianal abscess.

   **b.** neurologic disorder.

   **c.** pilonidal cyst.

   **d.** anorectal fistula.

___ **12.** While assessing the anus of an adult client, the nurse detects the presence of small nodules. The nurse should refer the client to a physician for possible

   **a.** polyps.

   **b.** anorectal fistula.

   **c.** hemorrhoids.

   **d.** rectocele.

___ **13.** While assessing the anus of an adult client, the nurse detects a peritoneal protrusion. The nurse should refer the client to a physician for possible

   **a.** anorectal fistula.

   **b.** polyps.

   **c.** prostate enlargement.

   **d.** peritoneal metastasis.

___ **14.** While examining the prostate gland of an older adult, the nurse detects hard fixed nodules. The nurse should refer the client to a physician for possible

   **a.** prostate cancer.

   **b.** benign prostatic hypertrophy.

   **c.** acute prostatitis.

   **d.** prostatocystitis.

**Activity G** **MATCHING**

*Match the terms in the left column with the correct descriptions in the right column.*

**Term**

_____ **1.** Constipation

_____ **2.** Diarrhea

_____ **3.** Hemorrhoids

_____ **4.** Pilonidal cyst

_____ **5.** Prostate-specific antigen (PSA) test

_____ **6.** Proctosigmoidoscopy

_____ **7.** Colonoscopy

_____ **8.** Laxatives

_____ **9.** Enema

_____ **10.** Valsalva maneuver

_____ **11.** Valves of Houston

_____ **12.** Steatorrhea

**Description**

**a.** Three semilunar transverse folds within the rectal interior

**b.** Examination of the rectum and sigmoid colon with the sigmoidoscope

**c.** Client holds the breath and bears down

**d.** Frequent loose stools

**e.** Medicines that loosen the bowel contents and encourage evacuation

**f.** Infrequent hard stool

**g.** Excessive fat in the stool

**h.** Blood test to detect prostate cancer

**i.** Endoscopic examination of the colon, either transabdominally during laparotomy or transanally by colonoscopy

**j.** A hair-containing cyst located in the midline over the coccyx or lower sacrum

**k.** A solution introduced into the rectum to promote evacuation of feces

**l.** Painless flabby papules due to varicose veins; two types, external or internal

**Activity H** **CRITICAL THINKING AND CASE STUDIES**

1. Describe your communication techniques nursing history questions, and physical examination of the anus, rectum, and prostate for a 26-year-old man who engages in anal sex. Include what and how you would teach about the risk factors for various diseases or conditions.

2. Read the following case study. Develop possible appropriate, nursing diagnoses and collaborative problems for Mrs. Cohen.

   Mrs. Cohen is 85 years old. She has a long history of chronic constipation, internal and external hemorrhoids, and heavy use of laxatives. She describes another bout of constipation with no bowel movement for 5 days, but with a feeling of fullness in her rectum. She says that she eats many vegetables when she feels better but gets too weak to cook or exercise, or even to get dressed, when she has these bouts of constipation. On examination, you note internal and external hemorrhoids, a moderate amount of hard formed stool in the rectum, and an area of hardness and irregularity about 2 cm in size in the distal portion of the rectum. The results of her stool test are positive for occult blood.

3. On the basis of the following assessment information, work through the steps of analyzing the data. Identify abnormal data and strengths in **subjective and objective findings**, assemble **cue clusters**, draw **inferences**, make possible **nursing diagnoses**, identify **defining characteristics**, **confirm or rule out** the nursing diagnosis, and **document** your conclusions. Use the blank diagnostic analysis charts provided at the end of this book to guide your thinking. You may want to write on the chart or use separate paper. Propose nursing diagnoses that are specific to the client in the case study. Identify collaborative problems, if any, for this client. Finally, identify data, if any, that point toward a medical problem requiring a referral.

Jim Czerniski, a 35-year-old white man, arrives at his primary care provider's office for his annual physical examination. At the start of the interview, he says to you, "My wife is a nurse and she makes me have a physical examination every year—especially with my family history." On questioning, you discover that his father died 4 years ago from colon cancer and that his brother has undergone three biopsies of rectal polyps. Mr. Czerniski states that he has undergone two rectal polyp biopsies, one last year and one 3 years ago. He denies recent changes in his bowel habits and has not noticed any blood in his stool. Jim looks a bit embarrassed when you ask how much water he drinks and how much fiber and roughage he eats. "I know I am supposed to eat a high-fiber diet and drink lots of water—my wife and I get in fights about it. I try real hard, but I am a Big Mac kinda guy, ya know? I eat what my wife fixes me for dinner, but I eat fast food for breakfast and lunch."

Your physical examination reveals a moist hairless anal opening with a tightly closed external sphincter. The perianal area is free of redness, lumps, ulcers, lesions, and rashes. No bulging or lesions appear when the client performs the Valsalva maneuver. The sacrococcygeal area is smooth and free of redness and hair. During palpation, the client can close the external sphincter around your gloved finger. The anus feels smooth and is free of nodules and hardness. The client reports that he feels no tenderness. As you palpate farther up in the rectum, you can just detect a small soft nodule on the rectal wall. The client says he feels no tenderness. Palpation of the peritoneal cavity area reveals a smooth nontender surface. The prostate gland is palpated as two smooth lobes, 2.5 cm long. They feel rubbery and are nontender. The median sulcus is palpated between the two lobes. When you withdraw your hand, you notice a small amount of semisolid brown stool on your glove. You send the stool to be tested for occult blood.

# SELF-REFLECTION AND EVALUATION OF LEARNER OBJECTIVES

After you have read Chapter 25 and completed the above quizzes and activities, please identify to what degree you have met each of the following chapter learning objectives. For those objectives that you have met partially or not at all, you will want to review the chapter content for that learning objective.

| Objective | Very Much | Somewhat | Not At All |
|---|---|---|---|
| 1. Describe the structures and function of the anus and rectum. | | | |
| 2. Discuss the risk factors for colorectal cancer and ways to reduce these risk factors. | | | |
| 3. Discuss the incidence of colorectal cancer across the cultures. | | | |
| 4. Describe the structures and functions of the prostate. | | | |
| 5. Discuss risk factors for prostate cancer and ways to reduce these risk factors. | | | |
| 6. Discuss the incidence of prostate cancer across the cultures. | | | |
| 7. Obtain an accurate history of the client's anus, rectum, and prostate health. | | | |
| 8. Explain how to prepare the client for an examination of the anus, rectum, and prostate. | | | |
| 9. Describe special care to be used with assessment of the anus, rectum, and prostate. | | | |
| 10. Describe the equipment necessary to perform an assessment of the anus, rectum, and prostate. | | | |

| Objective | Very Much | Somewhat | Not At All |
|---|---|---|---|
| 11. Describe the two physical examination techniques (inspection and palpation) used to assess the anus, rectum, and prostate. | | | |
| 12. Inspect the perianal area for lumps, ulcers, lesions, rashes, or redness and the sacrococcygeal area for swelling, redness, dimpling, or hair. | | | |
| 13. Palpate the anus for sphincter tone, tenderness or pain, nodules, and hardness. | | | |
| 14. Palpate the rectum for tenderness, irregularities, nodules, or hardness. | | | |
| 15. Palpate the peritoneal cavity and prostate (males) for tenderness or nodules. | | | |
| 16. Inspect stool for color and consistency; also test for occult blood. | | | |
| 17. Discuss various nursing diagnoses and collaborative problems commonly seen with assessment of the anus, rectum, and prostate. | | | |

# Musculoskeletal System

## Chapter Overview

Muscles, bones, joints, ligaments, and tendons are the body's infrastructure—the elements that allow humans an upright posture and extensive mobility. Changes that occur in other body systems may have a profound effect on the musculoskeletal system, and changes that occur in the musculoskeletal system itself affect the activities of daily living and quality of life across the life span, making careful and accurate assessment extremely important.

## CHAPTER PRETEST

### Activity A  MULTIPLE CHOICE

*Choose the one best answer for each of the following multiple-choice questions.*

 **1.** One of the functions of a bone is to

   **a.** store fat.

   **b.** produce secretions.

   **c.** produce blood cells.

   **d.** store protein.

 **2.** Bones contain yellow marrow that is composed mainly of

   **a.** fat.

   **b.** protein.

   **c.** cartilage.

   **d.** carbohydrates.

 **3.** The external covering of the bone that contains osteoblasts and blood vessels is termed the

   **a.** cartilage.

   **b.** synovial membrane.

   **c.** connective tissue.

   **d.** periosteum.

 **4.** Skeletal muscles are attached to bones by

   **a.** tendons.

   **b.** cartilage.

   **c.** fibrous connective tissue.

   **d.** ligaments.

_a_  **5.** Joints may be classified as cartilaginous, synovial, or
  **a.** articulate.
  **b.** flexible.
  **c.** immobile.
  **d.** fibrous.

_b_  **6.** Bones in synovial joints are joined together by
  **a.** cartilage.
  **b.** ligaments.
  **c.** tendons.
  **d.** periosteal tissue.

_d_  **7.** When the nurse moves the client's arm away from the midline of the body, the nurse is performing
  **a.** adduction.
  **b.** external rotation.
  **c.** retraction.
  **d.** abduction.

_____  **8.** When the nurse moves a client's leg upward, the nurse is performing
  **a.** supination.           **c.** eversion.
  **b.** external rotation.    **d.** internal rotation.

_b_  **9.** The subacromial bursae are contained in the
  **a.** temporomandibular joint.    **c.** elbow joint.
  **b.** shoulder joint.             **d.** wrist joint.

_d_  **10.** Articulation between the head of the femur and the acetabulum is in the
  **a.** knee joint.           **c.** ankle joint.
  **b.** tibial joint.         **d.** hip joint.

**Activity B** **LABELING ACTIVITIES**

*Label the major bones and joints of the shoulder and elbow.*

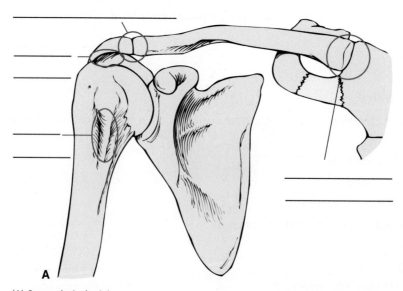

(A) Sternoclavicular joint.

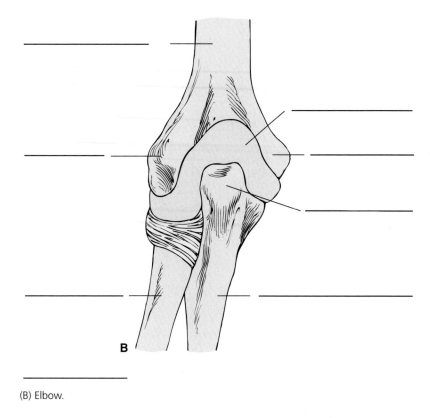

(B) Elbow.

*Label the structure indicated by the line; then match your answer with the label on the matching figure in Chapter 26 of your textbook.*

*Label the major bones and joints of the hip and knee.*

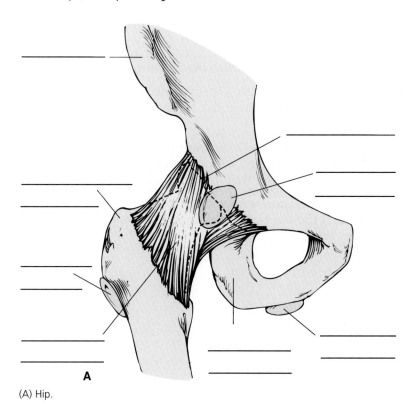

(A) Hip.

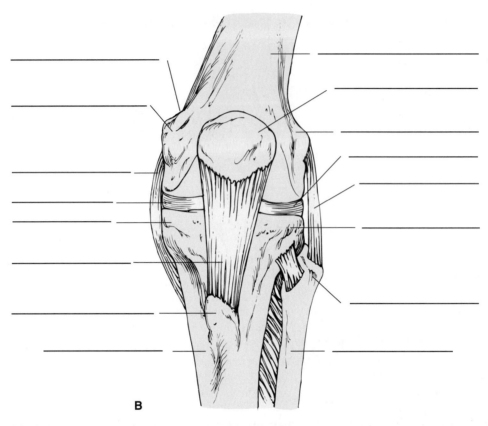

**B**

(B) Knee.

*Label the structure indicated by the line; then match your answer with the label on the matching figure in Chapter 26 of your textbook.*

**LEARNER ACTIVITIES**

*Working with peers in the learning lab*

*After reading Chapter 26, participate in the following learning activities.*

1. Review the information in "Promote Health: Osteoporosis" in Chapter 26. Determine your own risk for osteoporosis and ways to reduce these risk factors. Next, identify and discuss the ethnic groups that are at high risk for osteoporosis.

2. Obtain brochures and literature on osteoporosis from the county health department or your local health care facility for information. Discuss with your lab partner how best to give a presentation on this topic to college-aged women and then to a group of middle-aged women.

3. Find an elderly client, friend, or relative who will let you assess his or her musculoskeletal system. With your lab partner, discuss the assessment findings and compare them with the findings from an assessment of a younger person.

**Activity D**   **INTERVIEWING AND RECORDING ASSESSMENT FINDINGS**

Use the following Nursing History Checklist as your guide to interviewing and recording musculoskeletal assessment findings.

## Nursing History Checklist

| Questions | Normal Findings | Abnormal Findings | Additional Data Needed |
|---|---|---|---|
| *Current Symptoms* | | | |
| 1. Recent weight gain? | | | |
| 2. Difficulty chewing? | | | |
| 3. Joint, muscle, or bone throbbing? | | | |
| *Past History* | | | |
| 1. Past problems or injuries to joints, muscles, or bones? | | | |
| 2. Past treatment: surgery, medications, physical therapy, exercise, rest? | | | |
| 3. Tetanus and polio immunizations? | | | |
| 4. Diagnosed with diabetes mellitus, lupus, or sickle cell anemia? | | | |
| 5. How old at start of menstruation; started menopause; estrogen replacement therapy? | | | |
| *Family History* | | | |
| 1. Family history of rheumatoid arthritis, gout, osteoporosis, psoriasis, infectious tuberculosis? | | | |
| *Lifestyle and Health Practices* | | | |
| 1. Activities to promote musculoskeletal health? | | | |
| 2. Home remedies to relieve musculoskeletal problems? | | | |
| 3. Assistive devices to promote mobility? | | | |
| 4. Smoking? | | | |
| 5. Alcohol or caffeinated beverages? | | | |
| 6. Typical diet, drink milk, take calcium supplements? | | | |
| 7. Occupation? | | | |
| 8. Time in sunlight? | | | |
| 9. Routine exercise? | | | |
| 10. Difficulty with ADLs? | | | |
| 11. Typical posture? | | | |
| 12. Interference with sexual activities? | | | |
| 13. Ability to interact/socialize? | | | |
| 14. Body image? | | | |
| 15. Stress? | | | |

## Activity E  PERFORMING PHYSICAL ASSESSMENT

Use the following Physical Assessment Checklist as your guide to performing a musculoskeletal assessment. Column 1 can be used by you to guide your physical assessment. Column 2 may be used by your instructor to evaluate your skills as necessary.

### Physical Assessment Checklist

| Assessment Skill | Findings (Normal or Abnormal) and Notes | | Performance (Satisfactory, Needs Improvement, Unsatisfactory) | | |
| --- | --- | --- | --- | --- | --- |
| | N | A | S | N | U |
| 1. Gather equipment (tape measure, goniometer). | ☐ | ☐ | ☐ | ☐ | ☐ |
| 2. Explain procedure to client. | ☐ | ☐ | ☐ | ☐ | ☐ |
| 3. Ask client to put on a gown. | ☐ | ☐ | ☐ | ☐ | ☐ |
| *Gait* | | | | | |
| 1. Observe gait for base, weight-bearing stability, feet position, stride, arm swing, and posture. | ☐ | ☐ | ☐ | ☐ | ☐ |
| *Temporomandibular Joint* | | | | | |
| 1. Inspect, palpate, and test ROM. | ☐ | ☐ | ☐ | ☐ | ☐ |
| *Sternoclavicular Joint* | | | | | |
| 1. Inspect and palpate for midline location, color, swelling, and masses. | ☐ | ☐ | ☐ | ☐ | ☐ |
| *Spine* | | | | | |
| 1. Inspect and palpate cervical, thoracic, and lumbar spine for pain and tenderness. | ☐ | ☐ | ☐ | ☐ | ☐ |
| 2. Test ROM of cervical spine. | ☐ | ☐ | ☐ | ☐ | ☐ |
| 3. Test ROM of thoracic and lumbar spine. | ☐ | ☐ | ☐ | ☐ | ☐ |
| 4. Test for leg and back pain. | ☐ | ☐ | ☐ | ☐ | ☐ |
| 5. Measure leg length. | ☐ | ☐ | ☐ | ☐ | ☐ |
| *Shoulders* | | | | | |
| 1. Inspect and palpate shoulders for symmetry, color, swelling, and masses. | ☐ | ☐ | ☐ | ☐ | ☐ |
| 2. Test ROM of shoulders. | ☐ | ☐ | ☐ | ☐ | ☐ |
| *Elbows* | | | | | |
| 1. Inspect and palpate elbows for size, shape, deformities, redness, or swelling. | ☐ | ☐ | ☐ | ☐ | ☐ |
| 2. Test ROM of elbows. | ☐ | ☐ | ☐ | ☐ | ☐ |
| *Wrists* | | | | | |
| 1. Inspect and palpate wrists for size, shape, symmetry, color, swelling, tenderness, and nodules. | ☐ | ☐ | ☐ | ☐ | ☐ |
| 2. Test ROM of wrists. | ☐ | ☐ | ☐ | ☐ | ☐ |
| 3. Test for carpal tunnel syndrome. | ☐ | ☐ | ☐ | ☐ | ☐ |

| Assessment Skill | Findings (Normal or Abnormal) and Notes | | Performance (Satisfactory, Needs Improvement, Unsatisfactory) | | |
| --- | --- | --- | --- | --- | --- |
| | A | S | N | U | N |
| *Hands and Fingers* | | | | | |
| 1. Inspect and palpate hands and fingers for size, shape, symmetry, swelling, color, tenderness, and nodules. | ☐ | ☐ | ☐ | ☐ | ☐ |
| 2. Test ROM of hands and fingers. | ☐ | ☐ | ☐ | ☐ | ☐ |
| *Hips* | | | | | |
| 1. Inspect and palpate hips for shape and symmetry. | ☐ | ☐ | ☐ | ☐ | ☐ |
| 2. Test ROM of hips. | ☐ | ☐ | ☐ | ☐ | ☐ |
| *Knees* | | | | | |
| 1. Inspect and palpate knees for size, shape, symmetry, deformities, pain, and alignment. | ☐ | ☐ | ☐ | ☐ | ☐ |
| 2. Test knees for swelling. If small amount of fluid present, do "bulge test." If large amount of fluid present, do "ballottement test." | ☐ | ☐ | ☐ | ☐ | ☐ |
| 3. Test ROM of knees. | ☐ | ☐ | ☐ | ☐ | ☐ |
| 4. Perform McMurray's test if client complains of "clicking" in knee. | ☐ | ☐ | ☐ | ☐ | ☐ |
| *Ankles and Feet* | | | | | |
| 1. Inspect and palpate ankles and feet for position, alignment, shape, skin, tenderness, temperature, swelling, or nodules. | ☐ | ☐ | ☐ | ☐ | ☐ |
| 2. Test ROM of ankles and toes. | ☐ | ☐ | ☐ | ☐ | ☐ |
| *Analysis of Data* | | | | | |
| 1. Formulate nursing diagnoses (wellness, risk, actual). | ☐ | ☐ | ☐ | ☐ | ☐ |
| 2. Formulate collaborative problems. | ☐ | ☐ | ☐ | ☐ | ☐ |
| 3. Make necessary referrals. | ☐ | ☐ | ☐ | ☐ | ☐ |

# CHAPTER POSTTEST

**Activity F** MULTIPLE CHOICE

*Choose the one best answer for each of the following multiple-choice questions.*

_____ **1.** A client visits the clinic and tells the nurse that she has joint pain in her hands, especially in the morning. The nurse should assess the client further for signs and symptoms of

    **a.** arthritis.

    **b.** osteoporosis.

    **c.** carpal tunnel syndrome.

    **d.** a neurologic disorder.

*C* 2. A client with insulin-dependent diabetes visits the clinic and complains of painful hip joints. The nurse should assess the client carefully for signs and symptoms of

    **a.** arthritis.

    **b.** gait difficulties.

    **c.** osteomyelitis.

    **d.** scoliosis.

 3. A female client visits the clinic and tells the nurse that she began menarche at the age of 16 years. The nurse should instruct the client that she is at a higher risk for

    **a.** osteoporosis.

    **b.** osteomyelitis.

    **c.** rheumatoid arthritis.

    **d.** lordosis.

*C* 4. The nurse is planning a presentation on osteoporosis to a group of high school students. Which of the following should the nurse plan to include in the presentation?

    **a.** Bone density rises to a peak at age 50 for both sexes.

    **b.** Bone density in the Asian population is higher than in the white population.

    **c.** Moderate strenuous exercise tends to increase bone density.

    **d.** Approximately 5 million fractures in the United States are due to osteoporosis.

 5. The nurse is caring for an adult client who is in a cast because of a fractured arm. To promote healing of the bone and tissue, the nurse should instruct the client to eat a diet that is high in

    **a.** whole grains.

    **b.** vitamin B.

    **c.** vitamin E.

    **d.** vitamin C.

 6. An adult client tells the nurse that he eats sardines every day. The nurse should instruct the client that a diet high in purines can contribute to

    **a.** gouty arthritis.

    **b.** osteomalacia.

    **c.** bone fractures.

    **d.** osteomyelitis.

7. A client tells the nurse that his grandmother had a diagnosis of osteomalacia. The nurse should instruct the client that to decrease the risk factors for osteomalacia, the clients should have adequate amounts of

    **a.** vitamin E.

    **b.** riboflavin.

    **c.** β-carotene.

    **d.** vitamin D.

 8. The nurse is preparing to perform a musculoskeletal examination on an adult client. The nurse has explained the examination procedure to the client. The nurse determines that the client needs further instructions when the client says

    **a.** "You will be asking me to change positions often."

    **b.** "You'll be comparing bilateral joints."

    **c.** "You'll be assessing the size and strength of my joints."

    **d.** "You'll continue with range of motion even if I have discomfort."

**9.** While assessing muscle strength in an older adult client, the nurse determines that the client's knee joint has a rating of 3 and exhibits active motion against gravity. The nurse should document the client's muscle strength as being/having

a. normal.

b. slight weakness.

c. average weakness.

d. poor range of motion.

**10.** While assessing an adult client's jaw, the nurse hears a clicking popping sound, and the client expresses pain in the joint. The nurse should further assess the client for

a. arthritis.

b. TMJ dysfunction.

c. bruxism.

d. previous fracture.

**11.** While examining the spine of an adult client, the nurse notes that the client has a flattened lumbar curvature. The nurse should refer the client to a physician for possible

a. herniated disc.

b. scoliosis.

c. kyphosis.

d. cervical disc degeneration.

**12.** The nurse is assessing the spine of an adult client and detects lateral curvature of the thoracic spine with an increase in convexity on the left curved side. The nurse suspects that the client is experiencing

a. lordosis.

b. arthritis.

c. kyphosis.

d. scoliosis.

**13.** A client visits the clinic and tells the nurse that he has had lower back pain for the past several days. To perform Lasègue's test, the nurse should ask the client to

a. bend backward toward the nurse.

b. lean forward and touch his toes.

c. twist the shoulders in both directions.

d. lie flat and raise his leg to the point of pain.

**14.** An older adult client visits the clinic and tells the nurse that she has had shooting pains in both of her legs. The nurse should assess the client for signs and symptoms of

a. herniated intervertebral disc.

b. rheumatoid arthritis.

c. osteoporosis.

d. metastases.

**15.** While assessing the range of motion in an adult client's shoulders, the client expresses pain and exhibits limited abduction and muscle weakness. The nurse plans to refer the client to a physician for possible

a. rotator cuff tear.

b. nerve damage.

c. cervical disc degeneration.

d. tendonitis.

_____ **16.** While assessing an older adult client, the client complains of chronic pain and severe limitation of all shoulder movements. The nurse should refer the client to a physician for possible

    **a.** rotator cuff tendonitis.

    **b.** rheumatoid arthritis.

    **c.** calcified tendinitis.

    **d.** chronic bursitis.

_____ **17.** The nurse is examining an adult client's range of motion in the shoulders. The client is unable to shrug her shoulders against resistance. The nurse suspects that the client has a lesion of cranial nerve

    **a.** VIII.

    **b.** IX.

    **c.** X.

    **d.** XI.

_____ **18.** While assessing the elbow of an adult client, the client complains of pain and swelling. The nurse should further assess the client for

    **a.** arthritis.

    **b.** ganglion cyst.

    **c.** carpal tunnel syndrome.

    **d.** nerve damage.

_____ **19.** While reviewing a client's chart before seeing the client for the first time, the nurse notes that the client has a diagnosis of Dupuytren's contracture. The nurse anticipates that the client will exhibit

    **a.** inability to turn the wrists.

    **b.** ulnar deviation of the hands.

    **c.** flexion of the distal interphalangeal joints.

    **d.** inability to extend the ring and little finger.

_____ **20.** While assessing the musculoskeletal system of an adult client, the nurse observes hard painless nodules over the distal interphalangeal joints. The nurse should document the presence of

    **a.** osteoarthritis.

    **b.** bursitis.

    **c.** tendonitis.

    **d.** rheumatoid arthritis.

_____ **21.** A client visits the clinic and complains of wrist pain. To perform Phalen's test, the nurse should ask the client to

    **a.** move the hand inward with the wrists straight.

    **b.** place both palms on the examination table.

    **c.** flex both wrists against resistance.

    **d.** place the backs of both hands against each other.

_____ **22.** While assessing an adult client, the nurse tests the client for Tinel's sign. The nurse should instruct the client that numbness or tingling may indicate

    **a.** arthritis.

    **b.** carpal tunnel syndrome.

    **c.** tenosynovitis.

    **d.** crepitus.

___ **23.** While assessing the musculoskeletal system of an adult client, the nurse detects tenderness, warmth, and a boggy consistency of the client's knee. The nurse should refer the client to a physician for possible

   **a.** torn meniscus.

   **b.** malignancy.

   **c.** fracture.

   **d.** synovitis.

___ **24.** A client visits the clinic and complains of pain in his knees. The nurse explains that a ballottement test will be performed. To perform the ballottement test, the nurse should

   **a.** place the left thumb and index finger on either side of the patella.

   **b.** use the ball of the hand to firmly stroke the medial side of the knee.

   **c.** press the lateral side of the knee and inspect for swelling.

   **d.** palpate for tenderness 10 cm above the patella.

___ **25.** While assessing an older adult client, the nurse notes decreased range of motion and crepitation as the client tries to bend his knees to his chest. The nurse determines that the client is most likely experiencing

   **a.** flexion contractures.

   **b.** signs of aging.

   **c.** osteoarthritis.

   **d.** genu valgum.

___ **26.** A client visits the clinic and tells the nurse that after playing softball yesterday, he thinks his knee is "locking up." The nurse should perform the McMurray's test by asking the client to

   **a.** move from a standing to a squatting position.

   **b.** raise his leg while in a supine position.

   **c.** bend forward while trying to touch the toes.

   **d.** flex the knee and hip while in a supine position.

___ **27.** While assessing the feet of an adult client, the nurse notes that the client's great toes are deviated, with overlapping of the second toes. The client states that there is pain on the medial side. The nurse should refer the client to a physician for possible

   **a.** hallux valgus.

   **b.** pes planus.

   **c.** pes cavus.

   **d.** verruca vulgaris.

___ **28.** While reviewing a client's chart before seeing the client for the first time, the nurse notes that the client has a diagnosis of pes planus. The nurse anticipates that the client has

   **a.** high arches.

   **b.** bunions.

   **c.** calluses.

   **d.** flat feet.

___ 29. While assessing the feet of an older adult client the nurse observes that the metatarsopha-langeal joint to the client's great toe is tender, reddened, and painful. The nurse should refer the client to a physician for possible

   **a.** bunions.

   **b.** corns.

   **c.** hammer toe.

   **d.** gouty arthritis.

**30.** While assessing the feet of an adult client, the nurse observes hyperextension of the metatar-sophalangeal joint with flexion at the proximal interphalangeal joint on the client's second toes. The nurse should refer the client to a physician for possible

   **a.** hammer toes.

   **b.** gouty arthritis.

   **c.** calluses.

   **d.** hallux valgus.

___ **31.** While assessing the feet of an adult client, the nurse observes tiny dark spots under a painful callus on the client's foot. The nurse should document the presence of

   **a.** corns.

   **b.** bunions.

   **c.** plantar warts.

   **d.** gouty arthritis.

## Activity G　CROSSWORD PUZZLE

*Complete the following crossword puzzle to become more familiar with the terminology used with assessment of the musculoskeletal system.*

**ACROSS**

1. Goniometer is used to measure this; also phrase used to describe joint capability

5. Movement of the limbs or the trunk and head toward the median plane of the body

6. Outward turning of a limb: _____ rotation

8. Inflammation of a bursa

10. Spasmodic alternation of muscular contraction and relaxation

11. Fixation of a joint, often in an abnormal position; seen frequently with rheumatoid arthritis

14. Tenderness or pain in the muscle

15. Type of rigidity characterized by jerky movements when the muscle is passively stretched

17. Backward bending or flexion of a joint

18. Abnormal anterior concavity of the spine

**DOWN**

2. Movement of the limbs or the trunk and head, away from the median plane of the body

3. Dry crackling sound or sensation heard or felt as a joint is moved through ROM

4. Movement that brings a limb into or toward a bent condition

7. Circular movement of a limb

8. A fibrous, fluid-filled sac found between certain tendons and the bones beneath them

9. The localized uncoordinated twitching of a single muscle group

12. Movement that brings a limb into or toward a straight condition

13. Abnormal convexity of the posterior curve of the spine

16. Type of flexion associated with extension of the foot

### Activity H CRITICAL THINKING AND CASE STUDIES

1. Compare and contrast how you would assess for muscle strength, gait, and stability in a 25-year-old client versus those in a 75-year-old client.

2. Analyze the following client's risk for osteoporosis.

   A 52-year-old white woman, married, with two children, is 5 feet 8 inches tall and weighs 130 pounds. She quit smoking 15 years ago, drinks a lot of milk, went through final stages of menopause 1 year ago, and is thinking about using hormone (estrogen) replacement therapy.

3. On the basis of the following assessment information, work through the steps of analyzing the data. Identify abnormal data and strengths in **subjective and objective findings**, assemble **cue clusters**, draw **inferences**, make possible **nursing diagnoses**, identify **defining charactetristics, confirm or rule out** the nursing diagnosis, and **document** your conclusions. Use the blank diagnostic analysis charts provided at the end of this book to guide your thinking. You may want to write on the chart or use separate paper. Propose nursing diagnoses that are specific to the client in the case study. Identify collaborative problems, if any, for this client. Finally, identify data, if any, that point toward a medical problem requiring a referral.

Mrs. Clement is a 71-year-old woman who has had diabetes mellitus for 15 years. Her diabetes is controlled by diet and insulin. A retired schoolteacher, she has lived alone for the past 7 years since her husband died of liver cancer. Living in the upper level of a two-story apartment, she socializes with her neighbor and regularly attends church. She has a grown son and daughter, who both live out of state and call frequently but can visit only once a year. Because of her poor eyesight, her neighbor, a retired R.N., helps her draw up her insulin. When visited by the home health care nurse, Mrs. Clement states that she has had lower back and wrist pain for the past month.

During the interview, Mrs. Clement describes a sedentary lifestyle, spending much of her time watching TV, crocheting, or doing crossword puzzles. She uses a magnifying glass for close work. However, she has reduced her handwork because she has been having numbness and tingling in her right thumb and index finger. The pain is relieved by rest, but she often has sharp pain in the right wrist during the night. Mrs. Clement has never smoked, does not drink alcohol, and has five cups of coffee a day. She does little cooking. Her diet primarily consists of TV dinners and canned soups, vegetables, and fruits, with very few dairy products. She reports that constipation has become a more frequent problem over the past month. She has maintained her weight of 140 pounds for the past 10 years. She can do most activities of daily living unassisted, but her neighbor does the grocery shopping. She verbalizes embarrassment over the effects of the aging process and stooped posture, stating that she has noticed a decrease in her height over the past year. Mrs. Clement reports frequent low back aches with occasional sharp pains. She tries to avoid bending to prevent pain, uses a heating pad, and takes Tylenol two or three times a day, which temporarily relieves the pain. She experienced menopause at the age of 50 years and has never used estrogen replacement therapy.

Physical examination reveals her to be 5 feet 2 inches tall. Two years ago, her height was 5 feet 3½ inches. Her gait is wide-based and slow. Her temporomandibular joint (TMJ) has full range of motion (ROM) against resistance. She has apparent kyphosis of the cervical spine. Her paravertebrals are tender to palpation. Lower back pain is aggravated by ROM, is limited to the lower lumbar area, and does not radiate down the leg. The result of Lasègue's test is negative. No leg redness, nodules, tenderness, or swelling can be observed. The ROM of the cervical spine and upper extremities are within normal range against gravity but decreased against resistance. Lumbar flexion is 50 degrees; lateral bending is 25 degrees. The legs are equal in length. The shoulders, elbows, wrists, and fingers are symmetric, without redness, heat, swelling, or nodules. Some muscle atrophy is apparent in the upper extremities. The results of Phalen's test and Tinel's test are positive. The hips, knees, ankles, and toes are symmetric, without redness, swelling, heat, or nodules. The lower extremities have full ROM against gravity, but decreased ROM against resistance.

# SELF-REFLECTION AND EVALUATION OF LEARNER OBJECTIVES

After you have read Chapter 26 and completed the above quizzes and activities, please identify to what degree you have met each of the following chapter learning objectives. For those objectives that you have met partially or not at all, you will want to review the chapter content for that learning objective.

| Objective | Very Much | Somewhat | Not At All |
|---|---|---|---|
| 1. Describe the structure and functions of the bones, skeletal muscles, and joints. | | | |
| 2. Discuss risk factors for osteoporosis and ways to reduce these risk factors. | | | |
| 3. Discuss the incidence of osteoporosis across cultures. | | | |
| 4. Obtain an accurate nursing history of the client's muscles, joints, and bones. | | | |
| 5. Explain how to prepare the client for an examination of the muscles, joints, and bones. | | | |
| 6. Describe the equipment necessary to perform a musculoskeletal assessment. | | | |
| 7. Describe the two physical examination techniques (inspection and palpation) used to complete a musculoskeletal assessment. | | | |

| Objective | Very Much | Somewhat | Not At All |
|-----------|-----------|----------|------------|
| 8. Assess the client's gait. | | | |
| 9. Assess the client's joints for position, ROM, suppleness of movement, swelling, redness, tenderness or pain, bony overgrowths, alignment with other joints and bones, and associated muscle development and muscle strength. | | | |
| 10. Perform test for carpal tunnel syndrome. | | | |
| 11. Describe expected aging changes of the musculoskeletal system. | | | |

# Nervous System

## Chapter Overview

Just as the musculoskeletal system structures the body, so the neurologic system structures thought, movement and balance, sensation, and communication, among other life functions. Quality of life is significantly affected by the health of the neurologic system.

## CHAPTER PRETEST

### Activity A  MULTIPLE CHOICE

*Choose the one best answer for each of the following multiple-choice questions.*

_____ 1. The cerebrospinal fluid cushions the central nervous system (CNS), provides nourishment to the CNS, and

    **a.** transmits impulses.

    **b.** coats the brain.

    **c.** regulates heart rate.

    **d.** removes wastes.

_____ 2. The cerebrum is divided into right and left hemispheres, which are joined together by the

    **a.** corpus callosum.

    **b.** diencephalon.

    **c.** medulla oblongata.

    **d.** pons.

_____ 3. The portion of the brain that rims the surfaces of the cerebral hemispheres forming the cerebral cortex is the

    **a.** gray matter.

    **b.** cerebellum.

    **c.** diencephalon.

    **d.** brain stem.

____ **4.** The diencephalon of the brain consists of the

    **a.** pons and brain stem.

    **b.** medulla oblongata and cerebrum.

    **c.** cerebellum and midbrain.

    **d.** thalamus and hypothalamus.

____ **5.** The hypothalamus is responsible for regulating

    **a.** sleep cycles.

    **b.** nerve impulses.

    **c.** memory.

    **d.** eye reflexes.

**Activity B** **MATCHING**

*Match the terms in the left column with the correct descriptions in the right column.*

**Term**

____ **1.** Spinal accessory

____ **2.** Glossopharyngeal

____ **3.** Olfactory

____ **4.** Facial

____ **5.** Hypoglossal

____ **6.** Acoustic

____ **7.** Optic

____ **8.** Vagus

____ **9.** Abducens

____ **10.** Oculomotor

____ **11.** Trigeminal

____ **12.** Trochlear

**Description**

**a.** Carries sensations from the throat, larynx, heart, lungs, bronchi, gastrointestinal tract, and abdominal viscera

**b.** Innervates neck muscles that promote movement of the shoulders and head rotation

**c.** Carries visual impulses from the eye to the brain

**d.** Contracts eye muscles to control eye movement, constricts pupils, and elevates eyelids

**e.** Contains sensory fibers for taste on posterior one-third of the tongue; responsible for "gag reflex" when stimulated

**f.** Contracts one eye muscle to control inferomedial eye movement

**g.** Innervates tongue muscles that promote the movement of food and talking

**h.** Carries smell impulses from nasal mucous membrane to brain

**i.** Carries sensory impulses of pain, touch, and temperature from the face to the brain

**j.** Controls lateral eye movements

**k.** Contains sensory fibers for hearing and balance

**l.** Contains sensory fibers for taste on anterior two thirds of the tongue, and stimulates secretions from the salivary glands and tears from lacrimal glands

## Activity C  LABELING ACTIVITIES

*Label the structures of the brain.*

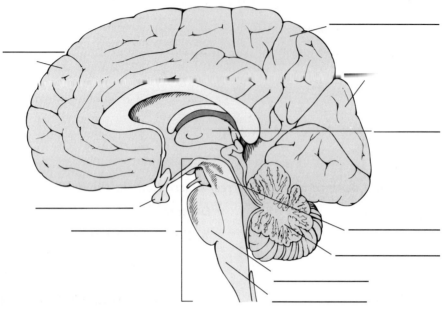

Structures of the brain.

*Label the structure indicated by the line; then match your answer with the label on the matching figure in Chapter 27 of your textbook.*

*Label this cross-section of the spinal cord.*

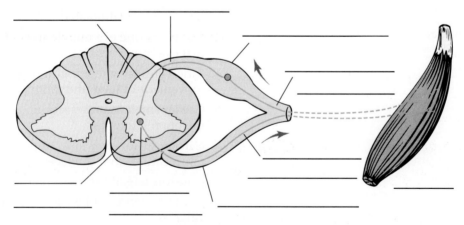

Cross-section of spinal cord.

*Label the structure indicated by the line; then match your answer with the label on the matching figure in Chapter 27 of your textbook.*

*Label the cranial nerves.*

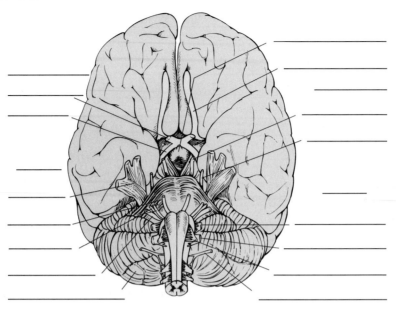

Twelve cranial nerves emerging from brain.

*Label the structure indicated by the line; then match your answer with the label on the matching figure in Chapter 27 of your textbook.*

**Activity D** **LEARNER ACTIVITIES**

### Working with peers in the learning lab

*After reading Chapter 27, participate in the following learning activities.*

1. Refer to "Promote Health: Cerebrovascular Accident (Stroke)" in Chapter 27. Then assess a lab partner's risk for cerebrovascular accident (CVA, stroke).

2. Assess the function of the 12 cranial nerves (labeled in the diagram above) of your lab partner.

3. Obtain the necessary equipment and assess your lab partner's sensory system for touch, vibrations, position, and tactile discrimination.

4. Use a reflex hammer to test your lab partner's deep tendon reflexes. Next, test for his or her superficial plantar and abdominal reflexes.

5. Practice testing balance and coordination safely with a lab partner.

**Activity E** **INTERVIEWING AND RECORDING ASSESSMENT FINDINGS**

Use the following Nursing History Checklist as your guide to interviewing and recording the findings from a neurologic assessment.

### Nursing History Checklist

| Questions | Normal Findings | Abnormal Findings | Additional Data Needed |
|-----------|-----------------|-------------------|------------------------|
| *Current Symptoms* | | | |
| 1. Headaches, numbness, or tingling? | | | |
| 2. Seizure activity? | | | |
| 3. Dizziness, lightheadedness, or problems with balance or coordination? | | | |

| Questions | Normal Findings | Abnormal Findings | Additional Data Needed |
|---|---|---|---|
| 4. Decrease in ability to smell or taste? | | | |
| 5. Ringing in ears? | | | |
| 6. Change in vision? | | | |
| 7. Difficulty understanding when people are talking to you or when you talk to others? | | | |
| 8. Difficulty swallowing? | | | |
| 9. Loss of bowel or bladder control? | | | |
| 10. Memory loss? | | | |
| 11. Tremors? | | | |
| *Past History* | | | |
| 1. Head injury? | | | |
| 2. Meningitis? | | | |
| 3. Encephalitis? | | | |
| 4. Spinal cord injury? | | | |
| 5. Stroke? | | | |
| 6. Treatment received? | | | |
| *Family History* | | | |
| 1. High blood pressure? | | | |
| 2. Stroke? | | | |
| 3. Alzheimer's disease? | | | |
| 4. Epilepsy? | | | |
| 5. Brain cancer? | | | |
| 6. Huntington's chorea? | | | |
| *Lifestyle and Health Practices* | | | |
| 1. Any prescription or nonprescription medications? | | | |
| 2. Smoking? | | | |
| 3. Wearing of seat belts/protective headgear? | | | |
| 4. Daily diet? | | | |
| 5. Exposure to lead, insecticides, pollutants, chemicals? | | | |
| 6. Lifting of heavy objects? | | | |
| 7. Frequent repetitive movements? | | | |
| 8. Functioning/daily activities? | | | |
| *Analysis of Data* | | | |
| 1. Formulate nursing diagnoses (wellness, risk, actual). | | | |
| 2. Formulate collaborative problems. | | | |
| 3. Make necessary referrals. | | | |

**Activity F** **PERFORMING PHYSICAL ASSESSMENT**

Use the following Physical Assessment Checklist as your guide to performing a neurologic assessment. Column 1 can be used by you to guide your physical assessment. Column 2 may be used by your instructor to evaluate your skills as necessary.

## Physical Assessment Checklist

| Assessment Skill | Findings (Normal or Abnormal) and Notes | | Performance (Satisfactory, Needs Improvement, Unsatisfactory) | | |
|---|---|---|---|---|---|
| | N | A | S | N | U |
| 1. Gather equipment, such as examination gloves, pencil and paper, cotton-tipped applicators, newsprint to read, ophthalmoscope, paper clip, penlight, Snellen chart, sterile cotton ball, substances to smell and taste, tongue blade, tuning fork, tape measure, cotton balls, objects to feel, test tubes with hot and cold water, tuning fork (low-pitched), and reflex hammer. | ☐ | ☐ | ☐ | ☐ | ☐ |
| 2. Explain procedure to client. | ☐ | ☐ | ☐ | ☐ | ☐ |
| 3. Ask client to put on a gown. | ☐ | ☐ | ☐ | ☐ | ☐ |
| *Mental Status* | | | | | |
| 1. Assess level of consciousness. | ☐ | ☐ | ☐ | ☐ | ☐ |
| 2. Observe appearance and behavior. | ☐ | ☐ | ☐ | ☐ | ☐ |
| 3. Observe mood, feelings, and expressions. | ☐ | ☐ | ☐ | ☐ | ☐ |
| 4. Observe thought processes and perceptions. | ☐ | ☐ | ☐ | ☐ | ☐ |
| 5. Observe cognitive abilities. | ☐ | ☐ | ☐ | ☐ | ☐ |
| *Cranial Nerves* | | | | | |
| 1. Test cranial nerve I—olfactory. | ☐ | ☐ | ☐ | ☐ | ☐ |
| 2. Test cranial nerve II—optic. | ☐ | ☐ | ☐ | ☐ | ☐ |
| 3. Test cranial nerve III—oculomotor. | ☐ | ☐ | ☐ | ☐ | ☐ |
| 4. Test cranial nerve IV—trochlear. | ☐ | ☐ | ☐ | ☐ | ☐ |
| 5. Test cranial nerve V—trigeminal. | ☐ | ☐ | ☐ | ☐ | ☐ |
| 6. Test cranial nerve VI—abducens. | ☐ | ☐ | ☐ | ☐ | ☐ |
| 7. Test cranial nerve VII—facial. | ☐ | ☐ | ☐ | ☐ | ☐ |
| 8. Test cranial nerve VIII—acoustic (vestibulocochlear). | ☐ | ☐ | ☐ | ☐ | ☐ |
| 9. Test cranial nerve IX—glossopharyngeal. | ☐ | ☐ | ☐ | ☐ | ☐ |
| 10. Test cranial nerve X—vagus. | ☐ | ☐ | ☐ | ☐ | U |
| 11. Test cranial nerve XI—spinal accessory. | ☐ | ☐ | ☐ | ☐ | ☐ |
| 12. Test cranial nerve XII—hypoglossal. | ☐ | ☐ | ☐ | ☐ | ☐ |

| Assessment Skill | Findings (Normal or Abnormal) and Notes | | Performance (Satisfactory, Needs Improvement, Unsatisfactory) | | |
|---|---|---|---|---|---|
| | N | A | S | N | U |
| *Motor and Cerebellar Systems* | | | | | |
| 1. Test condition and movement of muscles. | ☐ | ☐ | ☐ | ☐ | ☐ |
| 2. Test balance. | ☐ | ☐ | ☐ | ☐ | ☐ |
| 3. Test coordination. | ☐ | ☐ | ☐ | ☐ | ☐ |
| *Sensory System* | | | | | |
| 1. Test light touch, pain, and temperature sensations. | ☐ | ☐ | ☐ | ☐ | ☐ |
| 2. Test vibratory sensations. | ☐ | ☐ | ☐ | ☐ | ☐ |
| 3. Test position sensations. | ☐ | ☐ | ☐ | ☐ | ☐ |
| 4. Test tactile discrimination (fine touch). | ☐ | ☐ | ☐ | ☐ | ☐ |
| *Reflexes* | | | | | |
| 1. Test deep tendon reflexes (biceps, brachioradialis, triceps, patellar, Achilles, and ankle clonus). | ☐ | ☐ | ☐ | ☐ | ☐ |
| 2. Test superficial reflexes (plantar, abdominal, cremasteric). | ☐ | ☐ | ☐ | ☐ | ☐ |
| 3. Test for meningeal irritation/inflammation (Brudzinski's and Kernig's signs if indicated). | ☐ | ☐ | ☐ | ☐ | ☐ |

# CHAPTER POSTTEST

## Activity G  MULTIPLE CHOICE

*Choose the one best answer for each of the following multiple-choice questions.*

____ 1. Sensations of temperature, pain, and crude and light touch are carried by way of the
   a. extrapyramidal tract.
   b. corticospinal tract.
   c. spinothalamic tract.
   d. posterior tract.

____ 2. The cranial nerve that has sensory fibers for taste and fibers that result in the "gag reflex" is the
   a. vagus.
   b. hypoglossal.
   c. trigeminal.
   d. glossopharyngeal.

____ 3. The nurse is assessing an older adult client when the client tells the nurse that she has experienced transient blind spots for the last few days. The nurse should refer the client to a physician for possible
   a. vagus nerve damage.
   b. cerebral vascular accident.
   c. spinal cord compression.
   d. Parkinson's disease.

_____ **4.** The nurse is planning a presentation to a group of adults on the topic of cardiovascular accidents. Which of the following should the nurse plan to include in the teaching plan?

   **a.** Strokes are the number one cause of death in the United States.

   **b.** Smoking and high cholesterol levels are risk factors for CVA.

   **c.** Clients who smoke while taking oral contraceptives are not at higher risk.

   **d.** Postmenopausal women taking estrogen are at greater risk for CVA.

_____ **5.** The nurse is caring for a client during the immediate postoperative period after abdominal surgery. While performing a "neuro check" the nurse should assess the client's

   **a.** sensation in the extremities.

   **b.** deep tendon reflexes.

   **c.** ability to speak.

   **d.** recent memory.

_____ **6.** The nurse is preparing to percuss a client's reflexes in his arms. To use the reinforcement technique, the nurse should ask the client to

   **a.** clench his jaw.

   **b.** stretch the opposite arm.

   **c.** hold his neck toward the floor.

   **d.** straighten his legs forward.

_____ **7.** The Glasgow Coma Scale measures the level of consciousness in clients who are at high risk for rapid deterioration of the nervous system. A score of 13 indicates

   **a.** deep coma.

   **b.** severe impairment.

   **c.** no verbal response.

   **d.** some impairment.

_____ **8.** A client visits the clinic and tells the nurse that he has not been feeling very well. The nurse observes that the client's speech is slow, the client has a disheveled appearance, and he maintains poor eye contact with the nurse. The nurse should further assess the client for

   **a.** depression.

   **b.** delirium.

   **c.** hallucinations.

   **d.** schizophrenia.

_____ **9.** While assessing the neurologic system of a confused older adult, the nurse observes that the client is unable to recall past events. The nurse suspects that the client may be exhibiting signs of

   **a.** depression.

   **b.** anxiety.

   **c.** attention deficit disorder.

   **d.** cerebral cortex disorder.

_____ **10.** The nurse is assessing the neurologic system of an adult client. To test the client's use of memory to learn new information, the nurse should ask the client

   **a.** "What did you have for breakfast?"

   **b.** "How old were you when you began working?"

   **c.** "Can you repeat _rose, hose, nose, clothes_?"

   **d.** "Can you repeat _brown, chair, textbook, tomato_?"

_____ **11.** While assessing the pupils of a hospitalized adult client, the nurse observes that the client's pupils are dilated to 6 cm. The nurse suspects that the client is exhibiting signs of

   **a.** oculomotor nerve paralysis.

   **b.** damage to the pons.

   **c.** alcohol abuse.

   **d.** cocaine abuse.

_____ **12.** The nurse is assessing the neurologic system of an adult client. To test the client's motor function of the facial nerve, the nurse should

   **a.** ask the client to purse the lips.

   **b.** ask the client to open the mouth and say "ah."

   **c.** note the presence of a gag reflex.

   **d.** observe the client swallow a sip of water.

_____ **13.** The nurse is assessing the neurologic system of a client who has spastic muscle tone. The nurse should explain to the client that spastic muscle tone is associated with impairment to the

   **a.** extrapyramidal tract.

   **b.** spinothalamic tract.

   **c.** posterior columns.

   **d.** corticospinal tract.

_____ **14.** The nurse is preparing to perform the Romberg test on an adult male client. The nurse should instruct the client to

   **a.** squat down as far as he is able to do so.

   **b.** keep his eyes open while he bends at the knees.

   **c.** stand erect with arms at the sides and feet together.

   **d.** touch the tip of his nose with his finger.

_____ **15.** The nurse is planning to test position sensation in an adult female client. To perform this procedure, the nurse should ask the client to close her eyes while the nurse moves the client's

   **a.** arm away from the body.

   **b.** toes up or down.

   **c.** hand forward and then backward.

   **d.** leg away from the body.

_____ **16.** While assessing the Achilles reflex in an 84-year-old client, the nurse observes that the Achilles reflex is difficult to elicit. The nurse should

   **a.** refer the client to a physician for further evaluation.

   **b.** ask the client about injuries to the feet.

   **c.** determine whether the client is having any pain in the feet.

   **d.** document the finding in the client's record.

_____ **17.** While assessing the plantar reflex of an adult client, the nurse observes a positive Babinski reflex. The nurse suspects that the client may be exhibiting signs of

   **a.** meningeal irritation.

   **b.** diabetes mellitus.

   **c.** drug intoxication.

   **d.** lower motor neuron lesions.

**Activity H** **CRITICAL THINKING AND CASE STUDIES**

1. Read the following case study, and then formulate wellness, risk, and actual nursing diagnoses and identify collaborative problems for the client and his wife. Also develop nursing interventions to assist this family.

Mr. R., aged 74, has had Parkinson's disease for more than 10 years. His primary caregiver is his wife of 52 years, who is in good health except for rheumatoid arthritis. The couple's grown sons live in another state but visit the family once a year during the Christmas holidays. Recently Mr. R. has experienced a greater degree of twitching in his arms. He slurs his speech and is difficult to understand at times. He and his wife had enjoyed a wide range of activities, such as bowling, going to the movies, and trying new restaurants. However, since his condition has deteriorated they rarely leave the house. Mr. R. has also experienced difficulty walking and getting up from the bed or chair. His wife must assist him in all activities of daily living.

2. On the basis of the following assessment information, work through the steps analyzing the data. Identify abnormal data and strengths in **subjective and objective** findings, assemble **cue clusters**, draw **inferences**, make possible **nursing diagnoses**, identify **defining characteristics**, **confirm or rule out** the nursing diagnosis, and **document** your conclusions. Use the blank diagnostic analysis charts provided at the end of this book to guide your thinking. You may want to write on the chart or use separate paper. Propose nursing diagnoses that are specific to the client in the case study. Identify collaborative problems, if any, for this client. Finally, identify data, if any, that point toward a medical problem requiring a referral.

Mr. Kay is a 72-year-old man who had a right hemisphere thrombotic stroke 14 days ago and was discharged to his home from the 51st State Stroke Rehabilitation Center. His primary caregiver is his 68-year-old wife, who is in good health. He has a daughter and son, who live within a 50-mile radius and visit frequently. Before the CVA, Mr. Kay was very active and independent, a retired banker who loved to golf and travel. He received a diagnosis of hypertension 15 years ago but had poor compliance in taking prescribed medications. "When my blood pressure was checked, it was normal, so why take the medicine if I don't need it!" The CVA resulted in deficits in his visual, tactile, and kinesthetic senses. He denies his disabilities and frequently displays poor judgment and impulsive behavior. Mr. Kay requires partial assistance with activities of daily living, feeding, and mobility. While in rehabilitation he seemed to learn best if given brief simple cues. Because of visual disturbance, he has difficulty with visual cues.

When interviewed, Mr. Kay states he has weakness and numbness of his left arm and leg and that he often has to look at his left arm and leg to determine where they are. He also states that he frequently loses his balance and has occasional dizziness when getting up in the morning. He has difficulty with dressing and grooming and frequently confuses his comb with his toothbrush and puts his clothes on inside out. He is frustrated at not being able to care for himself. He has been prescribed a 2-gram-per-day sodium diet; however, he has a poor appetite. He states that the "food doesn't taste or smell good." His wife states that it often takes him a long time to complete a meal, and he frequently leaves food on the left side of the plate. When asked about changes in memory or concentration, his wife states, "Now, it's difficult for him to remember dates and phone numbers, but he knows people's names."

Your physical assessment reveals the following:

- Mental status: Awake, alert, oriented to person, place, and usually time. Communicates verbally, although comprehension is questionable at times. Eye contact poor. Mood seems anxious. Dress clean, shirt is on inside out. Difficulty in recalling recent dates and events. Unable to interpret written instructions. Reads a few sentences at a time; loses place on page frequently. Unable to recognize familiar objects such as toothbrush and comb. Unable to draw left side of clock. Saint Louis University Mental Status (SLUMS) Examination Score: 23.

- Cranial nerves: Intact except for cranial nerve II; loses place on page after reading a few sentences. Unable to record visual stimuli from the left side because of homonymous hemianopsia.

- Motor and cerebellar systems: Gait slow and unsteady with one person assisting; abnormal tandem walk. Muscle strength weak in left upper and lower extremities. Unable to assess finger coordination and fine motor function of left upper and lower extremities.

- Sensory system: Decreased light, sharp, dull touch; vibratory, two-point sensation in left upper and lower extremity; unable to identify safety pin and number traced on palm of left hand.

- Reflexes: 1+ left upper and lower extremities; 2+ right upper and lower extremities; down-going toes with plantar stimulation.

# SELF-REFLECTION AND EVALUATION OF LEARNER OBJECTIVES

After you have read Chapter 27 and completed the above quizzes and activities, please identify to what degree you have met each of the following chapter learning objectives. For those objectives that you have met partially or not at all, you will want to review chapter content for that learning objective.

| Objective | Very Much | Somewhat | Not At All |
|---|---|---|---|
| 1. Describe the structures and function of the central and peripheral nervous system. | | | |
| 2. Identify the 12 cranial nerves and name their functions. | | | |
| 3. Obtain an accurate nursing history of a client's neurologic system. | | | |
| 4. Identify the five major areas involved in a complete neurologic examination. | | | |
| 5. Explain how to prepare a client for a neurologic examination. | | | |
| 6. Describe the equipment necessary for examining the neurologic system. | | | |
| 7. Assess cranial nerve function of an adult client. | | | |
| 8. Assess the condition and movement of all muscle groups of the client. Also assess balance and coordination. | | | |
| 9. Assess light touch, pain, and temperature sensation of an adult. | | | |
| 10. Assess vibratory sensation, position sensation, and fine touch (tactile discrimination) of the client. | | | |
| 11. Assess deep tendon reflexes and then superficial reflexes of an adult client. | | | |
| 12. Assess the client for meningeal irritation. | | | |
| 13. Identify and discuss nursing diagnoses and collaborative problems for clients experiencing abnormalities of the neurologic system. | | | |

# 28

# Pulling It All Together

## Chapter Overview

Let the pages of this chapter help you review information on how to integrate the examination of all body systems into a routine organized process that flows comfortably for you and the client. A head-to-toe approach is used while examining some body systems in combination with others. Note that before performing a complete assessment, be familiar with your state's Nurse Practice Act to find out what you can legally assess and diagnose.

## CHAPTER PRETEST

### Activity A MULTIPLE CHOICE

*Choose the one best answer for each of the following multiple-choice questions.*

_____ **1.** The best approach to use when performing a total physical examination on a client is

    **a.** a toe-to-head integrated assessment of body systems.

    **b.** a head-to-toe integrated assessment of body systems.

    **c.** a total body system approach examining each body system individually.

    **d.** any approach that is convenient for you and the client.

_____ **2.** Before beginning a physical assessment it is important for the nurse to

    **a.** explain to the client in detail how each body system will be assessed.

    **b.** explain to the client the purpose of every physical assessment technique you will be using.

    **c.** acquire your client's verbal permission to perform the physical examination.

    **d.** acquire your client's written permission to perform the physical examination.

_____ **3.** Two body systems that may be logically integrated and assessed at the same time are the

    **a.** eye and ear exams.

    **b.** eye exam and cranial nerves II, III, IV, and VI.

    **c.** ear exam and cranial nerves IV, VI, and VIII.

    **d.** ear and nose exams.

_____ **4.** Examination of the skin should be

    **a.** integrated throughout the head-to-toe examination.

    **b.** completed at the beginning of the physical assessment before proceeding to other parts of the exam.

    **c.** performed at the very end of the physical assessment.

    **d.** integrated and completed only with the musculoskeletal examination.

**Activity B** **TRUE/FALSE**

**1. T F**   The Mental Status Exam should be performed after examining all other body systems.

**2. T F**   Assessment of cranial nerve I (olfactory) may be performed during examination of the nose, mouth, and throat.

**3. T F**   Assessment of the posterior and lateral chest should be completed before assessing the anterior chest.

**4. T F**   Examination of the legs should include assessment of lower peripheral vascular status.

**5. T F**   It is best to integrate the rectal examination with the abdominal examination.

**Activity C** **LEARNER ACTIVITIES**

### Working with peers in the learning lab

*After reading Chapter 28, participate in the learning activities.*

**1.** Practice performing an integrated head-to-toe examination on your lab partner without referring to the chapter. When you are finished, have your lab partner identify anything he or she feels you may have omitted during the examination. Check his or her report against the physical assessment checklist provided in this workbook chapter. Discuss which parts might have been better integrated for a smoother transition process for both the examiner and the client. Then repeat the process with you being the client and your lab partner being the examiner.

**Activity D** **INTERVIEWING AND RECORDING ASSESSMENT FINDINGS**

Use the following Nursing History Checklist as your guide to complete a total holistic health history of your lab partner or client before completing a head-to-toe assessment.

### Nursing History Checklist

| Questions | Normal Findings | Abnormal Findings | Data Missing |
|---|---|---|---|
| *Biographic Data* | | | |
| 1. Name? | | | |
| 2. Address? | | | |
| 3. Phone? | | | |
| 4. Birthdate? | | | |
| 5. Provider history? | | | |
| 6. Ethnicity? | | | |
| 7. Educational level? | | | |
| 8. Occupation? | | | |
| *Current Symptoms* | | | |
| 1. History of present concern (COLDSPA)? | | | |
| *Past History* | | | |
| 1. Birth problems? | | | |
| 2. Childhood illnesses? | | | |
| 3. Immunizations? | | | |
| 4. Illnesses? | | | |

| Questions | Normal Findings | Abnormal Findings | Data Missing |
|---|---|---|---|
| 5. Surgeries? | | | |
| 6. Accidents? | | | |
| 7. Pain? | | | |
| 8. Allergies? | | | |
| *Family History* | | | |
| 1. Family genogram? | | | |
| *Review of Body Systems* | | | |
| 1. Skin, hair, nails? | | | |
| 2. Ears? | | | |
| 3. Mouth, throat, nose, sinuses? | | | |
| 4. Thorax and lungs? | | | |
| 5. Breasts and regional lymph nodes? | | | |
| 6. Heart and neck vessels? | | | |
| 7. Peripheral vascular? | | | |
| 8. Abdomen? | | | |
| 9. Male/female genitalia? | | | |
| 10. Anus, rectum, and prostate? | | | |
| 11. Musculoskeletal? | | | |
| 12. Neurologic? | | | |
| *Lifestyle and Health Practices* | | | |
| 1. ADLs in a typical day? | | | |
| 2. Diet for past 24 hours? | | | |
| 3. Exercise regimen? | | | |
| 4. Sleep patterns? | | | |
| 5. Medications? | | | |
| 6. Use of recreation drugs, alcohol, nicotine, or caffeine? | | | |
| 7. Self-concept? | | | |
| 8. Life stressors and coping strategies? | | | |
| 9. Responsibilities and role at home and at work? | | | |
| 10. Type of work and level of satisfaction? | | | |
| 11. Finances? | | | |
| 12. Educational plans? | | | |
| 13. Social activities? | | | |
| 14. Relationships with others? | | | |

| Questions | Normal Findings | Abnormal Findings | Data Missing |
|---|---|---|---|
| 15. Values? | | | |
| 16. Spirituality? | | | |
| 17. Religious affiliations? | | | |
| 18. Environment, residency, and neighborhood? | | | |

## Activity E PERFORMING PHYSICAL ASSESSMENT

Use the following Physical Assessment Checklist as your guide to performing a head-to-toe assessment. Column 1 can be used by you to guide your physical assessment. Column 2 may be used by your instructor to evaluate your skills as necessary.

### Physical Assessment Checklist

| Assessment Skill | Findings (Normal or Abnormal) and Notes | | Performance (Satisfactory, Needs Improvement, Unsatisfactory) | | |
|---|---|---|---|---|---|
| | N | A | S | N | U |
| 1. Gather all equipment needed for a head-to-toe exam. | ☐ | ☐ | ☐ | ☐ | ☐ |
| 2. Prepare client by explaining what you will be doing. | ☐ | ☐ | ☐ | ☐ | ☐ |
| *General Survey* | | | | | |
| 1. Observe appearance. | ☐ | ☐ | ☐ | ☐ | ☐ |
| 2. Assess vital signs. | ☐ | ☐ | ☐ | ☐ | ☐ |
| 3. Take body measurements. | ☐ | ☐ | ☐ | ☐ | ☐ |
| 4. Calculate ideal body weight, body mass index, waist-to-hip ratio, mid-arm muscle area and circumference. | ☐ | ☐ | ☐ | ☐ | ☐ |
| 5. Test vision. | ☐ | ☐ | ☐ | ☐ | ☐ |
| *Mental Status Examination* | | | | | |
| 1. Observe LOC. | ☐ | ☐ | ☐ | ☐ | ☐ |
| 2. Observe posture and body movements. | ☐ | ☐ | ☐ | ☐ | ☐ |
| 3. Observe facial expressions. | ☐ | ☐ | ☐ | ☐ | ☐ |
| 4. Observe speech. | ☐ | ☐ | ☐ | ☐ | ☐ |
| 5. Observe mood, feelings, and expressions. | ☐ | ☐ | ☐ | ☐ | ☐ |
| 6. Observe thought processes and perceptions. | ☐ | ☐ | ☐ | ☐ | ☐ |
| 7. Assess cognitive abilities. | ☐ | ☐ | ☐ | ☐ | ☐ |
| 8. Give client a specimen cup if sample is needed, and ask client to empty bladder and change into gown. Ask client to sit on examination table. | ☐ | ☐ | ☐ | ☐ | ☐ |

| Assessment Skill | Findings (Normal or Abnormal) and Notes | | Performance (Satisfactory, Needs Improvement, Unsatisfactory) | | |
|---|---|---|---|---|---|
| | N | A | S | N | U |
| *Skin* | | | | | |
| 1. Throughout examination, assess skin for color variations, texture, temperature, turgor, edema, and lesions. | ☐ | ☐ | ☐ | ☐ | ☐ |
| 2. Teach skin self-examination. | ☐ | ☐ | ☐ | ☐ | ☐ |
| *Head and Face* | | | | | |
| 1. Inspect and palpate head. | ☐ | ☐ | ☐ | ☐ | ☐ |
| 2. Note consistency, distribution, color of hair. | ☐ | ☐ | ☐ | ☐ | ☐ |
| 3. Observe face for symmetry, features, expressions, condition of skin. | ☐ | ☐ | ☐ | ☐ | ☐ |
| 4. Have client smile, frown, show teeth, blow out cheeks, raise eyebrows, and tightly close eyes (CN VII). | ☐ | ☐ | ☐ | ☐ | ☐ |
| 5. Test sensations of forehead, cheeks, and chin (CN V). | ☐ | ☐ | ☐ | ☐ | ☐ |
| 6. Palpate temporal arteries for elasticity and tenderness. | ☐ | ☐ | ☐ | ☐ | ☐ |
| 7. Palpate temporomandibular joint. | ☐ | ☐ | ☐ | ☐ | ☐ |
| *Eyes* | | | | | |
| 1. Assess visual function. | ☐ | ☐ | ☐ | ☐ | ☐ |
| 2. Inspect external eye. | ☐ | ☐ | ☐ | ☐ | ☐ |
| 3. Test papillary reaction to light. | ☐ | ☐ | ☐ | ☐ | ☐ |
| 4. Test accommodation of pupils. | ☐ | ☐ | ☐ | ☐ | ☐ |
| 5. Assess corneal reflex (CN VII facial). | ☐ | ☐ | ☐ | ☐ | ☐ |
| 6. Use ophthalmoscope to inspect interior of eye. | ☐ | ☐ | ☐ | ☐ | ☐ |
| *Ears* | | | | | |
| 1. Inspect auricle, tragus, and lobule. | ☐ | ☐ | ☐ | ☐ | ☐ |
| 2. Palpate auricle and mastoid process. | ☐ | ☐ | ☐ | ☐ | ☐ |
| 3. Use otoscope to inspect auditory canal. | ☐ | ☐ | ☐ | ☐ | ☐ |
| 4. Use otoscope to inspect tympanic membrane. | ☐ | ☐ | ☐ | ☐ | ☐ |
| 5. Test hearing. | ☐ | ☐ | ☐ | ☐ | ☐ |
| *Nose and Sinuses* | | | | | |
| 1. Inspect external nose. | ☐ | ☐ | ☐ | ☐ | ☐ |
| 2. Palpate external nose for tenderness. | ☐ | ☐ | ☐ | ☐ | ☐ |
| 3. Check patency of airflow through nostrils. | ☐ | ☐ | ☐ | ☐ | ☐ |
| 4. Occlude each nostril and ask client to smell for soap, coffee, or vanilla (CN I). | ☐ | ☐ | ☐ | ☐ | ☐ |
| 5. Use otoscope to inspect internal nose. | ☐ | ☐ | ☐ | ☐ | ☐ |
| 6. Transilluminate maxillary sinuses. | ☐ | ☐ | ☐ | ☐ | ☐ |

| Assessment Skill | Findings (Normal or Abnormal) and Notes | | Performance (Satisfactory, Needs Improvement, Unsatisfactory) | | |
|---|:---:|:---:|:---:|:---:|:---:|
| | **N** | **A** | **S** | **N** | **U** |
| *Mouth and Throat* | | | | | |
| 1. Put on gloves. | ☐ | ☐ | ☐ | ☐ | ☐ |
| 2. Inspect lips. | ☐ | ☐ | ☐ | ☐ | ☐ |
| 3. Inspect teeth. | ☐ | ☐ | ☐ | ☐ | ☐ |
| 4. Check gums and buccal mucosa. | ☐ | ☐ | ☐ | ☐ | ☐ |
| 5. Inspect hard and soft palates. | ☐ | ☐ | ☐ | ☐ | ☐ |
| 6. Observe uvula. | ☐ | ☐ | ☐ | ☐ | ☐ |
| 7. Assess for gag reflex (CN X). | ☐ | ☐ | ☐ | ☐ | ☐ |
| 8. Inspect tonsils. | ☐ | ☐ | ☐ | ☐ | ☐ |
| 9. Inspect and palpate tongue. | ☐ | ☐ | ☐ | ☐ | ☐ |
| 10. Assess tongue strength (CN IX and X). | ☐ | ☐ | ☐ | ☐ | ☐ |
| 11. Check taste sensation (CN VII and IX). | ☐ | ☐ | ☐ | ☐ | ☐ |
| *Neck* | | | | | |
| 1. Inspect appearance of neck. | ☐ | ☐ | ☐ | ☐ | ☐ |
| 2. Test ROM of neck. | ☐ | ☐ | ☐ | ☐ | ☐ |
| 3. Palpate preauricular, postauricular, occipital, tonsillar, submandibular, and submental nodes. | ☐ | ☐ | ☐ | ☐ | ☐ |
| 4. Palpate trachea. | ☐ | ☐ | ☐ | ☐ | ☐ |
| 5. Palpate thyroid gland. | ☐ | ☐ | ☐ | ☐ | ☐ |
| 6. If enlarged, auscultate thyroid gland for bruits. | ☐ | ☐ | ☐ | ☐ | ☐ |
| 7. Palpate and auscultate carotid arteries. | ☐ | ☐ | ☐ | ☐ | ☐ |
| *Arms, Hands, and Fingers* | | | | | |
| 1. Inspect upper extremities. | ☐ | ☐ | ☐ | ☐ | ☐ |
| 2. Test shoulder shrug and ability to turn head against resistance (CN XI spinal). | ☐ | ☐ | ☐ | ☐ | ☐ |
| 3. Palpate arms. | ☐ | ☐ | ☐ | ☐ | ☐ |
| 4. Assess epitrochlear lymph nodes. | ☐ | ☐ | ☐ | ☐ | ☐ |
| 5. Test ROM of elbows. | ☐ | ☐ | ☐ | ☐ | ☐ |
| 6. Palpate brachial pulse. | ☐ | ☐ | ☐ | ☐ | ☐ |
| 7. Palpate ulnar and radial pulses. | ☐ | ☐ | ☐ | ☐ | ☐ |
| 8. Test ROM of wrist. | ☐ | ☐ | ☐ | ☐ | ☐ |
| 9. Inspect and palpate palms of hands. | ☐ | ☐ | ☐ | ☐ | ☐ |
| 10. Test ROM of fingers. | ☐ | ☐ | ☐ | ☐ | ☐ |

| Assessment Skill | Findings (Normal or Abnormal) and Notes | | Performance (Satisfactory, Needs Improvement, Unsatisfactory) | | |
|---|---|---|---|---|---|
| | N | A | S | N | U |
| 11. Use reflex hammer to test biceps, triceps, and brachioradialis reflexes. | ☐ | ☐ | ☐ | ☐ | ☐ |
| 12. Test rapid alternating movements of hands. | ☐ | ☐ | ☐ | ☐ | ☐ |
| 13. Test sensation in arms, hands, and fingers. | ☐ | ☐ | ☐ | ☐ | ☐ |
| *Posterior and Lateral Chest* | | | | | |
| 1. Ask client to continue sitting with arms at sides and stand behind client. Untie gown to expose posterior chest. | ☐ | ☐ | ☐ | ☐ | ☐ |
| 2. Inspect scapulae and chest wall. | ☐ | ☐ | ☐ | ☐ | ☐ |
| 3. Note use of accessory muscles when breathing. | ☐ | ☐ | ☐ | ☐ | ☐ |
| 4. Palpate chest. | ☐ | ☐ | ☐ | ☐ | ☐ |
| 5. Evaluate chest expansion at T9 or T10. | ☐ | ☐ | ☐ | ☐ | ☐ |
| 6. Percuss at posterior intercostals spaces. | ☐ | ☐ | ☐ | ☐ | ☐ |
| 7. Determine diaphragmatic excursion. | ☐ | ☐ | ☐ | ☐ | ☐ |
| 8. Auscultate posterior chest. | ☐ | ☐ | ☐ | ☐ | ☐ |
| 9. Test for two-point discrimination on back. | ☐ | ☐ | ☐ | ☐ | ☐ |
| 10. Auscultate apex and left sternal border of heart during exhalation. | ☐ | ☐ | ☐ | ☐ | ☐ |
| *Anterior Chest* | | | | | |
| 1. Inspect chest. | ☐ | ☐ | ☐ | ☐ | ☐ |
| 2. Note quality and pattern of respirations. | ☐ | ☐ | ☐ | ☐ | ☐ |
| 3. Observe intercostal spaces. | ☐ | ☐ | ☐ | ☐ | ☐ |
| 4. Palpate anterior chest. | ☐ | ☐ | ☐ | ☐ | ☐ |
| 5. Percuss anterior chest. | ☐ | ☐ | ☐ | ☐ | ☐ |
| 6. Auscultate anterior chest. | ☐ | ☐ | ☐ | ☐ | ☐ |
| 7. Test skin mobility and turgor. | ☐ | ☐ | ☐ | ☐ | ☐ |
| 8. Ask client to fold gown to waist and sit with arms hanging freely. | ☐ | ☐ | ☐ | ☐ | ☐ |
| *Female Breasts* | | | | | |
| 1. Inspect both breasts, areolas, and nipples. | ☐ | ☐ | ☐ | ☐ | ☐ |
| 2. Inspect for retractions and dimpling of nipples. | ☐ | ☐ | ☐ | ☐ | ☐ |
| 3. Palpate axillae. | ☐ | ☐ | ☐ | ☐ | ☐ |
| *Male Breasts* | | | | | |
| 1. Inspect breast tissue. | ☐ | ☐ | ☐ | ☐ | ☐ |
| 2. Palpate breast tissue and axillae. | ☐ | ☐ | ☐ | ☐ | ☐ |
| 3. Assist client to supine position with the head elevated to 30 to 45 degrees. Stand on client's right side. | ☐ | ☐ | ☐ | ☐ | ☐ |

| Assessment Skill | Findings (Normal or Abnormal) and Notes | | Performance (Satisfactory, Needs Improvement, Unsatisfactory) | | |
|---|---|---|---|---|---|
| | N | A | S | N | U |
| *Neck* | | | | | |
| 1. Evaluate jugular venous pressure. | ☐ | ☐ | ☐ | ☐ | ☐ |
| 2. Assist client to supine position (lower examination table). | ☐ | ☐ | ☐ | ☐ | ☐ |
| *Breasts (Female)* | | | | | |
| 1. Palpate breasts for masses and nipples for discharge. | ☐ | ☐ | ☐ | ☐ | ☐ |
| 2. Teach breast self-examination. | ☐ | ☐ | ☐ | ☐ | ☐ |
| *Heart* | | | | | |
| 1. Inspect and palpate for apical impulse. | ☐ | ☐ | ☐ | ☐ | ☐ |
| 2. Palpate the apex, left sternal border, and base of the heart. | ☐ | ☐ | ☐ | ☐ | ☐ |
| 3. Auscultate over aortic area, pulmonic area, Erb's point, tricuspid area, and apex. | ☐ | ☐ | ☐ | ☐ | ☐ |
| 4. Auscultate apex of heart as client lays on left side. | ☐ | ☐ | ☐ | ☐ | ☐ |
| *Abdomen* | | | | | |
| 1. Cover chest with gown and arrange draping to expose abdomen. | ☐ | ☐ | ☐ | ☐ | ☐ |
| 2. Inspect abdomen. | ☐ | ☐ | ☐ | ☐ | ☐ |
| 3. Auscultate abdomen. | ☐ | ☐ | ☐ | ☐ | ☐ |
| 4. Percuss abdomen. | ☐ | ☐ | ☐ | ☐ | ☐ |
| 5. Palpate abdomen. | ☐ | ☐ | ☐ | ☐ | ☐ |
| *Legs, Feet, and Toes* | | | | | |
| 1. Observe muscles. | ☐ | ☐ | ☐ | ☐ | ☐ |
| 2. Note hair distribution. | ☐ | ☐ | ☐ | ☐ | ☐ |
| 3. Palpate joints of hips and test ROM. | ☐ | ☐ | ☐ | ☐ | ☐ |
| 4. Palpate legs and feet. | ☐ | ☐ | ☐ | ☐ | ☐ |
| 5. Palpate knees. | ☐ | ☐ | ☐ | ☐ | ☐ |
| 6. Palpate ankles. | ☐ | ☐ | ☐ | ☐ | ☐ |
| 7. Assess capillary refill. | ☐ | ☐ | ☐ | ☐ | ☐ |
| 8. Test sensations (dull and sharp), two-point discrimination, reflexes, position sense, and vibratory sensation. | ☐ | ☐ | ☐ | ☐ | ☐ |
| 9. Perform heel-to-shin test. | ☐ | ☐ | ☐ | ☐ | ☐ |
| 10. Perform any special tests as warranted. | ☐ | ☐ | ☐ | ☐ | ☐ |
| 11. Secure gown and assist client to standing position. | ☐ | ☐ | ☐ | ☐ | ☐ |

| Assessment Skill | Findings (Normal or Abnormal) and Notes | | Performance (Satisfactory, Needs Improvement, Unsatisfactory) | | |
|---|---|---|---|---|---|
| | N | A | S | N | U |
| *Musculoskeletal and Neurologic Systems* | | | | | |
| 1. Observe for spinal curvatures and check for scoliosis. | ☐ | ☐ | ☐ | ☐ | ☐ |
| 2. Observe gait. | ☐ | ☐ | ☐ | ☐ | ☐ |
| 3. Observe tandem walk. | ☐ | ☐ | ☐ | ☐ | ☐ |
| 4. Observe hopping on each leg. | ☐ | ☐ | ☐ | ☐ | ☐ |
| 5. Perform Romberg's test. | ☐ | ☐ | ☐ | ☐ | ☐ |
| 6. Perform finger-to-nose test. | ☐ | ☐ | ☐ | ☐ | ☐ |
| *Female Genitalia* | | | | | |
| 1. Have female client assume the lithotomy position. Apply gloves. Apply lubricant as appropriate. | ☐ | ☐ | ☐ | ☐ | ☐ |
| 2. Inspect pubic hair. | ☐ | ☐ | ☐ | ☐ | ☐ |
| 3. Inspect mons pubis, labia majora, and perineum. | ☐ | ☐ | ☐ | ☐ | ☐ |
| 4. Inspect labia minora, clitoris, urethreal meatus, and vaginal opening. | ☐ | ☐ | ☐ | ☐ | ☐ |
| 5. Palpate Bartholin's glands, urethra, and Skene's glands. | ☐ | ☐ | ☐ | ☐ | ☐ |
| 6. Inspect cervix. | ☐ | ☐ | ☐ | ☐ | ☐ |
| 7. Inspect vagina. | ☐ | ☐ | ☐ | ☐ | ☐ |
| 8. Obtain cytologic smears and culture. | ☐ | ☐ | ☐ | ☐ | ☐ |
| 9. Palpate cervix. | ☐ | ☐ | ☐ | ☐ | ☐ |
| 10. Palpate uterus. | ☐ | ☐ | ☐ | ☐ | ☐ |
| 11. Palpate ovaries. | ☐ | ☐ | ☐ | ☐ | ☐ |
| 12. Discard gloves and apply clean gloves and lubricant. | ☐ | ☐ | ☐ | ☐ | ☐ |
| 13. Palpate rectovaginal septum. | ☐ | ☐ | ☐ | ☐ | ☐ |
| *Male Genitalia* | | | | | |
| 1. Sit on a stool and have client stand and face you with gown raised. Apply gloves. | ☐ | ☐ | ☐ | ☐ | ☐ |
| 2. Inspect penis. | ☐ | ☐ | ☐ | ☐ | ☐ |
| 3. Palpate for urethral discharge. | ☐ | ☐ | ☐ | ☐ | ☐ |
| 4. Inspect scrotum. | ☐ | ☐ | ☐ | ☐ | ☐ |
| 5. Palpate both testis and epididymis. | ☐ | ☐ | ☐ | ☐ | ☐ |
| 6. Transilluminate scrotal contents. | ☐ | ☐ | ☐ | ☐ | ☐ |
| 7. Inspect for bulges in inguinal and femoral areas. | ☐ | ☐ | ☐ | ☐ | ☐ |
| 8. Palpate for scrotal hernia. | ☐ | ☐ | ☐ | ☐ | ☐ |
| 9. Palpate for inguinal hernia. | ☐ | ☐ | ☐ | ☐ | ☐ |

| Assessment Skill | Findings (Normal or Abnormal) and Notes | | Performance (Satisfactory, Needs Improvement, Unsatisfactory) | | |
|---|---|---|---|---|---|
| | N | A | S | N | U |
| 10. Teach testicular self-examination. | ☐ | ☐ | ☐ | ☐ | ☐ |
| 11. Inspect perineal area. | ☐ | ☐ | ☐ | ☐ | ☐ |
| 12. Inspect sacrocaccygeal area. | ☐ | ☐ | ☐ | ☐ | ☐ |
| 13. Inspect for bulges or lesions as Valsalva maneuver is performed. | ☐ | ☐ | ☐ | ☐ | ☐ |
| *Rectal* | | | | | |
| 1. Ask the client to remain standing and to bend over the exam table. Change gloves. | ☐ | ☐ | ☐ | ☐ | ☐ |
| 2. Palpate anus. | ☐ | ☐ | ☐ | ☐ | ☐ |
| 3. Palpate external sphincter. | ☐ | ☐ | ☐ | ☐ | ☐ |
| 4. Palpate rectum. | ☐ | ☐ | ☐ | ☐ | ☐ |
| 5. Palpate peritoneal cavity. | ☐ | ☐ | ☐ | ☐ | ☐ |
| 6. Palpate prostate. | ☐ | ☐ | ☐ | ☐ | ☐ |
| 7. Inspect stool. | ☐ | ☐ | ☐ | ☐ | ☐ |

# CHAPTER POSTTEST

## Activity F  MATCHING

*Match the section of the head-to-toe examination on the left with the assessment on the right that would best be integrated there.*

**Section**

___ **1.** General survey

___ **2.** Mental Status Exam

___ **3.** Head and face

___ **4.** Eye

___ **5.** Ear

___ **6.** Mouth and throat

___ **7.** Neck

___ **8.** Arms, hands, and fingers

___ **9.** Male examination

**Assessment**

**a.** Biceps, triceps, and brachioradialis reflexes

**b.** Vital signs and anthropometric measurements

**c.** Mood, feelings, and perceptions

**d.** Cervical lymph nodes

**e.** Cranial nerve VII (facial)

**f.** Cranial nerve VIII

**g.** Cremasteric reflex

**h.** Cranial nerves IX and X

**i.** Cranial nerves II, III, IV, and VI

## Activity G  ESSAY QUESTIONS

1. Describe the equipment that is necessary to perform a total head-to-toe examination.

2. Describe two different ways that the nurse may integrate discrete parts of the physical examination to save time and to promote a smooth transition within the total physical examination.

# SELF-REFLECTION AND EVALUATION OF LEARNER OBJECTIVES

After you have read Chapter 28 and completed the above quizzes and activities, please identify to what degree you have met each of the following chapter learning objectives. For those objectives you have met partially or not at all, you will want to review the chapter content for that learning objective.

| Objective | Very Much | Somewhat | Not At All |
|---|---|---|---|
| 1. Explain how to prepare yourself and the client for a total physical examination. | | | |
| 2. List all the equipment needed for a total physical examination. | | | |
| 3. Describe parts of the physical examination that can be integrated within assessment of each of the body systems. | | | |
| 4. Perform a total head-to-toe integrated physical examination. | | | |

# UNIT IV

# Nursing Assessment of Special Groups

# Assessing Childbearing Women

## Chapter Overview

Women in the childbearing years have unique health care needs, particularly during pregnancy. The nursing assessment focuses generally on the various needs and changes specific to women and particularly on the related issues of hormones and hormonal balance.

## CHAPTER PRETEST

### Activity A  MULTIPLE CHOICE

*Choose the one best answer for each of the following multiple-choice questions.*

____ 1. While assessing the abdomen of a pregnant client, the nurse observes striae gravidarum. The nurse should instruct the client that after delivery, the striae gravidarum will

   **a.** completely disappear.

   **b.** remain the same.

   **c.** disappear if a special ointment is used.

   **d.** fade to a white or silvery color.

____ 2. While assessing the abdomen of a pregnant woman, the nurse observes a dark line from the client's umbilicus to the mons pubis. The nurse should explain to the client that this is called

   **a.** linea nigra.

   **b.** chloasma.

   **c.** melanin.

   **d.** epulis.

____ 3. During pregnancy, a relaxation of the ligaments and joints is caused by the increase in

   **a.** estrogen.

   **b.** chorionic gonadotropin.

   **c.** lactating hormone.

   **d.** progesterone.

____ **4.** The nurse is caring for a client who is 24 weeks pregnant. The client tells the nurse that she has been secreting colostrum for the past few days. The nurse should instruct the client that colostrum secretion

   **a.** does not normally occur until delivery of the baby.

   **b.** may be indicative of a problem with the breasts.

   **c.** is normal for some women in the second and third trimesters.

   **d.** may be indicative of preterm labor ensuing.

____ **5.** One cardiac change that commonly occurs in a pregnant client is

   **a.** an increase in maternal blood volume by 40% to 50%.

   **b.** a decrease in plasma volume by 20%.

   **c.** physiologic hypertension that stabilizes by 24 weeks' gestation.

   **d.** a decrease in the heart rate of the client.

____ **6.** As pregnancy progresses, the abdominal muscles may stretch to the point of separation. This condition is termed

   **a.** herniation.

   **b.** McDonald's sign.

   **c.** Goodell's sign.

   **d.** diastasis recti abdominis.

____ **7.** The nurse has instructed a pregnant client about changes that may occur to the client's gastrointestinal system during pregnancy. The nurse determines that the client needs further instructions when the client says

   **a.** "As a result of pregnancy, diarrhea may occur more often."

   **b.** "Gastric motility is decreased from the pressure of the fetus."

   **c.** "Constipation may occur because gastric tone is decreased."

   **d.** "Gallstone formation may occur because of prolonged emptying time of the gallbladder."

____ **8.** While interviewing a pregnant client, the nurse determines that the client has pica. The nurse should assess the client's

   **a.** blood sugar.

   **b.** teeth and gums.

   **c.** nutritional status.

   **d.** emotional status.

____ **9.** During pregnancy, the uterus enlarges as a result of hypertrophy of existing myometrial cells and hyperplasia of new cells. This growth is due to

   **a.** estrogen.

   **b.** progesterone.

   **c.** growth hormone.

   **d.** lactating hormone.

____ **10.** The nurse is caring for a pregnant client who is at approximately 20 weeks' gestation. The nurse is planning to measure the client's fundal height. At 20 weeks' gestation, the nurse should locate the top of the fundus

   **a.** at the top of the symphysis pubis.

   **b.** midway between the symphysis pubis and the umbilicus.

   **c.** at the level of the umbilicus.

   **d.** above the level of the umbilicus.

**LEARNER ACTIVITIES**

*Working with peers in the learning lab*

*After reading Chapter 29, participate in the following learning activities.*

**1.** With a lab partner, role-play nurse and childbearing client. Have the client present with common complaints of pregnancy. Have the nurse reassure the client, explain in layperson's terms the reasons for these symptoms, and offer recommendations for relief. (Also have the nurse refer any problems that are not normal to an appropriate health care provider, such as midwife or a physician.)

**Activity C** **INTERVIEWING AND RECORDING ASSESSMENT FINDINGS**

Use the following Nursing History Checklist as your guide for interviewing and recording the findings in an assessment of the childbearing woman.

**Nursing History Checklist**

| Questions | Satisfactory Data | Needs Additional Data | Data Missing |
|---|---|---|---|
| *Current Symptoms* | | | |
| 1. Weight changes? | | | |
| 2. Upper respiratory symptoms? | | | |
| 3. Stomach or bowel problems? | | | |
| 4. Urinary tract symptoms? | | | |
| 5. Vaginal discharge, bleeding, or leaking fluid? | | | |
| 6. Psychologic problems? | | | |
| 7. Breast changes? | | | |
| *Past History* | | | |
| 1. Past pregnancy history (include all previous deliveries and miscarriages)? | | | |
| 2. Neonatal problems at delivery or within the first 2 weeks of life? | | | |
| 3. Complicated pregnancies requiring termination, molar pregnancy, ectopic pregnancy, etc.? | | | |
| 4. LMP and duration, bleeding since that time? | | | |
| 5. Type of birth control used, if any? | | | |
| 6. Infertility problems? | | | |
| 7. Reproductive surgeries, abnormal Pap smears, etc.? | | | |
| 8. History of sexually transmitted diseases, treatment, vaginal infections, etc.? | | | |
| 9. Blood type? | | | |
| 10. Medical history? | | | |
| 11. Hospitalizations? | | | |
| 12. Surgeries? | | | |

| Questions | Satisfactory Data | Needs Additional Data | Data Missing |
|---|---|---|---|
| *Family History* | | | |
| 1. History of birth defects in the family? | | | |
| 2. Ethnic background? | | | |
| 3. Heart disease, lung disease, diabetes, asthma, cancer, birth defects, blood disorders, mental retardation, sickle cell disease? | | | |
| *Lifestyle and Health Practices* | | | |
| 1. Age at delivery? | | | |
| 2. Current medications? | | | |
| 3. Alcohol/cigarette use? | | | |
| 4. Street drug use? | | | |
| 5. Family members who consider social habits to be a problem? | | | |
| 6. Diet evaluation? | | | |
| 7. Weight/baseline? | | | |
| 8. Exercise routine? | | | |
| 9. Client's occupation/highest degree? | | | |
| 10. Work routine? | | | |
| 11. Chemical/radiation exposure? | | | |
| 12. Risk for toxoplasmosis? | | | |
| 13. Partner profile? | | | |
| 14. Social support systems? | | | |
| 15. Siblings? | | | |

## Activity D  PERFORMING PHYSICAL ASSESSMENT

Use the following Physical Assessment Checklist as your guide to performing an assessment examination of the childbearing woman. Column 1 can be used by you to guide your physical assessment. Column 2 may be used by your instructor to evaluate your skills as necessary.

### Physical Assessment Checklist

| Assessment Skill | Findings (Normal or Abnormal) and Notes | | Performance (Satisfactory, Needs Improvement, Unsatisfactory) | | |
|---|---|---|---|---|---|
| | N | A | S | N | U |
| 1. Gather equipment (ophthalmoscope, otoscope, stethoscope, speculum, sphygmomanometer, light, tape measure, fetal Doppler, gloves, lubricant, slides). | ☐ | ☐ | ☐ | ☐ | ☐ |
| 2. Explain procedure to client. | ☐ | ☐ | ☐ | ☐ | ☐ |

| Assessment Skill | Findings (Normal or Abnormal) and Notes | | Performance (Satisfactory, Needs Improvement, Unsatisfactory) | | |
|---|---|---|---|---|---|
| | N | A | S | N | U |
| 3. Ask client to put on a gown. | ☐ | ☐ | ☐ | ☐ | ☐ |
| 4. Assess vital signs. | ☐ | ☐ | ☐ | ☐ | ☐ |
| 5. Measure weight/height. | ☐ | ☐ | ☐ | ☐ | ☐ |
| 6. Observe behavior. | ☐ | ☐ | ☐ | ☐ | ☐ |
| 7. Inspect skin. | ☐ | ☐ | ☐ | ☐ | ☐ |
| 8. Inspect hair/nails. | ☐ | ☐ | ☐ | ☐ | ☐ |
| 9. Inspect neck. | ☐ | ☐ | ☐ | ☐ | ☐ |
| 10. Inspect mouth/nose/throat. | ☐ | ☐ | ☐ | ☐ | ☐ |
| 11. Inspect, palpate, percuss, and auscultate chest. | ☐ | ☐ | ☐ | ☐ | ☐ |
| 12. Inspect and palpate breasts. | ☐ | ☐ | ☐ | ☐ | ☐ |
| 13. Auscultate heart. | ☐ | ☐ | ☐ | ☐ | ☐ |
| 14. Inspect and palpate abdomen. | ☐ | ☐ | ☐ | ☐ | ☐ |
| 15. Measure fundal height. | ☐ | ☐ | ☐ | ☐ | ☐ |
| 16. Assess fetal position. | ☐ | ☐ | ☐ | ☐ | ☐ |
| 17. Auscultate fetal heart tones. | ☐ | ☐ | ☐ | ☐ | ☐ |
| 18. Inspect external genitalia. | ☐ | ☐ | ☐ | ☐ | ☐ |
| 19. Palpate Bartholin's and Skene's glands. | ☐ | ☐ | ☐ | ☐ | ☐ |
| 20. Inspect vaginal opening. | ☐ | ☐ | ☐ | ☐ | ☐ |
| 21. Perform speculum examination. | ☐ | ☐ | ☐ | ☐ | ☐ |
| 22. Obtain specimens. | ☐ | ☐ | ☐ | ☐ | ☐ |
| 23. Perform pelvic examination. | ☐ | ☐ | ☐ | ☐ | ☐ |
| 24. Inspect anus/rectum. | ☐ | ☐ | ☐ | ☐ | ☐ |
| 25. Auscultate blood pressure. | ☐ | ☐ | ☐ | ☐ | ☐ |
| 26. Inspect face and extremities. | ☐ | ☐ | ☐ | ☐ | ☐ |
| 27. Percuss deep tendon reflexes. | ☐ | ☐ | ☐ | ☐ | ☐ |
| 28. Determine pelvic adequacy. | ☐ | ☐ | ☐ | ☐ | ☐ |
| 29. Determine height/inclination of symphysis pubis. | ☐ | ☐ | ☐ | ☐ | ☐ |
| 30. Palpate lateral walls of pelvis. | ☐ | ☐ | ☐ | ☐ | ☐ |
| 31. Palpate ischial spines. | ☐ | ☐ | ☐ | ☐ | ☐ |
| 32. Palpate sacrum/coccyx. | ☐ | ☐ | ☐ | ☐ | ☐ |
| 33. Measure diagonal conjugate. | ☐ | ☐ | ☐ | ☐ | ☐ |
| 34. Calculate obstetric conjugate. | ☐ | ☐ | ☐ | ☐ | ☐ |

| Assessment Skill | Findings (Normal or Abnormal) and Notes | | Performance (Satisfactory, Needs Improvement, Unsatisfactory) | | |
|---|---|---|---|---|---|
| | N | A | S | N | U |
| 35. Measure transverse diameter of the pelvic outlet. | ☐ | ☐ | ☐ | ☐ | ☐ |
| 36. Assess for complaints of common neurologic discomforts during pregnancy. | ☐ | ☐ | ☐ | ☐ | ☐ |
| 37. Formulate nursing diagnoses (wellness, risk, actual). | ☐ | ☐ | ☐ | ☐ | ☐ |
| 38. Formulate collaborative problems. | ☐ | ☐ | ☐ | ☐ | ☐ |
| 39. Make necessary referrals. | ☐ | ☐ | ☐ | ☐ | ☐ |

# CHAPTER POSTTEST

**Activity E**  **MULTIPLE CHOICE**

*Choose the one best answer for each of the following multiple-choice questions.*

_____ 1. A pregnant client who is at approximately 36 weeks' gestation tells the nurse that she experiences dizziness while in bed. The nurse should instruct the client to avoid which position?

  **a.** side-lying.

  **b.** left lateral.

  **c.** prone.

  **d.** supine.

_____ 2. A client who is of normal weight just learned that she is 10 weeks pregnant. The client asks the nurse about weight gain during pregnancy. The nurse should instruct the client that the recommended weight gain is

  **a.** 15 to 20 pounds.

  **b.** 20 to 25 pounds.

  **c.** 25 to 35 pounds.

  **d.** 35 to 45 pounds.

_____ 3. A pregnant client at 12 weeks' gestation visits the clinic and tells the nurse that she has been vomiting severely for the past 5 days. The nurse should refer the client to a physician for possible

  **a.** hyperemesis gravidarum.

  **b.** viral infection.

  **c.** fetal anomalies.

  **d.** peptic ulcer.

_____ 4. A pregnant client visits the clinic for the first time. She tells the nurse that she has had two spontaneous abortions before this pregnancy. The nurse should refer the client to a physician for possible

  **a.** incompetent cervix.

  **b.** substance abuse.

  **c.** Rh incompatibility.

  **d.** hyperthyroidism.

_____ **5.** A pregnant client visits the clinic for the first time. The client tells the nurse that this is her first pregnancy and that she and her husband are Ashkenazi Jews and immigrated to the United States from Israel. The nurse should encourage the client to be tested for

**a.** sickle cell anemia.

**b.** cystic fibrosis.

**c.** cerebral palsy.

**d.** Tay–Sachs disease.

_____ **6.** A pregnant client near term is admitted to the hospital with scant vaginal bleeding and mild contractions. The client tells the nurse that she uses cocaine occasionally. The nurse should assess the client for signs and symptoms of

**a.** oligohydramnios.

**b.** polyhydramnios.

**c.** placenta previa.

**d.** abruptio placenta.

_____ **7.** A pregnant client visits the clinic for the first time. The nurse should explain to the client that she will have initial routine blood tests, which include testing for

**a.** $\alpha$-fetoprotein levels.

**b.** chromosomal anomalies.

**c.** cystic fibrosis.

**d.** Rh status.

_____ **8.** A pregnant client visits the clinic at 36 weeks' gestation. The nurse weighs the client and determines that the client has gained 5 pounds in 1 week. The nurse should assess the client's

**a.** dietary patterns.

**b.** edema of the lower extremities.

**c.** urinary patterns.

**d.** blood pressure.

_____ **9.** The nurse is planning to perform Leopold's maneuvers on a pregnant client. To perform the first maneuver, the nurse should place his or her hands on the

**a.** upper quadrant of the maternal abdomen.

**b.** lateral sides of the maternal abdomen.

**c.** presenting part.

**d.** top of the symphysis pubis.

_____ **10.** While caring for a pregnant client at 8 weeks' gestation, the client asks the nurse, "When can you hear the baby's heartbeat?" The nurse should instruct the client that when a Doppler device is used, the earliest time when the fetal heart rate can be heard is the gestational age of

**a.** 10 weeks.

**b.** 14 weeks.

**c.** 18 weeks.

**d.** 22 weeks.

____ **11.** While assessing a pregnant client, the nurse detects fetal heart rate decelerations that occur after a contraction. The nurse should notify the client's physician because this may be indicative of

   **a.** fetal demise.

   **b.** cardiac disease.

   **c.** head compression.

   **d.** poor placental perfusion.

____ **12.** The nurse is preparing to assess the fetal heart rate of a pregnant client near term. When the nurse hears the fetal heart rate above the maternal umbilicus, the fetus is most likely in which position?

   **a.** transverse.

   **b.** breech.

   **c.** vertex.

   **d.** face.

____ **13.** A pregnant client visits the clinic and complains of a thick purulent vaginal discharge. The nurse should obtain a specimen of the vaginal discharge because this type of discharge is usually indicative of

   **a.** gonorrhea.

   **b.** bacterial vaginosis.

   **c.** *Candida albicans* infection.

   **d.** chlamydial infection.

____ **14.** While assessing a pregnant client at 36 weeks' gestation, the nurse observes that the client's face is edematous and she has 3+ reflexes with mild clonus. The nurse should refer the client to a physician for possible

   **a.** hydatidiform mole.

   **b.** multiple gestation.

   **c.** pregnancy-induced hypertension.

   **d.** hyperthyroidism.

____ **15.** The nurse is caring for a pregnant client at 14 weeks' gestation and determines that the measurement between the client's ischial tuberosities is 10.5 cm. The nurse should

   **a.** instruct the client that a vaginal delivery is likely.

   **b.** refer the client to a physician for small pelvic size.

   **c.** measure the pubic arch to validate the measurement.

   **d.** estimate the size of the fetus.

**Activity F CROSSWORD PUZZLE**

*Complete the following crossword puzzle to become more familiar with the terminology used with assessment of the childbearing woman.*

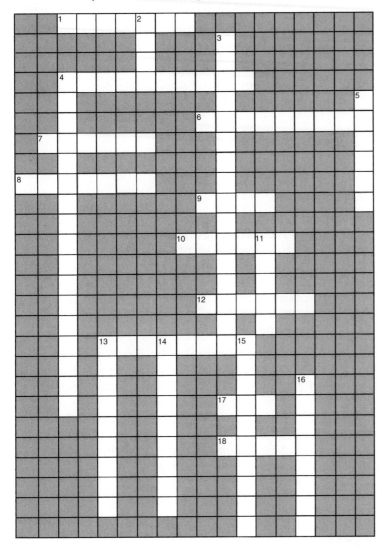

## ACROSS

**1.** Pregnancy in which the ovum is implanted outside the uterine cavity

**4.** The darker pigmentation appearing on the stomach that extends from the umbilicus to the symphysis pubis

**6.** The method used to assess uterine contractions

**7.** Tumor-like lesion that appears on the woman's gums

**8.** A nonsteroidal hormone that influences the pelvic joints and ligaments to loosen up during pregnancy

## DOWN

**2.** A craving for nonnutritional substances, such as dirt, clay, etc.

**3.** "Stretch marks" during pregnancy

**4.** Technique used to determine the presentation, position, and presenting part of the fetus

**5.** Women may develop physiologic _____ during pregnancy, often because the disproportionate increase in blood volume when compared with red blood cell production

**11.** How many trimesters are there in a pregnancy?

9. Fetal heart tones are best heard through the _____ of the fetus

10. At 30 weeks' gestation, the uterus should measure approximately _____ cm

12. The presentation in which the buttocks appear first in the vaginal canal

13. The facial mask of pregnancy

17. In the longitudinal _____ the fetal spine axis is parallel to the mother's spinal axis

18. True or false: Systolic murmurs are not a normal variant during pregnancy

13. Fluid secreted from the breasts, especially during the third trimester

14. The _____ conjugate is the smallest opening through which the fetal head must pass

15. Conflicting feelings and emotions felt by many women during the first trimester

16. Most common type of pelvis found in women

**Activity G** **CRITICAL THINKING AND CASE STUDIES**

1. On the basis of the following assessment information, work through the steps of analyzing the data. Identify abnormal data and strengths in **subjective and objective findings**, assemble **cue clusters**, draw **inferences**, make possible **nursing diagnoses**, identify **defining characteristics**, **confirm or rule out** the nursing diagnosis, and **document** your conclusions. Use the blank diagnostic analysis charts provided at the end of this book to guide your thinking. You may want to write on the chart or use separate paper. Propose nursing diagnoses that are specific to the client in the case study. Identify collaborative problems, if any, for this client. Finally, identify data, if any, that point toward a medical problem requiring a referral.

Kaitlin presents to your office today, thinking that she may be pregnant. Kaitlin is a 20-year-old primigravida who remembers her last menstrual period (LMP) as having been November 13, 2008, which would make her at approximately 20 weeks' gestation. She states that she did have some irregular spotting in December for approximately 2 days.

Kaitlin's medical and surgical history is unremarkable. Her family history is also noncontributory. Her social history is negative for alcohol and drugs. She is single and lives at home with her parents while attending college. The father of the baby is involved but is unsure about his feelings regarding the pregnancy. This pregnancy was not planned, and he wants to finish college and develop his career. Marriage plans are not in the father's schedule at this time.

# SELF-REFLECTION AND EVALUATION
# OF LEARNER OBJECTIVES

After you have read Chapter 29 and completed the above quizzes and activities, please identify to what degree you have met each of the following chapter learning objectives. For those objectives that you have met partially or not at all, you will want to review the chapter content for that learning objective.

| Objective | Very Much | Somewhat | Not At All |
|---|---|---|---|
| 1. Explain the dynamic cardiovascular changes that occur during pregnancy. | | | |
| 2. Describe the skin changes that occur during pregnancy. | | | |
| 3. Measure the progressional growth of the uterus during pregnancy. | | | |
| 4. Discuss common concerns and complaints experienced by the pregnant client. | | | |
| 5. Obtain an accurate nursing history by conducting a prenatal interview. | | | |
| 6. Demonstrate how to correctly perform Leopold's maneuvers. | | | |

# Assessing Newborns and Infants

During the first year of life, the newborn undergoes rapid physical and mental growth and development. Routine preventive health care is important for early detection of medical disorders/abnormalities and intervention that may grossly affect proper growth and development of the newborn.

## CHAPTER PRETEST

**Activity A** **MULTIPLE CHOICE**

*Choose the one best answer for each of the following multiple-choice questions.*

_____ **1.** The anterior fontanelle of a neonate closes between

    **a.** 2 and 3 months.

    **b.** 4 and 6 months.

    **c.** 7 and 11 months.

    **d.** 12 and 18 months.

_____ **2.** The nurse is planning to instruct a first-time mother about her newborn. The nurse should plan to instruct the mother that the newborn

    **a.** is an obligatory nose breather.

    **b.** will have deciduous teeth by 3 months.

    **c.** who drools is preparing for tooth eruption.

    **d.** will develop permanent teeth in the jaw by 6 years of age.

_____ **3.** Normal breathing pattern for a full-term infant may include

    **a.** abdominal breathing with a rate of 80–100 breaths/minute.

    **b.** chest breathing with nasal flaring of 20–40 breaths/minute.

    **c.** shallow and irregular breathing with a rate of 80–100 breaths/minute.

    **d.** abdominal/chest breathing movements at a rate of 30–60 breaths/minute.

_____ **4.** The Moro Reflex is

    **a.** a response to sudden stimulation or an abrupt change in position.

    **b.** fanning of the toes.

    **c.** stepping of the feet.

    **d.** extension of one arm and leg when turning the head.

## Activity B   LEARNER ACTIVITIES

### Working with peers in the learning lab

*After reading Chapter 30, participate in the following learning activities.*

**1.** A 4-month-old is brought in for well-child care. The mother asks, "What is my baby going to have done today?" Discuss with a lab partner what you would include in your reply.

## Activity C   INTERVIEWING AND RECORDING ASSESSMENT FINDINGS

Use the following Nursing History Checklist as your guide to interviewing and recording the findings of a pediatric assessment.

### Nursing History Checklist

| Questions | Normal Findings | Abnormal Findings | Additional Data Needed |
|---|---|---|---|
| *Current Symptoms* | | | |
| 1. Parent's (informant's) reason for seeking health care for the newborn or infant? | | | |
| *Current Health/Illness Status* | | | |
| 1. Symptom analysis of chief complaint? | | | |
| 2. Other current or recurrent illnesses or problems? | | | |
| 3. Any other health concerns? | | | |
| 4. Current medication used? | | | |
| *Past History* | | | |
| 1. Birth history (pregnancy, labor and delivery, perinatal history)? | | | |
| 2. Previous illnesses, injuries, or surgeries? | | | |
| 3. Allergies (and reactions to same)? | | | |
| 4. Immunization status? | | | |
| 5. Growth and developmental milestones? | | | |
| 6. Habits? | | | |
| *Review of Systems* | | | |
| 1. General: overall health status? | | | |
| 2. Integument: lesions, bruising, care habits? | | | |
| 3. Head: trauma? | | | |
| 4. Eyes: visual acuity, last eye exam, drainage, infections? | | | |
| 5. Ears: hearing acuity, last hearing exam, drainage, infections? | | | |

| Questions | Normal Findings | Abnormal Findings | Additional Data Needed |
|---|---|---|---|
| 6. Nose: bleeding, congestion, discharge? | | | |
| 7. Mouth: lesions, tooth eruption, last dental exam? | | | |
| 8. Throat: hoarseness, difficulty swallowing? | | | |
| 9. Neck: limited range of motion? | | | |
| 10. Chest: cough, wheezing, shortness of breath, asthma, infections? | | | |
| 11. Breasts: lesions, discharge, swelling? | | | |
| 12. Cardiovascular: history of murmurs, congenital defects? | | | |
| 13. Gastrointestinal: change in appetite, bowel habits, food intolerances, nausea, vomiting, history of parasites? | | | |
| 14. Genitourinary: discharge, urinary tract infections? | | | |
| 15. Musculoskeletal: pain, swelling, fractures, mobility problems, scoliosis? | | | |
| 16. Neurologic: ataxia, tremors, unusual movements, seizures? | | | |
| 17. Lymphatic: pain, swelling or tenderness, enlargement of spleen or liver? | | | |
| 18. Endocrine/metabolic: growth patterns, polyuria, polydypsia, polyphagia? | | | |
| 19. Psychiatric history: any psychiatric, developmental, substance abuse, or eating disorder? | | | |
| *Family History* | | | |
| 1. Family genetic traits or diseases with familial tendencies? | | | |
| 2. Communicable diseases? | | | |
| 3. Psychiatric disorders? | | | |
| 4. Substance abuse? | | | |
| *Nutritional History* | | | |
| 1. Quantity and the types of food or formula ingested daily (use 24-hour recall, food diary for 3 days [2 weekdays and 1 weekend day], or food frequency record)? | | | |
| 2. Newborn or infant has any problem with feeding? | | | |
| *Sleep History* | | | |
| 1. Sleep patterns of newborn or infant? | | | |
| *Developmental Assessment* | | | |
| 1. Reflexes? | | | |
| 2. Denver Developmental Screening Test results? | | | |

## Activity D   PERFORMING PHYSICAL ASSESSMENT

Use the following Physical Assessment Checklist as your guide to performing a pediatric assessment examination. Column 1 can be used by you to guide your physical assessment. Column 2 may be used by your instructor to evaluate your skills as necessary.

### Physical Assessment Checklist

| Assessment Skill | Findings (Normal or Abnormal) and Notes | | Performance (Satisfactory, Needs Improvement, Unsatisfactory) | | |
|---|---|---|---|---|---|
| | N | A | S | N | U |
| 1. In most cases, physical assessment involves a head-to-toe examination that covers each body system. | ☐ | ☐ | ☐ | ☐ | ☐ |
| *General Appearance* | | | | | |
| 1. Inspect physical appearance. | ☐ | ☐ | ☐ | ☐ | ☐ |
| 2. Assess nutritional state. | ☐ | ☐ | ☐ | ☐ | ☐ |
| 3. Assess behavior. | ☐ | ☐ | ☐ | ☐ | ☐ |
| 4. Assess overall development. | ☐ | ☐ | ☐ | ☐ | ☐ |
| *Vital Signs* | | | | | |
| 1. Measure blood pressure. | ☐ | ☐ | ☐ | ☐ | ☐ |
| 2. Measure pulse rate. | ☐ | ☐ | ☐ | ☐ | ☐ |
| 3. Measure respirations. | ☐ | ☐ | ☐ | ☐ | ☐ |
| 4. Measure temperature. | ☐ | ☐ | ☐ | ☐ | ☐ |
| 5. Measure height and weight. | ☐ | ☐ | ☐ | ☐ | ☐ |
| 6. Measure head circumference. | ☐ | ☐ | ☐ | ☐ | ☐ |
| *Skin, Hair, and Nails* | | | | | |
| 1. Inspect and palpate skin. | ☐ | ☐ | ☐ | ☐ | ☐ |
| 2. Inspect and palpate hair (distribution, characteristics). | ☐ | ☐ | ☐ | ☐ | ☐ |
| 3. Inspect and palpate nails (texture, shape, color, condition). | ☐ | ☐ | ☐ | ☐ | ☐ |
| *Head, Neck, and Cervical Lymph Nodes* | | | | | |
| 1. Inspect and palpate the head (symmetry, condition of fontanelles). | ☐ | ☐ | ☐ | ☐ | ☐ |
| 2. Inspect and palpate the face. | ☐ | ☐ | ☐ | ☐ | ☐ |
| 3. Inspect and palpate the neck (suppleness, lymph nodes for swelling, mobility, temperature, and tenderness). | ☐ | ☐ | ☐ | ☐ | ☐ |
| *Mouth, Throat, Nose, and Sinuses* | | | | | |
| 1. Inspect mouth and throat (tooth eruption, condition of gums, lips, teeth, palpates, tonsils, tongue, buccal mucosa). | ☐ | ☐ | ☐ | ☐ | ☐ |
| 2. Inspect nose and sinuses (discharge, tenderness, turbinates [color, swelling]). | ☐ | ☐ | ☐ | ☐ | ☐ |

| Assessment Skill | Findings (Normal or Abnormal) and Notes | | Performance (Satisfactory, Needs Improvement, Unsatisfactory) | | |
|---|---|---|---|---|---|
| | N | A | S | N | U |
| *Eyes* | | | | | |
| 1. Inspect external eye. | ☐ | ☐ | ☐ | ☐ | ☐ |
| 2. Perform visual acuity tests. | ☐ | ☐ | ☐ | ☐ | ☐ |
| 3. Perform extraocular muscle tests. | ☐ | ☐ | ☐ | ☐ | ☐ |
| 4. Perform internal (ophthalmoscopic) examination. | ☐ | ☐ | ☐ | ☐ | ☐ |
| *Ears* | | | | | |
| 1. Inspect external ears. | ☐ | ☐ | ☐ | ☐ | ☐ |
| 2. Perform otoscopic examination. | ☐ | ☐ | ☐ | ☐ | ☐ |
| 3. Assess hearing acuity. | ☐ | ☐ | ☐ | ☐ | ☐ |
| *Thorax and Lungs* | | | | | |
| 1. Inspect shape of thorax and respiratory effort. | ☐ | ☐ | ☐ | ☐ | ☐ |
| 2. Percuss the lungs. | ☐ | ☐ | ☐ | ☐ | ☐ |
| 3. Auscultate for breath sounds and adventitious sounds. | ☐ | ☐ | ☐ | ☐ | ☐ |
| *Breasts* | | | | | |
| 1. Inspect and palpate breasts (shape, discharge, lesions). | ☐ | ☐ | ☐ | ☐ | ☐ |
| *Heart* | | | | | |
| 1. Inspect and palpate the precordium. | ☐ | ☐ | ☐ | ☐ | ☐ |
| 2. Auscultate heart sounds. | ☐ | ☐ | ☐ | ☐ | ☐ |
| *Abdomen* | | | | | |
| 1. Inspect shape. | ☐ | ☐ | ☐ | ☐ | ☐ |
| 2. Inspect umbilicus. | ☐ | ☐ | ☐ | ☐ | ☐ |
| 3. Auscultate bowel sounds. | ☐ | ☐ | ☐ | ☐ | ☐ |
| 4. Palpate softness. | ☐ | ☐ | ☐ | ☐ | ☐ |
| 5. Palpate for masses and tenderness. | ☐ | ☐ | ☐ | ☐ | ☐ |
| 6. Palpate liver. | ☐ | ☐ | ☐ | ☐ | ☐ |
| 7. Palpate spleen. | ☐ | ☐ | ☐ | ☐ | ☐ |
| 8. Palpate kidneys. | ☐ | ☐ | ☐ | ☐ | ☐ |
| 9. Palpate bladder. | ☐ | ☐ | ☐ | ☐ | ☐ |
| *Male Genitalia* | | | | | |
| 1. Inspect penis and urinary meatus. | ☐ | ☐ | ☐ | ☐ | ☐ |
| 2. Inspect and palpate scrotum and testes. | ☐ | ☐ | ☐ | ☐ | ☐ |
| 3. Inspect and palpate inguinal area for hernias. | ☐ | ☐ | ☐ | ☐ | ☐ |

| Assessment Skill | Findings (Normal or Abnormal) and Notes | | Performance (Satisfactory, Needs Improvement, Unsatisfactory) | | |
|---|---|---|---|---|---|
| | N | A | S | N | U |
| *Female Genitalia* | | | | | |
| 1. Inspect external genitalia. | ☐ | ☐ | ☐ | ☐ | ☐ |
| 2. Inspect internal genitalia. | ☐ | ☐ | ☐ | ☐ | ☐ |
| *Anus and Rectum* | | | | | |
| 1. Inspect anus. | ☐ | ☐ | ☐ | ☐ | ☐ |
| 2. Palpate rectum. | ☐ | ☐ | ☐ | ☐ | ☐ |
| *Musculoskeletal* | | | | | |
| 1. Assess feet and legs. | ☐ | ☐ | ☐ | ☐ | ☐ |
| 2. Assess for congenital hip dysplasia. | ☐ | ☐ | ☐ | ☐ | ☐ |
| 3. Assess spine and posture. | ☐ | ☐ | ☐ | ☐ | ☐ |
| 4. Assess gait. | ☐ | ☐ | ☐ | ☐ | ☐ |
| 5. Assess joints. | ☐ | ☐ | ☐ | ☐ | ☐ |
| 6. Assess muscles. | ☐ | ☐ | ☐ | ☐ | ☐ |
| *Neurologic* | | | | | |
| 1. Perform newborn assessment. | ☐ | ☐ | ☐ | ☐ | ☐ |
| 2. Test cranial nerve function. | ☐ | ☐ | ☐ | ☐ | ☐ |
| 3. Test deep tendon and superficial reflexes. | ☐ | ☐ | ☐ | ☐ | ☐ |
| 4. Test sensory function. | ☐ | ☐ | ☐ | ☐ | ☐ |
| 5. Test motor function and infantile reflexes. | ☐ | ☐ | ☐ | ☐ | ☐ |
| 6. Observe for "soft" signs. | ☐ | ☐ | ☐ | ☐ | ☐ |
| *Analysis of Data* | | | | | |
| 1. Formulate nursing diagnoses (wellness, risk, actual). | ☐ | ☐ | ☐ | ☐ | ☐ |
| 2. Formulate collaborative problems. | ☐ | ☐ | ☐ | ☐ | ☐ |
| 3. Make necessary referrals. | ☐ | ☐ | ☐ | ☐ | ☐ |

# CHAPTER POSTTEST

**Activity E** **MULTIPLE CHOICE**

*Choose the one best answer for each of the following multiple-choice questions.*

____ **1.** While assessing a young infant's musculoskeletal system, the nurse anticipates that the anterior curve in the cervical region will be developed by
  **a.** 1 to 2 months.
  **b.** 3 to 4 months.
  **c.** 6 to 8 months.
  **d.** 9 to 12 months.

___ **2.** The nurse is assessing a 1-year-old infant who weighed 8 pounds at birth. When the nurse prepares to weigh the infant, the nurse anticipates that this infant should weigh approximately

   **a.** 16 pounds.

   **b.** 20 pounds.

   **c.** 24 pounds.

   **d.** 28 pounds.

___ **3.** A mother visits the clinic with her 2-month-old son for a routine visit. The mother has been bottle-feeding the infant and asks the nurse, "When can I start giving him solid foods?" The nurse should instruct the mother that solid foods can be introduced when the infant is

   **a.** 2 to 4 months old.

   **b.** 4 to 6 months old.

   **c.** 6 to 8 months old.

   **d.** 8 to 10 months old.

___ **4.** The nurse is assessing a newborn with the mother present. When the nurse observes an irregularly shaped red patch on the back of the newborn's neck, the nurse should explain to the mother that this is termed

   **a.** port wine stain.

   **b.** hemangioma.

   **c.** cafe au lait spot.

   **d.** storkbite.

___ **5.** While assessing a newborn infant, the nurse observes yellow-white retention cysts in the newborn's mouth. The nurse should explain to the infant's parents that these spots are usually indicative of

   **a.** Epstein's pearls.

   **b.** thrush.

   **c.** allergic reactions.

   **d.** dehydration.

___ **6.** The nurse is preparing to inspect a newborn's inner ear with an otoscope. The nurse should pull the pinna

   **a.** down and back.

   **b.** up and back.

   **c.** down and forward.

   **d.** sideways and forward.

### Activity F  CRITICAL THINKING AND CASE STUDIES

On the basis of the assessment information in the following case studies, work through the steps of analyzing the data. Identify abnormal data and strengths in **subjective and objective findings**, assemble **cue clusters**, draw **inferences**, make possible **nursing diagnoses**, identify **defining characteristics**, **confirm or rule out** the diagnoses, and **document** your conclusions. Use the blank diagnostic analysis charts provided at the end of this book to guide your thinking. You may want to write on the chart or use separate paper. In either case, propose nursing diagnoses that are specific to the client in the case study. Identify collaborative problems, if any, for this client. Finally, identify data, if any, that point toward a medical problem requiring a referral.

**1.** Carsen is a 2-week-old infant brought into the clinic today for a weight check and his regular 2-week visit. His mother, a 22-year-old gravida 1, is concerned that he is not eating well. She started out breast-feeding him but had difficulty and stopped breast-feeding 2 days ago. She is not sure how much formula he should be taking now. She is here for his physical exam and to learn how to determine if he is getting the proper nutrition he needs.

2. Kaylee, an 18-month-old, returns to the operating room 4 days post-op for cauterization of post-tonsillectomy bleed. Vital signs upon returning to the pediatric floor after surgery are weight 11.83 kg, BP 109/71, apical heart rate 144, respiratory rate 28, temperature 99.4°F axillary, and pulse ox 96% room air. An IV is in place with an initial D5LR 200cc bolus followed by D5.225% NS at 60 cc/hour. Initial lab results indicate moderate dehydration and moderate anemia. Physical exam reveals pale skin tones, tacky mucous membranes, with no active tonsillectomy bleeding. Tylenol with Codeine $\frac{3}{4}$ teaspoon is ordered q4h prn pain. Kaylee remains on the floor for 4 subsequent days—continuing to refuse PO fluids even with regular administration of analgesic. Two days after admission, a trial of locking IV fluids is initiated with plan to discharge if Kaylee tolerates PO fluids through supper. If unable to tolerate PO, restart IV fluids at 50 cc/hour. This trial fails this day and the following day has a total PO intake of sips and urine output of 141 cc for the 24-hour period. A repeat IV bolus is given and the same course of action is taken the next day. Again, this trial fails and IV fluids are re-initiated. Several days after returning to the OR for cauterization, Kaylee still refused to drink anything at all. Kaylee's behavior consisted of continually holding a blue blanket and watching the door, crying "Bubby … Bubby" repeatedly. After having much interaction with Kaylee and her family, and assessing the situation, the nurse realized that Kaylee was missing her twin brother so much that it was affecting everything she could see or do. Apparently, these siblings had never been separated. The brother's visitation had been restricted by the other shifts—because of his age—he was well below the required 6 years of age to visit on the pediatric floor. Two evenings in a row, the nurse allowed the parents to bring him into the room to visit with the understanding that he was not allowed in the hallway, but would always remain in the room. During both of these visits, Kaylee began to drink normally during a "pretend picnic" on the floor with her brother. She was discharged home on the fourth post-op day of hospitalization with optimal PO intake.

## SELF-REFLECTION AND EVALUATION OF LEARNER OBJECTIVES

After you have read Chapter 30 and completed the above quizzes and activities, please identify to what degree you have met each of the following chapter learning objectives. For those objectives that you have met partially or not at all, you will want to review the chapter content for that learning objective.

| Objective | Very Much | Somewhat | Not At All |
|---|---|---|---|
| 1. Evaluate the growth and development patterns of infants. | | | |
| 2. Describe the components needed in the assessment of the general appearance, and differentiate between norms, variations of normal, and abnormal general appearances. | | | |
| 3. Demonstrate proper method for assessing vital signs and temperature in newborns and infants. Discuss the normal ranges for each measurement. | | | |
| 4. Explain technique used to measure head circumference and why it is measured. | | | |
| 5. Explain how skin, hair, and nails are assessed in newborns and infants, and discuss possible norms, variations, and abnormalities that may be noted. | | | |

| Objective | Very Much | Somewhat | Not At All |
|---|---|---|---|
| 6. Explain how head, neck, and cervical lymph nodes are assessed in newborns and infants, and discuss possible norms, variations, and abnormalities that may be noted. | | | |
| 7. Explain how eyes are assessed in newborns and infants, and discuss possible norms, variations, and abnormalities that may be noted. | | | |
| 8. Explain how ears are assessed in newborns and infants, and discuss possible norms, variations, and abnormalities that may be noted. | | | |
| 9. Explain how mouth, throat, nose, and sinuses are assessed in newborns and infants, and discuss possible norms, variations, and abnormalities that may be noted. | | | |
| 10. Explain how thorax is assessed in newborns and infants, and discuss possible norms, variations, and abnormalities that may be noted. | | | |
| 11. Explain how breasts are assessed in newborns and infants, and discuss possible norms, variations, and abnormalities that may be noted. | | | |
| 12. Explain how heart is assessed in newborns and infants, and discuss possible norms, variations, and abnormalities that may be noted. | | | |
| 13. Explain how abdomen is assessed in newborns and infants, and discuss possible norms, variations, and abnormalities that may be noted. | | | |
| 14. Explain how male and female genitalia are assessed in newborns and infants, and discuss possible norms, variations, and abnormalities that may be noted. | | | |
| 15. Explain how the anus and rectum are assessed in newborns and infants, and discuss possible norms, variations, and abnormalities that may be noted. | | | |
| 16. Explain how to assess the musculoskeletal system in newborns and infants, and discuss possible variations. | | | |
| 17. Explain how to assess the neurologic system in newborns and infants, and discuss possible variations. | | | |
| 18. Explain the common infantile reflexes. | | | |
| 19. Explain how to document and interpret assessment findings. | | | |
| 20. Discuss various nursing diagnoses and collaborative problems commonly seen with assessment of infants and children. | | | |

# Assessing Children and Adolescents

The special data collected during the nursing assessment of children and adolescents play a key role in supporting the health of these growing young people. The nurse should be aware of the differences between a child/adolescent and an adult and incorporate the special needs of both the pediatric client and his or her parent into the assessment.

## CHAPTER PRETEST

### Activity A  MULTIPLE CHOICE

*Choose the one best answer for each of the following multiple-choice questions.*

_____ **1.** While assessing the skin, hair, and nails of a 4-year-old boy, the nurse can anticipate that the child will have

    **a.** functioning apocrine glands.

    **b.** a thin layer of subcutaneous fat.

    **c.** fine, downy hairs on his body.

    **d.** smooth-textured skin.

_____ **2.** The nurse is planning a presentation on childhood growth and development to a group of new parents. Which of the following should the nurse include in the teaching plan?

    **a.** A child's head reaches 90% of its full growth by 6 years of age.

    **b.** Half of a child's postnatal brain growth is achieved by 3 years of age.

    **c.** During the school-aged years, the cranium grows faster than the face.

    **d.** Lymphoid tissue reaches adult size by 4 years of age.

_____ **3.** The nurse is preparing to assess the heart sounds in a 3-year-old child. To locate the apical impulse, the nurse should plan to place the stethoscope at the child's

    **a.** second intercostal space.

    **b.** third intercostal space.

    **c.** fourth intercostal space.

    **d.** fifth intercostal space.

**Activity B** **MATCHING**

*Match the following descriptions with the appropriate age group.*

**Description**

_____ **1.** Engages in parallel play

_____ **2.** Likes explanations and demonstrations in health teaching

_____ **3.** Peak age group for separation anxiety

_____ **4.** Confidentiality a must

_____ **5.** Gains 15 to 65 pounds during this stage

_____ **6.** Girls surpass boys in growth during this period

_____ **7.** Visual capacity reaches adult level of 20/20

_____ **8.** Sensorimotor stage is completed in this period

_____ **9.** Ability to listen and comprehend starts during this stage

_____ **10.** Vocabulary ranges from 900 to 2,100 words

_____ **11.** Develops ability to think beyond the present

_____ **12.** Has ability to decide between two socially accepted standards

_____ **13.** The age of "magical thinking"

_____ **14.** Learns rules and competition

_____ **15.** Develops lifelong eating patterns

**Age Group**

**a.** Toddlers

**b.** Preschoolers

**c.** School-agers

**d.** Adolescents

**Activity C** **LEARNER ACTIVITIES**

*After reading Chapter 31, participate in the following learning activities.*

**1.** Describe how you would perform the following:

   **a.** an otoscopic examination on a feisty 2-year-old

   **b.** the patellar reflex on a 4-year-old who kicks before you strike

   **c.** abdominal palpation on a ticklish 9-year-old

   **d.** the psychosocial history of a 16-year-old

### Working with peers in the learning lab

Discuss with a lab partner how you would handle the following situations.

**1.** While performing an assessment of a 15-year-old girl, you note that she is quiet and withdrawn. She complains of multiple vague physical complaints and gives you her favorite watch, stating, "I know you'll take real good care of this." Discuss what you would do next.

**2.** You are going to give a 30-minute talk to a PTA group on the health needs of school-aged children. Considering that you are addressing a group whose children's ages range from 6 to 12 years, discuss what you would include in your talk.

**Activity D**   **INTERVIEWING AND RECORDING ASSESSMENT FINDINGS**

Use the following Nursing History Checklist as your guide to interviewing and recording the findings of a pediatric assessment.

### Nursing History Checklist

| Questions | Normal Findings | Abnormal Findings | Additional Data Needed |
|---|---|---|---|
| *Current Symptoms* | | | |
| 1. Child's reason for seeking health care or the parent's (informant's) reason for seeking health care for the child? | | | |
| *Current Health/Illness Status* | | | |
| 1. Symptom analysis of chief complaint? | | | |
| 2. Other current or recurrent illnesses or problems? | | | |
| 3. Any other health concerns? | | | |
| 4. Current medication used? | | | |
| *Past History* | | | |
| 1. Birth history (pregnancy, labor and delivery, perinatal history)? | | | |
| 2. Previous illnesses, injuries, or surgeries? | | | |
| 3. Allergies (and reactions to same)? | | | |
| 4. Immunization status? | | | |
| 5. Growth and developmental milestones? | | | |
| 6. Habits? | | | |
| *Review of Systems* | | | |
| 1. General: overall health status? | | | |
| 2. Integument: lesions, bruising, care habits? | | | |
| 3. Head: trauma, headaches? | | | |
| 4. Eyes: visual acuity, last eye exam, drainage, infections? | | | |
| 5. Ears: hearing acuity, last hearing exam, drainage, infections? | | | |
| 6. Nose: bleeding, congestion, discharge? | | | |
| 7. Mouth: lesions, soreness, tooth eruption, patterns of dental care, last dental exam? | | | |
| 8. Throat: sore throat frequency, hoarseness, difficulty swallowing? | | | |
| 9. Neck: stiffness, tenderness? | | | |
| 10. Chest: pain, cough, wheezing, shortness of breath, asthma, infections? | | | |
| 11. Breasts: thelarche, lesions, discharge, performance of breast self-examination (BSE)? | | | |

| Questions | Normal Findings | Abnormal Findings | Additional Data Needed |
|---|---|---|---|
| 12. Cardiovascular: history of murmurs, exercise tolerance, dizziness, palpitations, congenital defects? | | | |
| 13. Gastrointestinal: appetite, bowel habits, food intolerances, nausea, vomiting, pain, history of parasites? | | | |
| 14. Genitourinary: urgency, frequency, discharge, urinary tract infections, sexually transmitted diseases, enuresis, sexual problems or dysfunctions (male), performance of testicular self-examination? | | | |
| 15. Gynecologic: menarche, menstrual history, sexual problems or dysfunctions? | | | |
| 16. Musculoskeletal: pain, swelling, fractures, mobility problems, scoliosis? | | | |
| 17. Neurologic: ataxia, tremors, unusual movements, seizures? | | | |
| 18. Lymphatic: pain, swelling or tenderness, enlargement of spleen or liver? | | | |
| 19. Endocrine/metabolic: growth patterns, polyuria, polydypsia, polyphagia? | | | |
| 20. Psychiatric history: any psychiatric, developmental, substance abuse, or eating disorder? | | | |
| *Family History* | | | |
| 1. Family genetic traits or diseases with familial tendencies? | | | |
| 2. Communicable diseases? | | | |
| 3. Psychiatric disorders? | | | |
| 4. Substance abuse? | | | |
| *Nutritional History* | | | |
| 1. Determine the quantity and the types of food or formula ingested daily: use 24-hour recall, food diary for 3 days (2 weekdays and 1 weekend day), or food frequency record. | | | |
| 2. Ask if child has any problem with feeding. | | | |
| 3. Ask if child uses any vitamin supplements. | | | |
| 4. Ask if child is on special diet. | | | |
| 5. Ask if there are any cultural or religious preferences. | | | |
| 6. Assess dieting behaviors: include body image, types of diets, frequency of weighing, and use of self-induced vomiting, laxatives, and diuretics. | | | |

| Questions | Normal Findings | Abnormal Findings | Additional Data Needed |
|---|---|---|---|
| *Sleep History* | | | |
| 1. Time child goes to bed and awakens? | | | |
| 2. Quality of sleep? | | | |
| 3. Nap history? | | | |
| 4. Sleep aids (blanket, toy)? | | | |
| *Psychosocial History* | | | |
| 1. Home: composition of family members, occupation/education of members, culture and religion, communication patterns, family roles and relationships, financial status? | | | |
| 2. School: grades, behavior, relationship with teachers and peers? | | | |
| 3. Activities: types of play, number of hours of TV viewing per day, amount of non–school-related reading, hobbies? | | | |
| 4. Discipline: type and frequency used at home? | | | |
| 5. Sex: child's/adolescent's concerns, abuse history, sexual activity patterns, number of partners, use of condoms and contraceptives, AIDS awareness? | | | |
| 6. Substance use: amount, frequency, and circumstances of use for tobacco, alcohol, licit and illicit drugs, steroids, and substances such as inhalants? | | | |
| 7. Violence: domestic violence, self-abusive behaviors, suicide ideation and attempts, violence perpetrated on others by child/adolescent being interviewed? | | | |
| *Developmental Assessment* | | | |
| 1. Assess developmental milestones in<br>a. gross motor skills.<br>b. fine motor skills.<br>c. language development.<br>d. cognitive development.<br>e. social and affective development. | | | |
| 2. Observe the child's behavior before structured interaction for spontaneous activity; observe the child's responses to the environment. | | | |
| 3. Administer developmental tests as appropriate for age (Denver Developmental Screening Test, Brazelton Neonatal Behavior Assessment Scale, Goodeneough-Harris Draw-A-Person Test, temperament questionnaires). | | | |

**Activity E** **PERFORMING PHYSICAL ASSESSMENT**

Use the following Physical Assessment Checklist as your guide to performing a pediatric assessment examination. Column 1 can be used by you to guide your physical assessment. Column 2 may be used by your instructor to evaluate your skills as necessary.

## Physical Assessment Checklist

| Assessment Skill | Findings (Normal or Abnormal) and Notes | | Performance (Satisfactory, Needs Improvement, Unsatisfactory) | | |
|---|---|---|---|---|---|
| | N | A | S | N | U |
| 1. Uses general principles:<br>a. In most cases, physical assessment involves a head-to-toe examination that covers each body system. | ☐ | ☐ | ☐ | ☐ | ☐ |
| b. Complete less threatening and least intrusive procedures first, to secure child's trust. | ☐ | ☐ | ☐ | ☐ | ☐ |
| c. Explain what you will be doing and what the child can expect to feel; allow the child to manipulate equipment before it is used. | ☐ | ☐ | ☐ | ☐ | ☐ |
| 2. Uses developmental approaches:<br>a. Toddlers: Allow to sit on parent's lap, enlist parent's aid, use play, praise cooperation. | ☐ | ☐ | ☐ | ☐ | ☐ |
| b. Preschoolers: Use story telling, use doll and puppet play, give choices when able. | ☐ | ☐ | ☐ | ☐ | ☐ |
| c. School-age: Maintain privacy, use gown, explain procedures and equipment, teach about their bodies. | ☐ | ☐ | ☐ | ☐ | ☐ |
| d. Adolescents: Provide privacy and confidentiality, provide option of having parent present or not, emphasize normality, provide health teaching. | ☐ | ☐ | ☐ | ☐ | ☐ |
| *General Appearance* | | | | | |
| 1. Inspect physical appearance. | ☐ | ☐ | ☐ | ☐ | ☐ |
| 2. Assess nutritional state. | ☐ | ☐ | ☐ | ☐ | ☐ |
| 3. Assess hygiene. | ☐ | ☐ | ☐ | ☐ | ☐ |
| 4. Assess behavior. | ☐ | ☐ | ☐ | ☐ | ☐ |
| 5. Assess interactions with parents and nurse. | ☐ | ☐ | ☐ | ☐ | ☐ |
| 6. Assess overall development and speech. | ☐ | ☐ | ☐ | ☐ | ☐ |
| *Vital Signs* | | | | | |
| 1. Measure blood pressure. | ☐ | ☐ | ☐ | ☐ | ☐ |
| 2. Measure pulse rate. | ☐ | ☐ | ☐ | ☐ | ☐ |
| 3. Measure respirations. | ☐ | ☐ | ☐ | ☐ | ☐ |
| 4. Measure temperature. | ☐ | ☐ | ☐ | ☐ | ☐ |
| 5. Measure height and weight. | ☐ | ☐ | ☐ | ☐ | ☐ |
| *Skin, Hair, and Nails* | | | | | |
| 1. Inspect and palpate skin. | ☐ | ☐ | ☐ | ☐ | ☐ |
| 2. Inspect and palpate hair (distribution, characteristics). | ☐ | ☐ | ☐ | ☐ | ☐ |
| 3. Inspect and palpate nails (texture, shape, color, condition). | ☐ | ☐ | ☐ | ☐ | ☐ |

| Assessment Skill | Findings (Normal or Abnormal) and Notes | | Performance (Satisfactory, Needs Improvement, Unsatisfactory) | | |
|---|---|---|---|---|---|
| | N | A | S | N | U |
| *Head, Neck, and Cervical Lymph Nodes* | | | | | |
| 1. Inspect and palpate the head (symmetry, condition of fontanelles). | ☐ | ☐ | ☐ | ☐ | ☐ |
| 2. Inspect and palpate the face. | ☐ | ☐ | ☐ | ☐ | ☐ |
| 3. Inspect and palpate the neck (suppleness, lymph nodes for swelling, mobility, temperature, and tenderness). | ☐ | ☐ | ☐ | ☐ | ☐ |
| *Mouth, Throat, Nose, and Sinuses* | | | | | |
| 1. Inspect mouth and throat (tooth eruption, condition of gums, lips, teeth, palpates, tonsils, tongue, buccal mucosa). | ☐ | ☐ | ☐ | ☐ | ☐ |
| 2. Inspect nose and sinuses (discharge, tenderness, turbinates [color, swelling]). | ☐ | ☐ | ☐ | ☐ | ☐ |
| *Eyes* | | | | | |
| 1. Inspect external eye. | ☐ | ☐ | ☐ | ☐ | ☐ |
| 2. Perform visual acuity tests. | ☐ | ☐ | ☐ | ☐ | ☐ |
| 3. Perform extraocular muscle tests. | ☐ | ☐ | ☐ | ☐ | ☐ |
| 4. Perform internal (ophthalmoscopic) examination. | ☐ | ☐ | ☐ | ☐ | ☐ |
| *Ears* | | | | | |
| 1. Inspect external ears. | ☐ | ☐ | ☐ | ☐ | ☐ |
| 2. Perform internal (otoscopic) examination. | ☐ | ☐ | ☐ | ☐ | ☐ |
| 3. Assess hearing acuity. | ☐ | ☐ | ☐ | ☐ | ☐ |
| *Thorax and Lungs* | | | | | |
| 1. Inspect shape of thorax and respiratory effort. | ☐ | ☐ | ☐ | ☐ | ☐ |
| 2. Percuss the lungs. | ☐ | ☐ | ☐ | ☐ | ☐ |
| 3. Auscultate for breath sounds and adventitious sounds. | ☐ | ☐ | ☐ | ☐ | ☐ |
| *Breasts* | | | | | |
| 1. Inspect and palpate breasts (shape, discharge, lesions). | ☐ | ☐ | ☐ | ☐ | ☐ |
| 2. Assess stage of sexual development (for girls). | ☐ | ☐ | ☐ | ☐ | ☐ |
| *Heart* | | | | | |
| 1. Inspect and palpate the precordium. | ☐ | ☐ | ☐ | ☐ | ☐ |
| 2. Auscultate heart sounds. | ☐ | ☐ | ☐ | ☐ | ☐ |
| *Abdomen* | | | | | |
| 1. Inspect shape. | ☐ | ☐ | ☐ | ☐ | ☐ |
| 2. Inspect umbilicus. | ☐ | ☐ | ☐ | ☐ | ☐ |
| 3. Auscultate bowel sounds. | ☐ | ☐ | ☐ | ☐ | ☐ |
| 4. Palpate softness. | ☐ | ☐ | ☐ | ☐ | ☐ |

| Assessment Skill | Findings (Normal or Abnormal) and Notes | | Performance (Satisfactory, Needs Improvement, Unsatisfactory) | | |
|---|---|---|---|---|---|
| | N | A | S | N | U |
| 5. Palpate for masses and tenderness. | ☐ | ☐ | ☐ | ☐ | ☐ |
| 6. Palpate liver. | ☐ | ☐ | ☐ | ☐ | ☐ |
| 7. Palpate spleen. | ☐ | ☐ | ☐ | ☐ | ☐ |
| 8. Palpate kidneys. | ☐ | ☐ | ☐ | ☐ | ☐ |
| 9. Palpate bladder. | ☐ | ☐ | ☐ | ☐ | ☐ |
| *Male Genitalia* | | | | | |
| 1. Inspect penis and urinary meatus. | ☐ | ☐ | ☐ | ☐ | ☐ |
| 2. Inspect and palpate scrotum and testes. | ☐ | ☐ | ☐ | ☐ | ☐ |
| 3. Inspect and palpate inguinal area for hernias. | ☐ | ☐ | ☐ | ☐ | ☐ |
| 4. Assess sexual development. | ☐ | ☐ | ☐ | ☐ | ☐ |
| *Female Genitalia* | | | | | |
| 1. Inspect external genitalia. | ☐ | ☐ | ☐ | ☐ | ☐ |
| 2. Inspect internal genitalia. | ☐ | ☐ | ☐ | ☐ | ☐ |
| 3. Assess sexual development. | ☐ | ☐ | ☐ | ☐ | ☐ |
| *Anus and Rectum* | | | | | |
| 1. Inspect anus. | ☐ | ☐ | ☐ | ☐ | ☐ |
| 2. Palpate rectum. | ☐ | ☐ | ☐ | ☐ | ☐ |
| *Musculoskeletal* | | | | | |
| 1. Assess feet and legs. | ☐ | ☐ | ☐ | ☐ | ☐ |
| 2. Assess for congenital hip dysplasia. | ☐ | ☐ | ☐ | ☐ | ☐ |
| 3. Assess spine and posture. | ☐ | ☐ | ☐ | ☐ | ☐ |
| 4. Assess gait. | ☐ | ☐ | ☐ | ☐ | ☐ |
| 5. Assess joints. | ☐ | ☐ | ☐ | ☐ | ☐ |
| 6. Assess muscles. | ☐ | ☐ | ☐ | ☐ | ☐ |
| *Neurologic* | | | | | |
| 1. Test cerebral function (language, memory, cognition). | ☐ | ☐ | ☐ | ☐ | ☐ |
| 2. Test cranial nerve function. | ☐ | ☐ | ☐ | ☐ | ☐ |
| 3. Test deep tendon and superficial reflexes. | ☐ | ☐ | ☐ | ☐ | ☐ |
| 4. Test balance and coordination. | ☐ | ☐ | ☐ | ☐ | ☐ |
| 5. Test sensory function. | ☐ | ☐ | ☐ | ☐ | ☐ |
| 6. Test motor function and infantile reflexes. | ☐ | ☐ | ☐ | ☐ | ☐ |
| 7. Observe for "soft" signs. | ☐ | ☐ | ☐ | ☐ | ☐ |

| Assessment Skill | Findings (Normal or Abnormal) and Notes | | Performance (Satisfactory, Needs Improvement, Unsatisfactory) | | |
|---|---|---|---|---|---|
| | N | A | S | N | U |
| *Analysis of Data* | | | | | |
| 1. Formulate nursing diagnoses (wellness, risk, actual). | ☐ | ☐ | ☐ | ☐ | ☐ |
| 2. Formulate collaborative problems. | ☐ | ☐ | ☐ | ☐ | ☐ |
| 3. Make necessary referrals. | ☐ | ☐ | ☐ | ☐ | ☐ |

# CHAPTER POSTTEST

### Activity F MULTIPLE CHOICE

*Choose the one best answer for each of the following multiple-choice questions.*

_____ 1. The nurse is assessing a young adolescent female client using Tanner's Sexual Maturity Rating for Breast Development. The nurse determines that the client has enlargement of the breasts and areolae, with no separation of contours. The client is in Tanner Stage

   a. two.

   b. three.

   c. four.

   d. five.

_____ 2. A mother brings her 12-year-old son to the clinic for a routine physical. The mother tells the nurse that her son seems to be growing taller recently. The nurse should instruct the mother that the peak growth spurt in boys usually occurs by age

   a. 12 years.

   b. 13 years.

   c. 14 years.

   d. 15 years.

_____ 3. A parent visits the clinic with her 4-year-old child. While communicating with the child, the nurse should

   a. touch the child gently but frequently during the interview.

   b. stand in front of the child so the child can see the nurse.

   c. use standard medical terminology so the child is not confused.

   d. talk to the child in simple terms at the child's eye level.

_____ 4. While communicating with an ill 5-year-old child, one of the most valuable communication techniques that the nurse can use is

   a. play.

   b. direct communication.

   c. indirect communication.

   d. closed-ended questions.

___ 5. A mother visits the clinic with her toddler, who has injured himself in a fall. The nurse caring for the toddler should
   a. tell the child it is okay to cry in the clinic.
   b. play a game with the child.
   c. allow the child to identify the nurse with the parent.
   d. use demonstrations when providing health teaching to the child.

___ 6. The nurse is caring for an 11-year-old child who was hospitalized after an auto accident. While communicating with this child, the nurse should
   a. use simple questions.
   b. provide simple explanations.
   c. use peers as examples.
   d. allow the child to engage in the discussions.

___ 7. The nurse is caring for a hospitalized adolescent with sickle cell crisis. While communicating with the client, the nurse should
   a. give the client control whenever possible.
   b. provide simple explanations.
   c. use concrete terminology.
   d. provide concrete answers to questions.

___ 8. A mother visits the clinic for a routine visit with her 5-year-old son. The mother asks the nurse when the child's permanent teeth will erupt. The nurse should explain to the mother that permanent teeth usually begin to erupt by age
   a. $5\frac{1}{2}$ years.
   b. 6 years.
   c. $6\frac{1}{2}$ years.
   d. 7 years.

___ 9. A mother visits the clinic for a routine visit with her 11-year-old daughter. The mother tells the nurse that her daughter has just started puberty. The mother asks the nurse when she can expect the daughter to begin menstruation. The nurse should explain to the mother that menstruation usually begins about
   a. 1 year after the onset of puberty.
   b. 18 months after the onset of puberty.
   c. 24 months after the onset of puberty.
   d. 30 months after the onset of puberty.

___ 10. The nurse is preparing to assess the gross motor development of a 4-year-old child. The nurse should ask the child to
   a. hop on one foot.
   b. skip a rope.
   c. throw a ball.
   d. balance on alternate feet with eyes closed.

___ 11. The nurse is planning to assess the cognitive development of a 3-year-old child. The nurse plans to assess whether or not the child can
   a. classify complex objects.
   b. quantify objects.
   c. sort objects.
   d. make simple classifications.

____ **12.** A young mother visits the clinic with her 18-month-old child. The mother asks the nurse when she should begin toilet training with the child. The nurse should explain to the mother that

    **a.** she can begin bowel training as soon as the child appears ready.

    **b.** bladder training usually begins at 18 months of age.

    **c.** nighttime bladder control is usually achieved by 3 years of age.

    **d.** bowel training is usually started when the child is 3 years of age.

____ **13.** While assessing a 4-year-old child, the nurse observes that the child's nails are concave in shape. The nurse should assess the child for a deficiency of

    **a.** magnesium.

    **b.** vitamin C.

    **c.** zinc.

    **d.** iron.

____ **14.** The nurse is assessing a 4-year-old child with a temperature of 100°F. The nurse observes that the client has Koplik's spots on his buccal mucosa. The nurse should explain to the client's parents that the child is most likely exhibiting signs of

    **a.** measles.

    **b.** mumps.

    **c.** chickenpox.

    **d.** tonsillitis.

____ **15.** The nurse is preparing to assess a 5-year-old child. To perform the Hirschberg test, the nurse should

    **a.** ask the child to cover one eye.

    **b.** shine a light directly into the pupils.

    **c.** use an ophthalmoscope to check the eyes.

    **d.** ask the child to name various colors.

### Activity G CRITICAL THINKING AND CASE STUDIES

On the basis of the following assessment information, work through the steps of analyzing the data. Identify abnormal data and strengths in **subjective and objective findings**, assemble **cue clusters**, draw **inferences**, make possible **nursing diagnoses**, identify **defining characteristics**, **confirm or rule out** the nursing diagnosis, and **document** your conclusions. Use the blank diagnostic analysis charts provided at the end of this book to guide your thinking. You may want to write on the chart or use separate paper. Propose nursing diagnoses that are specific to the client in the case study. Identify collaborative problems, if any, for this client. Finally, identify data, if any, that point toward a medical problem requiring a referral.

**1.** You are the home health nurse assigned to visit 12-year-old Sara Smith, who has mild cerebral palsy and a seizure disorder. Sara has difficulty with gross and fine motor movement and must wear leg braces. However, she is a very intelligent child, who makes up for her disability with her gift for creativity. Recently she has experienced an increase in seizure activity. Her physician has related this to the changes of puberty and has altered her medications. You are making this home visit to see how she is adjusting to her new medications.

During your interview, you find that Sara has just moved to this town. She states that she hates her new house and her new school. She tells you that everyone teases her because of the way she speaks and moves and because of her braces. She also states that she has not told her mother about this because she does not want to upset her. Sara has no siblings. Her mother is a single parent, who works full time and who still expresses some guilt over Sara's "condition," which has existed from birth.

2. **Kaylee, an 18-month-old**, returns to the operating room 4 days post-op for cauterization of post-tonsillectomy bleed. Upon returning to the pediatric floor after surgery.

**Vital Signs** are BP 109/71, apical heart rate 144, respirations 28, temperature 99.4°F axillary, and pulse ox 96% room air and weight 11.83 kg. **IV is in place** with an initial D5LR 200cc bolus followed by D5.225% NS at 60 cc/hour. Lab results indicate moderate dehydration and moderate anemia.

**Physical exam**: pale skin tones, tacky mucous membranes, no active tonsillectomy bleeding.

Four days postoperative, Kaylee continues to refuse PO fluids even with regular administration of Tylenol with Codeine $\frac{3}{4}$ teaspoon as ordered q4h prn pain. Two days after admission, a trial of locking IV fluids is initiated with plan to discharge if Kaylee tolerates PO fluids through supper. If unable to tolerate PO, restart IV fluids at 50 cc/hour. This trial fails the first day but takes sips of fluids and has a urine output of 141 cc for the 24-hour period the second day. A repeat IV bolus is given and the same course of action is taken the next day. Again, this trial fails and IV fluids are re-initiated. Several days after returning to the OR for cauterization, Kaylee still refused to drink anything at all.

Kaylee's behavior consisted of continually holding a blue blanket and watching the door, crying "Bubby ... Bubby" repeatedly. After having much interaction with Kaylee and her family, and assessing the situation, the nurse realized that Kaylee was missing her twin brother so much that it was affecting everything she could see or do within her activities of daily living, including eating and drinking. Apparently, these siblings had never been separated. The brother's visitation had been restricted by hospital staff because he was well below the required 6 years of age to visit on the pediatric floor. Next for two consecutive evenings, the pediatric nurse allowed the parents to bring him into the room to visit with the understanding that he was not allowed in the hallway, but would always remain in the room with their supervision. During both of these visits, Kaylee began to drink normally during a "pretend picnic" on the floor with her brother. She was discharged home on the fourth post-op day of hospitalization with optimal PO intake.

### Subjective data

- Refuses PO fluids.
- Continually holding a blue blanket.
- Crying and repeating "Bubby."
- Watching the door.

### Objective data

- Returned to OR for cauterization of post-tonsillectomy bleed.
- Vital signs: Weight 11.83 kg, BP 109/71, apical heart rate 144, respiratory rate 28, temperature 99.4°F axillary, and pulse ox 96% room air.
- IV in place.
- Lab results indicate moderate dehydration and anemia.
- Pale skin tones.
- Tacky mucous membranes.
- Failed trials of locking IV fluids.
- Brother's visitation restricted.

### Identify cue clusters

- Admitted after cauterization of post-tonsillectomy bleed.
- Vital signs: Weight 11.83 kg, BP 109/71, apical heart rate 144, respiratory rate 28, temperature 99.4°F axillary, and pulse ox 96% room air.

- Physical exam reveals pale skin tones, tacky mucous membranes, with no active tonsillectomy bleeding.
- Kaylee remains on the floor for 4 subsequent days, continuing to refuse PO fluids even with regular administration of analgesic.
- Failed trials of locking IV fluids with possible discharge.
- Following day has a total PO intake of sips and urine output of 141 cc for the 24-hour period.
- Continual crying and watching the door.
- Never been separated from twin brother.
- Began to drink normally with visit from twin brother.

### List possible nursing diagnoses

**1.** Fluid volume deficit related to decreased PO intake secondary to S/P tonsillectomy.

**2.** Acute pain related to crying secondary to invasive procedure.

**3.** Fear related to absence of twin brother due to hospital policies.

**4.** Delayed surgical recovery related to perceived loss of sibling.

### Check for defining characteristics

**1.** *Major*
   - Vital signs (slightly elevated HR and temperature).
   - Labs indicate moderate dehydration and anemia.
   - Pale skin tones, tacky mucous membranes, no active tonsillectomy bleeding.
   - Following day total PO intake of sips and urine output of 141 cc for 24-hour period.

   *Minor*
   - Refuses PO fluids even with regular administration of analgesic.

**2.** *Major*
   - Crying.
   - Refuses PO fluids even with regular administration of analgesic.

   *Minor*
   - Pale skin tones.
   - S/P invasive procedure.

**3.** *Major*
   - Continual crying, repeating "Bubby" and watching the door.
   - Brother's visitation restricted due to hospital policies.
   - Began to drink normally with visit from twin brother.

   *Minor*
   - Never been separated from twin brother.

**4.** *Major*
   - Returns to OR for cauterization of post-tonsillectomy bleed.
   - Failed trials of locking IV fluids.

   *Minor*
   - Hospitalized 4 days postoperatively.

### Confirm or rule out diagnoses

1. Confirm—meets defining characteristics.

2. Confirm—meets defining characteristics but further assessment required—characteristics may be related to another problem.

3. Confirm—meets some defining characteristics.

4. Rule out—does not meet defining characteristics—these characteristics best describe the characteristics of another nursing diagnosis.

### Document conclusions

*Nursing diagnoses appropriate at this time:*

Fluid volume deficit related to decreased PO intake secondary to S/P tonsillectomy.

Acute pain related to crying secondary to invasive procedure.

Fear related to absence of twin brother due to hospital policies.

# SELF-REFLECTION AND EVALUATION OF LEARNER OBJECTIVES

After you have read Chapter 31 and completed the above quizzes and activities, please identify to what degree you have met each of the following chapter learning objectives. For those objectives that you have met partially or not at all, you will want to review the chapter content for that learning objective.

| Objective | Very Much | Somewhat | Not At All |
|---|---|---|---|
| 1. Briefly describe how children differ in structure and function from adults, and discuss how these differences affect physical assessment. | | | |
| 2. Differentiate the interviewing techniques used for parents, toddlers, preschoolers, school-agers, and adolescents. | | | |
| 3. Explain how play techniques can be used for distraction purposes during assessment. | | | |
| 4. Explain the components of the pediatric history. | | | |
| 5. Evaluate the growth and development patterns of toddlers. | | | |
| 6. Evaluate the growth and development patterns of preschoolers. | | | |
| 7. Evaluate the growth and development patterns of school-aged children. | | | |
| 8. Evaluate the growth and development patterns of adolescents. | | | |
| 9. Describe the components needed in the assessment of the general appearance, and differentiate between norms, variations of normal, and abnormal general appearances. | | | |

| Objective | Very Much | Somewhat | Not At All |
|---|---|---|---|
| 10. Demonstrate proper method for assessing vital signs and temperature in children and adolescents. Discuss the normal ranges for each measurement for children and adolescents. | | | |
| 11. Explain technique used to measure head circumference in toddlers younger than 2 years. | | | |
| 12. Explain how skin, hair, and nails are assessed in children and adolescents, and discuss the possible norms, variations, and abnormalities that may be noted. | | | |
| 13. Explain how head, neck, and cervical lymph nodes are assessed in children and adolescents, and discuss the possible norms, variations, and abnormalities that may be noted. | | | |
| 14. Explain how eyes are assessed in children and adolescents, and discuss the possible norms, variations, and abnormalities that may be noted. | | | |
| 15. Explain how ears are assessed in children and adolescents, and discuss the possible norms, variations, and abnormalities that may be noted. | | | |
| 16. Explain how thorax and lungs are assessed in children and adolescents, and discuss the possible norms, variations, and abnormalities that may be noted. | | | |
| 17. Explain how heart is assessed in children and adolescents, and discuss the possible norms, variations, and abnormalities that may be noted. | | | |
| 18. Explain how breasts are assessed in children and adolescents, and discuss the possible norms, variations, and abnormalities that may be noted. Explain the Tanner stages of female breast development and the method of teaching breast self-examination to adolescents. | | | |
| 19. Explain how abdomen is assessed in children and adolescents, and discuss the possible norms, variations, and abnormalities that may be noted. | | | |
| 20. Explain how male genitalia are assessed in children and adolescents, and discuss the possible norms, variations, and abnormalities that may be noted. Explain the Tanner stages of male pubic hair and genital development and the method of teaching testicular self-examination to male adolescents. | | | |
| 21. Explain how female genitalia are assessed in children and adolescents, and discuss the possible norms, variations, and abnormalities that may be noted. Explain the Tanner stages of female pubic hair development. | | | |

| Objective | Very Much | Somewhat | Not At All |
|---|---|---|---|
| 22. Explain how the anus and rectum are assessed in children and adolescents, and discuss the possible norms, variations, and abnormalities that may be noted. | | | |
| 23. Explain how to assess the musculoskeletal system in children and adolescents, and discuss the possible norms, variations, and abnormalities that may be noted. | | | |
| 24. Explain how to assess the neurologic system in children and adolescents, and discuss the possible norms, variations, and abnormalities that may be noted. | | | |
| 25. Explain how to document and interpret assessment findings. | | | |
| 26. Discuss various nursing diagnoses and collaborative problems commonly seen with assessment of children and adolescents. | | | |

# Assessing Frail Elderly Clients

## Chapter Overview

What distinguishes a frail elderly adult from an elderly adult is his or her delicate balance of health and independence, which can easily be compromised by an acute illness, accidents such as a fall, or adverse medication reactions.

## CHAPTER PRETEST

### Activity A  MULTIPLE CHOICE

*Choose the one best answer for each of the following multiple-choice questions.*

_____ **1.** The physical declines of aging often first become noticeable when

    **a.** approximately 50% of function is lost.

    **b.** the person is at least 75 years old.

    **c.** acute or chronic illness places excessive demands on the body.

    **d.** cognitive declines become significant.

_____ **2.** A benign skin lesion commonly seen in the aged is

    **a.** squamous cell carcinoma.

    **b.** shingles.

    **c.** actinic keratosis.

    **d.** lentigenes.

_____ **3.** Diminished vibratory sensations and slowed motor responses in advanced age result in

    **a.** stiffness and rigidity.

    **b.** paresthesia.

    **c.** postural instability.

    **d.** tremors.

____ **4.** A sign of infection in the elder that is more common than fever is

    **a.** pain.

    **b.** confusion.

    **c.** diarrhea.

    **d.** cough.

____ **5.** By age 90, renal blood flow has usually decreased by approximately

    **a.** 5%.

    **b.** 10%.

    **c.** 25%.

    **d.** 50%.

____ **6.** A neurologic change associated with normal aging is

    **a.** loss of long-term memory.

    **b.** a decrease in reaction time.

    **c.** swaying or shuffling gait.

    **d.** a significant decline in judgment and cognition.

## Activity B  MATCHING

*Match the terms in the left column with the correct descriptions in the right column.*

**Term**

____ **1.** Calcification, stiffening, and dilation of the aortic valve

____ **2.** Decreased ventricular compliance

____ **3.** Loss of elasticity in aorta and arteries

____ **4.** Decreased baroreceptor sensitivity

**Description**

**a.** Rise in systolic blood pressure

**b.** Soft systolic murmur at base of heart

**c.** $S_4$

**d.** Orthostatic hypotension

## Activity C  LEARNER ACTIVITIES

### Working with peers in the learning lab

*After reading Chapter 32, participate in the following learning activities.*

**1.** Practice the timed Get Up and Go test on your lab partner. Then do the test again with your lab partner, using crutches to walk. Do it one more time with your partner's arm in a sling. How do these disabilities affect gait stability and timing?

**2.** Identify and discuss with your lab partner two risk factors for each problem included in the acronym SPICES.

**3.** Find a frail elder 80 years or older who is not completely independent in some aspect of everyday life. Assess the degree to which he or she is dependent in activities of daily living (ADLs) and instrumental activities of daily living (IADLs). Also address this person's physical and social environment for barriers and for resources related to independent function.

**4.** Visit a retail supplier of rehabilitative aids or home medical equipment. Locate items that assist persons with various degrees of immobility. Itemize at least 10 of them from least to most expensive.

**5.** Visit an intensive care unit. Identify as many factors as you can in the physical environment or the nursing practices that may contribute to delirium in a frail elder.

**6.** Review the medication profile of five hospitalized elders over the age of 80. Identify all the medications they are taking that have anticholinergic side effects. Describe the assessment parameters that are indicated.

**Activity D** **INTERVIEWING AND RECORDING ASSESSMENT FINDINGS**

Use the following Functional Status Checklist as your guide to adapting the nursing health history and physical examination for the frail elder client. Record your findings.

**Functional Status Checklist**

| Function | Findings |
|---|---|
| *Activities of Daily Living (ADLs)* | |
| 1. Bathing | |
| 2. Dressing | |
| 3. Toileting | |
| 4. Transferring | |
| 5. Continence | |
| 6. Feeding | |
| *Instrumental Activities of Daily Living (IADLs)* | |
| 1. Ability to use the telephone | |
| 2. Shopping | |
| 3. Food preparation | |
| 4. Housekeeping | |
| 5. Laundry | |
| 6. Transportation | |
| 7. Medication management | |
| 8. Ability to handle finances | |
| *Geriatric Syndromes* | |
| 1. Skin impairment | |
| 2. Poor nutrition | |
| 3. Incontinence | |
| 4. Cognitive impairment | |
| 5. Evidence of falls or functional decline | |
| 6. Sleep disturbances | |
| *Special Tests Indicated by History or Physical Examination* | |
| 1. Assessment of swallowing | |
| 2. Voice-whisper examination | |
| 3. Get Up and Go test | |
| 4. 24-hour food and fluid diary | |
| 5. Mini-Nutritional Assessment | |
| 6. Short Blessed Test for memory and concentration | |
| 7. Geriatric depression scale | |
| 8. Assessment of urinary continence | |

# CHAPTER POSTTEST

**Activity E** **MULTIPLE CHOICE**

*Choose the one best answer for each of the following multiple-choice questions.*

_____ **1.** A risk factor for sinusitis in the frail elderly is

    **a.** a nasogastric feeding tube.

    **b.** an accumulation of ear wax.

    **c.** decreased ability to detect odors.

    **d.** conductive hearing loss.

_____ **2.** Common signs or symptoms of disease in the oldest-old include all of the below *except*

    **a.** weakness.

    **b.** confusion.

    **c.** falls.

    **d.** fever.

_____ **3.** Any new onset of incontinence in the frail elder should be investigated for

    **a.** prostatitis.

    **b.** stroke.

    **c.** fecal impaction.

    **d.** urinary tract infection.

_____ **4.** An objective assessment that is frequently indicated when the subjective assessment reveals a history of falling is

    **a.** a 24-hour food diary.

    **b.** a Get Up and Go test.

    **c.** a tonometry exam.

    **d.** palpation of the joints for crepitus.

_____ **5.** A gastrointestinal problem that often requires emergency treatment in the frail elder is

    **a.** lactose intolerance.

    **b.** hiatal hernia

    **c.** diverticulitis.

    **d.** Crohn's disease.

_____ **6.** To compensate for a stooped posture and less flexible knee, hip, and shoulder joints, the elderly person often walks

    **a.** with a waddling type of gait.

    **b.** with one leg slightly dragging behind the other.

    **c.** with the feet farther apart and the knees slightly bent.

    **d.** with a slight swaying side-to-side motion.

_____ **7.** A common sign or symptom of depression in the elderly is

    **a.** rambling or incoherent speech.

    **b.** illusion or hallucinations.

    **c.** insomnia.

    **d.** cognitive impairment or pseudodementia.

____ **8.** A key area to assess in older adults with chronic respiratory or cardiac problems and some constant degree of dyspnea is

  **a.** nutritional deficiency.

  **b.** dysphagia.

  **c.** the degree to which dyspnea affects daily function.

  **d.** a possible history of immunosuppression.

____ **9.** A characteristic sign of delirium is

  **a.** a significant decline in memory.

  **b.** a chronic low mood.

  **c.** a rapid decline in level of alertness.

  **d.** disorientation to self.

____ **10.** All of the following are accurate signs of dehydration in the frail elder *except*

  **a.** a furrowed tongue.

  **b.** tenting of the skin when pinched.

  **c.** dry warm skin.

  **d.** sunken eyes.

____ **11.** Signs of arterial insufficiency in the very old include all of the following *except*

  **a.** paleness of the leg when elevated.

  **b.** dusky or mottled appearance of the leg in a dependent position.

  **c.** hair loss on the skin.

  **d.** cool, thin, shiny skin.

**Activity F** **MATCHING**

*In Part 1, match the sign or symptom with the corresponding eye disorder (only one response per question). In Part 2, match the medication with the adverse side effect that it may cause (possibly more than one answer per question; some responses may not be used at all).*

**Part 1. Eye Symptoms and Disorders**

____ **1.** Noticeable loss of vision and distortion of familiar objects and occasional floaters

____ **2.** Floaters associated with flashes of light

____ **3.** Blurriness of words in center of the page

____ **4.** Significant decrease in central vision

  **a.** Macular degeneration

  **b.** Retinal detachment

  **c.** Cataract

  **d.** Diabetic retinopathy

  **e.** Oral corticosteroid

  **f.** Steroidal inhalant

**Part 2. Medications and Adverse Effects**

____ **5.** Whitish or yellow-tinged patches in mouth

____ **6.** Orthostatic hypotension

____ **7.** Erectile dysfunction

____ **8.** GI bleeding

____ **9.** Constipation

  **g.** Antidepressants

  **h.** Anticoagulants

  **i.** Anticholinergics

  **j.** Antihypertensives

**Activity G** **CRITICAL THINKING AND CASE STUDIES**

1. Explain the various ways in which falls or a history of falls should be assessed in the frail elder.

2. Identify an acute pathologic condition that may manifest as a decline in functional ability. Explain how you might identify the condition.

3. Compare and contrast the steps of a musculoskeletal and neurologic examination of a young adult with those for an adult over the age of 85. Pay close attention to the significance of those steps that assess functional status.

4. You are a nurse in the emergency room. An 88-year-old woman is brought in by her daughter-in-law. Upon initial examination, you notice that this thin, frail, elderly woman has bruises on her back, buttocks, and upper chest. She follows your actions with her eyes but mainly groans or cries out, "Oh take it away ... take it away." When you try to find out why she has been brought to the E.R. today, her daughter-in-law tells you that the client fell in the bathtub and she is worried that she may have broken a bone.

   How would you adjust the interview to adapt to the needs of this elderly woman? Describe key features of the musculoskeletal and neurologic exams that need to be undertaken. What aspects of a functional and psychosocial assessment should you perform?

# SELF-REFLECTION AND EVALUATION OF LEARNER OBJECTIVES

After you have read Chapter 32 and completed the above quizzes and activities, please identify to what degree you have met each of the following chapter learning objectives. For those objectives that you have met partially or not at all, you will want to review the chapter content for that learning objective.

| Objective | Very Much | Somewhat | Not At All |
|---|---|---|---|
| 1. Describe the common structural changes brought on by aging in the various body systems. | | | |
| 2. Recognize the unique presentation of disease and illness in the very old (often referred to as the geriatric syndromes). | | | |
| 3. Effectively interview the frail elderly client by modifying interview techniques used for the adult client. | | | |
| 4. Effectively examine the frail elderly client by modifying the physical examination techniques used for the adult client. | | | |
| 5. Describe assessment abnormalities in the frail elderly client that may be the result of adverse drug effects. | | | |
| 6. Explain how to incorporate assessment of functional status when collecting subjective and objective data on the frail elderly client to accurately evaluate findings. | | | |

# Assessing Families

## Chapter Overview

In assessing the family, many nurses focus on the individual as client and the family as context for the client's health and care. This requires assessing family strengths and problem areas as they affect the family support system. If the whole family is viewed as the client, then nursing assessment is directed toward the family unit as a dynamic system.

## CHAPTER PRETEST

### Activity A MULTIPLE CHOICE

*Choose the one best answer for each of the following multiple-choice questions.*

_____ 1. A broad definition of the family includes two or more persons who
   a. are related by blood.
   b. live in the same household.
   c. are married.
   d. have mutual decision making.

_____ 2. The internal structure of a family includes
   a. the gender of the members.
   b. ethnic identity.
   c. religious practices.
   d. social class.

_____ 3. An example of a subsystem of a family is
   a. father–renter.
   b. mother–chairperson.
   c. father–leader.
   d. mother–son.

_____ 4. According to the theory by Minuchin, disengaged families have boundaries that are
   a. open.
   b. diffuse.
   c. permeable.
   d. rigid.

____ **5.** In the most functional families, parents have power that

  **a.** rests with the father.

  **b.** rests with the mother.

  **c.** is shared by both parents.

  **d.** is shared by all of the family members.

## Activity B  MATCHING

*Match the terms in the left column with the correct descriptions in the right column.*

**Term**

____ **1.** Ecomap

____ **2.** Self-differentiation

____ **3.** Circular communication

____ **4.** Gender role

____ **5.** Multigenerational patterns

**Description**

**a.** Feedback system of reciprocal communication between people

**b.** Similarity of illness or behaviors that run through the family from one generation to the next

**c.** Diagram of the family's contact with larger systems

**d.** Behaviors expected of family members based on their sex and family beliefs about masculinity and femininity

**e.** Young adult's shift toward separation from the family of origin

## Activity C  LEARNER ACTIVITIES

### Working with peers in the learning lab

*After reading Chapter 33, participate in the following learning activities.*

**1.** Have a group of lab partners and make lists of words that each associates with family. Discuss the patterns and definitions of family revealed by the words.

**2.** Make a genogram of your family over three or four generations. Add causes and dates of illness or death for each family member. Note any repeating patterns.

## Activity D  INTERVIEWING AND RECORDING ASSESSMENT FINDINGS

Use the following Nursing History Checklist as your guide to interviewing a peer and recording your findings in a family assessment.

### Nursing History Checklist

| Questions | Normal Findings | Abnormal Findings | Data Missing |
|---|---|---|---|
| *Internal Family Structure* | | | |
| 1. Construct genogram of family composition. | | | |
| 2. Family type and who is considered to be family? | | | |
| 3. Recent movement in or out? | | | |
| 4. Gender role? | | | |
| 5. Rank order? | | | |
| 6. Family subsystems? | | | |
| 7. Family boundaries (permeable, rigid, or diffuse)? | | | |
| 8. Family power structure? | | | |

| Questions | Normal Findings | Abnormal Findings | Data Missing |
|---|---|---|---|
| *External Family Structure* | | | |
| 1. Construct an ecomap. | | | |
| 2. Extended family? | | | |
| 3. External systems? | | | |
| 4. Context? | | | |
| *Family Development* | | | |
| 1. Life cycle stages and tasks? | | | |
| *Instrumental Function* | | | |
| 1. Ability to carry out activities of daily living? | | | |
| *Affecting and Socialization Function* | | | |
| 1. Support and nurturance of family members? | | | |
| 2. Parenting practices for socialization of children? | | | |
| 3. Subgroups for triangles and boundaries (permeable, rigid, diffuse boundaries; level of self-differentiation of family members)? | | | |
| *Expressive Function* | | | |
| 1. Construct a family attachment diagram. | | | |
| 2. Emotional communication? | | | |
| 3. Verbal communication? | | | |
| 4. Nonverbal communication? | | | |
| 5. Circular communication? | | | |
| *Health Care Function* | | | |
| 1. Family's health care function (beliefs and practices)? | | | |
| *Multigenerational Patterns* | | | |
| 1. Data for multigenerational patterns of positive and negative behaviors? | | | |
| *Analysis of Data* | | | |
| 1. Formulate nursing diagnoses (wellness, risk, actual). | | | |
| 2. Formulate collaborative problems (if present). | | | |
| 3. Make necessary referrals. | | | |

# CHAPTER POSTTEST

**Activity E** **MULTIPLE CHOICE**

*Choose the one best answer for each of the following multiple-choice questions.*

_____ **1.** The nurse is preparing to draw a genogram of a client's family. The symbol for male members of the family is a

    **a.** triangle.

    **b.** circle.

    **c.** oval.

    **d.** square.

_____ **2.** One element of the context of a family's structure is

    **a.** ethnicity.

    **b.** extended family members.

    **c.** gender.

    **d.** power.

_____ **3.** The ability of a family to carry out activities of daily living is a family function termed

    **a.** employment.

    **b.** exchanging.

    **c.** differentiation.

    **d.** instrumental.

_____ **4.** According to Bowen's family theory, differentiation of self is assessed by

    **a.** determining the number of members in the family.

    **b.** looking at the communication patterns of the family.

    **c.** documenting the roles of each family member.

    **d.** determining the boundaries of the subsystems in the family structure.

_____ **5.** Families with poorly differentiated members will exhibit

    **a.** rigid patterns of interactions.

    **b.** difficulties in delaying gratification.

    **c.** difficulties in maintaining intimate personal relations.

    **d.** family roles that are based on skills and interests.

_____ **6.** Cybernetics, as applied to families, combines communication with

    **a.** Minuchin's theory.

    **b.** general systems theory.

    **c.** Friedman's theory.

    **d.** Bowen's theory.

_____ **7.** One example of a complementary birth order of spouses is

    **a.** youngest son marries youngest daughter.

    **b.** middle son marries middle daughter.

    **c.** oldest son marries youngest daughter.

    **d.** oldest son marries oldest daughter.

_____ **8.** In the assessment of the family's home environment, an important characteristic for the nurse to assess is the

   **a.** neighborhood's safety.

   **b.** school system.

   **c.** public transportation.

   **d.** availability of churches.

_____ **9.** While assessing a family, the nurse determines that the family's parental practices are based on control, coercion, and punishment. These parenting practices discourage

   **a.** self-fulfillment.

   **b.** self-differentiation.

   **c.** circular communication.

   **d.** socialization.

_____ **10.** The nurse visits a family at home after the 16-year-old only son was injured severely in an automobile accident. The client is in a wheelchair and requires 24-hour care. The client's mother is the sole caregiver, and she tells the nurse that she is saddened because "my son was such a wonderful basketball player." A priority family nursing diagnosis is

   **a.** depression related to youthful family member's health status.

   **b.** ineffective community coping related to mother being sole caregiver.

   **c.** immobility related to severe injuries from automobile accident.

   **d.** risk for dysfunctional grieving related to loss of health status of youthful family member.

## Activity F  MATCHING

*Match the terms in the left column with the correct descriptions in the right column.*

**Term**

_____ **1.** Genogram

_____ **2.** Nuclear family

_____ **3.** Rank order

_____ **4.** Emotional communication

_____ **5.** Nonverbal communication

**Description**

**a.** Messages sent through body position, eye contact, touch, gestures, tone of voice, crying, stammering, etc.

**b.** The position of the children within a family based on age and gender

**c.** The range and types of feelings that are openly expressed or acceptable to be communicated within a family

**d.** A diagram of the family tree showing genetics, generational information, and relationships of family members

**e.** Usually considered to include father, mother, and children

## Activity G  CRITICAL THINKING AND CASE STUDIES

**1.** On the basis of the following assessment information, work through the steps of analyzing the data. Identify abnormal data and strengths in **subjective and objective** findings, assemble **cue clusters**, draw **inferences**, make possible **nursing diagnoses**, identify **defining characteristics**, **confirm or rule out** the nursing diagnosis, and **document** your conclusions. Use the blank diagnostic analysis charts provided at the end of this book to guide your thinking. You may want to write on the chart or use separate paper. Propose nursing diagnoses that are specific to the client in the case study. Identify collaborative problems, if any, for this client. Finally, identify data, if any, that point toward a medical problem requiring a referral.

The Harrison family has come to the clinic for a renewal of prescriptions. Mary Harrison begins to talk to the nurse about the increasing stress that she is under because of her parents' illnesses. In the course of the conversation, the nurse asks whether Mary believes that she and the family need help with deciding how to handle the many problems associated with caring for her mother with

Alzheimer's disease and her father with congestive heart failure. The Harrison family decides to arrange to meet with the nurse to discuss these problems.

The Harrison family is composed of a couple (Mary and Richard), Mary's mother and father (Nan and Ned), and two grown children (Maria and Stan), who live and work in other cities. Mary is a 52-year-old schoolteacher who has had to take a leave of absence to care for her mother, Nan. Nan is 78 years old and has advancing Alzheimer's disease. Richard, 53 years old, works in construction and on occasion is out of work. Ned is 80 years old and has congestive heart failure, which makes it difficult for him to care for his wife. Nan and Ned moved in with Mary and Richard when Maria and Stan moved away 2 years ago. Financial pressures are increasing because of Mary's 3-month leave of absence and Richard's variable annual income. Nan and Ned have no income other than Ned's social security.

Mary describes herself as less and less able to keep up with the house, the meals, and her mother's personal care needs. Richard says that Mary is becoming very grouchy and unpleasant and that she rarely wants to have sex. Mary accuses Richard of not doing anything to help her around the house. Richard says that housework and caring for people is women's work. No one in the family wants to put Nan in a nursing home.

# SELF-REFLECTION AND EVALUATION OF LEARNER OBJECTIVES

After you have read Chapter 33 and completed the above quizzes and activities, please identify to what degree you have met each of the following chapter learning objectives. For those objectives that you have met partially or not at all, you will want to review the chapter content for that learning objective.

| Objective | Very Much | Somewhat | Not At All |
|---|---|---|---|
| 1. Define *family*. | | | |
| 2. List the three essential components of a family assessment (structure, development, and function) and the major elements of each component. | | | |
| 3. Determine a family's life cycle stage and the related tasks. | | | |
| 4. Construct a genogram for a three-generational family. | | | |
| 5. Construct a family attachment diagram. | | | |
| 6. Construct a family ecomap. | | | |
| 7. Discuss theoretic concepts of family function, including systems theory, Bowen's family system theory, and communication theory. | | | |
| 8. Use Bowen's theory to determine the level of self-differentiation of a family and its members and to detect triangles within a family. | | | |
| 9. Describe the importance of communication to family function. | | | |
| 10. Discuss various nursing diagnoses and collaborative problems commonly seen with assessment of the family. | | | |

# Assessing Communities

## Chapter Overview

Community may be defined and classified in various ways depending on one's perspective. A nursing assessment of a community, however, aims to determine the health-related concerns of its members, regardless of the type of the community.

## CHAPTER PRETEST

**Activity A** **MULTIPLE CHOICE**

*Choose the one best answer for each of the following multiple-choice questions.*

_____ 1. The number one cause of childhood mortality in the United States for children between the ages of 5 and 14 years is

   **a.** malignant neoplasms.

   **b.** congenital anomalies.

   **c.** motor vehicle accidents.

   **d.** burns.

_____ 2. The number one cause of mortality in the United States for people between the ages of 45 and 64 is

   **a.** cerebrovascular diseases.

   **b.** diseases of the heart.

   **c.** accidents.

   **d.** malignant neoplasms.

_____ 3. The number one cause of mortality in the United States for people 65 and older is

   **a.** diseases of the heart.

   **b.** malignant neoplasms.

   **c.** cerebrovascular diseases.

   **d.** accidents.

_____ **4.** Since 1970, the number of divorces in the United States has

   **a.** declined.

   **b.** doubled.

   **c.** tripled.

   **d.** quadrupled.

_____ **5.** In the United States, single parents are at a greater risk for health problems, especially those related to

   **a.** finances.

   **b.** housing.

   **c.** role overload.

   **d.** basic needs.

_____ **6.** In the United States, the growing number of homeless individuals and families is related to the community's

   **a.** disregard for these individuals.

   **b.** lack of resources for assistance.

   **c.** high unemployment rates.

   **d.** lack of affordable housing.

_____ **7.** Many communities, especially those in rural areas, cannot provide needed health care services, particularly those related to

   **a.** cardiac care.

   **b.** orthopedic care.

   **c.** dental care.

   **d.** obstetric care.

_____ **8.** The primary purpose of a community assessment is to

   **a.** determine the tax base.

   **b.** determine health-related concerns.

   **c.** obtain federal funding for new programs.

   **d.** collect census data.

_____ **9.** In many rural areas of the United States, one major problem that makes many social service programs inaccessible is

   **a.** a lack of community awareness.

   **b.** reliance on federal support monies.

   **c.** a lack of transportation.

   **d.** a limited number of welfare programs.

_____ **10.** One major concern associated with higher morbidity and mortality rates in a community is

   **a.** limited athletic programs in schools.

   **b.** the number of long-term care facilities.

   **c.** the religious beliefs of the population.

   **d.** poverty.

## Activity B  CROSSWORD PUZZLE

*Complete the following crossword puzzle to become more familiar with the terminology used with assessment of the community.*

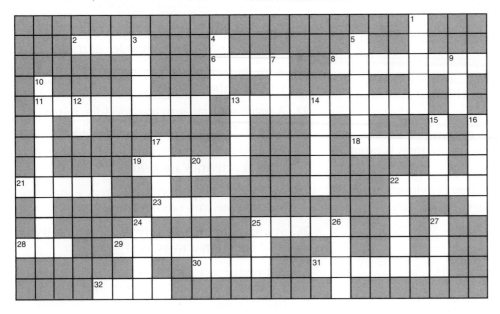

### ACROSS

**2.** Community recreation programs usually provide for both individual and _____ sports

**6.** A weather-related condition often associated with accidents and other health problems

**8.** Food _____ are often provided by local religious organizations

**11.** Another term for "disease" data

**13.** A type of anemia prevalent in African-Americans

**18.** A natural boundary often used to separate geographic regions

**19.** U.S. department where demographic information may be obtained

**21.** U.S. department involved in data collection related to unemployment information

**22.** A title that may be given to the chief elected official of a city or town

**23.** Program available through some local police departments, designed to help combat drug use among adolescents

**25.** Birth and death records are examples of _____ statistics

### DOWN

**1.** Access to health care is a concern to those in remote _____ areas.

**3.** A community group organized to combat driving under the influence of alcohol (acronym)

**4.** Abbreviation for Social Security Administration

**5.** Leading cause of death in U.S. adults aged 45 to 54

**7.** Federal program designed to provide nutritional supplements and education for women and children (acronym)

**9.** Federal agency responsible for environmental concerns (abbreviation)

**10.** A component of emergency care, which may not be available in some rural areas

**12.** An abbreviation associated with train travel

**13.** Second leading cause of infant mortality in the United States in 1991 (acronym)

**14.** A tick-borne illness associated with certain geographic regions of the United States

28. Abbreviation for degree awarded to an individual who did not complete high school but later returns to classes to receive a diploma

29. Disposal of hazardous _____ is a serious environmental concern for many communities

30. A voluntary agency that provides social programs and activities for children and adults (abbreviation)

31. An economical means of transportation available in many large urban areas is rapid _____

32. A body of water that often provides a site for recreation in many communities

15. A voluntary agency found in many areas is the Salvation _____

16. A means of communication in many small towns is a community bulletin _____

17. Type of poisoning often associated with ingestion of paint from older homes

20. A method of collecting information from large numbers of people

22. A program that provides food for home-bound individuals is _____ on Wheels

24. An area in a community where many recreational activities are held

25. An example of a nonprofit agency that provides home care (abbreviation)

26. Stories about the history of a community may be referred to as local _____

27. Abbreviation for state department responsible for highway construction and maintenance

## Activity C LEARNER ACTIVITIES

### Working with peers in the learning lab

*After reading Chapter 34, participate in the following learning activities.*

1. With a group of lab partners, assess the health and social services of a selected part of your community. Include items 1 through 5 on the Community Assessment Checklist below. Discuss your findings regarding whether the resources are adequate for that community.

2. With a group of lab partners, have each group member take a specific age group and list the forms of recreation that might be of interest to that age group and how they might contribute to health.

3. Go to an inner-city health clinic or a rural health clinic. Interview clients about their means of transportation to reach health and social service agencies. Note the difficulties and identify resources that would be needed to improve access to these agencies.

## Activity D INTERVIEWING AND RECORDING ASSESSMENT FINDINGS

Complete the following Community Assessment Checklist for a selected community. Choose a small community or a section of a larger community, for example, an institution such as a university, a suburb, or an inner-city residential section. Analyze the data as indicated.

### Community Assessment Checklist

| Questions | Normal Findings | Abnormal Findings | Additional Data Needed |
|---|---|---|---|
| *Community of People* | | | |
| 1. Assess history. | | | |
| 2. Assess age/gender distribution of community members. | | | |
| 3. Assess racial/ethnic groups. | | | |

| Questions | Normal Findings | Abnormal Findings | Additional Data Needed |
|---|---|---|---|
| 4. Assess vital statistics (birth and death records). | | | |
| 5. Assess household size/marital status/mobility. | | | |
| 6. Assess values/religious beliefs. | | | |
| 7. Assess geographic boundaries. | | | |
| 8. Assess neighborhoods. | | | |
| 9. Assess housing. | | | |
| 10. Assess climate and terrain. | | | |
| *Health and Social Services* | | | |
| 1. Assess hospitals/clinics/emergency care/private practitioners. | | | |
| 2. Assess public health and home services. | | | |
| 3. Assess social service agencies. | | | |
| 4. Assess long-term care. | | | |
| 5. Assess economics. | | | |
| 6. Assess safety. | | | |
| 7. Assess transportation. | | | |
| 8. Assess education. | | | |
| 9. Assess government and politics. | | | |
| 10. Assess communication. | | | |
| 11. Assess recreation. | | | |
| *Analysis of Data* | | | |
| 1. Formulate nursing diagnoses (wellness, risk, and actual). | | | |
| 2. Formulate collaborative problems. | | | |
| 3. Make necessary referrals. | | | |

# CHAPTER POSTTEST

## Activity E  MULTIPLE CHOICE

*Choose the one best answer for each of the following multiple-choice questions.*

____ **1.** From a sociologic perspective, a community is defined as a group, population, or cluster of people with

    **a.** common geographic boundaries.

    **b.** a time–space relationship.

    **c.** similar religious practices.

    **d.** at least one common characteristic.

_____ 2. The definition of a community as defined by the World Health Organization includes
   **a.** a community functioning within a particular social structure.
   **b.** an open social system that is characterized by people in a place.
   **c.** a cluster of people with similar political preferences.
   **d.** a group of people with at least one common characteristic.

_____ 3. One example of a boundary for a geopolitical community is a
   **a.** religious organization.
   **b.** special-interest group.
   **c.** subway system.
   **d.** river.

_____ 4. The "Community as Partner" model is based on the work by the nursing theorist
   **a.** Madeline Leininger.
   **b.** Sister Callista Roy.
   **c.** Imogene King.
   **d.** Betty Neuman.

_____ 5. The nurse is assessing demographic information about a particular community. To assess the risk factors for health-related problems, the nurse should assess the community members'
   **a.** ethnicity.
   **b.** age.
   **c.** housing density.
   **d.** growth within the population.

_____ 6. A nurse is assessing a community of Native Americans. One important piece of health-related information that the nurse should obtain is the incidence of
   **a.** tuberculosis.
   **b.** congenital abnormalities.
   **c.** pregnancy-induced hypertension.
   **d.** diabetes mellitus.

_____ 7. The number one cause of infant mortality in the United States is
   **a.** sudden infant death syndrome.
   **b.** low birth weight/prematurity.
   **c.** respiratory distress syndrome.
   **d.** congenital anomalies.

_____ 8. The number one cause of childhood mortality in the United States for children between the ages of 1 and 4 years is
   **a.** unintentional injuries.
   **b.** malignant neoplasms.
   **c.** homicide.
   **d.** congenital anomalies.

_____ 9. Occupational-related deaths and injuries in the United States are usually due to
   **a.** musculoskeletal injuries.
   **b.** burns.
   **c.** chemical injuries.
   **d.** poisonings.

____ **10.** In the assessment of a community, it is important for the nurse to assess the educational institutions. One indicator that there are problems in the high school system is the

    **a.** low absenteeism of the teachers.

    **b.** number of GED programs available.

    **c.** special education programs available.

    **d.** low graduation rate.

____ **11.** After assessing a local community, the nurse determines that there is a lack of community areas for exercise and socialization, particularly for the elderly members of the population. A priority nursing diagnosis for this community is

    **a.** potential for enhanced community coping.

    **b.** ineffective community coping related to lack of funding.

    **c.** ineffective management of therapeutic regimen related to elderly population.

    **d.** risk for social isolation related to a lack of recreational activities and facilities.

## Activity F  CRITICAL THINKING AND CASE STUDIES

**1.** On the basis of the following assessment information, work through the steps of analyzing the data. Identify abnormal data and strengths in **subjective and objective findings**, assemble **cue clusters**, draw **inferences**, make possible **nursing diagnoses**, identify **defining characteristics**, **confirm or rule out** the nursing diagnosis, and **document** your conclusions. Use the blank diagnostic analysis charts provided at the end of this book to guide your thinking. You may want to write on the chart or use separate paper. Propose nursing diagnoses that are specific to the client in the case study. Identify collaborative problems, if any, for this client. Finally, identify data, if any, that point toward a medical problem requiring a referral.

### History

The area known as Evansboro was first settled by French explorers and established as a military outpost. Soon afterward, the area was settled by other French immigrants because of its rich farmland. It was a busy trading post in the 1800s because of its location on the St. Croix River.

### Demographics

The total population of Evansboro, as of the 2000 census, was 9,156. Of the total residents, the female-to-male ratio is 1.1:1. There are 1,767 persons who are 65 years of age or older and 2,287 who are 18 years or younger. Racial distribution data reveal that 64.2% of the residents are African-American, 34.5% are white, 0.8% are Native American, and 0.5% belong to other racial groups. Most of Evansboro's residents are married (71.6%), 23.1% are single, and the remainder are either separated, divorced, or widowed. The leading causes of death are cardiovascular disease and lung cancer. Several religious denominations are represented in Evansboro; those with the greatest percentage of members include Southern Baptist, African Methodist Episcopal, and United Methodist.

### Physical

Evansboro is bordered on the west by the St. Croix River and is otherwise surrounded by farmland. It lies within the flood plain of the river and as a result is periodically threatened by flooding. The last time that homes were affected by flood waters was 3 years ago. Evansboro is located in Washington County. State Highway 25 borders the eastern limits of the town and intersects with U.S. Highway 62 along the northern border of Evansboro. The average temperature during the month of January is 60.3°F; during the month of July it is 95.1°F.

### Health and social services

Evansboro has a small 50-bed general hospital with a 5-bed special care unit, an emergency room, and limited surgical services. No obstetric services are available. The hospital also provides hospice and home health services. Additional home health services are provided to the area through Housecalls, Inc. Twelve physicians provide services in Evansboro; seven are family practice specialists and the others include an internist, two pediatricians, and two general surgeons. There are also four dentists and three optometrists. The main office of the Washington County Health Department is in Evansboro and offers several services, including Women, Infants, and Children (WIC), immunizations, surveillance for sexually transmitted diseases (STDs), screening for chronic diseases, and a smoking cessation program. The health department does not provide family planning services and does not currently employ an environmental sanitarian. There is a small community counseling center that employs three full-time counselors, one full-time psychologist, and one part-time psychiatrist. Evansboro is the county seat and offers limited social welfare programs through government agencies such as Family and Children's Services. There are two long-term care facilities (with 100 beds and 65 beds), and both provide skilled nursing care. The county provides ambulance/EMT service but does not have a 911 system in place. The community has a Meals on Wheels program for the homebound. Civic and fraternal organizations, such as the Lions Club and the Business and Professional Women's Club, provide many services as well.

### Economics

The median household income for Evansboro is $28,586; the median individual income is $15,356. Of the total population of Evansboro, 5.6% fall below the federal poverty guidelines. The major occupations in Evansboro are manufacturing, farming, and business, including agribusiness. The major crops include peanuts and tobacco. The manufacturers include Johnson's Peanut Processing Plant, Jordan Tobacco, Inc., and Pinewood Paper Mill. None of these companies employs a health nurse. The unemployment rate is 6.9%, which is near the state average.

### Safety and transportation

Evansboro employs seven full-time and four part-time policemen. The most frequently reported crimes are domestic assault, traffic violations, and vandalism. The crime rate is slightly lower than that for the state. The police department provides the D.A.R.E. program to the local middle school. The local fire department includes six full-time and six part-time employees and has recently purchased a new fire truck. There are also several volunteers trained by the fire department who offer their services when needed. The primary means of transportation is the private automobile. There is a taxi service in Evansboro, and the local senior citizen's center provides transportation to seniors within the city. There is a small county airport about 15 miles away, which provides commuter service to larger airports in the region.

### Education

There are three elementary schools (grades K through 3), one middle school (grades 4 through 6), one junior high school (grades 7 and 8), and one senior high school (grades 9 through 12). Together the schools have an enrollment of approximately 1,900 students. One school nurse provides services for the three elementary schools, one nurse provides services between the middle school and the junior high school, and one school nurse is employed at the high school. The elementary and middle schools have an after-school program, and all schools have a school lunch program. The schools require physical education for all grades. The junior high offers programs in softball, baseball, basketball, and track. The high school also offers these same athletic programs as well as golf, wrestling, football, and volleyball. There is a variety of other extracurricular school-sponsored activities as well. The nurses employed at the high school and the junior high expressed some concern about what they believe is a growing problem with illicit drug and alcohol use among students. The high school offers GED classes, and the district's junior college, which is 30 miles away, offers some night classes in Evansboro. There is a community library, which is open 6 days a week. School officials and others in Evansboro are concerned about the condition of the junior high, which was built 70 years ago; the building is in need of many repairs and cannot adequately accommodate the number of students enrolled. The school board is considering a school bond referendum, but is not optimistic because of the reluctance of voters to pass any tax increase.

## Recreation

Evansboro has a city park with ball fields, tennis courts, soccer fields, picnic facilities, hiking trails, and a municipal pool. The park district provides several programs, including Red Cross swimming instruction, water aerobics for seniors, a swim team, Little League baseball and softball, soccer teams, and a tag football program for children aged 8 to 14. Evansboro has a movie theater, a bowling alley, a senior citizens' center, and several Boy Scout and Girl Scout troops. There are several other activities, such as the county fair and "Christmas in the Park," when businesses in town provide a light display in the city park. Other special-interest groups include a fishing club, a 4-H club, and a club for those interested in collecting. Church groups also offer a variety of recreational opportunities.

## Politics and government

Evansboro has an aldermanic type of local government. The city council is composed of eight elected members, two from each ward. The chair of the council is the mayor, who is also elected. There is a city attorney, a city treasurer, and a city clerk. The mayor is quite positive about the ability of the city council members to work together as well as about the response of the community to the city government. Both major political parties are represented in the city.

## Communication

Evansboro has one local AM radio station, which primarily broadcasts local news and country music, and various other AM and FM stations broadcast in the area. There is a weekly newspaper, the *Evansboro Chronicle*. The city has cable television access, and Internet services are provided through Apex Internet, Inc. Evansboro has a post office and telephone services.

# SELF-REFLECTION AND EVALUATION OF LEARNER OBJECTIVES

After you have read Chapter 34 and completed the above quizzes and activities, please identify to what degree you have met each of the following chapter learning objectives. For those objectives that you have met partially or not at all, you will want to review the chapter content for that learning objective.

| Objective | Very Much | Somewhat | Not At All |
|---|---|---|---|
| 1. Discuss how the history of a community may affect its current health status. | | | |
| 2. Describe the types of demographic information necessary to complete a community assessment and the sources of this information. | | | |
| 3. Discuss ways in which cultural and religious values affect health behaviors and attitudes. | | | |
| 4. Describe factors that make up the physical environment of the community. | | | |
| 5. Describe types of primary care facilities and providers that should be available in a community. | | | |
| 6. Discuss the types of programs/services that public health/home agencies can provide. | | | |
| 7. Describe the types of agencies needed to provide necessary services within a community. | | | |

| Objective | Very Much | Somewhat | Not At All |
|---|---|---|---|
| 8.  Describe types of long-term care options that may be available in a community. | | | |
| 9.  Discuss how economic factors can affect health of a community. | | | |
| 10. Describe services and programs essential to provide for the safety needs of a community. | | | |
| 11. Discuss forms of transportation that may be available in a community and how lack of adequate transportation may impact health. | | | |
| 12. Assess education-related factors in a community, and discuss the relationship between education and health. | | | |
| 13. Describe the relationship of government officials and leaders to the overall welfare of the community. | | | |
| 14. Identify formal and informal means of communication that may exist within a community. | | | |
| 15. Describe ways in which recreation affects the health of individuals in a community. | | | |
| 16. Complete a community assessment. | | | |

# Answers

## CHAPTER 1

### CHAPTER PRETEST
#### Activity A MATCHING
**1.** f    **2.** i    **3.** a    **4.** b    **5.** e    **6.** g    **7.** c    **8.** j    **9.** h    **10.** d

### CHAPTER POSTTEST
#### Activity C MULTIPLE CHOICE
1. **a.** physiologic status.
2. **d.** formulation of nursing diagnoses.
3. **a.** continuous.
4. **d.** comprehensive.
5. **d.** includes a brief reassessment of the client's normal body system.
6. **c.** review the client's health care record.
7. **c.** avoid premature judgments about the client.
8. **a.** arrive at conclusions about the client's health.
9. **d.** check for the presence of defining characteristics.
10. **b.** rapid advances in biomedical knowledge and technology.

## CHAPTER 2

### CHAPTER PRETEST
#### Activity A MULTIPLE CHOICE
1. **a.** perception of pain.
2. **d.** using closed-ended questions.
3. **a.** indicate acceptance of the client's cultural differences.
4. **c.** knowledge of his or her own thoughts and feelings about these issues.
5. **a.** use very basic lay terminology.
6. **d.** encourage the client to quit smoking.
7. **a.** avoids excessive eye contact with the client.
8. **b.** provide the client with information as questions arise.
9. **a.** maintain eye contact while asking the questions from the form.
10. **a.** assess the client's hearing acuity.

### CHAPTER POSTTEST
#### Activity D MULTIPLE CHOICE
1. **b.** rephrasing the client's statements.
2. **c.** working.
3. **d.** explain the role and purpose of the nurse.
4. **a.** allow the client to ventilate his or her feelings.
5. **d.** expressing interest in a neutral manner.
6. **b.** provide structure and set limits with the client.

7. **d.** identify risk factors to the client and his or her significant others.
8. **b.** review the food pyramid with the client.
9. **d.** "How do you manage your stress?"

**Activity E** **MATCHING**

**1.** g      **2.** d      **3.** b      **4.** h      **5.** f      **6.** a      **7.** c      **8.** e

# CHAPTER 3

## CHAPTER PRETEST

**Activity A** **MATCHING**

**1.** b      **2.** c      **3.** d      **4.** f      **5.** h      **6.** k      **7.** g      **8.** i      **9.** a      **10.** j      **11.** e

## CHAPTER POSTTEST

**Activity C** **MULTIPLE CHOICE**

1. **a.** wash both hands with soap and water.
2. **b.** explain each procedure being performed and the reason for the procedure.
3. **d.** use minimal position changes.
4. **d.** inspection.
5. **c.** dorsal surface of the hand.
6. **c.** deep palpation.
7. **d.** percussion.
8. **d.** blunt percussion.
9. **d.** blunt percussion.
10. **c.** indirect percussion.
11. **a.** hyperresonance.
12. **b.** bone.
13. **b.** $1\frac{1}{2}$-inch diaphragm.

# CHAPTER 4

## CHAPTER PRETEST

**Activity A** **MULTIPLE CHOICE**

1. **d.** draw a line through the error, writing "error" and initialing.
2. **b.** avoid slang terms or labels unless they are direct quotes.
3. **a.** "Bilateral lung sounds clear."
4. **d.** vital signs.
5. **d.** pain relief measures.
6. **c.** requires a lot of time to complete.
7. **a.** prevents missed questions during data collection.
8. **b.** may be easily used by different levels of caregivers, which enhances communication.
9. **a.** establishes comparability of nursing data across clinical populations.
10. **d.** focused.
11. **a.** validate all data before documentation of the data.

## CHAPTER POSTTEST

**Activity C** **MATCHING**

**1.** S      **2.** O      **3.** S      **4.** O      **5.** O      **6.** S      **7.** O      **8.** O      **9.** S      **10.** O

# CHAPTER 5

## CHAPTER PRETEST

**Activity A** **MATCHING**

**1.** f      **2.** e      **3.** a      **4.** b      **5.** h      **6.** i      **7.** c      **8.** d      **9.** g

## CHAPTER POSTTEST
### Activity C  MULTIPLE CHOICE
1.  **d.** validate information and judgments.
2.  **d.** perform the steps of the assessment process accurately.
3.  **a.** fatigue related to excessive noise levels as manifested by client's statements of chronic fatigue.
4.  **d.** quickly make a diagnosis without hypothesizing several diagnoses.

# CHAPTER 6

## CHAPTER PRETEST
### Activity A  MATCHING
1. e    2. d    3. f    4. a    5. b    6. c    7. h    8. g    9. j    10. i

## CHAPTER POSTTEST
### Activity E  MULTIPLE CHOICE
1.  **a.** eye opening, and appropriateness of verbal and motor responses.
2.  **c.** depression often mimics signs and symptoms of dementia.
3.  **b.** orientation, memory, speech, and cognitive function.
4.  **b.** Orientation to time is usually lost first and orientation to person is usually lost last.
5.  **d.** abstract reasoning.
6.  **c.** generativity.

# CHAPTER 7

## CHAPTER PRETEST
### Activity A  MULTIPLE CHOICE
1.  **c.** lacking adequate finances.
2.  **a.** decreased body metabolism.
### Activity B  MATCHING
1. c    2. f    3. e    4. g    5. b    6. h    7. i    8. j    9. d    10. a

## CHAPTER POSTTEST
### Activity E  MULTIPLE CHOICE
1.  **c.** vital signs.
2.  **a.** normal changes that occur with the aging process.
3.  **b.** observe for equal bilateral chest expansion of 1 to 2 inches.
4.  **a.** shorter inspiratory phase.
5.  **c.** "Are you having pain from your surgery?"
6.  **b.** 30 to 50 mm Hg.

# CHAPTER 8

## CHAPTER PRETEST
### Activity A  MULTIPLE CHOICE
1.  **c.** believe the client when he or she claims to be in pain.
2.  **b.** acute pain is associated with a recent onset of illness or injury with a duration of less than 6 months, whereas chronic pain persists longer than 6 months.
3.  **c.** diaphoresis.
4.  **a.** documents the exact description given by client.

## CHAPTER POSTTEST

### Activity E  MATCHING

**1.** e          **2.** f          **3.** d          **4.** b          **5.** g          **6.** a          **7.** c

### Activity F  CROSSWORD PUZZLE

**Across**
 **1.** pricking
 **3.** perception
 **6.** aggravating
 **8.** transduction
**10.** acute
**11.** Spinoreticular
**14.** Spinothalamic
**16.** A-delta
**17.** chronic
**18.** stress

**Down**
 **2.** gate control model
 **3.** pain
 **4.** transmission
 **5.** mast
 **7.** modulation
 **9.** vasodilatation
**12.** substance P
**13.** VAS
**15.** C-fibers

# CHAPTER 9

## CHAPTER PRETEST

### Activity A  TRUE/FALSE

**1.** F          **2.** F          **3.** F          **4.** T          **5.** T          **6.** F          **7.** T          **8.** T          **9.** T

## CHAPTER POSTTEST

### Activity E  MULTIPLE CHOICE

**1.**  **b.** remain calm and accepting in response to any information the client discloses.
**2.**  **b.** make sure that the assessment includes questions to ensure that Mr. Jenkins has access to food and needed medication.
**3.**  **c.** period of reconciliation.

# CHAPTER 10

## CHAPTER PRETEST

### Activity A  MATCHING

**1.** b          **2.** c          **3.** e          **4.** a          **5.** d

## CHAPTER POSTTEST

### Activity D  MULTIPLE CHOICE

**1.**  **d.** expecting all members of a cultural group to hold the same beliefs and behave in the same way.
**2.**  **c.** The family values taking sick roles and caregiver roles.
**3.**  **a.** Both genetics and environment produce biological variation.

### Activity E  CHOOSING

**a.** do          **b.** don't          **c.** don't          **d.** do          **e.** do          **f.** do          **g.** do

### Activity F  MATCHING

**1.** c          **2.** a          **3.** b          **4.** e          **5.** f          **6.** d

# CHAPTER 11

## CHAPTER PRETEST

### Activity A  MATCHING

**1.** c          **2.** a          **3.** b          **4.** c

## CHAPTER POSTTEST

### Activity D MULTIPLE CHOICE

1. **d.** reveal beliefs that might affect client care.
2. **b.** spiritual distress.
3. **c.** promote harmony between health and spirituality.
4. **a.** individualizing interventions to meet specific needs.

### Activity E TRUE/FALSE

1. T    2. T    3. T    4. F    5. F    6. T

# CHAPTER 12

## CHAPTER PRETEST

### Activity A MATCHING

1. d    2. c    3. a    4. b

## CHAPTER POSTTEST

### Activity E MULTIPLE CHOICE

1. **a.** heart attack.
2. **c.** body mass index.
3. **b.** females with 35 inches or greater waist circumference.
4. **a.** waist circumference.
5. **d.** who is a bodybuilder.
6. **b.** altered nutrition, more than body requirements, related to intake greater than calories expended.
7. **c.** repeat the procedure three times and average the measurements.

# CHAPTER 13

## CHAPTER PRETEST

### Activity A MULTIPLE CHOICE

1. **d.** subcutaneous tissue.
2. **d.** D.
3. **a.** innermost layer of the epidermis.
4. **b.** volume of blood circulating in the dermis.
5. **d.** dermis.
6. **a.** areola of the breast.
7. **a.** vellus.
8. **b.** filter for dust.
9. **c.** keratinized epidermal cells.

## CHAPTER POSTTEST

### Activity F MULTIPLE CHOICE

1. **d.** domestic abuse.
2. **a.** symptoms of stress.
3. **d.** squamous cell carcinomas are most common on body sites with heavy sun exposure.
4. **a.** overall amount of sun exposure.
5. **c.** chronic discoid lupus erythematosus.
6. **a.** hypothyroidism.
7. **d.** malignant melanoma.
8. **d.** fluid intake.
9. **b.** oral mucosa.
10. **b.** ashen.
11. **a.** a great degree of cyanosis.

12. **d.** sclera.
13. **b.** caused by aging of the skin in older adults.
14. **a.** blue.
15. **b.** stage II.
16. **d.** use two fingers to pinch the skin under the clavicle.
17. **c.** a recent illness.
18. **a.** hypoxia.
19. **a.** macules.
20. **a.** plaque.
21. **c.** vesicles.
22. **d.** fissures.
23. **d.** keloid.
24. **d.** risk for ineffective health maintenance related to deficient knowledge of effects of sunlight on skin lesions.

### Activity G CROSSWORD PUZZLE

**Across**
1. papule
7. induration
10. fissure
11. macule
12. diffuse
14. contusion
17. annular
20. tumor
22. excoriation
24. vesicle
25. petechiae

**Down**
1. pustule
2. plaque
3. erosion
4. nevus
5. lichenification
6. bulla
8. nodule
9. keloid
13. confluent
15. crust
16. atrophy
18. scale
19. urticaria
21. ulcer
23. wheal

# CHAPTER 14

## CHAPTER PRETEST

### Activity A MATCHING

| 1. d | 2. h | 3. a | 4. i | 5. b | 6. f | 7. c | 8. e | 9. j | 10. g |
|------|------|------|------|------|------|------|------|------|-------|

## CHAPTER POSTTEST

### Activity F MULTIPLE CHOICE

1. **a.** reduction of the blood supply to the brain.
2. **b.** meningeal irritation.
3. **d.** trigeminal neuralgia.
4. **a.** migraine headache.
5. **a.** cluster headaches.
6. **d.** tension headaches.
7. **d.** tumor-related headache.
8. **b.** ask the client if touching the head is permissible.
9. **b.** acromegaly.
10. **c.** Paget's disease.
11. **d.** parotid gland enlargement.
12. **b.** swallow a small sip of water.
13. **c.** refer the client to a physician for further evaluation.
14. **b.** approach the client posteriorly.
15. **d.** sit in an upright position.
16. **c.** health-seeking behaviors related to verbalization of wanting to stay healthy.

# CHAPTER 15

## CHAPTER PRETEST

### Activity A MULTIPLE CHOICE

1. **c.** protector.
2. **a.** meibomian glands.
3. **d.** bulbar portion.
4. **d.** rectus muscles.
5. **a.** choroid layer.
6. **c.** retina.
7. **a.** an oily substance to lubricate the eyes.
8. **d.** cleanse the cornea and the lens.
9. **a.** optic chiasma.
10. **b.** accommodation.

## CHAPTER POSTTEST

### Activity F MULTIPLE CHOICE

1. **d.** corneal reflexes.
2. **d.** head trauma.
3. **c.** check the client's blood pressure.
4. **a.** tell the client that these often occur with aging.
5. **a.** glaucoma.
6. **b.** refer the client to an ophthalmologist.
7. **d.** vitamin A deficiency.
8. **b.** increased intracranial pressure.
9. **d.** allergies.
10. **d.** a foreign body in the eye.
11. **d.** lacrimal obstruction.
12. **b.** 2 years.
13. **d.** corneal damage.
14. **b.** ultraviolet light exposure.
15. **a.** position the client 20 feet away from the chart.
16. **d.** refer the client to an optometrist.
17. **d.** document the findings in the client's records.
18. **b.** decreased accommodation.
19. **a.** esotropia.
20. **c.** requires the covering of each eye separately.

# CHAPTER 16

## CHAPTER PRETEST

### Activity A MULTIPLE CHOICE

1. **c.** external ear.
2. **d.** stapes.
3. **a.** vestibule.
4. **a.** fluid.
5. **b.** conductive hearing.
6. **d.** perceptive hearing.

## CHAPTER POSTTEST

### Activity F MULTIPLE CHOICE

1. **c.** taking antibiotics.
2. **c.** "It is difficult to prevent hearing loss or worsening of hearing."
3. **d.** observe the client's response to the explanations.
4. **d.** firmly pull the auricle out, up, and back.

5. **d.** refer the client to a physician.
6. **a.** infection.
7. **d.** strike a tuning fork and place it on the center of the client's head or forehead.
8. **c.** conductive hearing loss.

**Activity G** MATCHING

| 1. g | 2. i | 3. a | 4. c | 5. e | 6. d | 7. h | 8. b | 9. f |

# CHAPTER 17

## CHAPTER PRETEST

**Activity A** MULTIPLE CHOICE

1. **d.** soft palate.
2. **a.** uvula.
3. **b.** frenulum.
4. **c.** Wharton's ducts.
5. **d.** warm the inspired air.

## CHAPTER POSTTEST

**Activity F** MULTIPLE CHOICE

1. **c.** maxillary sinuses.
2. **d.** aphthous stomatitis.
3. **a.** refer the client for further evaluation.
4. **d.** refer the client for further evaluation.
5. **a.** aspiration.
6. **d.** stress and anxiety.
7. **a.** Diets low in fruits and vegetables are a possible risk factor for oral cancer.
8. **d.** don clean gloves for the procedure.
9. **d.** riboflavin.
10. **a.** *Candida albicans* infection.
11. **b.** area underneath the tongue.
12. **a.** depress the tongue blade slightly off center.
13. **c.** touching each other.
14. **a.** position the handle of the otoscope to one side.
15. **d.** an upper respiratory infection.

**Activity G** MATCHING

| 1. e | 2. h | 3. m | 4. j | 5. p | 6. c | 7. k | 8. n | 9. b | 10. g |
| 11. i | 12. a | 13. f | 14. l | 15. d | 16. o | | | | |

# CHAPTER 18

## CHAPTER PRETEST

**Activity A** MULTIPLE CHOICE

1. **d.** manubrium.
2. **a.** angle.
3. **c.** seventh.
4. **b.** area slightly above the clavicle.
5. **a.** parietal pleura.
6. **d.** cilia.
7. **d.** hypercapnia.

## CHAPTER POSTTEST

**Activity F** MULTIPLE CHOICE

1. **d.** infection.
2. **d.** tuberculosis.

3.  **d.** Studies have indicated that there is a genetic component in the development of lung cancer.
4.  **d.** chronic obstructive pulmonary disease.
5.  **d.** asking the client to exhale forcefully and hold his breath.
6.  **c.** ask the client to breathe deeply through her mouth.
7.  **a.** repeat the phrase "ninety-nine."
8.  **b.** pectus excavatum.
9.  **a.** chronic bronchitis.
10. **a.** pneumonia.
11. **d.** bronchitis.
12. **a.** diabetic ketoacidosis.

### Activity G  MATCHING

**1.** d      **2.** g      **3.** j      **4.** h      **5.** b      **6.** i      **7.** c      **8.** f      **9.** a      **10.** e

# CHAPTER 19

## CHAPTER PRETEST

### Activity A  MULTIPLE CHOICE

1.  **a.** progesterone.
2.  **d.** areolas.
3.  **b.** glandular.
4.  **d.** Cooper's ligaments.
5.  **d.** fatty tissue.
6.  **a.** lateral lymph nodes.

## CHAPTER POSTTEST

### Activity F  MULTIPLE CHOICE

1.  **c.** upper outer quadrant.
2.  **c.** fibrocystic breast disease.
3.  **a.** having a baby before the age of 20 years.
4.  **c.** physical stress.
5.  **d.** breast cancer patients of the same race.
6.  **d.** contraceptives.
7.  **b.** depression.
8.  **d.** grapefruit juice.
9.  **d.** right after menstruation.
10. **a.** blocked lymphatic drainage.
11. **c.** refer the client for a cytology examination
12. **b.** tumor.
13. **c.** an infectious process.
14. **d.** disturbed body image related to mastectomy.

### Activity G  MATCHING

**1.** i      **2.** f      **3.** l      **4.** h      **5.** d      **6.** m      **7.** k      **8.** b      **9.** e      **10.** n
**11.** a     **12.** j     **13.** g     **14.** c

# CHAPTER 20

## CHAPTER PRETEST

### Activity A  MULTIPLE CHOICE

1.  **a.** precordium.
2.  **a.** between the left atrium and the left ventricle.
3.  **a.** at the exit of each ventricle at the beginning of the great vessels.
4.  **a.** posterior wall of the right atrium.
5.  **a.** conduction of the impulse throughout the atria.

## CHAPTER POSTTEST
### Activity F  MULTIPLE CHOICE

1.  **c.** apex of the heart.
2.  **d.** can be heard during diastole.
3.  **b.** angina.
4.  **a.** high serum level of low-density lipoproteins.
5.  **d.** Estrogen replacement therapy in postmenopausal women decreases the risk of heart attack.
6.  **a.** apical pulse.
7.  **a.** ask the client to hold her breath.
8.  **c.** associated with occlusive arterial disease.
9.  **d.** increased central venous pressure.
10. **a.** cardiac murmur.
11. **b.** third to fifth intercostal space at the left sternal border.
12. **d.** refer the client to a physician.
13. **d.** recognize that this finding is normal in adolescents.
14. **c.** mitral valve stenosis.
15. **a.** obstructive lung disease.
16. **d.** heart rate speeds up and slows down during a cycle.
17. **a.** low-frequency sound best heard with the bell of the stethoscope.

### Activity G  CROSSWORD PUZZLE

**Across**
1.  pulmonic
4.  diaphragm
6.  infarct
9.  auscultation
10. pedis
11. thrill
13. PMI
14. mitral
15. radial
17. systole
23. aortic
24. heave
26. splitting
27. bradycardia

**Down**
2.  murmur
3.  tibial
5.  peripheral
6.  ischemia
7.  pulse
8.  bell
12. diastole
16. apex
18. tricuspid
19. ERBS
20. bruit
21. angina
22. thrombus
24. Homan's
25. NSR

# CHAPTER 21

## CHAPTER PRETEST
### Activity A  MULTIPLE CHOICE

1.  **d.** brachial artery.
2.  **a.** knee.
3.  **d.** ankle.
4.  **c.** 70%.

## CHAPTER POSTTEST
### Activity F  MULTIPLE CHOICE

1.  **d.** arterial insufficiency.
2.  **a.** venous insufficiency.
3.  **b.** intermittent claudication.
4.  **d.** getting regular exercise.
5.  **a.** apply K-Y jelly to the client's skin.
6.  **a.** lymphedema.
7.  **c.** brachial pulse.
8.  **c.** flex his elbow about 90 degrees.

9.  **d.** venous insufficiency.
10. **d.** malignancy.
11. **d.** flex the client's knee, then dorsiflex the foot.
12. **c.** competence of the saphenous vein valves.

**Activity G** **MATCHING**

**1.** i    **2.** d    **3.** k    **4.** m    **5.** g    **6.** l    **7.** b    **8.** j    **9.** f    **10.** c
**11.** e    **12.** a    **13.** h

# CHAPTER 22

## CHAPTER PRETEST

**Activity A** **MULTIPLE CHOICE**

1.  **c.** abdominal oblique.
2.  **b.** left lower quadrant.
3.  **d.** deep in the upper abdomen and is not normally palpable.
4.  **a.** store and excrete bile.
5.  **a.** right lower quadrant.

## CHAPTER POSTTEST

**Activity F** **MULTIPLE CHOICE**

1.  **a.** right upper quadrant.
2.  **d.** right lower quadrant.
3.  **b.** left upper quadrant.
4.  **d.** costovertebral angle.
5.  **a.** stomach ulcers.
6.  **c.** appetite changes.
7.  **a.** "I can decrease the constipation if I eat foods high in fiber and drink water."
8.  **c.** disturbed body image related to temporary colostomy.
9.  **d.** inspect the abdominal area.
10. **a.** ask the client to empty his bladder.
11. **d.** internal bleeding.
12. **d.** masses.
13. **a.** umbilical hernia.
14. **d.** peritoneal irritation.
15. **b.** paralytic ileus.
16. **a.** intestinal obstruction.
17. **c.** use the diaphragm of the stethoscope.
18. **b.** place the right hand below the left costal margin.
19. **d.** palpate deeply while quickly releasing pressure.
20. **c.** raise the client's right leg from the hip.

# CHAPTER 23

## CHAPTER PRETEST

**Activity A** **MULTIPLE CHOICE**

1.  **c.** sweat glands.
2.  **d.** glans.
3.  **a.** vestibule.
4.  **a.** pink squamous epithelium and connective tissue.
5.  **d.** estrogen.

## CHAPTER POSTTEST

**Activity F** **MULTIPLE CHOICE**

1.  **b.** "Do you experience mood swings or bloating?"
2.  **a.** hot flashes.

3.  **d.** infection.
4.  **b.** sexually transmitted disease.
5.  **a.** decreased urethral elasticity.
6.  **a.** refrain from douching 48 hours before the examination.
7.  **c.** warm tap water.
8.  **a.** bear down.
9.  **d.** cystocele.
10. **a.** stress incontinence.
11. **a.** infection.
12. **a.** herpes simplex virus infection.
13. **d.** genital warts.
14. **a.** *Trichomonas vaginalis* infection.
15. **d.** ectopic pregnancy.

**Activity G** **MATCHING**

| 1. g | 2. e | 3. k | 4. f | 5. c | 6. h | 7. l | 8. b | 9. j | 10. d |
|------|------|------|------|------|------|------|------|------|-------|
| 11. a | 12. i | | | | | | | | |

# CHAPTER 24

## CHAPTER PRETEST

### Activity A MULTIPLE CHOICE

1.  **a.** glans.
2.  **d.** foreskin.
3.  **b.** suspended by the spermatic cord.
4.  **a.** just above and parallel to the inguinal ligament.

## CHAPTER POSTTEST

### Activity F MULTIPLE CHOICE

1.  **d.** prostate enlargement.
2.  **c.** 3 years.
3.  **a.** transient periods of erectile dysfunction are common.
4.  **c.** inguinal hernia.
5.  **d.** has anal intercourse with other males.
6.  **d.** continue the examination in an unhurried manner.
7.  **a.** ask the client to empty his bladder.
8.  **b.** herpes infection.
9.  **b.** syphilis.
10. **a.** urethritis.
11. **c.** cryptorchidism.
12. **c.** epididymitis.
13. **d.** varicocele.
14. **d.** bowel sounds at the bulge.
15. **a.** refer the client to an emergency room.

**Activity G** **MATCHING**

| 1. c | 2. e | 3. g | 4. f | 5. a | 6. h | 7. b | 8. d |
|------|------|------|------|------|------|------|------|

# CHAPTER 25

## CHAPTER PRETEST

### Activity A MULTIPLE CHOICE

1.  **a.** composed of smooth muscle.
2.  **d.** intersphincteric groove.
3.  **d.** hemorrhoids.
4.  **a.** median sulcus.

**5. b.** secrete a milky substance that neutralizes female acidic secretions.
**6. c.** empty into the urethra.

## CHAPTER POSTTEST

### Activity F  MULTIPLE CHOICE

**1. a.** gastrointestinal infection.
**2. d.** gastrointestinal bleeding.
**3. a.** biliary disease.
**4. a.** year.
**5. c.** Diets high in fat and low in fiber are associated with colorectal cancer.
**6. d.** advanced age.
**7. a.** African-American.
**8. b.** left lateral position.
**9. d.** bear down.
**10. c.** a fungal infection.
**11. c.** pilonidal cysts.
**12. a.** polyps.
**13. d.** peritoneal metastasis.
**14. a.** prostate cancer.

### Activity G  MATCHING

**1.** f      **2.** d      **3.** l      **4.** j      **5.** h      **6.** b      **7.** i      **8.** e      **9.** k      **10.** c
**11.** a      **12.** g

# CHAPTER 26

## CHAPTER PRETEST

### Activity A  MULTIPLE CHOICE

**1. c.** produce blood cells.
**2. a.** fat.
**3. d.** periosteum.
**4. a.** tendons.
**5. d.** fibrous.
**6. b.** ligaments.
**7. d.** abduction.
**8. a.** supination.
**9. b.** shoulder joint.
**10. d.** hip joint.

## CHAPTER POSTTEST

### Activity F  MULTIPLE CHOICE

**1. a.** arthritis.
**2. c.** osteomyelitis.
**3. a.** osteoporosis.
**4. c.** Moderate strenuous exercise tends to increase bone density.
**5. d.** vitamin C.
**6. a.** gouty arthritis.
**7. d.** vitamin D.
**8. d.** "You'll continue with range of motion even if I have discomfort."
**9. c.** average weakness.
**10. b.** TMJ dysfunction.
**11. a.** herniated disc.
**12. d.** scoliosis.
**13. d.** lie flat and raise his leg to the point of pain.
**14. a.** herniated intervertebral disc.
**15. a.** rotator cuff tear.

16. **c.** calcified tendinitis.
17. **d.** XI.
18. **a.** arthritis.
19. **d.** inability to extend the ring and little finger.
20. **a.** osteoarthritis.
21. **d.** place the backs of both hands against each other.
22. **b.** carpal tunnel syndrome.
23. **d.** synovitis.
24. **a.** place the left thumb and index finger on either side of the patella.
25. **c.** osteoarthritis.
26. **d.** flex the knee and hip while in a supine position.
27. **a.** hallux valgus.
28. **d.** flat feet.
29. **d.** gouty arthritis.
30. **a.** hammer toes.
31. **c.** plantar warts.

## Activity G CROSSWORD PUZZLE

**Across**
1. range of motion
5. adduction
6. external
8. bursitis
10. clonus
11. ankylosis
14. myalgia
15. cogwheel
17. dorsiflexion
18. lordosis

**Down**
2. abduction
3. crepitus
4. flexion
7. circumduction
8. bursa
9. fasciculation
12. extension
13. kyphosis
16. plantar

# CHAPTER 27

## CHAPTER PRETEST

### Activity A MULTIPLE CHOICE

1. **d.** removes wastes.
2. **a.** corpus callosum.
3. **a.** gray matter.
4. **d.** thalamus and hypothalamus.
5. **a.** sleep cycles.

### Activity B MATCHING

| 1. b | 2. e | 3. h | 4. l | 5. g | 6. k | 7. c | 8. a | 9. j | 10. d |
|------|------|------|------|------|------|------|------|------|-------|
| 11. i | 12. f | | | | | | | | |

## CHAPTER POSTTEST

### Activity G MULTIPLE CHOICE

1. **c.** spinothalamic tract.
2. **d.** glossopharyngeal.
3. **b.** cerebral vascular accident.
4. **b.** Smoking and high cholesterol levels are risk factors for CVA.
5. **a.** sensation in the extremities.
6. **a.** clench his jaw.
7. **d.** some impairment.
8. **a.** depression.
9. **d.** cerebral cortex disorder.
10. **d.** "Can you repeat *brown, chair, textbook, tomato*?"
11. **a.** oculomotor nerve paralysis.
12. **a.** ask the client to purse the lips.

13. **d.** corticospinal tract.
14. **c.** stand erect with arms at the sides and feet together.
15. **b.** toes up or down.
16. **d.** document the finding in the client's record.
17. **c.** drug intoxication.

# CHAPTER 28

## CHAPTER PRETEST

### Activity A  MULTIPLE CHOICE

1. **b.** a head-to-toe integrated assessment of body systems.
2. **c.** acquire your client's verbal permission to perform the physical examination.
3. **b.** eye exam and cranial nerves II, III, IV, VI.
4. **a.** integrated throughout the head-to-toe examination.

### Activity B  TRUE/FALSE

1. F    2. T    3. T    4. T    5. F

## CHAPTER POSTTEST

### Activity F  MATCHING

1. b    2. c    3. e    4. i    5. f    6. h    7. d    8. a    9. g

# CHAPTER 29

## CHAPTER PRETEST

### Activity A  MULTIPLE CHOICE

1. **d.** fade to a white or silvery color.
2. **a.** linea nigra.
3. **d.** progesterone.
4. **c.** is normal for some women in the second and third trimesters.
5. **a.** an increase in maternal blood volume by 40% to 50%.
6. **d.** diastasis recti abdominis.
7. **a.** "As a result of pregnancy, diarrhea may occur more often."
8. **c.** nutritional status.
9. **a.** estrogen.
10. **c.** at the level of the umbilicus.

## CHAPTER POSTTEST

### Activity E  MULTIPLE CHOICE

1. **d.** supine.
2. **c.** 25 to 35 pounds.
3. **a.** hyperemesis gravidarum.
4. **a.** incompetent cervix.
5. **d.** Tay-Sachs disease.
6. **d.** abruptio placenta.
7. **d.** Rh status.
8. **d.** blood pressure.
9. **a.** upper quadrant of the maternal abdomen.
10. **a.** 10 weeks.
11. **d.** poor placental perfusion.
12. **b.** breech.
13. **a.** gonorrhea.
14. **c.** pregnancy-induced hypertension.
15. **a.** instruct the client that a vaginal delivery is likely.

## Activity F CROSSWORD PUZZLE

**Across**
1. ectopic
4. linea nigra
6. palpation
7. epulis
8. relaxin
9. back
10. 30
12. breech
13. chloasma
17. lie
18. false

**Down**
2. pica
3. striae gravidarum
4. Leopold's maneuvers
5. anemia
11. three
13. colostrums
14. obstetric
15. ambivalent
16. gynecoid

# CHAPTER 30

## CHAPTER PRETEST

### Activity A MULTIPLE CHOICE

1. **d.** 12 and 18 months.
2. **a.** is an obligatory nose breather.
3. **d.** abdominal/chest breathing movements at a rate of 30–60 breaths/minute.
4. **a.** a response to sudden stimulation or an abrupt change in position.

## CHAPTER POSTTEST

### Activity E MULTIPLE CHOICE

1. **b.** 3 to 4 months.
2. **c.** 24 pounds.
3. **b.** 4 to 6 months old.
4. **d.** storkbite.
5. **a.** Epstein's pearls.
6. **a.** down and back.

# CHAPTER 31

## CHAPTER PRETEST

### Activity A MULTIPLE CHOICE

1. **d.** smooth-textured skin.
2. **a.** A child's head reaches 90% of its full growth by 6 years of age.
3. **c.** fourth intercostal space.

### Activity B MATCHING

| 1. a | 2. c | 3. a | 4. d | 5. d | 6. c | 7. c | 8. a | 9. a | 10. b |
|------|------|------|------|------|------|------|------|------|-------|
| 11. d | 12. d | 13. b | 14. c | 15. c | | | | | |

## CHAPTER POSTTEST

### Activity F MULTIPLE CHOICE

1. **b.** three.
2. **c.** 14 years.
3. **d.** talk to the child in simple terms at the child's eye level.
4. **a.** play.
5. **a.** tell the child it is okay to cry in the clinic.
6. **d.** allow the child to engage in the discussions.
7. **a.** give the client control whenever possible.

8. **b.** 6 years.
9. **d.** 30 months after the onset of puberty.
10. **a.** hop on one foot.
11. **d.** make simple classifications.
12. **a.** she can begin bowel training as soon as the child appears ready.
13. **d.** iron.
14. **a.** measles.
15. **b.** shine a light directly onto the pupils.

# CHAPTER 32

## CHAPTER PRETEST

### Activity A MULTIPLE CHOICE

1. **c.** acute or chronic illness places excessive demands on the body.
2. **d.** lentigenes.
3. **c.** postural instability.
4. **b.** confusion.
5. **d.** 50%.
6. **b.** a decrease in reaction time.

### Activity B MATCHING

**1.** b        **2.** c        **3.** a        **4.** d

## CHAPTER POSTTEST

### Activity E MULTIPLE CHOICE

1. **a.** a nasogastric feeding tube.
2. **d.** fever.
3. **d.** urinary tract infection.
4. **b.** a Get Up and Go test.
5. **c.** diverticulitis.
6. **c.** with the feet farther apart and the knees slightly bent.
7. **d.** cognitive impairment or pseudodementia.
8. **c.** the degree to which dyspnea affects daily function.
9. **c.** a rapid decline in level of alertness.
10. **b.** tenting of skin when pinched.
11. **c.** hair loss on the skin.

### Activity F MATCHING

| Part 1 | Part 2 |
|--------|--------|
| **1.** d | **5.** e, f |
| **2.** b | **6.** g, i, j |
| **3.** a | **7.** g, j |
| **4.** c | **8.** h |
|          | **9.** g, i |

# CHAPTER 33

## CHAPTER PRETEST

### Activity A MULTIPLE CHOICE

1. **d.** have mutual decision making.
2. **a.** the gender of the members.
3. **d.** mother–son.
4. **d.** rigid.
5. **c.** is shared by both parents.

## Activity B MATCHING

**1.** c     **2.** e     **3.** a     **4.** d     **5.** b

## CHAPTER POSTTEST

### Activity E MULTIPLE CHOICE

1. **d.** square.
2. **a.** ethnicity.
3. **d.** instrumental.
4. **d.** determining the boundaries of the subsystems in the family structure.
5. **a.** rigid patterns of interactions.
6. **b.** general systems theory.
7. **c.** oldest son marries youngest daughter.
8. **a.** neighborhood's safety.
9. **d.** socialization.
10. **d.** risk for dysfunctional grieving related to loss of health status of youthful family member.

### Activity F MATCHING

**1.** d     **2.** e     **3.** b     **4.** c     **5.** a

# CHAPTER 34

## CHAPTER PRETEST

### Activity A MULTIPLE CHOICE

1. **c.** motor vehicle accidents.
2. **d.** malignant neoplasms.
3. **a.** diseases of the heart.
4. **d.** quadrupled
5. **c.** role overload.
6. **d.** lack of affordable housing.
7. **d.** obstetric care.
8. **b.** determine health-related concerns.
9. **c.** a lack of transportation.
10. **d.** poverty.

### Activity B CROSSWORD PUZZLE

**Across**

2. team
6. snow
8. pantries
11. morbidity
13. sickle cell
18. river
19. Census
21. Labor
22. mayor
23. DARE
25. vital
28. GED
29. waste
30. YMCA
31. transit
32. lake

**Down**

1. rural
3. MADD
4. SSA
5. cancer
7. WIC
9. EPA
10. ambulance
12. RR
13. SIDS
14. Lyme
15. Army
16. board
17. lead
20. survey
22. Meals
24. park
25. VNA
26. lore
27. DOT

## CHAPTER POSTTEST

**Activity E** **MULTIPLE CHOICE**

1. **d.** at least one common characteristic.
2. **a.** a community functioning within a particular social structure.
3. **d.** river.
4. **d.** Betty Neuman.
5. **b.** age.
6. **d.** diabetes mellitus.
7. **d.** congenital anomalies.
8. **a.** unintentional injuries.
9. **a.** musculoskeletal injuries.
10. **d.** low graduation rate.
11. **d.** risk for social isolation related to a lack of recreational activities and facilities.

# Diagnostic Reasoning Guides

The following pages are included for use with the case studies in this book. They are designed to help guide your thinking and assist you in arriving at appropriate conclusions. Use them to work through the steps of data analysis. You may also want to refer to the concept maps in your textbook for examples of how these will look after you fill them out.

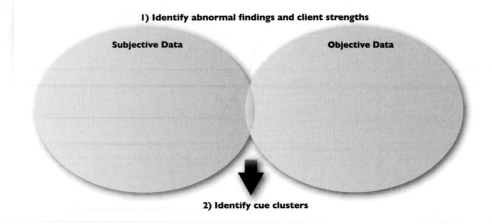

**1) Identify abnormal findings and client strengths**

Subjective Data        Objective Data

**2) Identify cue clusters**

**3) Draw Inferences**

**4) List possible nursing diagnoses**

**5) Check for defining characteristics**

**6) Confirm or rule out diagnoses**

**7) Document conclusions**

Nursing diagnoses that are appropriate for this client include:          Potential collaborative problems include the following:

**1) Identify abnormal findings and client strengths**

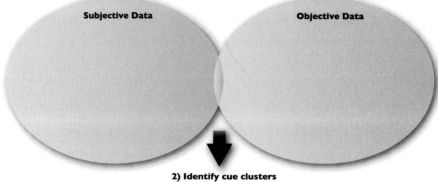

Subjective Data                          Objective Data

**2) Identify cue clusters**

**3) Draw Inferences**

**4) List possible nursing diagnoses**

**5) Check for defining characteristics**

**6) Confirm or rule out diagnoses**

**7) Document conclusions**

**Nursing diagnoses that are appropriate for this client include:**          **Potential collaborative problems include the following:**

**I) Identify abnormal findings and client strengths**

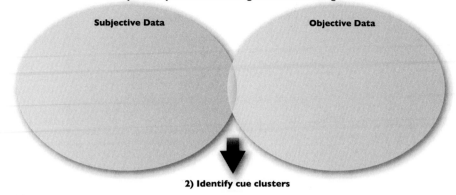

**Subjective Data**        **Objective Data**

**2) Identify cue clusters**

**3) Draw Inferences**

**4) List possible nursing diagnoses**

**5) Check for defining characteristics**

**6) Confirm or rule out diagnoses**

**7) Document conclusions**

**Nursing diagnoses that are appropriate for this client include:**        **Potential collaborative problems include the following:**

**1) Identify abnormal findings and client strengths**

**Subjective Data**                    **Objective Data**

**2) Identify cue clusters**

**3) Draw Inferences**

**4) List possible nursing diagnoses**

**5) Check for defining characteristics**

**6) Confirm or rule out diagnoses**

**7) Document conclusions**

**Nursing diagnoses that are appropriate for this client include:**          **Potential collaborative problems include the following:**